C000215784

BIG EASY READ
BRITAIN

Atlas contents

Scale 1:160,000
or 2.52 miles to 1 inch

13th edition June 2017

© AA Media Limited 2017

Original edition printed 1991.

Cartography: All cartography in this atlas edited, designed and produced by the Mapping Services Department of AA Publishing (A05503).

This atlas contains Ordnance Survey data © Crown copyright and database right 2017.

Publisher's Notes: Published by AA Publishing (a trading name of AA Media Limited, whose registered office is Fanum House, Basing View, Basingstoke, Hampshire RG21 4EA, UK. Registered number 06112600).

ISBN: 978 0 7495 7853 4 (spiral bound)
ISBN: 978 0 7495 7852 7 (paperback)

A CIP catalogue record for this book is available from The British Library.

Disclaimer: The contents of this atlas are believed to be correct at the time of the latest revision, it will not contain any subsequent amended, new or temporary information including diversions and traffic control or enforcement systems. The publishers cannot be held responsible or liable for any loss or damage occasioned to any person acting or refraining from action as a result of any use or reliance on material in this atlas, nor for any errors, omissions or changes in such material. This does not affect your statutory rights.

The publishers would welcome information to correct any errors or omissions and to keep this atlas up to date. Please write to the Atlas Editor, AA Publishing, The Automobile Association, Fanum House, Basing View, Basingstoke, Hampshire RG21 4EA, UK.
E-mail: roadatlasfeedback@theaa.com

Acknowledgements: AA Publishing would like to thank the following for their assistance in producing this atlas:
Crematoria data provided by the Cremation Society of Great Britain. Cadw, English Heritage, Forestry Commission, Historic Scotland, Johnsons, National Trust and National Trust for Scotland, RSPB, The Wildlife Trust, Scottish Natural Heritage, Natural England, The Countryside Council for Wales (road maps). Award winning beaches from 'Blue Flag' and 'Keep Scotland Beautiful' (summer 2016 data): for latest information visit www.blueflag.org and www.keepscotlandbeautiful.org

Road signs are © Crown Copyright 2017. Reproduced under the terms of the Open Government Licence.

Printer: Leo Paper Products, China

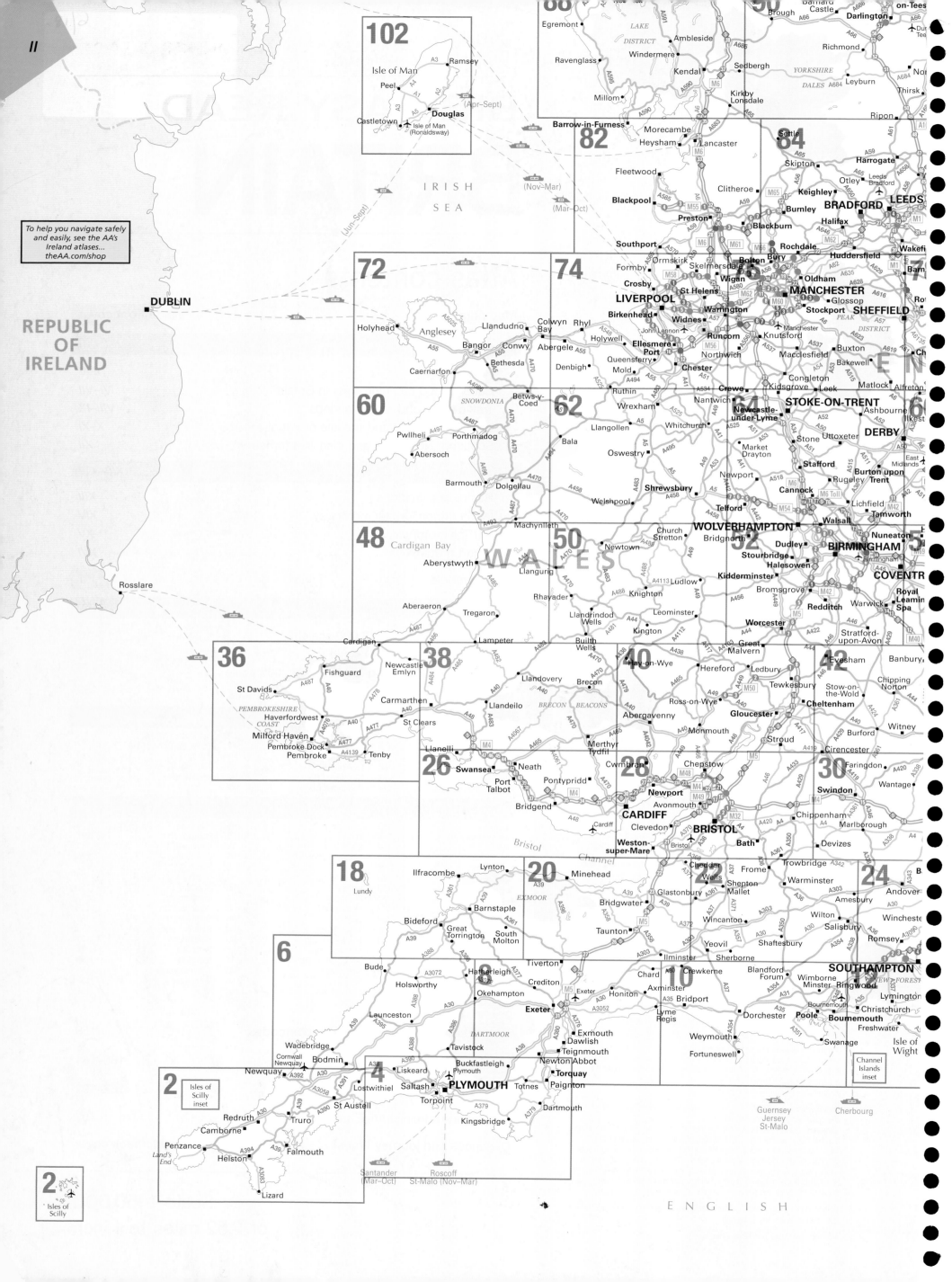

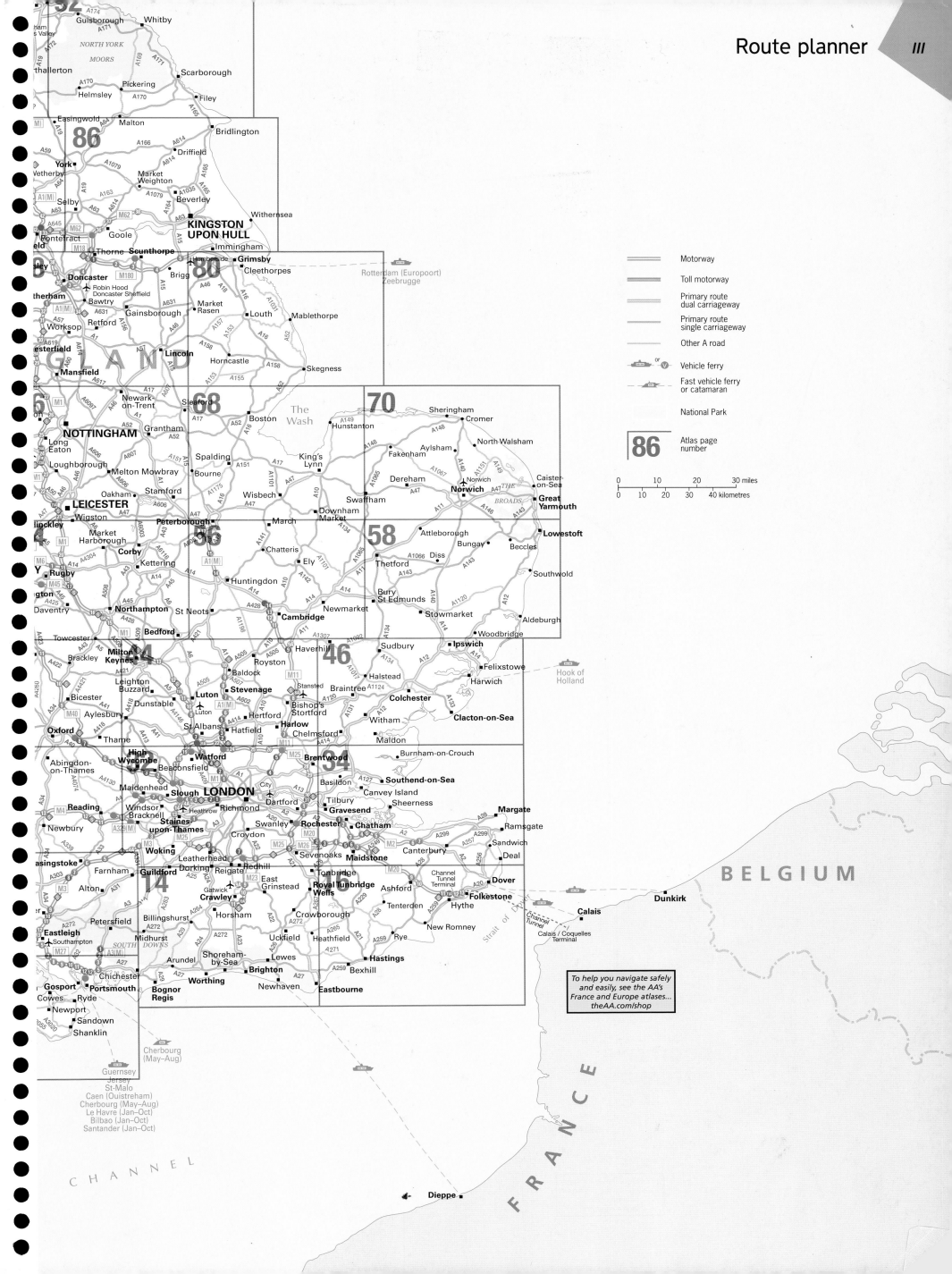

Legend:

Motorway

Toll motorway

Primary route
dual carriageway

Primary route
single carriageway

Other A road

Vehicle ferry

Fast vehicle ferry
or catamaran

National Park

86 Atlas page
number

0   10   20   30 miles
0 10 20 30 40 kilometres

To help you navigate safely
and easily, see the AA's
France and Europe atlases...
theAA.com/shop

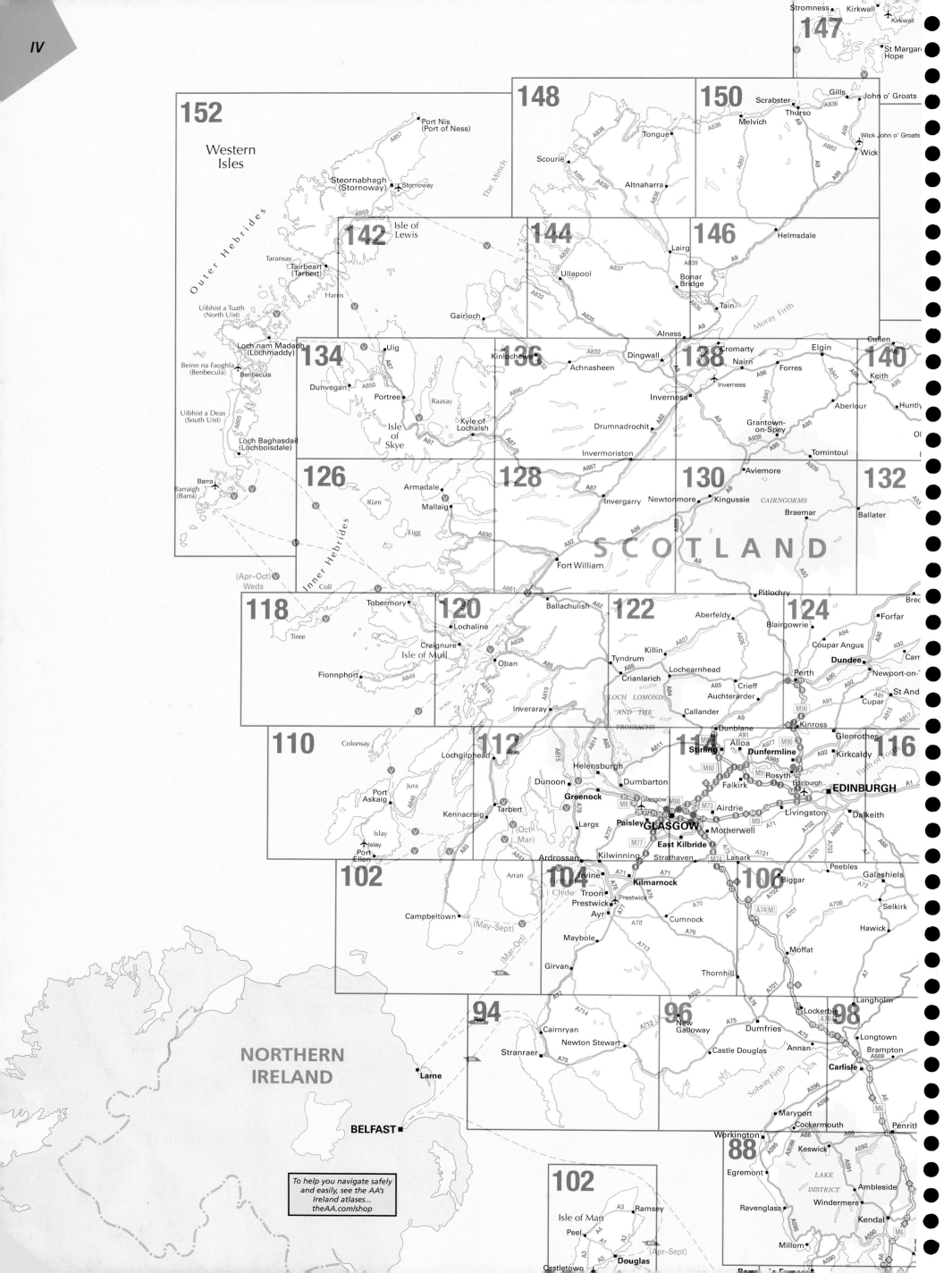

152 Western Isles

Outer Hebrides

Port Nis (Port of Ness)

Steornabhagh (Stornoway)

Taransay
Tairbeart (Tarbert)
Harris

Uibhist a Tuath (North Uist)
Benbecula
Beinn na Faoghla (Benbecula)

Loch nam Madadh (Lochmaddy)

Uibhist a Deas (South Uist)

Loch Baghasdail (Lochboisdale)

Barra
Barraigh (Barra)

142 Isle of Lewis

134

Uig
Dunvegan
Portree
Raasay
Isle of Skye
Kyle of Lochalsh

126

Rùm
Armadale
Mallaig
Eigg

(Apr–Oct) Weds
Coll

118

Tiree
Tobermory
Craignure
Isle of Mull
Fionnphort

110

Colonsay
Jura
Port Askaig
Islay
Port Ellen

Kennacraig

148

Tongue
Scourie
Altnaharra

144

Ullapool
Gairloch

136

Kinlochewe
Achnasheen
Dingwall

150

Scrabster
Melvich
Thurso
Gills
John o' Groats
Wick John o' Groats
Wick

146

Lairg
Bonar Bridge
Helmsdale
Tain
Alness
Moray Firth

138

Cromarty
Inverness
Nairn
Forres
Elgin
Cullen
Drumnadrochit
Invermoriston
Grantown-on-Spey
Tomintoul

140

Keith
Aberlour
Huntly

SCOTLAND

130

Aviemore
Newtonmore
Kingussie
CAIRNGORMS
Braemar

132

Ballater

128

Invergarry
Fort William

122

Ballachulish
Aberfeldy
Blairgowrie
Killin
Tyndrum
Crianlarich
Lochearnhead
Crieff
Callander
LOCH LOMOND AND THE TROSSACHS
Auchterarder

124

Coupar Angus
Perth
Dundee
Newport-on-
St And
Cupar
Forfar
Bred

120

Lochaline
Oban
Inveraray

112

Lochgilphead
Helensburgh
Dunoon
Dumbarton
Greenock
Largs
Tarbert
(Oct / Mar)

114 Stirling
Alloa
Dunblane
Dunfermline
Rosyth
Falkirk
Glasgow
Airdrie
Paisley
Motherwell
East Kilbride
Livingston
EDINBURGH

116

Glenrothes
Kirkcaldy
Firth of

102

Campbeltown
Arran
Ardrossan
Kilwinning
Troon
Prestwick
Ayr
Maybole
Girvan
(May–Sept)
(Mar–Oct)

104

Irvine
Kilmarnock
Strathaven
Lanark

106

Biggar
Peebles
Galashiels
Selkirk
Hawick
Cumnock
Thornhill
Moffat

94

Cairnryan
Stranraer
Newton Stewart

96

New Galloway
Dumfries
Castle Douglas
Annan

98

Lockerbie
Longtown
Brampton
Carlisle

NORTHERN IRELAND

Larne

BELFAST

88

Solway Firth
Maryport
Cockermouth
Penrith
Workington
Keswick
Egremont
LAKE DISTRICT
Ravenglass
Windermere
Ambleside
Kendal
Millom

102

Isle of Man
Ramsey
Peel
Douglas
Castletown
(Apr–Sept)

147

Stromness
Kirkwall
St Margare Hope

To help you navigate safely and easily, see the AA's Ireland atlases... theAA.com/shop

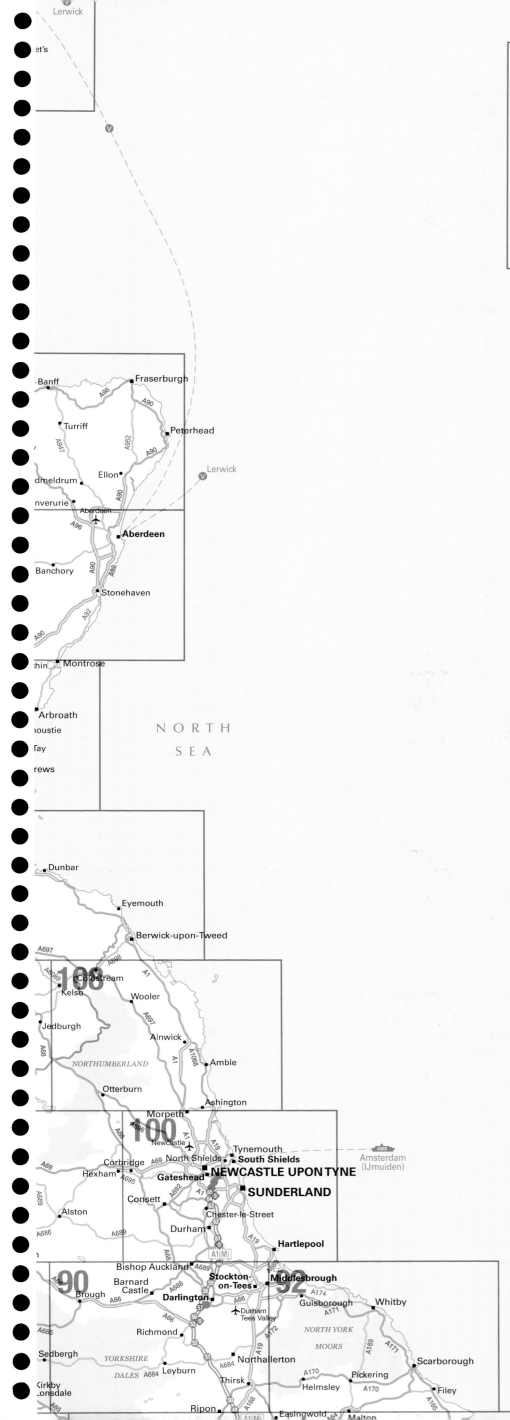

147
Orkney Islands

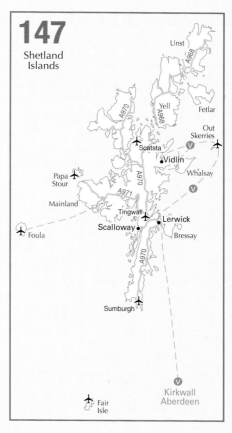

147
Shetland Islands

EMERGENCY DIVERSION ROUTES

In an emergency it may be necessary to close a section of motorway or other main road to traffic, so a temporary sign may advise drivers to follow a diversion route. To help drivers navigate the route, black symbols on yellow patches may be permanently displayed on existing direction signs, including motorway signs. Symbols may also be used on separate signs with yellow backgrounds.

For further information see *theaa.com/motoring_advice/ general-advice/emergency-diversion-routes.html*

FERRY INFORMATION

Information on ferry routes and operators can be found on pages *X–XII*.

═══════	Motorway
═══════	Toll motorway
═══════	Primary route dual carriageway
───────	Primary route single carriageway
───────	Other A road
	Vehicle ferry
	Fast vehicle ferry or catamaran
	National Park
96	Atlas page number

0   10   20   30 miles
0   10   20   30   40 kilometres

Caravan and camping sites in Britain

These pages list the top 300 AA-inspected Caravan and Camping (C & C) sites in the Pennant rating scheme. **Five Pennant Premier sites are shown in green,** **Four Pennant sites are shown in blue.**

Listings include addresses, telephone numbers and websites together with page and grid references to locate the sites in the atlas. The total number of touring pitches is also included for each site, together with the type of pitch available.
The following abbreviations are used: **C = Caravan CV = Campervan T = Tent**

To find out more about the AA's Pennant rating scheme and other rated caravan and camping sites not included on these pages please visit ***theAA.com***

ENGLAND

Alders Caravan Park
Home Farm, Alne, York
YO61 1RY
Tel: 01347 838722 **85 P2**
alderscaravanpark.co.uk
Total Pitches: 87 (C, CV & T)

Andrewshayes Holiday Park
Dalwood, Axminster
EX13 7DY
Tel: 01404 831225 **9 N5**
andrewshayes.co.uk
Total Pitches: 150 (C, CV & T)

Apple Tree Park C & C Site
A38, Claypits, Stonehouse
GL10 3AL
Tel: 01452 742362 **41 M10**
appletreepark.co.uk
Total Pitches: 65 (C, CV & T)

Appuldurcombe Gardens Holiday Park
Appuldurcombe Road, Wroxall, Isle of Wight
PO38 3EP
Tel: 01983 852597 **13 J8**
appuldurcombegardens.co.uk
Total Pitches: 130 (C, CV & T)

Atlantic Bays Holiday Park
St Merryn, Padstow
PL28 8PY
Tel: 01841 520855 **6 C10**
atlanticbaysholidaypark.co.uk
Total Pitches: 70 (C, CV & T)

Ayr Holiday Park
St Ives, Cornwall
TR26 1EJ
Tel: 01736 795855 **2 E6**
ayrholidaypark.co.uk
Total Pitches: 40 (C, CV & T)

Back of Beyond Touring Park
234 Ringwood Road, St Leonards, Dorset
BH24 2SB
Tel: 01202 876968 **11 Q4**
backofbeyondtouringpark.co.uk
Total Pitches: 80 (C, CV & T)

Bagwell Farm Touring Park
Knights in the Bottom, Chickerell, Weymouth
DT3 4EA
Tel: 01305 782575 **10 G8**
bagwellfarm.co.uk
Total Pitches: 320 (C, CV & T)

Bardsea Leisure Park
Priory Road, Ulverston
LA12 9QE
Tel: 01229 584712 **89 J11**
bardsealeisure.co.uk
Total Pitches: 83 (C & CV)

Barlings Country Holiday Park
Barlings Lane, Langworth
LN3 5DF
Tel: 01522 753200 **79 Q8**
barlingscountrypark.co.uk
Total Pitches: 84 (C, CV & T)

Barn Farm Campsite
Barn Farm, Birchover, Matlock
DE4 2BL
Tel: 01629 650245 **77 N11**
barnfarmcamping.com
Total Pitches: 62 (C, CV & T)

Bath Chew Valley Caravan Park
Ham Lane, Bishop Sutton
BS39 5TZ
Tel: 01275 332127 **29 J10**
bathchewvalley.co.uk
Total Pitches: 45 (C, CV & T)

Bay View Holiday Park
Bolton le Sands, Carnforth
LA5 9TN
Tel: 01524 732854 **83 L1**
holgates.co.uk
Total Pitches: 100 (C, CV & T)

Beaconsfield Farm Caravan Park
Battlefield, Shrewsbury
SY4 4AA
Tel: 01939 210370 **63 N8**
beaconsfieldholidaypark.co.uk
Total Pitches: 60 (C & CV)

Beech Croft Farm
Beech Croft, Blackwell in the Peak, Buxton
SK17 9TQ
Tel: 01298 85330 **77 L9**
beechcroftfarm.co.uk
Total Pitches: 30 (C, CV & T)

Bellingham C & C Club Site
Brown Rigg, Bellingham
NE48 2JY
Tel: 01434 220175 **99 N2**
campingandcaravanningclub.co.uk/bellingham
Total Pitches: 64 (C, CV & T)

Beverley Parks C & C Park
Goodrington Road, Paignton
TQ4 7JE
Tel: 01803 661961 **5 Q5**
beverley-holidays.co.uk
Total Pitches: 172 (C, CV & T)

Bingham Grange Touring & Camping Park
Melplash, Bridport
DT6 3TT
Tel: 01308 488234 **10 D5**
binghamgrange.co.uk
Total Pitches: 150 (C, CV & T)

Blackmore Vale C & C Park
Sherborne Causeway, Shaftesbury
SP7 9PX
Tel: 01747 851523 **23 J8**
blackmorevalecaravanpark.co.uk
Total Pitches: 13 (C, CV & T)

Blue Rose Caravan Country Park
Star Carr Lane, Brandesburton
YO25 8RU
Tel: 01964 543366 **87 L6**
bluerosepark.com
Total Pitches: 58 (C & CV)

Briarfields Motel & Touring Park
Gloucester Road, Cheltenham
GL51 0SX
Tel: 01242 235324 **41 P7**
briarfields.net
Total Pitches: 72 (C, CV & T)

Broadhembury C & C Park
Steeds Lane, Kingsnorth, Ashford
TN26 1NQ
Tel: 01233 620859 **16 H3**
broadhembury.co.uk
Total Pitches: 110 (C, CV & T)

Brokerswood Country Park
Brokerswood, Westbury
BA13 4EH
Tel: 01373 822238 **23 J3**
brokerswoodcountrypark.co.uk
Total Pitches: 69 (C, CV & T)

Brompton Caravan Park
Brompton-on-Swale, Richmond
DL10 7EZ
Tel: 01748 824629 **91 K7**
bromptoncaravanpark.co.uk
Total Pitches: 177 (C, CV & T)

Budemeadows Touring Park
Widemouth Bay, Bude
EX23 0NA
Tel: 01288 361646 **7 J4**
budemeadows.com
Total Pitches: 145 (C, CV & T)

Burrowhayes Farm C & C Site & Riding Stables
West Luccombe, Porlock, Minehead
TA24 8HT
Tel: 01643 862463 **20 D4**
burrowhayes.co.uk
Total Pitches: 120 (C, CV & T)

Burton Constable Holiday Park & Arboretum
Old Lodges, Sproatley, Hull
HU11 4LJ
Tel: 01964 562508 **87 M8**
burtonconstable.co.uk
Total Pitches: 105 (C, CV & T)

Cakes & Ale
Abbey Lane, Theberton, Leiston
IP16 4TE
Tel: 01728 831655 **59 N8**
cakesandale.co.uk
Total Pitches: 55 (C, CV & T)

Calloose C & C Park
Leedstown, Hayle
TR27 5ET
Tel: 01736 850431 **2 F7**
calloose.co.uk
Total Pitches: 109 (C, CV & T)

Camping Caradon Touring Park
Trelawne, Looe
PL13 2NA
Tel: 01503 272388 **4 C6**
campingcaradon.co.uk
Total Pitches: 75 (C, CV & T)

Capesthorne Hall
Congleton Road, Siddington, Macclesfield
SK11 9JY
Tel: 01625 861221 **76 F9**
capesthorne.com
Total Pitches: 50 (C & CV)

Carlyon Bay C & C Park
Bethesda, Cypress Avenue, Carlyon Bay
PL25 3RE
Tel: 01726 812735 **3 P4**
carlyonbay.net
Total Pitches: 180 (C, CV & T)

Carnon Downs C & C Park
Carnon Downs, Truro
TR3 6JJ
Tel: 01872 862283 **3 K6**
carnon-downs-caravanpark.co.uk
Total Pitches: 150 (C, CV & T)

Carvynick Country Club
Summercourt, Newquay
TR8 5AF
Tel: 01872 510716 **3 L3**
carvynick.co.uk
Total Pitches: 47 (C & CV)

Castlerigg Hall C & C Park
Castlerigg Hall, Keswick
CA12 4TE
Tel: 017687 74499 **89 J2**
castlerigg.co.uk
Total Pitches: 68 (C, CV & T)

Cayton Village Caravan Park
Mill Lane, Cayton Bay, Scarborough
YO11 3NN
Tel: 01723 583171 **93 L10**
caytontouring.co.uk
Total Pitches: 310 (C, CV & T)

Charris C & C Park
Candy's Lane, Corfe Mullen, Wimborne
BH21 3EF
Tel: 01202 885970 **11 N5**
charris.co.uk
Total Pitches: 45 (C, CV & T)

Cheddar Mendip Heights C & C Club Site
Townsend, Priddy, Wells
BA5 3BP
Tel: 01749 870241 **22 C3**
campingandcaravanningclub.co.uk/cheddar
Total Pitches: 90 (C, CV & T)

Chy Carne Holiday Park
Kuggar, Ruan Minor, Helston
TR12 7LX
Tel: 01326 290200 **2 H11**
chycarne.co.uk
Total Pitches: 30 (C, CV & T)

Clippesby Hall
Hall Lane, Clippesby, Great Yarmouth
NR29 3BL
Tel: 01493 367800 **71 N9**
clippesby.com
Total Pitches: 120 (C, CV & T)

Cofton Country Holidays
Starcross, Dawlish
EX6 8RP
Tel: 01626 890111 **8 H8**
coftonholidays.co.uk
Total Pitches: 450 (C, CV & T)

Concierge Camping
Ratham Estate, Ratham Lane, West Ashling, Chichester
PO18 8DL
Tel: 01243 573118 **13 P3**
conciergecamping.co.uk
Total Pitches: 15 (C, CV & T)

Concierge Glamping
Ratham Estate, Ratham Lane, West Ashling, Chichester
PO18 8DL
Tel: 01243 573118 **13 P3**
conciergecamping.co.uk
Total Pitches: 4 (T)

Coombe Touring Park
Race Plain, Netherhampton, Salisbury
SP2 8PN
Tel: 01722 328451 **23 N7**
coombecaravanpark.co.uk
Total Pitches: 50 (C, CV & T)

Corfe Castle C & C Club Site
Bucknowle, Wareham
BH20 5PQ
Tel: 01929 480280 **11 M8**
campingandcaravanningclub.co.uk/corfecastle
Total Pitches: 80 (C, CV & T)

Cornish Farm Touring Park
Shoreditch, Taunton
TA3 7BS
Tel: 01823 327746 **21 K9**
cornishfarm.com
Total Pitches: 50 (C, CV & T)

Cosawes Park
Perranarworthal, Truro
TR3 7QS
Tel: 01872 863724 **3 J7**
cosawestouringandcamping.co.uk
Total Pitches: 59 (C, CV & T)

Cote Ghyll C & C Park
Osmotherley, Northallerton
DL6 3AH
Tel: 01609 883425 **91 Q7**
coteghyll.com
Total Pitches: 77 (C, CV & T)

Country View Holiday Park
Sand Road, Sand Bay, Weston-super-Mare
BS22 9UJ
Tel: 01934 627595 **28 D9**
cvhp.co.uk
Total Pitches: 190 (C, CV & T)

Crafty Camping
Woodland Workshop, Yonder Hill, Holditch
TA20 4NL
Tel: 01460 221102 **9 Q4**
mallinson.co.uk
Total Pitches: 8 (T)

Crealy Meadows C & C Park
Sidmouth Road, Clyst St Mary, Exeter
EX5 1DR
Tel: 01395 234888 **9 J7**
crealymeadows.co.uk
Total Pitches: 120 (C, CV & T)

Crows Nest Caravan Park
Gristhorpe, Filey
YO14 9PS
Tel: 01723 582206 **93 M10**
crowsnestcaravanpark.com
Total Pitches: 49 (C, CV & T)

Dell Touring Park
Beyton Road, Thurston, Bury St Edmunds
IP31 3RB
Tel: 01359 270121 **58 D8**
thedellcaravanpark.co.uk
Total Pitches: 50 (C, CV & T)

Dolbeare Park C & C
St Ive Road, Landrake, Saltash
PL12 5AF
Tel: 01752 851332 **4 E4**
dolbeare.co.uk
Total Pitches: 60 (C, CV & T)

Dornafield
Dornafield Farm, Two Mile Oak, Newton Abbot
TQ12 6DD
Tel: 01803 812732 **5 P3**
dornafield.com
Total Pitches: 135 (C, CV & T)

Dorset Country Holidays
Sherborne Causeway, Shaftesbury
SP7 9PX
Tel: 01747 851523 **23 J8**
blackmorevalecaravanandcampingpark.co.uk
Total Pitches: 7 (T)

East Fleet Farm Touring Park
Chickerell, Weymouth
DT3 4DW
Tel: 01305 785768 **10 G9**
eastfleet.co.uk
Total Pitches: 400 (C, CV & T)

Eden Valley Holiday Park
Lanlivery, Nr Lostwithiel
PL30 5BU
Tel: 01208 872277 **3 Q3**
edenvalleyholidaypark.co.uk
Total Pitches: 56 (C, CV & T)

Eskdale C & C Club Site
Boot, Holmrook
CA19 1TH
Tel: 019467 23253 **88 G6**
campingandcaravanningclub.co.uk/eskdale
Total Pitches: 100 (CV & T)

Exe Valley Caravan Site
Mill House, Bridgetown, Dulverton
TA22 9JR
Tel: 01643 851432 **20 E7**
exevalleycamping.co.uk
Total Pitches: 48 (C, CV & T)

Fields End Water Caravan Park & Fishery
Benwick Road, Doddington, March
PE15 0TY
Tel: 01354 740199 **56 G2**
fieldsendcaravans.co.uk
Total Pitches: 52 (C, CV & T)

Flusco Wood
Flusco, Penrith
CA11 0JB
Tel: 017684 80020 **98 F12**
fluscowood.co.uk
Total Pitches: 36 (C & CV)

Globe Vale Holiday Park
Radnor, Redruth
TR16 4BH
Tel: 01209 891183 **2 H5**
globevale.co.uk
Total Pitches: 138 (C, CV & T)

Golden Cap Holiday Park
Seatown, Chideock, Bridport
DT6 6JX
Tel: 01308 422139 **10 C6**
wdlh.co.uk
Total Pitches: 108 (C, CV & T)

Golden Square C & C Park
Oswaldkirk, Helmsley
YO62 5YQ
Tel: 01439 788269 **92 C10**
goldensquarecaravanpark.com
Total Pitches: 129 (C, CV & T)

Goosewood Holiday Park
Sutton-on-the-Forest, York
YO61 1ET
Tel: 01347 810829 **86 B3**
flowerofmay.com
Total Pitches: 100 (C & CV)

Green Acres Caravan Park
High Knells, Houghton, Carlisle
CA6 4JW
Tel: 01228 675418 **98 E6**
caravanpark-cumbria.com
Total Pitches: 35 (C, CV & T)

Greenacres Touring Park
Haywards Lane, Chelston, Wellington
TA21 9PH
Tel: 01823 652844 **21 J9**
greenacres-wellington.co.uk
Total Pitches: 40 (C & CV)

Greenhill Farm C & C Park
Greenhill Farm, New Road, Landford, Salisbury
SP5 2AZ
Tel: 01794 324117 **24 D9**
greenhillfarm.co.uk
Total Pitches: 160 (C, CV & T)

Greenhill Leisure Park
Greenhill Farm, Station Road, Bletchingdon, Oxford
OX5 3BQ
Tel: 01869 351600 **43 K8**
greenhill-leisure-park.co.uk
Total Pitches: 92 (C, CV & T)

Grouse Hill Caravan Park
Flask Bungalow Farm, Fylingdales, Robin Hood's Bay
YO22 4QH
Tel: 01947 880543 **93 J7**
grousehill.co.uk
Total Pitches: 175 (C, CV & T)

Gunvenna Holiday Park
St Minver, Wadebridge
PL27 6QN
Tel: 01208 862405 **6 D9**
gunvenna.com
Total Pitches: 75 (C, CV & T)

Gwithian Farm Campsite
Gwithian Farm, Gwithian, Hayle
TR27 5BX
Tel: 01736 753127 **2 F6**
gwithianfarm.co.uk
Total Pitches: 87 (C, CV & T)

Harbury Fields
Harbury Fields Farm, Harbury, Nr Leamington Spa
CV33 9JN
Tel: 01926 612457 **54 B8**
harburyfields.co.uk
Total Pitches: 59 (C & CV)

Haw Wood Farm Caravan Park
Hinton, Saxmundham
IP17 3QT
Tel: 01502 359550 **59 N6**
hawwoodfarm.co.uk
Total Pitches: 60 (C, CV & T)

Heathfield Farm Camping
Heathfield Road, Freshwater, Isle of Wight
PO40 9SH
Tel: 01983 407822 **12 E7**
heathfieldcamping.co.uk
Total Pitches: 75 (C, CV & T)

Heathland Beach Caravan Park
London Road, Kessingland
NR33 7PJ
Tel: 01502 740337 **59 Q3**
heathlandbeach.co.uk
Total Pitches: 63 (C, CV & T)

Hele Valley Holiday Park
Hele Bay, Ilfracombe
EX34 9RD
Tel: 01271 862460 **19 K4**
helevalley.co.uk
Total Pitches: 50 (C, CV & T)

Hendra Holiday Park
Newquay
TR8 4NY
Tel: 01637 875778 **3 K2**
hendra-holidays.com
Total Pitches: 548 (C, CV & T)

Herding Hill Farm
Shield Hill, Haltwhistle
NE49 9NW
Tel: 01434 320175 **99 K5**
herdinghillfarm.co.uk
Total Pitches: 22 (C, CV & T)

Herding Hill Farm Glamping Site
Shield Hill, Haltwhistle
NE49 9NW
Tel: 01434 320175 **99 K5**
herdinghillfarm.co.uk
Total Pitches: 24 (T)

Hidden Valley Park
West Down, Braunton, Ilfracombe
EX34 8NU
Tel: 01271 813837 **19 K5**
hiddenvalleypark.com
Total Pitches: 100 (C, CV & T)

High Moor Farm Park
Skipton Road, Harrogate
HG3 2LT
Tel: 01423 563637 **85 K4**
highmoorfarmpark.co.uk
Total Pitches: 320 (C & CV)

Highfield Farm Touring Park
Long Road, Comberton, Cambridge
CB23 7DG
Tel: 01223 262308 **56 H9**
highfieldfarmtouringpark.co.uk
Total Pitches: 120 (C, CV & T)

Highlands End Holiday Park
Eype, Bridport, Dorset
DT6 6AR
Tel: 01308 422139 **10 C6**
wdlh.co.uk
Total Pitches: 195 (C, CV & T)

Hill Cottage Farm C & C Park
Sandleheath Road, Alderholt, Fordingbridge
SP6 3EG
Tel: 01425 650513 **23 P10**
hillcottagefarmcampingandcaravanpark.co.uk
Total Pitches: 95 (C, CV & T)

Hill Farm Caravan Park
Branches Lane, Sherfield English, Romsey
SO51 6FH
Tel: 01794 340402 **24 E8**
hillfarmpark.com
Total Pitches: 100 (C, CV & T)

Hill of Oaks & Blakeholme
Windermere
LA12 8NR
Tel: 015395 31578 **89 K9**
hillofoaks.co.uk
Total Pitches: 43 (C & CV)

Hillside Caravan Park
Canvas Farm, Moor Road, Knayton, Thirsk
YO7 4BR
Tel: 01845 537349 **91 Q9**
hillsidecaravanpark.co.uk
Total Pitches: 50 (C & CV)

Hollins Farm C & C
Far Arnside, Carnforth
LA5 0SL
Tel: 01524 701767 **89 M11**
holgates.co.uk
Total Pitches: 12 (C, CV & T)

Holmans Wood Holiday Park
Harcombe Cross, Chudleigh
TQ13 0DZ
Tel: 01626 853785 **8 G8**
holmanswood.co.uk
Total Pitches: 73 (C, CV & T)

Honeybridge Park
Honeybridge Lane, Dial Post, Horsham
RH13 8NX
Tel: 01403 710923 **14 H7**
honeybridgepark.co.uk
Total Pitches: 130 (C, CV & T)

Hurley Riverside Park
Park Office, Hurley, Nr Maidenhead
SL6 5NE
Tel: 01628 824493 **32 B5**
hurleyriversidepark.co.uk
Total Pitches: 200 (C, CV & T)

Hylton Caravan Park
Eden Street, Silloth
CA7 4AY
Tel: 016973 31707 **97 M7**
stanwix.com
Total Pitches: 90 (C, CV & T)

Island Lodge C & C Site
Stumpy Post Cross, Kingsbridge
TQ7 4BL
Tel: 01548 852956 **5 M7**
islandlodgesite.co.uk
Total Pitches: 30 (C, CV & T)

Isle of Avalon Touring Caravan Park
Godney Road, Glastonbury
BA6 9AF
Tel: 01458 833618 **22 C5**
avaloncaravanpark.co.uk
Total Pitches: 120 (C, CV & T)

Jacobs Mount Caravan Park
Jacobs Mount, Stepney Road, Scarborough
YO12 5NL
Tel: 01723 361178 **93 L9**
jacobsmount.com
Total Pitches: 156 (C, CV & T)

Jasmine Caravan Park
Cross Lane, Snainton, Scarborough
YO13 9BE
Tel: 01723 859240 **93 J10**
jasminepark.co.uk
Total Pitches: 68 (C, CV & T)

Juliot's Well Holiday Park
Camelford, Cornwall
PL32 9RF
Tel: 01840 213302 **6 G8**
southwestholidayparks.co.uk/parks/juliots-well
Total Pitches: 39 (C, CV & T)

Kenneggy Cove Holiday Park
Higher Kenneggy, Rosudgeon, Penzance
TR20 9AU
Tel: 01736 763453 **2 E9**
kenneggycove.co.uk
Total Pitches: 40 (C, CV & T)

Kings Down Tail C & C Park
Salcombe Regis, Sidmouth
EX10 0PD
Tel: 01297 680313 **9 M6**
kingsdowntail.co.uk
Total Pitches: 80 (C, CV & T)

King's Lynn C & C Park
New Road, North Runcton, King's Lynn
PE33 0RA
Tel: 01553 840004 **69 M9**
kl-cc.co.uk
Total Pitches: 150 (C, CV & T)

Kits Coty Glamping
84 Collingwood Road, Kits Coty Estate, Aylesford
ME20 7ER
Tel: 01634 685862 **34 C10**
kitscotyglamping.co.uk
Total Pitches: 4 (T)

Kneps Farm Holiday Park
River Road, Stanah, Thornton-Cleveleys, Blackpool
FY5 5LR
Tel: 01253 823632 **83 J6**
knepsfarm.co.uk
Total Pitches: 40 (C & CV)

Knight Stainforth Hall Caravan & Campsite
Stainforth, Settle
BD24 0DP
Tel: 01729 822200 **84 B2**
knightstainforth.co.uk
Total Pitches: 100 (C, CV & T)

Ladycross Plantation Caravan Park
Egton, Whitby
YO21 1UA
Tel: 01947 895502 **92 G5**
ladycrossplantation.co.uk
Total Pitches: 130 (C, CV & T)

Lady's Mile Holiday Park
Dawlish, Devon
EX7 0LX
Tel: 01626 863411 **8 H9**
ladysmile.co.uk
Total Pitches: 570 (C, CV & T)

Lamb Cottage Caravan Park
Dalefords Lane, Whitegate, Northwich
CW8 2BN
Tel: 01606 882302 **75 Q10**
lambcottage.co.uk
Total Pitches: 45 (C & CV)

Langstone Manor C & C Park
Moortown, Tavistock
PL19 9JZ
Tel: 01822 613371 **7 P10**
langstone-manor.co.uk
Total Pitches: 40 (C, CV & T)

Lanyon Holiday Park
Loscombe Lane, Four Lanes, Redruth
TR16 6LP
Tel: 01209 313474 **2 H7**
lanyonholidaypark.co.uk
Total Pitches: 25 (C, CV & T)

Lebberston Touring Park
Filey Road, Lebberston, Scarborough
YO11 3PE
Tel: 01723 585723 **93 M10**
lebberstontouring.co.uk
Total Pitches: 125 (C & CV)

Lee Valley Campsite
Sewardstone Road, Chingford, London
E4 7RA
Tel: 020 8529 5689 **33 M3**
visitleevalley.org.uk/wheretostay
Total Pitches: 81 (C, CV & T)

Lickpenny Caravan Site
Lickpenny Lane, Tansley, Matlock
DE4 5GF
Tel: 01629 583040 **77 Q11**
lickpennycaravanpark.co.uk
Total Pitches: 80 (C & CV)

Lime Tree Park
Dukes Drive, Buxton
SK17 9RP
Tel: 01298 22988 **77 K9**
limetreeparkbuxton.com
Total Pitches: 106 (C, CV & T)

Lincoln Farm Park Oxfordshire
High Street, Standlake
OX29 7RH
Tel: 01865 300239 **43 J11**
lincolnfarmpark.co.uk
Total Pitches: 90 (C, CV & T)

Long Acres Touring Park
Station Road, Old Leake, Boston
PE22 9RF
Tel: 01205 871555 **68 G2**
long-acres.co.uk
Total Pitches: 40 (C, CV & T)

Longnor Wood Holiday Park
Newtown, Longnor, Nr Buxton
SK17 0NG
Tel: 01298 83648 **77 K11**
longnorwood.co.uk
Total Pitches: 47 (C, CV & T)

Lower Polladras Touring Park
Carleen, Breage, Helston
TR13 9NX
Tel: 01736 762220 **2 F8**
lower-polladras.co.uk
Total Pitches: 39 (C, CV & T)

Lowther Holiday Park
Eamont Bridge, Penrith
CA10 2JB
Tel: 01768 863631 **89 N1**
lowther-holidaypark.co.uk
Total Pitches: 180 (C, CV & T)

Manor Farm Holiday Centre
Charmouth, Bridport
DT6 6QL
Tel: 01297 560226 **10 B6**
manorfarmholidaycentre.co.uk
Total Pitches: 400 (C, CV & T)

Manor Wood Country Caravan Park
Manor Wood, Coddington, Chester
CH3 9EN
Tel: 01829 782990 **63 M1**
cheshire-caravan-sites.co.uk
Total Pitches: 45 (C, CV & T)

Mayfield Park
Cheltenham Road, Cirencester
GL7 7BH
Tel: 01285 831301 **42 B10**
mayfieldpark.co.uk
Total Pitches: 105 (C, CV & T)

Meadowbank Holidays
Stour Way, Christchurch
BH23 2PQ
Tel: 01202 483597 **12 B6**
meadowbank-holidays.co.uk
Total Pitches: 41 (C & CV)

Middlewick Farm
Wick Lane, Glastonbury
BA6 8JW
Tel: 01458 832351 **22 C5**
middlewickholidaycottages.co.uk
Total Pitches: 3 (T)

Middlewood Farm Holiday Park
Middlewood Lane, Fylingthorpe, Robin Hood's Bay, Whitby
YO22 4UF
Tel: 01947 880414 **93 J6**
middlewoodfarm.com
Total Pitches: 100 (C, CV & T)

Minnows Touring Park
Holbrook Lane, Sampford Peverell
EX16 7EN
Tel: 01884 821770 **20 G10**
minnowstouringpark.co.uk
Total Pitches: 59 (C, CV & T)

Moon & Sixpence
Newbourn Road, Waldringfield, Woodbridge
IP12 4PP
Tel: 01473 736650 **47 N3**
moonandsixpence.eu
Total Pitches: 50 (C & CV)

Moor Lodge Park
Blackmoor Lane, Bardsey, Leeds
LS17 9DZ
Tel: 01937 572424 **85 M7**
moorlodgecaravanpark.co.uk
Total Pitches: 12 (C & CV)

Moss Wood Caravan Park
Crimbles Lane, Cockerham
LA2 0ES
Tel: 01524 791041 **83 L5**
mosswood.co.uk
Total Pitches: 25 (C, CV & T)

Naburn Lock Caravan Park
Naburn
YO19 4RU
Tel: 01904 728697 **86 B6**
naburnlock.co.uk
Total Pitches: 100 (C, CV & T)

New Lodge Farm C & C Site
New Lodge Farm, Bulwick, Corby
NN17 3DU
Tel: 01780 450493 **55 N2**
newlodgefarm.com
Total Pitches: 72 (C, CV & T)

Newberry Valley Park
Woodlands, Combe Martin
EX34 0AT
Tel: 01271 882334 **19 L4**
newberryvalleypark.co.uk
Total Pitches: 110 (C, CV & T)

Newlands Holidays
Charmouth, Bridport
DT6 6RB
Tel: 01297 560259 **10 B6**
newlandsholidays.co.uk
Total Pitches: 240 (C, CV & T)

Newperran Holiday Park
Rejerrah, Newquay
TR8 5QJ
Tel: 01872 572407 **3 K4**
newperran.co.uk
Total Pitches: 357 (C, CV & T)

Ninham Country Holidays
Ninham, Shanklin, Isle of Wight
PO37 7PL
Tel: 01983 864243 **13 J8**
ninham-holidays.co.uk
Total Pitches: 135 (C, CV & T)

North Morte Farm C & C Park
North Morte Road, Mortehoe, Woolacombe
EX34 7EG
Tel: 01271 870381 **19 J4**
northmortefarm.co.uk
Total Pitches: 180 (C, CV & T)

Northam Farm Caravan & Touring Park
Brean, Burnham-on-Sea
TA8 2SE
Tel: 01278 751244 **21 M2**
northamfarm.co.uk
Total Pitches: 350 (C, CV & T)

Oakdown Country Holiday Park
Gatedown Lane, Weston, Sidmouth
EX10 0PT
Tel: 01297 680387 **9 M7**
oakdown.co.uk
Total Pitches: 150 (C, CV & T)

Old Hall Caravan Park
Capernwray, Carnforth
LA6 1AD
Tel: 01524 733276 **83 M1**
oldhallcaravanpark.co.uk
Total Pitches: 38 (C & CV)

Orchard Park
Frampton Lane, Hubbert's Bridge, Boston
PE20 3QU
Tel: 01205 290328 **68 E3**
orchardpark.co.uk
Total Pitches: 87 (C, CV & T)

Ord House Country Park
East Ord, Berwick-upon-Tweed
TD15 2NS
Tel: 01289 305288 **117 L11**
ordhouse.co.uk
Total Pitches: 79 (C, CV & T)

Oxon Hall Touring Park
Welshpool Road, Shrewsbury
SY3 5FB
Tel: 01743 340868 **63 M9**
morris-leisure.co.uk
Total Pitches: 105 (C, CV & T)

Padstow Touring Park
Padstow
PL28 8LE
Tel: 01841 532061 **6 C10**
padstowtouringpark.co.uk
Total Pitches: 150 (C, CV & T)

Park Cliffe C & C Estate
Birks Road, Tower Wood, Windermere
LA23 3PG
Tel: 015395 31344 **89 L8**
parkcliffe.co.uk
Total Pitches: 60 (C, CV & T)

Parkers Farm Holiday Park
Higher Mead Farm, Ashburton, Devon
TQ13 7LJ
Tel: 01364 654869 8 E10
parkersfarmholidays.co.uk
Total Pitches: 100 (C, CV & T)

Parkland C & C Site
Sorley Green Cross, Kingsbridge
TQ7 4AF
Tel: 01548 852723 5 M7
parklandsite.co.uk
Total Pitches: 50 (C, CV & T)

Penrose Holiday Park
Goonhavern, Truro
TR4 9QF
Tel: 01872 573185 3 K4
penroseholidaypark.com
Total Pitches: 110 (C, CV & T)

Pentire Haven Holiday Park
Stibb Road, Kilkhampton, Bude
EX23 9QY
Tel: 01288 321601 7 J3
pentirehaven.co.uk
Total Pitches: 120 (C, CV & T)

Petwood Caravan Park
Off Stixwould Road, Woodhall Spa
LN10 6QH
Tel: 01526 354799 80 D11
petwoodcaravanpark.com
Total Pitches: 98 (C, CV & T)

Polmanter Touring Park
Halsetown, St Ives
TR26 3LX
Tel: 01736 795640 2 E7
polmanter.co.uk
Total Pitches: 270 (C, CV & T)

Porlock Caravan Park
Porlock, Minehead
TA24 8ND
Tel: 01643 862269 20 D4
porlockcaravanpark.co.uk
Total Pitches: 40 (C, CV & T)

Porthtowan Tourist Park
Mile Hill, Porthtowan, Truro
TR4 8TY
Tel: 01209 890256 2 H5
porthtowantouristpark.co.uk
Total Pitches: 80 (C, CV & T)

Quantock Orchard Caravan Park
Flaxpool, Crowcombe, Taunton
TA4 4AW
Tel: 01984 618618 21 J6
quantock-orchard.co.uk
Total Pitches: 60 (C, CV & T)

Ranch Caravan Park
Station Road, Honeybourne, Evesham
WR11 7PR
Tel: 01386 830744 42 C3
ranch.co.uk
Total Pitches: 120 (C & CV)

Riddings Wood C & C Park
Bullock Lane, Riddings, Alfreton
DE55 4BP
Tel: 01773 605160 66 C2
riddingswoodcaravanandcampingpark.co.uk
Total Pitches: 75 (C, CV & T)

Ripley Caravan Park
Knaresborough Road, Ripley, Harrogate
HG3 3AU
Tel: 01423 770050 85 L3
ripleycaravanpark.com
Total Pitches: 60 (C, CV & T)

River Dart Country Park
Holne Park, Ashburton
TQ13 7NP
Tel: 01364 652511 5 M3
riverdart.co.uk
Total Pitches: 170 (C, CV & T)

River Valley Holiday Park
London Apprentice, St Austell
PL26 7AP
Tel: 01726 73533 3 N4
rivervalleyholidaypark.co.uk
Total Pitches: 45 (C, CV & T)

Riverside C & C Park
Marsh Lane, North Molton Road, South Molton
EX36 3HQ
Tel: 01769 579269 19 P8
exmoorriverside.co.uk
Total Pitches: 58 (C, CV & T)

Riverside Caravan Park
High Bentham, Lancaster
LA2 7FJ
Tel: 015242 61272 83 P1
riversidecaravanpark.co.uk
Total Pitches: 61 (C & CV)

Riverside Caravan Park
Leigham Manor Drive, Marsh Mills, Plymouth
PL6 8LL
Tel: 01752 344122 4 H5
riversidecaravanpark.com
Total Pitches: 259 (C, CV & T)

Riverside Meadows Country Caravan Park
Ure Bank Top, Ripon
HG4 1JD
Tel: 01765 602964 91 N12
flowerofmay.com
Total Pitches: 80 (C, CV & T)

Robin Hood C & C Park
Green Dyke Lane, Slingsby
YO62 4AP
Tel: 01653 628391 92 E11
robinhoodcaravanpark.co.uk
Total Pitches: 32 (C, CV & T)

Rose Farm Touring & Camping Park
Stepshort, Belton, Nr Great Yarmouth
NR31 9JS
Tel: 01493 780896 71 P11
rosefarmtouringpark.co.uk
Total Pitches: 145 (C, CV & T)

Rosedale C & C Park
Rosedale Abbey, Pickering
YO18 8SA
Tel: 01751 417272 92 E7
flowerofmay.com
Total Pitches: 100 (C, CV & T)

Ross Park
Park Hill Farm, Ipplepen, Newton Abbot
TQ12 5TT
Tel: 01803 812983 5 P3
rossparkcaravanpark.co.uk
Total Pitches: 110 (C, CV & T)

Rudding Holiday Park
Follifoot, Harrogate
HG3 1JH
Tel: 01423 870439 85 L4
ruddingholidaypark.co.uk
Total Pitches: 86 (C, CV & T)

Run Cottage Touring Park
Alderton Road, Hollesley, Woodbridge
IP12 3RQ
Tel: 01394 411309 47 P3
runcottage.co.uk
Total Pitches: 45 (C, CV & T)

Rutland C & C
Park Lane, Greetham, Oakham
LE15 7FN
Tel: 01572 813520 67 M9
rutlandcaravanandcamping.co.uk
Total Pitches: 130 (C, CV & T)

St Helens Caravan Park
Wykeham, Scarborough
YO13 9QD
Tel: 01723 862771 93 K10
sthelenscaravanpark.co.uk
Total Pitches: 250 (C, CV & T)

St Mabyn Holiday Park
Longstone Road, St Mabyn, Wadebridge
PL30 3BY
Tel: 01208 841677 6 F10
stmabynholidaypark.co.uk
Total Pitches: 120 (C, CV & T)

Sandy Balls Holiday Village
Sandy Balls Estate Ltd, Godshill, Fordingbridge
SP6 2JZ
Tel: 0844 693 1336 24 B10
sandyballs.co.uk
Total Pitches: 225 (C, CV & T)

Seaview International Holiday Park
Boswinger, Mevagissey
PL26 6LL
Tel: 01726 843425 3 N6
seaviewinternational.com
Total Pitches: 201 (C, CV & T)

Severn Gorge Park
Bridgnorth Road, Tweedale, Telford
TF7 4JB
Tel: 01952 684789 64 D11
severngorgepark.co.uk
Total Pitches: 12 (C & CV)

Shamba Holidays
East Moors Lane, St Leonards, Ringwood
BH24 2SB
Tel: 01202 873302 11 Q4
shambaholidays.co.uk
Total Pitches: 150 (C, CV & T)

Shrubbery Touring Park
Rousdon, Lyme Regis
DT7 3XW
Tel: 01297 442227 9 P6
shrubberypark.co.uk
Total Pitches: 120 (C, CV & T)

Silverbow Park
Perranwell, Goonhavern
TR4 9NX
Tel: 01872 572347 3 J4
silverbowpark.co.uk
Total Pitches: 90 (C, CV & T)

Silverdale Caravan Park
Middlebarrow Plain, Cove Road, Silverdale, Nr Carnforth
LA5 0SH
Tel: 01524 701508 89 M11
holgates.co.uk
Total Pitches: 80 (C, CV & T)

Skelwith Fold Caravan Park
Ambleside, Cumbria
LA22 0HX
Tel: 015394 32277 89 K6
skelwith.com
Total Pitches: 150 (C & CV)

Somers Wood Caravan Park
Somers Road, Meriden
CV7 7PL
Tel: 01676 522978 53 N4
somerswood.co.uk
Total Pitches: 48 (C & CV)

South Lytchett Manor C & C Park
Dorchester Road, Lytchett Minster, Poole
BH16 6JB
Tel: 01202 622577 11 M6
southlytchettmanor.co.uk
Total Pitches: 150 (C, CV & T)

South Meadows Caravan Park
South Road, Belford
NE70 7DP
Tel: 01668 213326 109 J3
southmeadows.co.uk
Total Pitches: 83 (C, CV & T)

Stanmore Hall Touring Park
Stourbridge Road, Bridgnorth
WV15 6DT
Tel: 01746 761761 52 D2
morris-leisure.co.uk
Total Pitches: 129 (C, CV & T)

Stowford Farm Meadows
Berry Down, Combe Martin
EX34 0PW
Tel: 01271 882476 19 L5
stowford.co.uk
Total Pitches: 700 (C, CV & T)

Stroud Hill Park
Fen Road, Pidley, St Ives
PE28 3DE
Tel: 01487 741333 56 G5
stroudhillpark.co.uk
Total Pitches: 60 (C, CV & T)

Summers Ponds Fishery & Campsite
Chapel Road, Barns Green, Horsham
RH13 0PR
Tel: 01403 732539 14 G5
summersponds.co.uk
Total Pitches: 86 (C, CV & T)

Sun Valley Resort
Pentewan Road, St Austell
PL26 6DJ
Tel: 01726 843266 3 N5
sunvalleyresort.co.uk
Total Pitches: 29 (C, CV & T)

Swiss Farm Touring & Camping
Marlow Road, Henley-on-Thames
RG9 2HY
Tel: 01491 573419 31 Q6
swissfarmcamping.co.uk
Total Pitches: 140 (C, CV & T)

Tanner Farm Touring C & C Park
Tanner Farm, Goudhurst Road, Marden
TN12 9ND
Tel: 01622 832399 16 C3
tannerfarmpark.co.uk
Total Pitches: 120 (C, CV & T)

Tattershall Lakes Country Park
Sleaford Road, Tattershall
LN4 4LR
Tel: 01526 348800 80 D12
tattershall-lakes.com
Total Pitches: 186 (C, CV & T)

Tehidy Holiday Park
Harris Mill, Illogan, Portreath
TR16 4JQ
Tel: 01209 216489 2 H6
tehidy.co.uk
Total Pitches: 18 (C, CV & T)

Teversal C & C Club Site
Silverhill Lane, Teversal
NG17 3JJ
Tel: 01623 551838 78 D11
campingandcaravanningclub.co.uk/teversal
Total Pitches: 126 (C, CV & T)

The Inside Park
Down House Estate, Blandford Forum
DT11 9AD
Tel: 01258 453719 11 L4
theinsidepark.co.uk
Total Pitches: 125 (C, CV & T)

The Laurels Holiday Park
Padstow Road, Whitecross, Wadebridge
PL27 7JQ
Tel: 01209 313474 6 D10
thelaurelsholidaypark.co.uk
Total Pitches: 30 (C, CV & T)

The Old Brick Kilns
Little Barney Lane, Barney, Fakenham
NR21 0NL
Tel: 01328 878305 70 E5
old-brick-kilns.co.uk
Total Pitches: 65 (C, CV & T)

The Old Oaks Touring Park
Wick Farm, Wick, Glastonbury
BA6 8JS
Tel: 01458 831437 22 C5
theoldoaks.co.uk
Total Pitches: 98 (C, CV & T)

The Orchards Holiday Caravan Park
Main Road, Newbridge, Yarmouth, Isle of Wight
PO41 0TS
Tel: 01983 531331 12 G7
orchards-holiday-park.co.uk
Total Pitches: 160 (C, CV & T)

The Quiet Site
Ullswater, Watermillock
CA11 0LS
Tel: 07768 727016 89 L2
thequietsite.co.uk
Total Pitches: 100 (C, CV & T)

The Ranch Caravan Park
Cliffe Common, Selby
YO8 6PA
Tel: 01757 638984 86 C8
theranchcaravanpark.co.uk
Total Pitches: 44 (C, CV & T)

Treago Farm Caravan Site
Crantock, Newquay
TR8 5QS
Tel: 01637 830277 3 J2
treagofarm.co.uk
Total Pitches: 90 (C, CV & T)

Tregoad Park
St Martin, Looe
PL13 1PB
Tel: 01503 262718 4 D5
tregoadpark.co.uk
Total Pitches: 200 (C, CV & T)

Treloy Touring Park
Newquay
TR8 4JN
Tel: 01637 872063 3 L2
treloy.co.uk
Total Pitches: 223 (C, CV & T)

Trencreek Holiday Park
Hillcrest, Higher Trencreek, Newquay
TR8 4NS
Tel: 01637 874210 3 K2
trencreekholidaypark.co.uk
Total Pitches: 194 (C, CV & T)

Trethem Mill Touring Park
St Just-in-Roseland, Nr St Mawes, Truro
TR2 5JF
Tel: 01872 580504 3 L7
trethem.com
Total Pitches: 84 (C, CV & T)

Trevalgan Touring Park
Trevalgan, St Ives
TR26 3BJ
Tel: 01736 791892 2 D6
trevalgantouringpark.co.uk
Total Pitches: 135 (C, CV & T)

Trevella Park
Crantock, Newquay
TR8 5EW
Tel: 01637 830308 3 K3
trevella.co.uk
Total Pitches: 165 (C, CV & T)

Trevornick
Holywell Bay, Newquay
TR8 5PW
Tel: 01637 830531 3 J3
trevornick.co.uk
Total Pitches: 688 (C, CV & T)

Truro C & C Park
Truro
TR4 8QN
Tel: 01872 560274 3 J5
trurocaravanandcampingpark.co.uk
Total Pitches: 51 (C, CV & T)

Tudor C & C
Shepherds Patch, Slimbridge, Gloucester
GL2 7BP
Tel: 01453 890483 41 L11
tudorcaravanpark.com
Total Pitches: 75 (C, CV & T)

Two Mills Touring Park
Yarmouth Road, North Walsham
NR28 9NA
Tel: 01692 405829 71 K6
twomills.co.uk
Total Pitches: 81 (C, CV & T)

Ulwell Cottage Caravan Park
Ulwell Cottage, Ulwell, Swanage
BH19 3DG
Tel: 01929 422823 11 N8
ulwellcottagepark.co.uk
Total Pitches: 77 (C, CV & T)

Vale of Pickering Caravan Park
Carr House Farm, Allerston, Pickering
YO18 7PQ
Tel: 01723 859280 92 H10
valeofpickering.co.uk
Total Pitches: 120 (C, CV & T)

Wagtail Country Park
Cliff Lane, Marston, Grantham
NG32 2HU
Tel: 01400 251955 67 M4
wagtailcountrypark.co.uk
Total Pitches: 76 (C & CV)

Warcombe Farm C & C Park
Station Road, Mortehoe, Woolacombe
EX34 7EJ
Tel: 01271 870690 19 J4
warcombefarm.co.uk
Total Pitches: 250 (C, CV & T)

Wareham Forest Tourist Park
North Trigon, Wareham
BH20 7NZ
Tel: 01929 551393 11 L6
warehamforest.co.uk
Total Pitches: 200 (C, CV & T)

Waren C & C Park
Waren Mill, Bamburgh
NE70 7EE
Tel: 01668 214366 109 J3
meadowhead.co.uk
Total Pitches: 150 (C, CV & T)

Watergate Bay Touring Park
Watergate Bay, Tregurrian
TR8 4AD
Tel: 01637 860387 6 B11
watergatebaytouringpark.co.uk
Total Pitches: 171 (C, CV & T)

Waterrow Touring Park
Wiveliscombe, Taunton
TA4 2AZ
Tel: 01984 623464 20 G8
waterrowpark.co.uk
Total Pitches: 44 (C, CV & T)

Wayfarers C & C Park
Relubbus Lane, St Hilary, Penzance
TR20 9EF
Tel: 01736 763326 2 E8
wayfarerspark.co.uk
Total Pitches: 32 (C, CV & T)

Wells Touring Park
Haybridge, Wells
BA5 1AJ
Tel: 01749 676869 22 C4
wellstouringpark.co.uk
Total Pitches: 72 (C, CV & T)

Wheathill Touring Park
Wheathill, Bridgnorth
WV16 6QT
Tel: 01584 823456 51 Q4
wheathillpark.co.uk
Total Pitches: 25 (C & CV)

Whitefield Forest Touring Park
Brading Road, Ryde, Isle of Wight
PO33 1QL
Tel: 01983 617069 13 K7
whitefieldforest.co.uk
Total Pitches: 90 (C, CV & T)

Widdicombe Farm Touring Park
Marldon, Paignton
TQ3 1ST
Tel: 01803 558325 5 P4
widdicombefarm.co.uk
Total Pitches: 180 (C, CV & T)

Widemouth Fields C & C Park
Park Farm, Poundstock, Bude
EX23 0NA
Tel: 01288 361351 7 J4
peterbullresorts.co.uk/widemouth-fields
Total Pitches: 156 (C, CV & T)

Wight Glamping Holidays
Everland, Long Lane, Newport, Isle of Wight
PO30 2NW
Tel: 01983 532507 13 J7
wightglampingholidays.co.uk
Total Pitches: 4 (T)

Wild Rose Park
Ormside, Appleby-in-Westmorland
CA16 6EJ
Tel: 017683 51077 90 A3
harrisonholidayhomes.co.uk
Total Pitches: 226 (C & CV)

Wilksworth Farm Caravan Park
Cranborne Road, Wimborne Minster
BH21 4HW
Tel: 01202 885467 11 N4
wilksworthfarmcaravanpark.co.uk
Total Pitches: 85 (C, CV & T)

Willowbank Holiday Home & Touring Park
Coastal Road, Ainsdale, Southport
PR8 3ST
Tel: 01704 571566 75 K2
willowbankcp.co.uk
Total Pitches: 87 (C & CV)

Wolds View Touring Park
115 Brigg Road, Caistor
LN7 6RX
Tel: 01472 851099 80 B3
woldsviewtouringpark.co.uk
Total Pitches: 60 (C, CV & T)

Wood Farm C & C Park
Axminster Road, Charmouth
DT6 6BT
Tel: 01297 560697 9 Q6
woodfarm.co.uk
Total Pitches: 175 (C, CV & T)

Wooda Farm Holiday Park
Poughill, Bude
EX23 9HJ
Tel: 01288 352069 7 J3
wooda.co.uk
Total Pitches: 200 (C, CV & T)

Woodclose Caravan Park
High Casterton, Kirkby Lonsdale
LA6 2SE
Tel: 015242 71597 89 Q11
woodclosepark.com
Total Pitches: 22 (C, CV & T)

Woodhall Country Park
Stixwold Road, Woodhall Spa
LN10 6UJ
Tel: 01526 353710 80 D10
woodhallcountrypark.co.uk
Total Pitches: 115 (C, CV & T)

Woodland Springs Adult Touring Park
Venton, Drewsteignton
EX6 6PG
Tel: 01647 231695 8 D6
woodlandsprings.co.uk
Total Pitches: 81 (C, CV & T)

Woodlands Grove C & C Park
Blackawton, Dartmouth
TQ9 7DQ
Tel: 01803 712598 5 N6
woodlands-caravanpark.com
Total Pitches: 350 (C, CV & T)

Woodovis Park
Gulworthy, Tavistock
PL19 8NY
Tel: 01822 832968 7 N10
woodovis.com
Total Pitches: 50 (C, CV & T)

Yeatheridge Farm Caravan Park
East Worlington, Crediton
EX17 4TN
Tel: 01884 860330 8 E3
yeatheridge.co.uk
Total Pitches: 103 (C, CV & T)

SCOTLAND

Aviemore Glamping
Eriskay, Craignagower Avenue, Aviemore
PH22 1RW
Tel: 01479 810717 130 G2
aviemoreglamping.com
Total Pitches: 4 (T)

Banff Links Caravan Park
Inverboyndie, Banff
AB45 2JJ
Tel: 01261 812228 140 G3
banfflinkscaravanpark.co.uk
Total Pitches: 55 (C, CV & T)

Beecraigs C & C Site
Beecraigs Country Park, The Visitor Centre, Linlithgow
EH49 6PL
Tel: 01506 844516 115 J6
beecraigs.com
Total Pitches: 36 (C, CV & T)

Blair Castle Caravan Park
Blair Atholl, Pitlochry
PH18 5SR
Tel: 01796 481263 130 F11
blaircastlecaravanpark.co.uk
Total Pitches: 226 (C, CV & T)

Brighouse Bay Holiday Park
Brighouse Bay, Borgue, Kirkcudbright
DG6 4TS
Tel: 01557 870267 96 D9
gillespie-leisure.co.uk
Total Pitches: 190 (C, CV & T)

Cairnsmill Holiday Park
Largo Road, St Andrews
KY16 8NN
Tel: 01334 473604 125 K10
cairnsmill.co.uk
Total Pitches: 62 (C, CV & T)

Craigtoun Meadows Holiday Park
Mount Melville, St Andrews
KY16 8PQ
Tel: 01334 475959 125 J10
craigtounmeadows.co.uk
Total Pitches: 56 (C, CV & T)

Gart Caravan Park
The Gart, Callander
FK17 8LE
Tel: 01877 330002 122 G11
theholidaypark.co.uk
Total Pitches: 128 (C & CV)

Glen Nevis C & C Park
Glen Nevis, Fort William
PH33 6SX
Tel: 01397 702191 128 F10
glen-nevis.co.uk
Total Pitches: 380 (C, CV & T)

Glenearly Caravan Park
Dalbeattie
DG5 4NE
Tel: 01556 611393 96 G6
glenearlycaravanpark.co.uk
Total Pitches: 39 (C, CV & T)

Hoddom Castle Caravan Park
Hoddom, Lockerbie
DG11 1AS
Tel: 01576 300251 97 N4
hoddomcastle.co.uk
Total Pitches: 200 (C, CV & T)

Huntly Castle Caravan Park
The Meadow, Huntly
AB54 4UJ
Tel: 01466 794999 140 E8
huntlycastle.co.uk
Total Pitches: 90 (C, CV & T)

Linnhe Lochside Holidays
Corpach, Fort William
PH33 7NL
Tel: 01397 772376 128 F9
linnhe-lochside-holidays.co.uk
Total Pitches: 85 (C, CV & T)

Loch Ken Holiday Park
Parton, Castle Douglas
DG7 3NE
Tel: 01644 470282 96 E4
lochkenholidaypark.co.uk
Total Pitches: 40 (C, CV & T)

Loch Shin Wigwams
Forge Cottage, Achfrish, Shinness, Lairg
IV27 4DN
Tel: 01549 402936 145 N3
wigwamholidays.com
Total Pitches: 2 (T)

Lomond Woods Holiday Park
Old Luss Road, Balloch, Loch Lomond
G83 8QP
Tel: 01389 755000 113 M5
holiday-parks.co.uk
Total Pitches: 115 (C & CV)

Milton of Fonab Caravan Park
Bridge Road, Pitlochry
PH16 5NA
Tel: 01796 472882 123 N1
fonab.co.uk
Total Pitches: 154 (C, CV & T)

River Tilt Caravan Park
Blair Atholl, Pitlochry
PH18 5TE
Tel: 01796 481467 130 G11
rivertiltpark.co.uk
Total Pitches: 30 (C, CV & T)

Runach Arainn
The Old Manse, Kilmory, Isle of Arran
KA27 8PH
Tel: 01770 870515 103 P5
runacharainn.com
Total Pitches: 3 (T)

Sands of Luce Holiday Park
Sands of Luce, Sandhead, Stranraer
DG9 9JN
Tel: 01776 830456 94 G8
sandsofluceholidaypark.co.uk
Total Pitches: 80 (C, CV & T)

Seaward Caravan Park
Dhoon Bay, Kirkudbright
DG6 4TJ
Tel: 01557 870267 96 D8
gillespie-leisure.co.uk
Total Pitches: 25 (C, CV & T)

Shieling Holidays
Craignure, Isle of Mull
PA65 6AY
Tel: 01680 812496 120 D5
shielingholidays.co.uk
Total Pitches: 90 (C, CV & T)

Silver Sands Holiday Park
Covesea, West Beach, Lossiemouth
IV31 6SP
Tel: 01343 813262 147 M11
silver-sands.co.uk
Total Pitches: 140 (C, CV & T)

Skye C & C Club Site
Loch Greshornish, Borve, Arnisort, Edinbane, Isle of Skye
IV51 9PS
Tel: 01470 582230 134 F5
campingandcaravanningclub.co.uk/skye
Total Pitches: 105 (C, CV & T)

Strathfillan Wigwam Village
Auchtertyre Farm, Tyndrum, Crianlarich
FK20 8RU
Tel: 01838 400251 122 B7
wigwamholidays.com
Total Pitches: 23 (T)

Thurston Manor Leisure Park
Innerwick, Dunbar
EH42 1SA
Tel: 01368 840643 116 G6
thurstonmanor.co.uk
Total Pitches: 120 (C & CV)

Trossachs Holiday Park
Aberfoyle
FK8 3SA
Tel: 01877 382614 113 Q2
trossachsholidays.co.uk
Total Pitches: 66 (C, CV & T)

Witches Craig C & C Park
Blairlogie, Stirling
FK9 5PX
Tel: 01786 474947 114 E2
witchescraig.co.uk
Total Pitches: 60 (C, CV & T)

WALES

Bron Derw Touring Caravan Park
Llanrwst
LL26 0YT
Tel: 01492 640494 73 N11
bronderw-wales.co.uk
Total Pitches: 48 (C & CV)

Bron-Y-Wendon Caravan Park
Wern Road, Llanddulas, Colwyn Bay
LL22 8HG
Tel: 01492 512903 74 B8
northwales-holidays.co.uk
Total Pitches: 130 (C & CV)

Bryn Gloch C & C Park
Betws Garmon, Caernarfon
LL54 7YY
Tel: 01286 650216 73 J12
campwales.co.uk
Total Pitches: 160 (C, CV & T)

Caerfai Bay Caravan & Tent Park
Caerfai Bay, St Davids, Haverfordwest
SA62 6QT
Tel: 01437 720274 36 E5
caerfaibay.co.uk
Total Pitches: 106 (C, CV & T)

Cenarth Falls Holiday Park
Cenarth, Newcastle Emlyn
SA38 9JS
Tel: 01239 710345 37 P2
cenarth-holipark.co.uk
Total Pitches: 30 (C, CV & T)

Daisy Bank Caravan Park
Snead, Montgomery
SY15 6EB
Tel: 01588 620471 51 K2
daisy-bank.co.uk
Total Pitches: 80 (C, CV & T)

Deucoch Touring & Camping Park
Sarn Bach, Abersoch
LL53 7LD
Tel: 01758 713293 60 E7
deucoch.com
Total Pitches: 70 (C, CV & T)

Dinlle Caravan Park
Dinas Dinlle, Caernarfon
LL54 5TW
Tel: 01286 830324 72 G12
thornleyleisure.co.uk
Total Pitches: 175 (C, CV & T)

Eisteddfa
Eisteddfa Lodge, Pentrefelin, Criccieth
LL52 0PT
Tel: 01766 522696 61 J4
eisteddfapark.co.uk
Total Pitches: 100 (C, CV & T)

Erwlon C & C Park
Brecon Road, Llandovery
SA20 0RD
Tel: 01550 721021 39 J5
erwlon.co.uk
Total Pitches: 75 (C, CV & T)

Fforest Fields C & C Park
Hundred House, Builth Wells
LD1 5RT
Tel: 01982 570406 50 F10
fforestfields.co.uk
Total Pitches: 120 (C, CV & T)

Hendre Mynach Touring C & C Park
Llanaber Road, Barmouth
LL42 1YR
Tel: 01341 280262 61 K8
hendremynach.co.uk
Total Pitches: 240 (C, CV & T)

Home Farm Caravan Park
Marian-Glas, Isle of Anglesey
LL73 8PH
Tel: 01248 410614 72 H7
homefarm-anglesey.co.uk
Total Pitches: 102 (C, CV & T)

Islawrffordd Caravan Park
Tal-y-bont, Barmouth
LL43 2AQ
Tel: 01341 247269 61 K8
islawrffordd.co.uk
Total Pitches: 105 (C, CV & T)

Llys Derwen C & C Site
Ffordd Bryngwyn, Llanrug, Caernarfon
LL55 4RD
Tel: 01286 673322 73 J11
llysderwen.co.uk
Total Pitches: 20 (C, CV & T)

Moelfryn C & C Park
Ty-Cefn, Pant-y-Bwlch, Newcastle Emlyn
SA38 9JE
Tel: 01559 371231 37 Q3
moelfryncaravanpark.co.uk
Total Pitches: 25 (C, CV & T)

Pencelli Castle C & C Park
Pencelli, Brecon
LD3 7LX
Tel: 01874 665451 39 P7
pencelli-castle.com
Total Pitches: 80 (C, CV & T)

Penhein Glamping
Penhein, Llanvair Discoed, Chepstow
NP16 6RB
Tel: 01633 400581 28 F4
penhein.co.uk
Total Pitches: 6 (T)

Penisar Mynydd Caravan Park
Caerwys Road, Rhuallt, St Asaph
LL17 0TY
Tel: 01745 582227 74 F8
penisarmynydd.co.uk
Total Pitches: 71 (C, CV & T)

Plas Farm Caravan Park
Betws-yn-Rhos, Abergele
LL22 8AU
Tel: 01492 680254 74 B9
plasfarmcaravanpark.co.uk
Total Pitches: 54 (C, CV & T)

Plassey Holiday Park
The Plassey, Eyton, Wrexham
LL13 0SP
Tel: 01978 780277 63 K3
plassey.com
Total Pitches: 90 (C, CV & T)

Pont Kemys C & C Park
Chainbridge, Abergavenny
NP7 9DS
Tel: 01873 880688 40 D10
pontkemys.com
Total Pitches: 65 (C, CV & T)

Red Kite Touring Park
Van Road, Llanidloes
SY18 6NG
Tel: 01686 412122 50 C4
redkitetouringpark.co.uk
Total Pitches: 66 (C & CV)

River View Touring Park
The Dingle, Llanedi, Pontarddulais
SA4 0FH
Tel: 01635 844876 38 E10
riverviewtouringpark.com
Total Pitches: 60 (C, CV & T)

Riverside Camping
Seiont Nurseries, Pont Rug, Caernarfon
LL55 2BB
Tel: 01286 678781 72 H11
riversidecamping.co.uk
Total Pitches: 73 (C, CV & T)

St David's Park
Red Wharf Bay, Pentraeth, Isle of Anglesey
LL75 8RJ
Tel: 01248 852341 73 J7
stdavidspark.com
Total Pitches: 45 (C, CV & T)

The Little Yurt Meadow
Bay Tree Barns, Mill Road, Bronington
SY13 3HJ
Tel: 01948 780136 63 N4
thelittleyurtmeadow.co.uk
Total Pitches: 3 (T)

Trawsdir Touring C & C Park
Llanaber, Barmouth
LL42 1RR
Tel: 01341 280999 61 K8
barmouthholidays.co.uk
Total Pitches: 70 (C, CV & T)

Trefalun Park
Devonshire Drive, St Florence, Tenby
SA70 8RD
Tel: 01646 651514 37 L10
trefalunpark.co.uk
Total Pitches: 90 (C, CV & T)

Tyddyn Isaf Caravan Park
Lligwy Bay, Dulas, Isle of Anglesey
LL70 9PQ
Tel: 01248 410203 72 H6
tyddynisaf.co.uk
Total Pitches: 80 (C, CV & T)

White Tower Caravan Park
Llandwrog, Caernarfon
LL54 5UH
Tel: 01286 830649 72 G12
whitetowerpark.co.uk
Total Pitches: 52 (C & CV)

CHANNEL ISLANDS

Beuvelande Camp Site
Beuvelande, St Martin, Jersey
JE3 6EZ
Tel: 01534 853575 13 d2
campingjersey.com
Total Pitches: 150 (C, CV & T)

Durrell Wildlife Camp
Les Augres Manor, La Profonde Rue, Trinity, Jersey
JE3 5BP
Tel: 01534 860095 13 c1
durrell.org/camp
Total Pitches: 12 (T)

Fauxquets Valley Campsite
Castel, Guernsey
GY5 7QL
Tel: 01481 255460 12 c2
fauxquets.co.uk
Total Pitches: 120 (C, CV & T)

Rozel Camping Park
Summerville Farm, St Martin, Jersey
JE3 6AX
Tel: 01534 855200 13 d1
rozelcamping.com
Total Pitches: 100 (C, CV & T)

Traffic signs

Signs giving orders

Signs with red circles are mostly prohibitive. Plates below signs qualify their message.

 Entry to 20mph zone

 End of 20mph zone

Maximum speed

National speed limit applies

School crossing patrol

Stop and give way

Give way to traffic on major road

Manually operated temporary STOP and GO signs

No entry for vehicular traffic

No vehicles except bicycles being pushed

No cycling

No motor vehicles

No buses (over 8 passenger seats)

No overtaking

No towed caravans

No vehicles carrying explosives

No vehicle or combination of vehicles over length shown

No vehicles over height shown

No vehicles over width shown

Give priority to vehicles from opposite direction

No right turn

No left turn

No U-turns

No goods vehicles over maximum gross weight shown (in tonnes) except for loading and unloading

No vehicles over maximum gross weight shown (in tonnes)

Parking restricted to permit holders

No stopping during period indicated except for buses

No stopping during times shown except for as long as necessary to set down or pick up passengers

No waiting

No stopping (Clearway)

Signs with blue circles but no red border mostly give positive instruction.

Ahead only

Turn left ahead (right if symbol reversed)

Turn left (right if symbol reversed)

Keep left (right if symbol reversed)

Vehicles may pass either side to reach same destination

Mini-roundabout (roundabout circulation – give way to vehicles from the immediate right)

Route to be used by pedal cycles only

Segregated pedal cycle and pedestrian route

Minimum speed

End of minimum speed

Buses and cycles only

Trams only

Pedestrian crossing point over tramway

One-way traffic (note: compare circular 'Ahead only' sign)

With-flow bus and cycle lane

Contraflow bus lane

With-flow pedal cycle lane

Note: The signs shown in this road atlas are those most commonly in use and are not all drawn to the same scale. In Scotland and Wales bilingual versions of some signs are used, showing both English and Gaelic or Welsh spellings. Some older designs of signs may still be seen on the roads. A comprehensive explanation of the signing system illustrating the vast majority of road signs can be found in the AA's handbook *Know Your Road Signs*. Where there is a reference to a rule number, this refers to *The Highway Code*. Both of these publications are on sale at theaa.com/shop and booksellers.

Warning signs

Mostly triangular

Distance to 'STOP' line ahead

Dual carriageway ends

Road narrows on right (left if symbol reversed)

Road narrows on both sides

Distance to 'Give Way' line ahead

Crossroads

Junction on bend ahead

T-junction with priority over vehicles from the right

Staggered junction

Traffic merging from left ahead

The priority through route is indicated by the broader line.

Double bend first to left (symbol may be reversed)

Bend to right (or left if symbol reversed)

Roundabout

Uneven road

Plate below some signs (REDUCE SPEED NOW)

Two-way traffic crosses one-way road

Two-way traffic straight ahead

Opening or swing bridge ahead

Low-flying aircraft or sudden aircraft noise

Falling or fallen rocks

Traffic signals not in use

Traffic signals

Slippery road

Steep hill downwards

Steep hill upwards

Gradients may be shown as a ratio i.e. 20% = 1:5

Tunnel ahead

Trams crossing ahead

Level crossing with barrier or gate ahead

Level crossing without barrier or gate ahead

Level crossing without barrier

School crossing patrol ahead (some signs have amber lights which flash when crossings are in use) (Patrol)

Frail (or blind or disabled if shown) pedestrians likely to cross road ahead

Pedestrians in road ahead (No footway for 400 yds)

Zebra crossing

Overhead electric cable; plate indicates maximum height of vehicles which can pass safely (Safe height 16'-6")

Available width of headroom indicated

Sharp deviation of route to left (or right if chevrons reversed)

Light signals ahead at level crossing, airfield or bridge (STOP when lights show)

Miniature warning lights at level crossings (Red/Green STOP/Clear — IF NO LIGHT - PHONE CROSSING OPERATOR)

Cattle

Wild animals

Wild horses or ponies

Accompanied horses or ponies

Cycle route ahead

Risk of ice (Ice)

Traffic queues likely ahead (Queues likely)

Distance over which road humps extend (Humps for ½ mile)

Other danger; plate indicates nature of danger (Hidden dip)

Soft verges (Soft verges for 2 miles)

Side winds

Hump bridge

Ford (Worded warning sign)

Quayside or river bank

Risk of grounding

Direction signs

Mostly rectangular

Signs on motorways – blue backgrounds

 At a junction leading directly into a motorway (junction number may be shown on a black background)

 On approaches to junctions (junction number on black background)

 Route confirmatory sign after junction

 Downward pointing arrows mean 'Get in lane' The left-hand lane leads to a different destination from the other lanes.

 The panel with the inclined arrow indicates the destinations which can be reached by leaving the motorway at the next junction

Signs on primary routes - green backgrounds

 On approaches to junctions

 At the junction

 On approaches to junctions

Route confirmatory sign after junction

 On approach to a junction in Wales (bilingual)

Blue panels indicate that the motorway starts at the junction ahead. Motorways shown in brackets can be reached along the route indicated. White panels indicate local or non-primary routes leading from the junction ahead. Brown panels show the route to tourist attractions. The name of the junction may be shown at the top of the sign. The aircraft symbol indicates the route to an airport. A symbol may be included to warn of a hazard or restriction along that route.

 Primary route forming part of a ring road

 (R)

Signs on non-primary and local routes - black borders

 On approaches to junctions

 At the junction

Direction to toilets with access for the disabled

Green panels indicate that the primary route starts at the junction ahead. Route numbers on a blue background show the direction to a motorway. Route numbers on a green background show the direction to a primary route.

Other direction signs

 Picnic site

 Ancient monument in the care of English Heritage (Wrest Park)

 Direction to a car park (Saturday only)

 Tourist attraction (Zoo)

Direction to camping and caravan site (300 yds)

Advisory route for lorries

Route for pedal cycles forming part of a network

Recommended route for pedal cycles to place shown (Marton 3)

Route for pedestrians (Public library Council offices)

Emergency diversion routes

  Symbols showing emergency diversion route for motorway and other main road traffic

 Diversion route (Northtown)

In an emergency it may be necessary to close a section of motorway or other main road to traffic, so a temporary sign may advise drivers to follow a diversion route. To help drivers navigate the route, black symbols on yellow patches may be permanently displayed on existing direction signs, including motorway signs. Symbols may also be used on separate signs with yellow backgrounds.

For further information see
www.theaa.com/motoring_advice/general-advice/emergency-diversion-routes.html

Information signs

All rectangular

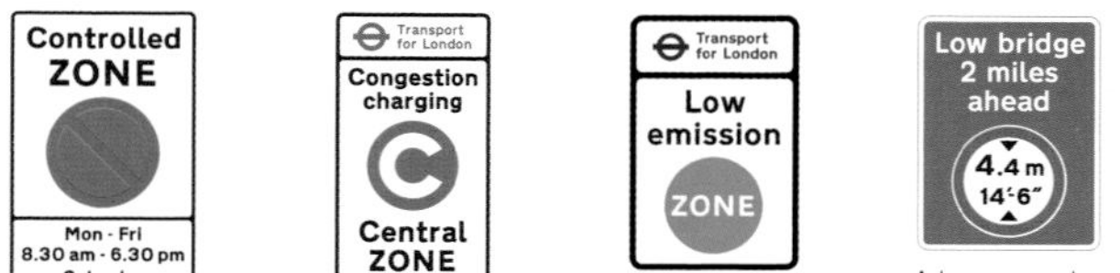
Controlled
ZONE
Mon - Fri
8.30 am - 6.30 pm
Saturday
8.30 am - 1.30 pm
Congestion
charging
Central
ZONE
Mon - Fri
7 am - 6 pm
Low
emission
ZONE
Low bridge
2 miles
ahead
4.4 m
14'6"

Entrance to controlled parking zone

Entrance to congestion charging zone

Greater London Low Emission Zone (LEZ)

Advance warning of restriction or prohibition ahead

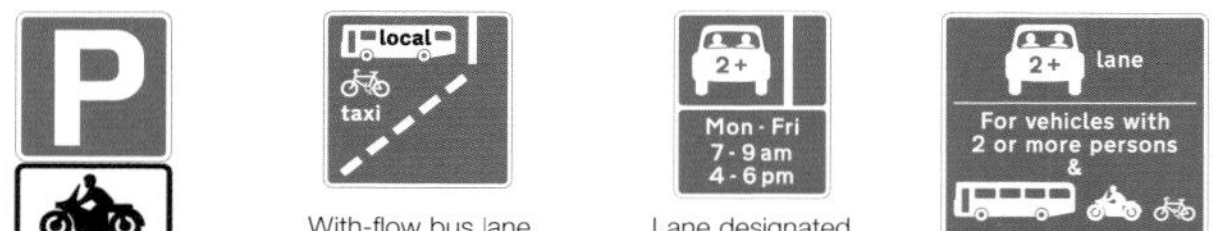
P
local
taxi
2+
Mon - Fri
7 - 9 am
4 - 6 pm
lane
For vehicles with
2 or more persons
No HGVs
over 7.5T

Parking place for solo motorcycles

With-flow bus lane ahead which pedal cycles and taxis may also use

Lane designated for use by high occupancy vehicles (HOV) - see rule 142

Vehicles permitted to use an HOV lane ahead

M62
Except
buses

End of motorway

Start of motorway and point from which motorway regulations apply

Appropriate traffic lanes at junction ahead

Traffic on the main carriageway coming from right has priority over joining traffic

Additional traffic joining from left ahead. Traffic on main carriageway has priority over joining traffic from right hand lane of slip road.

Traffic in right hand lane of slip road joining the main carriageway has prority over left hand lane

'Countdown' markers at exit from motorway (each bar represents 100 yards to the exit). Green-backed markers may be used on primary routes and white-backed markers with black bars on other routes. At approaches to concealed level crossings white-backed markers with red bars may be used. Although these will be erected at equal distances the bars do not represent 100 yard intervals.

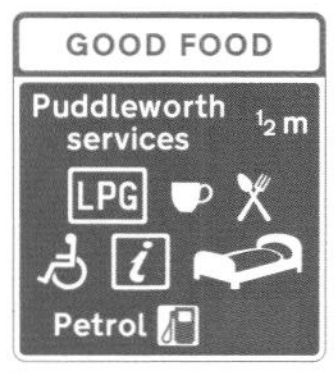
GOOD FOOD
Puddleworth
services
½ m
LPG
Petrol

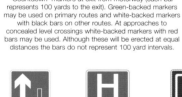

Motorway service area sign showing the operator's name

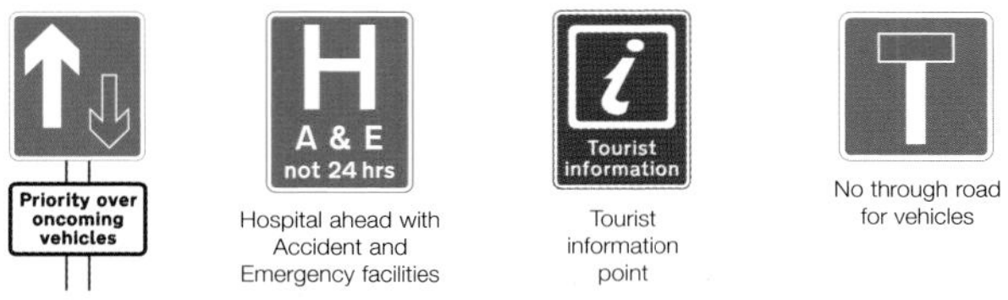
Priority over
oncoming
vehicles
H
A & E
not 24 hrs
Tourist
information

Traffic has priority over oncoming vehicles

Hospital ahead with Accident and Emergency facilities

Tourist information point

No through road for vehicles

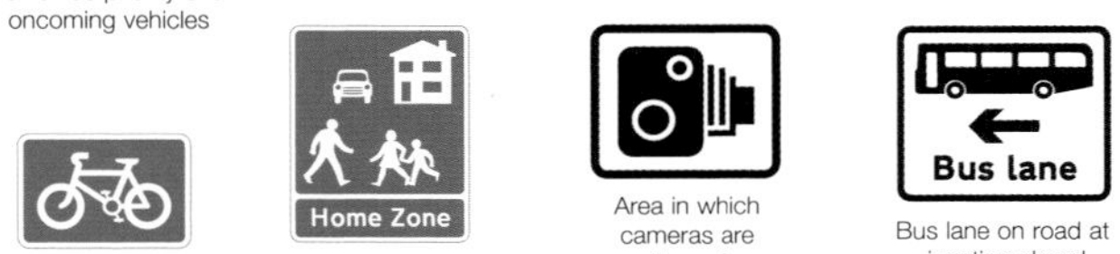
Home Zone
Bus lane

Recommended route for pedal cycles

Home Zone Entry*

Area in which cameras are used to enforce traffic regulations

Bus lane on road at junction ahead

*Home Zone Entry – You are entering an area where people could be using the whole street for a range of activities. You should drive slowly and carefully and be prepared to stop to allow people time to move out of the way.

Roadworks signs

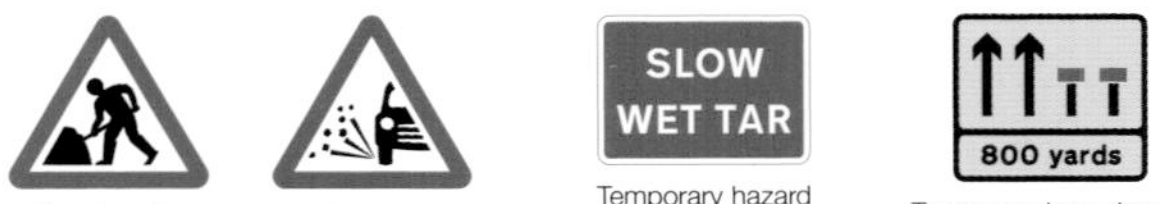
SLOW
WET TAR
800 yards

Road works

Loose chippings

Temporary hazard at roadworks

Temporary lane closure (the number and position of arrows and red bars may be varied according to lanes open and closed)

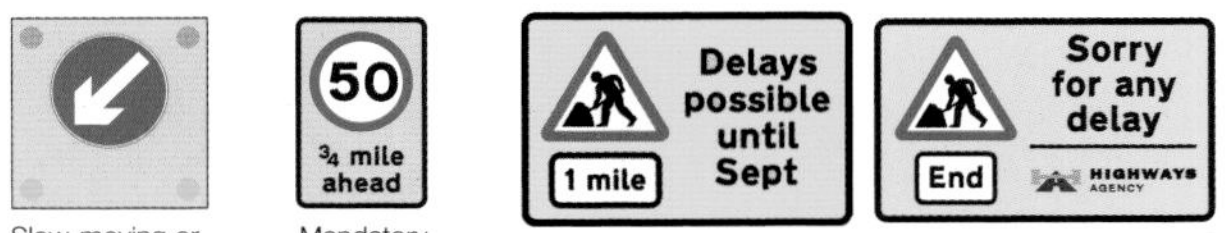
50
¾ mile
ahead
Delays
possible
until
Sept
1 mile
Sorry
for any
delay
End

Slow-moving or stationary works vehicle blocking a traffic lane. Pass in the direction shown by the arrow.

Mandatory speed limit ahead

Roadworks 1 mile ahead

End of roadworks and any temporary restrictions including speed limits

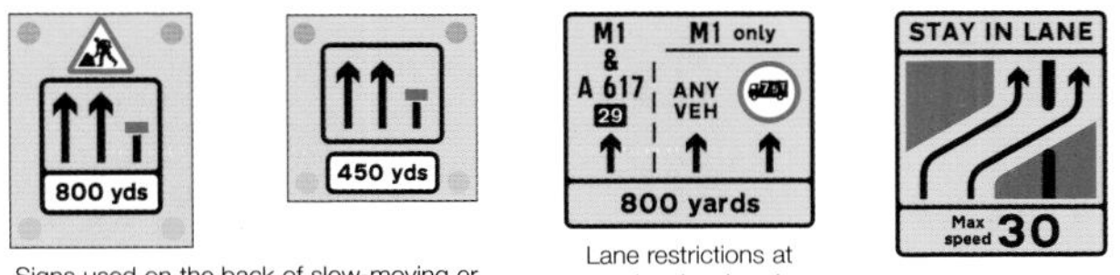
800 yds
450 yds
M1
&
A 617
M1 only
ANY
VEH
800 yards
STAY IN LANE
Max
speed
30

Signs used on the back of slow-moving or stationary vehicles warning of a lane closed ahead by a works vehicle. There are no cones on the road.

Lane restrictions at roadworks ahead

One lane crossover at contraflow roadworks

Road markings

Across the carriageway

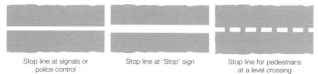

Stop line at signals or police control

Stop line at 'Stop' sign

Stop line for pedestrians at a level crossing

Give way to traffic on major road (can also be used at mini roundabouts)

Give way to traffic from the right at a roundabout

Give way to traffic from the right at a mini-roundabout

Along the carriageway

Edge line

Centre line See Rule 127

Hazard warning line See Rule 127

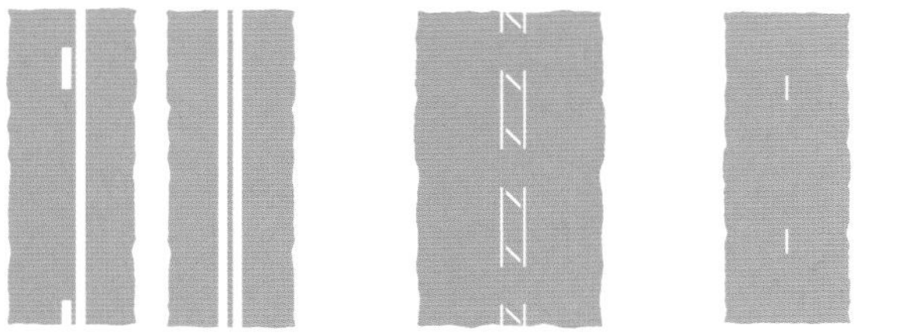

Double white lines See Rules 128 and 129

See Rule 130

Lane line See Rule 131

Along the edge of the carriageway

Waiting restrictions

Waiting restrictions indicated by yellow lines apply to the carriageway, pavement and verge. You may stop to load or unload (unless there are also loading restrictions as described below) or while passengers board or alight. Double yellow lines mean no waiting at any time, unless there are signs that specifically indicate seasonal restrictions. The times at which the restrictions apply for other road markings are shown on nearby plates or on entry signs to controlled parking zones. If no days are shown on the signs, the restrictions are in force every day including Sundays and Bank Holidays. White bay markings and upright signs (see below) indicate where parking is allowed.

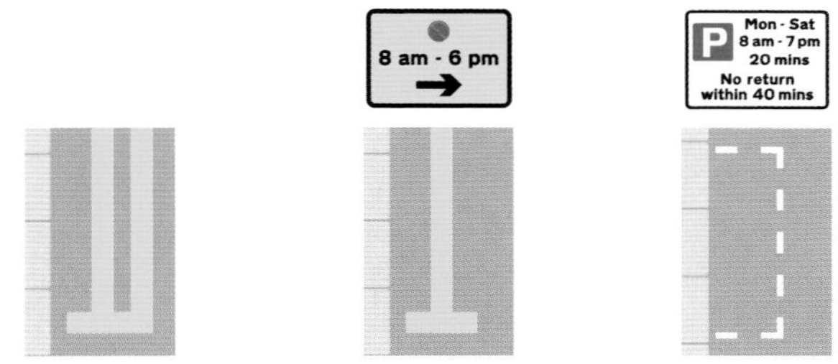
8 am - 6 pm
P
Mon - Sat
8 am - 7 pm
20 mins
No return
within 40 mins

No waiting at any time

No waiting during times shown on sign

Waiting is limited to the duration specified during the days and times shown

Red Route stopping controls

Red lines are used on some roads instead of yellow lines. In London the double and single red lines used on Red Routes indicate that stopping to park, load/unload or to board and alight from a vehicle (except for a licensed taxi or if you hold a Blue Badge) is prohibited. The red lines apply to the carriageway, pavement and verge. The times that the red line prohibitions apply are shown on nearby signs, but the double red line ALWAYS means no stopping at any time. On Red Routes you may stop to park, load/unload in specially marked boxes and adjacent signs specify the times and purposes and duration allowed. A box MARKED IN RED indicates that it may only be available for the purpose specified for part of the day (e.g. between busy peak periods). A box MARKED IN WHITE means that it is available throughout the day.

RED AND SINGLE YELLOW LINES CAN ONLY GIVE A GUIDE TO THE RESTRICTIONS AND CONTROLS IN FORCE AND SIGNS, NEARBY OR AT A ZONE ENTRY, MUST BE CONSULTED.

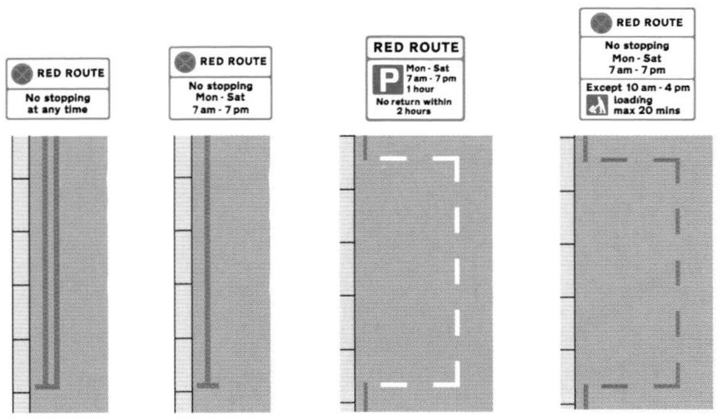
RED ROUTE
No stopping
at any time
RED ROUTE
No stopping
Mon - Sat
7 am - 7 pm
RED ROUTE
P
Mon - Sat
7 am - 7 pm
1 hour
No return within
2 hours
RED ROUTE
No stopping
Mon - Sat
7 am - 7 pm
Except 10 am - 4 pm
loading
max 20 mins

No stopping at any time

No stopping during times shown on sign

Parking is limited to the duration specified during the days and times shown

Only loading may take place at the times shown for up to a maximum duration of 20 mins

On the kerb or at the edge of the carriageway

Loading restrictions on roads other than Red Routes

Yellow marks on the kerb or at the edge of the carriageway indicate that loading or unloading is prohibited at the times shown on the nearby black and white plates. You may stop while passengers board or alight. If no days are indicated on the signs the restrictions are in force every day including Sundays and Bank Holidays.

ALWAYS CHECK THE TIMES SHOWN ON THE PLATES.

Lengths of road reserved for vehicles loading and unloading are indicated by a white 'bay' marking with the words 'Loading Only' and a sign with the white on blue 'trolley' symbol. This sign also shows whether loading and unloading is restricted to goods vehicles and the times at which the bay can be used. If no times or days are shown it may be used at any time. Vehicles may not park here if they are not loading or unloading.

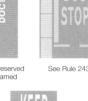

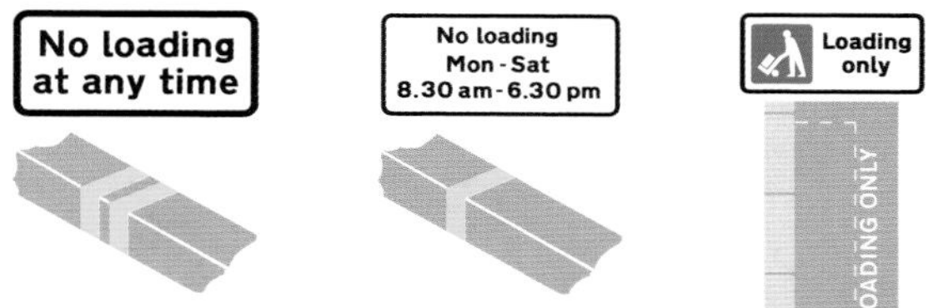
No loading
at any time
No loading
Mon - Sat
8.30 am - 6.30 pm
Loading
only
LOADING ONLY

No loading or unloading at any time

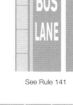

No loading or unloading at the times shown

Loading bay

Other road markings

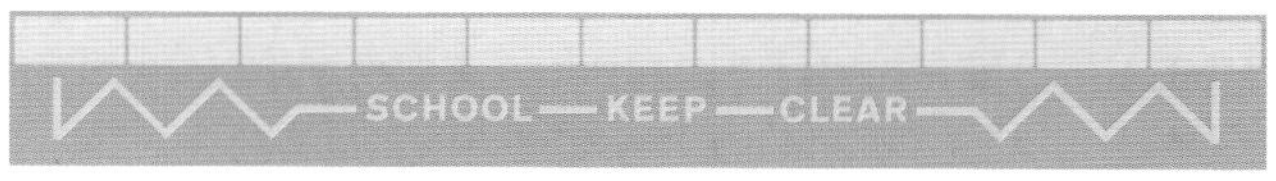
SCHOOL — KEEP — CLEAR

Keep entrance clear of stationary vehicles, even if picking up or setting down children

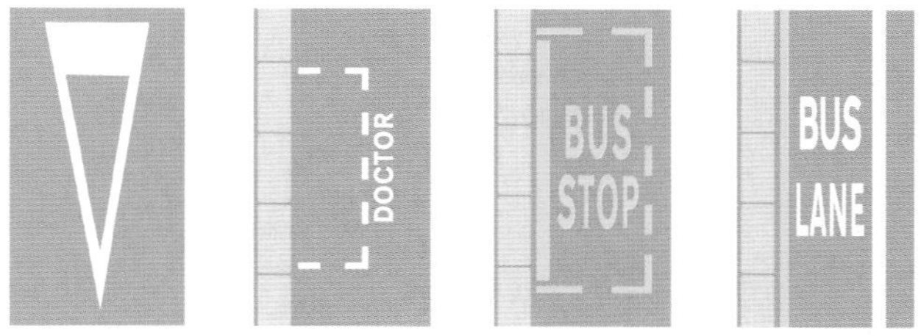
DOCTOR
BUS
STOP
BUS
LANE

Warning of 'Give Way' just ahead

Parking space reserved for vehicles named

See Rule 243

See Rule 141

KEEP
CLEAR
CITY
A3
YORK
ST

Box junction - See Rule 174

Do not block that part of the carriageway indicated

Indication of traffic lanes

Light signals controlling traffic

Traffic Light Signals

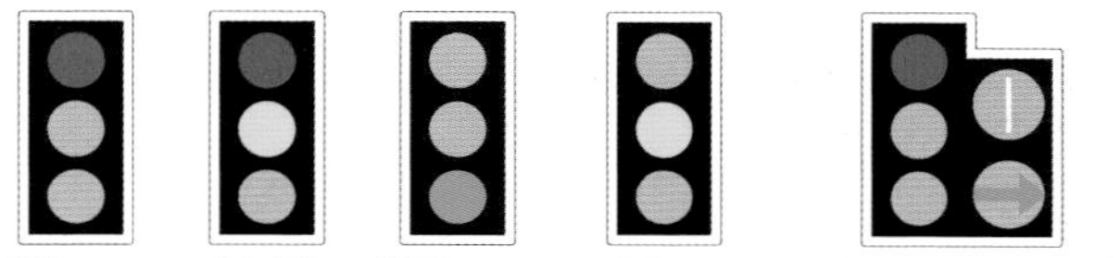

RED means 'Stop'. Wait behind the stop line on the carriageway.

RED AND AMBER also means 'Stop'. Do not pass through or start until GREEN shows.

GREEN means you may go on if the way is clear. Take special care if you intend to turn left or right and give way to pedestrians who are crossing.

AMBER means 'Stop' at the stop line. You may go on only if the AMBER appears after you have crossed the stop line or are so close to it that to pull up might cause an accident.

A GREEN ARROW may be provided in addition to the full green signal if movement in a certain direction is allowed before or after the full green phase. If the way is clear you may go but only in the direction shown by the arrow. You may do this whatever other lights may be showing. White light signals may be provided for trams.

Flashing red lights

Alternately flashing red lights mean YOU MUST STOP

At level crossings, lifting bridges, airfields, fire stations, etc.

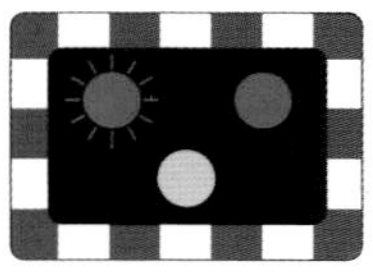

Motorway signals

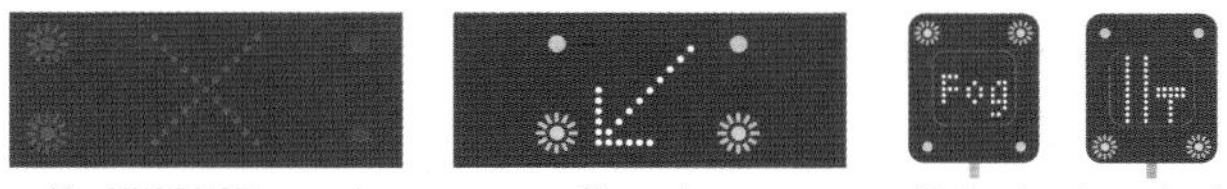
Fog

You MUST NOT proceed further in this lane

Change lane

Reduced visibility ahead

Lane ahead closed

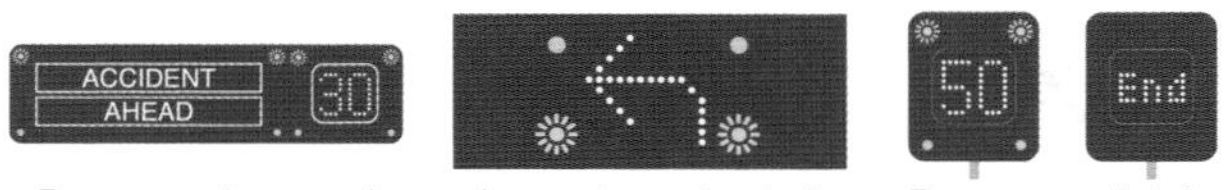
ACCIDENT
AHEAD
30
50
End

Temporary maximum speed advised and information message

Leave motorway at next exit

Temporary maximum speed advised

End of restriction

Lane control signals

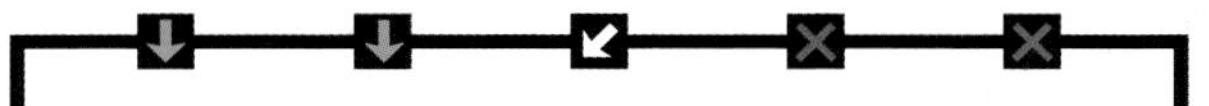

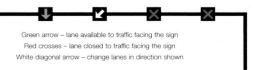

Green arrow – lane available to traffic facing the sign

Red crosses – lane closed to traffic facing the sign

White diagonal arrow – change lanes in direction shown

Channel hopping and the Isle of Wight

For business or pleasure, hopping on a ferry across to France, the Channel Islands or Isle of Wight has never been easier.

The vehicle ferry services listed in the table give you all the options, together with detailed port plans to help you navigate to and from the ferry terminals. Simply choose your preferred route, not forgetting the fast sailings (see 🚢). Bon voyage!

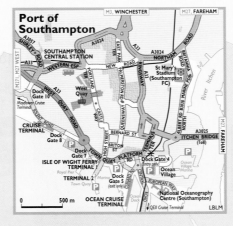

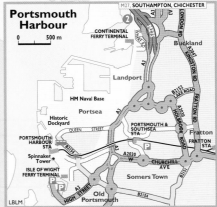

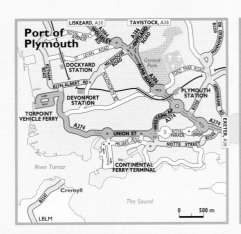

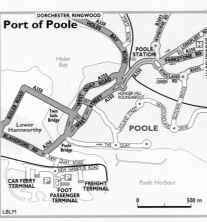

ENGLISH CHANNEL AND ISLE OF WIGHT FERRY CROSSINGS

From	To	Journey time	Operator website
Dover	Calais	1 hr 30 mins	dfdsseaways.co.uk
Dover	Calais	1 hr 30 mins	poferries.com
Dover	Dunkirk	2 hrs	dfdsseaways.co.uk
Folkestone	Calais (Coquelles)	35 mins	eurotunnel.com
Lymington	Yarmouth (IOW)	40 mins	wightlink.co.uk
Newhaven	Dieppe	4 hrs	dfdsseaways.co.uk
Plymouth	Roscoff	6–8 hrs	brittany-ferries.co.uk
Plymouth	St-Malo	10 hrs 15 mins (Nov–Mar)	brittany-ferries.co.uk
Poole	Cherbourg	4 hrs 15 mins	brittany-ferries.co.uk
Poole	Guernsey	3 hrs 🚢	condorferries.co.uk
Poole	Jersey	4 hrs 30 mins 🚢	condorferries.co.uk
Poole	St-Malo	7–12 hrs (via Channel Is.) 🚢	condorferries.co.uk
Portsmouth	Caen (Ouistreham)	6–7 hrs	brittany-ferries.co.uk
Portsmouth	Cherbourg	3 hrs (May–Aug) 🚢	brittany-ferries.co.uk
Portsmouth	Cherbourg	5 hrs 30 mins (May–Aug)	condorferries.co.uk
Portsmouth	Fishbourne (IOW)	45 mins	wightlink.co.uk
Portsmouth	Guernsey	7 hrs	condorferries.co.uk
Portsmouth	Jersey	8–11 hrs	condorferries.co.uk
Portsmouth	Le Havre	8 hrs (Jan–Oct)	brittany-ferries.co.uk
Portsmouth	St-Malo	9–11 hrs	brittany-ferries.co.uk
Southampton	East Cowes (IOW)	60 mins	redfunnel.co.uk

The information listed is provided as a guide only, as services are liable to change at short notice. Services shown are for vehicle ferries only, operated by conventional ferry unless indicated as a fast ferry service (🚢). Please check sailings before planning your journey.

Travelling further afield? For ferry services to Northern Spain see brittany-ferries.co.uk.

ENGLISH

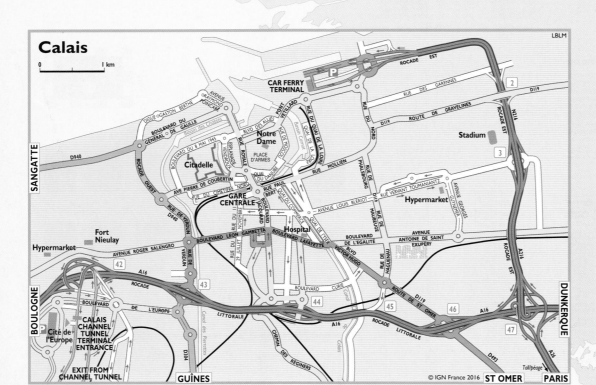

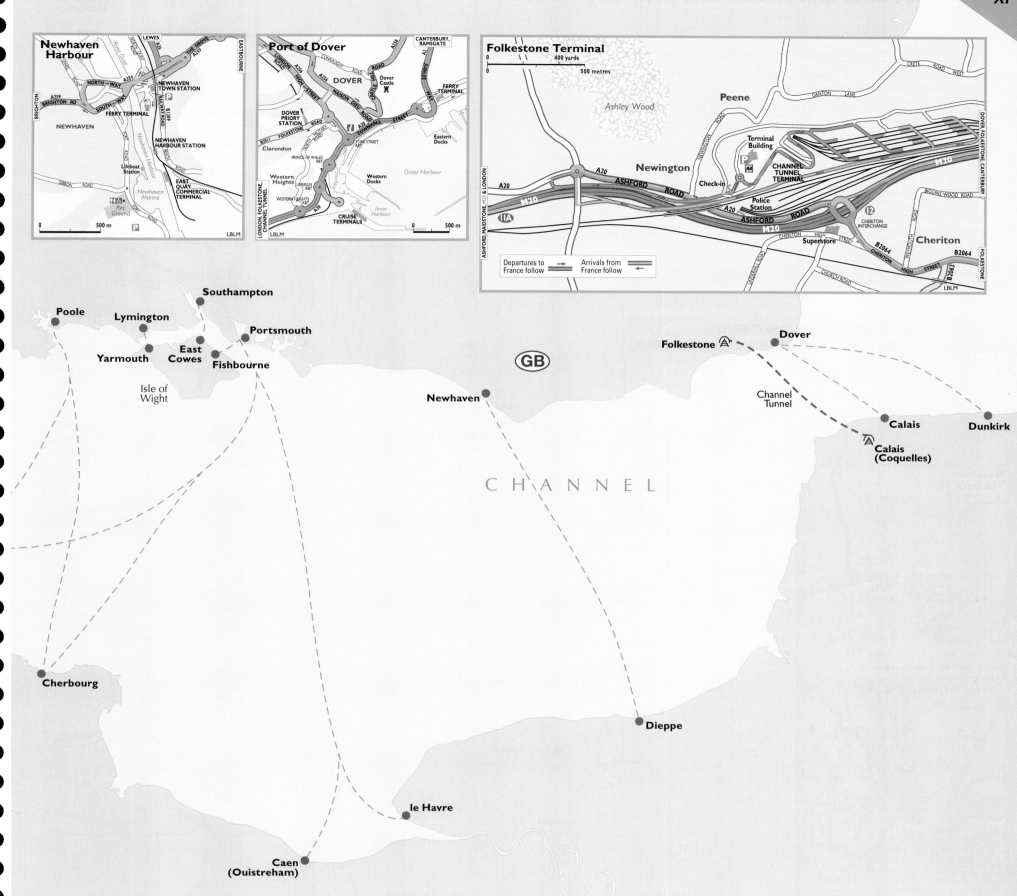

Newhaven Harbour

LEWES
NORTH WAY
SOUTH WAY
BRIGHTON
A259
BRIGHTON RD
A26
NEWHAVEN
NEWHAVEN TOWN STATION
THE DROVE
FERRY TERMINAL
River Ouse
EASTBOURNE
RAILWAY ROAD
NEWHAVEN HARBOUR STATION
Newhaven Harbour
Lifeboat Station
EAST QUAY COMMERCIAL TERMINAL
GIBBON ROAD
Rec Ground
Newhaven Marina
0   500 m
LBLM

Port of Dover

LONDON, FOLKESTONE, CHANNEL TUNNEL
CANTERBURY, RAMSGATE
CONNAUGHT ROAD
A256
DOVER
Dover Castle
MAISON DIEU RD
FERRY TERMINAL
DOVER PRIORY STATION
Clarendon
FOLKESTONE ROAD
A20
PRINCE OF WALES RBT
YORK STREET
TOWNWALL STREET
A2
Eastern Docks
Western Heights
WESTERN HEIGHTS RBT
LIMEKILN RBT
Western Docks
Outer Harbour
Inner Harbour
CRUISE TERMINALS
0   500 m
LBLM

Folkestone Terminal

0   400 yards
0   500 metres
Ashley Wood
Peene
DANTON LANE
CRETE ROAD WEST
Newington
Terminal Building
P
CHANNEL TUNNEL TERMINAL
M20
DOVER, FOLKESTONE, CANTERBURY
ASHFORD, MAIDSTONE, M25 & LONDON
A20
M20
ASHFORD ROAD
Check-in
Police Station
ASHFORD ROAD
BIGGINS WOOD ROAD
11A
M20
CHERITON HIGH STREET
Superstore
CHERITON INTERCHANGE
12
Cheriton
B2064
B2064
FOLKESTONE
CHURCH ROAD
Departures to France follow →
Arrivals from France follow
LBLM

Poole
Lymington
Southampton
Yarmouth
East Cowes
Fishbourne
Portsmouth
Isle of Wight
Cherbourg
Newhaven
CHANNEL
GB
F
Folkestone
Dover
Channel Tunnel
Calais
Calais (Coquelles)
Dunkirk
Dieppe
le Havre
Caen (Ouistreham)

Calais / Coquelles Terminal

0   400 yards
0   500 metres
Coquelles
D243E
Freight only
ibis Hotel
ibis Budget Hotel
Novotel
Cité Europe
P
P
PASSENGER TERMINAL
Petrol Station
Check-in
Frontier Controls
Freight only
A16 (E402) ROCADE LITTORALE
BOULEVARD DE L'EUROPE
BOULEVARD DE LA CÔTE D'OPALE
CALAIS
BOULOGNE
A16 (E402) ROCADE LITTORALE
Eurotunnel Administration Headquarters
Parc d'activites les Terrasses
Arrivals Platforms
Departures Platforms
HGV Fuel Station
Freight Terminal
Freight only
DUNKIRK A11 (PARIS)
D940
Departures to England follow →
Arrivals from England follow
LBLM

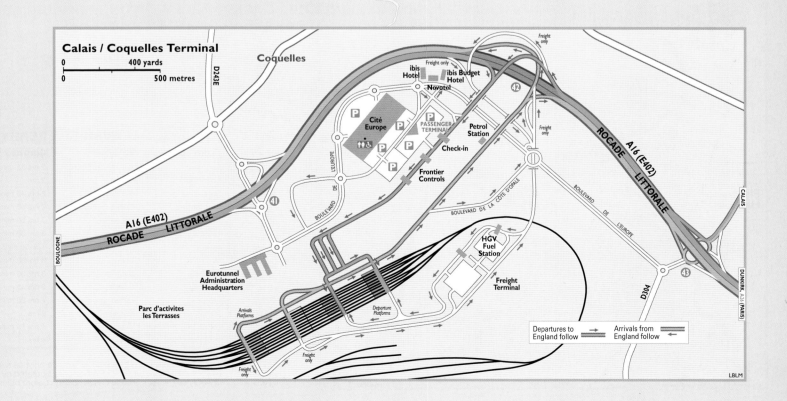

SCOTLAND FERRIES

From	To	Journey time	Operator website
Scottish Islands/west coast of Scotland			
Gourock	Dunoon	20 mins	western-ferries.co.uk
Glenelg	Skye	20 mins (Easter–Oct)	skyeferry.co.uk

Numerous and varied sailings from the west coast of Scotland to Scottish islands are provided by Caledonian MacBrayne. Please visit calmac.co.uk for all ferry information, including those of other operators.

From	To	Journey time	Operator website
Orkney Islands			
Aberdeen	Kirkwall	6 hrs	northlinkferries.co.uk
Gills	St Margaret's Hope	1 hr	pentlandferries.co.uk
Scrabster	Stromness	1 hr 30 mins	northlinkferries.co.uk
Lerwick	Kirkwall	5 hrs 30 mins	northlinkferries.co.uk

Inter-island services are operated by Orkney Ferries. Please see orkneyferries.co.uk for details.

From	To	Journey time	Operator website
Shetland Islands			
Aberdeen	Lerwick	12 hrs 30 mins	northlinkferries.co.uk
Kirkwall	Lerwick	7 hrs 45 mins	northlinkferries.co.uk

Inter-island services are operated by Shetland Island Council Ferries. Please see shetland.gov.uk/ferries for details.

Please note that some smaller island services are day dependent and reservations are required for some routes. Book and confirm sailing schedules by contacting the operator.

NORTH SEA FERRY CROSSINGS

From	To	Journey time	Operator website
Harwich	Hook of Holland	7–8 hrs	stenaline.co.uk
Kingston upon Hull	Rotterdam (Europoort)	10 hrs 45 mins	poferries.com
Kingston upon Hull	Zeebrugge	13 hrs 15 mins	poferries.com
Newcastle upon Tyne	Amsterdam (IJmuiden)	15 hrs 30 mins	dfdsseaways.co.uk

Heysham Harbour

Liverpool Docks

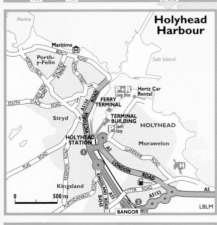

Holyhead Harbour

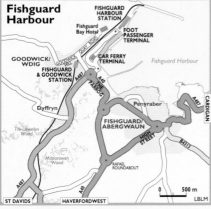

Fishguard Harbour

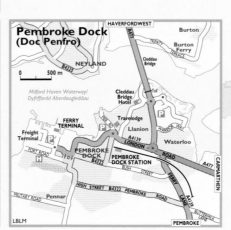

Pembroke Dock (Doc Penfro)

Aberdeen Harbour

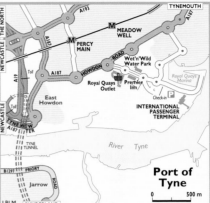

Port of Tyne

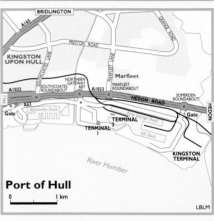

Port of Hull

Harwich International Port

IRISH SEA FERRY CROSSINGS

From	To	Journey time	Operator website
Cairnryan	Belfast	2 hrs 15 mins	stenaline.co.uk
Cairnryan	Larne	2 hrs	poferries.com
Douglas	Belfast	2 hrs 45 mins (April–Sept)	steam-packet.com
Douglas	Dublin	2 hrs 55 mins (April–Aug)	steam-packet.com
Fishguard	Rosslare	3 hrs 30 mins – 4 hrs	stenaline.co.uk
Heysham	Douglas	3 hrs 30 mins	steam-packet.com
Holyhead	Dublin	1 hr 50 mins	irishferries.com
Holyhead	Dublin	3 hrs 30 mins	irishferries.com
Holyhead	Dublin	3 hrs 30 mins	stenaline.co.uk
Liverpool	Douglas	2 hrs 45 mins (Mar–Oct)	steam-packet.com
Liverpool	Dublin	7 hrs 30 mins – 8 hrs 30 mins	poferries.com
Liverpool (Birkenhead)	Belfast	8 hrs	stenaline.co.uk
Liverpool (Birkenhead)	Douglas	4 hrs 15 mins (Nov–Mar)	steam-packet.com
Pembroke Dock	Rosslare	4 hrs	irishferries.com

The information listed is provided as a guide only, as services are liable to change at short notice. Services shown are for vehicle ferries only, operated by conventional ferry unless indicated as a fast ferry service. Please check sailings before planning your journey.

Motorway and Primary Route junctions which have access or exit restrictions are shown on the map pages thus:

M1 London - Leeds

Junction	Northbound	Southbound
2	Access only from A1 *(northbound)*	Exit only to A1 *(southbound)*
4	Access only from A41 *(northbound)*	Exit only to A41 *(southbound)*
6A	Access only from M25 (no link from A405)	Exit only to M25 (no link from A405)
7	Access only from A414	Exit only to A414
17	Exit only to M45	Access only from M45
19	Exit only to M6 *(northbound)*	Exit only to A14 *(southbound)*
21A	Exit only, no access	Access only, no exit
23A	Access only from A42	No restriction
24A	Access only, no exit	Exit only, no access
35A	Exit only, no access	Access only, no exit
43	Exit only to M621	Access only from M621
48	Exit only to A1(M) *(northbound)*	Access only from A1(M) *(southbound)*

M2 Rochester - Faversham

Junction	Westbound	Eastbound
1	No exit to A2 *(eastbound)*	No access from A2 *(westbound)*

M3 Sunbury - Southampton

Junction	Northeastbound	Southwestbound
8	Access only from A303, no exit	Exit only to A303, no access
10	Exit only, no access	Access only, no exit
14	Access from M27 only, no exit	No access to M27 *(westbound)*

M4 London - South Wales

Junction	Westbound	Eastbound
1	Access only from A4 *(westbound)*	Exit only to A4 *(eastbound)*
2	Access only from A4 *(westbound)*	Access only from A4 *(eastbound)*
21	Exit only to M48	Access only from M48
23	Access only from M48	Exit only to M48
25	Exit only, no access	Access only, no exit
25A	Exit only, no access	Access only, no exit
29	Exit only to A48(M)	Access only from A48(M)
38	Exit only, no access	No restriction
39	Access only, no exit	No access or exit
42	Exit only to A483	Access only from A483

M5 Birmingham - Exeter

Junction	Northeastbound	Southwestbound
10	Access only, no exit	Exit only, no access
11A	Access only from A417 *(westbound)*	Exit only to A417 *(eastbound)*
18A	Exit only to M49	Access only from M49
18	Exit only, no access	Access only, no exit

M6 Toll Motorway

Junction	Northwestbound	Southeastbound
T1	Access only, no exit	No access or exit
T2	No access or exit	Exit only, no access
T5	Access only, no exit	Exit only to A5148 *(northbound)*, no access
T7	Exit only, no access	Access only, no exit
T8	Exit only, no access	Access only, no exit

M6 Rugby - Carlisle

Junction	Northbound	Southbound
3A	Exit only to M6 Toll	Access only from M6 Toll
4	Exit only to M42 *(southbound)* & A446	Exit only to A446
4A	Access only from M42 *(southbound)*	Exit only to M42
5	Exit only, no access	Access only, no exit
10A	Exit only to M54	Access only from M54
11A	Access only from M6 Toll	Exit only to M6 Toll
with M56 (jct 20A)	No restriction	Access only from M56 *(eastbound)*
20	Exit only to M56 *(westbound)*	Access only from M56 *(eastbound)*
24	Access only, no exit	Exit only, no access
25	Exit only, no access	Access only, no exit
30	Access only from M61	Exit only to M61
31A	Exit only, no access	Access only, no exit
45	Exit only, no access	Access only, no exit

M8 Edinburgh - Bishopton

Junction	Westbound	Eastbound
6	Exit only, no access	Access only, no exit
6A	Access only, no exit	Exit only, no access
7	Access only, no exit	Exit only, no access
7A	Exit only, no access	Access only from A725 *(northbound)*, no exit
8	No access from M73 *(southbound)* or from A8 *(eastbound)* & A89	No exit to M73 *(northbound)* or to A8 *(westbound)* & A89
9	Access only, no exit	Exit only, no access
13	Access only from M80 *(southbound)*	Exit only to M80 *(northbound)*
14	Access only, no exit	Exit only, no access
16	Exit only to A804	Access only from A879
17	Exit only to A82	No restriction
18	Access only from A82 *(eastbound)*	Exit only to A814
19	No access from A814 *(westbound)*	Exit only to A814 *(westbound)*
20	Exit only, no access	Access only, no exit
21	Access only, no exit	Exit only to A8
22	Exit only to M77 *(southbound)*	Access only from M77 *(northbound)*
23	Exit only to B768	Access only from B768
25	No access or exit from or to A8	No access or exit from or to A8
25A	Exit only, no access	Access only, no exit
28	Exit only, no access	Access only, no exit
28A	Exit only to A737	Access only from A737

M9 Edinburgh - Dunblane

Junction	Northwestbound	Southeastbound
2	Access only, no exit	Exit only, no access
3	Exit only, no access	Access only, no exit
6	Access only, no exit	Exit only to A905
8	Exit only to M876 *(southwestbound)*	Access only from M876 *(northeastbound)*

M11 London - Cambridge

Junction	Northbound	Southbound
4	Access only from A406 *(eastbound)*	Exit only to A406
5	Exit only, no access	Access only, no exit
8A	Exit only, no access	No direct access, use jct 8
9	Exit only to A11	Access only from A11
13	Exit only, no access	Access only, no exit
14	Exit only, no access	Access only, no exit

M20 Swanley - Folkestone

Junction	Northwestbound	Southeastbound
2	Staggered junction; follow signs - access only	Staggered junction; follow signs - exit only
3	Exit only to M26 *(westbound)*	Access only from M26 *(eastbound)*
5	Access only from A20	For access follow signs - exit only to A20
6	No restriction	For exit follow signs
11A	Access only, no exit	Exit only, no access

M23 Hooley - Crawley

Junction	Northbound	Southbound
7	Exit only to A23 *(northbound)*	Access only from A23 *(southbound)*
10A	Access only, no exit	Exit only, no access

M25 London Orbital Motorway

Junction	Clockwise	Anticlockwise
1B	No direct access, use slip road to jct 2 Exit only	Access only, no exit
5	No exit to M26 *(eastbound)*	No access from M26
19	Exit only, no access	Access only, no exit
21	Access only from M1 *(southbound)* Exit only to M1 *(northbound)*	Access only from M1 *(southbound)* Exit only to M1 *(northbound)*
31	No exit (use slip road via jct 30), access only	No access (use slip road via jct 30), exit only

M26 Sevenoaks - Wrotham

Junction	Westbound	Eastbound
with M25 (jct 5)	Exit only to clockwise M25 *(westbound)*	Access only from anticlockwise M25 *(eastbound)*
with M20 (jct 3)	Access only from M20 *(northwestbound)*	Exit only to M20 *(southeastbound)*

M27 Cadnam - Portsmouth

Junction	Westbound	Eastbound
4	Staggered junction; follow signs - access only from M3 *(southbound)*. Exit only to M3 *(northbound)*	Staggered junction; follow signs - access only from M3 *(southbound)*. Exit only to M3 *(northbound)*
10	Exit only, no access	Access only, no exit
12	Staggered junction; follow signs - exit only to M275 *(southbound)*	Staggered junction; follow signs - access only from M275 *(northbound)*

M40 London - Birmingham

Junction	Northwestbound	Southeastbound
3	Exit only, no access	Access only, no exit
7	Exit only, no access	Access only, no exit
8	Exit only to M40/A40	Access only from M40/A40
13	Exit only, no access	Access only, no exit
14	Access only, no exit	Exit only, no access
16	Access only, no exit	Exit only, no access

M42 Bromsgrove - Measham

Junction	Northeastbound	Southwestbound
1	Access only, no exit	Exit only, no access
7	Exit only to M6 *(northwestbound)*	Access only from M6 *(northwestbound)*
7A	Exit only to M6 *(southeastbound)*	No access or exit
8	Access only from M6 *(southeastbound)*	Exit only to M6 *(northwestbound)*

M45 Coventry - M1

Junction	Westbound	Eastbound
Dunchurch (unnumbered)	Access only from A45	Exit only, no access
with M1 (jct 17)	Access only from M1 *(northbound)*	Exit only to M1 *(southbound)*

M48 Chepstow

Junction	Westbound	Eastbound
21	Access only from M4 *(westbound)*	Exit only to M4 *(eastbound)*
23	No exit to M4 *(eastbound)*	No access from M4 *(westbound)*

M53 Mersey Tunnel - Chester

Junction	Northbound	Southbound
11	Access only from M56 *(westbound)* Exit only to M56 *(eastbound)*	Access only from M56 *(westbound)* Exit only to M56 *(eastbound)*

M54 Telford - Birmingham

Junction	Westbound	Eastbound
with M6 (jct 10A)	Access only from M6 *(northbound)*	Exit only to M6 *(southbound)*

M56 Chester - Manchester

Junction	Westbound	Eastbound
1	Access only from M60 *(westbound)*	Exit only to M60 *(eastbound)* & A34 *(northbound)*
2	Exit only, no access	Access only, no exit
3	Access only, no exit	Exit only, no access
4	Exit only, no access	Access only, no exit
7	Exit only, no access	No restriction
8	Access only, no exit	No access or exit
9	No exit to M6 *(southbound)*	No access from M6 *(northbound)*
15	Exit only to M53	Access only from M53
16	No access or exit	No restriction

M57 Liverpool Outer Ring Road

Junction	Northwestbound	Southeastbound
3	Access only, no exit	Exit only, no access
5	Access only from A580 *(westbound)*	Exit only, no access

M58 Liverpool - Wigan

Junction	Westbound	Eastbound
1	Exit only, no access	Access only, no exit

M60 Manchester Orbital

Junction	Clockwise	Anticlockwise
2	Access only, no exit	Exit only, no access
3	No access from M56	Access only from A34 *(northbound)*
4	Access only from A34 *(northbound)*. Exit only to M56	Access only from M56 *(eastbound)*. Exit only to A34 *(southbound)*
5	Access and exit only from and to A5103 *(northbound)*	Access and exit only from and to A5103 *(southbound)*
7	No direct access, use slip road to jct 8. Exit only to A56	Access only from A56. No exit, use jct 8
14	Access from A580 *(eastbound)*	Exit only to A580 *(westbound)*
16	Access only, no exit	Exit only, no access
20	Exit only, no access	Access only, no exit
22	No restriction	Exit only, no access
25	Exit only, no access	No restriction
26	No restriction	Exit only, no access
27	Access only, no exit	Exit only, no access

M61 Manchester - Preston

Junction	Northwestbound	Southeastbound
3	No access or exit	Exit only, no access
with M6 (jct 30)	Exit only to M6 *(northbound)*	Access only from M6 *(southbound)*

M62 Liverpool - Kingston upon Hull

Junction	Westbound	Eastbound
23	Access only, no exit	Exit only, no access
32A	No access to A1(M) *(southbound)*	No restriction

M65 Preston - Colne

Junction	Northeastbound	Southwestbound
9	Exit only, no access	Access only, no exit
11	Access only, no exit	Exit only, no access

M66 Bury

Junction	Northbound	Southbound
with A56	Exit only to A56 *(northbound)*	Access only from A56 *(southbound)*
1	Exit only, no access	Access only, no exit

M67 Hyde Bypass

Junction	Westbound	Eastbound
1	Access only, no exit	Exit only, no access
2	Exit only, no access	Access only, no exit
3	Exit only, no access	No restriction

M69 Coventry - Leicester

Junction	Northbound	Southbound
2	Access only, no exit	Exit only, no access

M73 East of Glasgow

Junction	Northbound	Southbound
1	No exit to A74 & A721	No exit to A74 & A721
2	No access from or exit to A89. No access from *(eastbound)*	No access from or exit to A89. No exit to M8 *(westbound)*

M74 and A74(M) Glasgow - Gretna

Junction	Northbound	Southbound
3	Exit only, no access	Access only, no exit
3A	Access only, no exit	Exit only, no access
4	No access from A74 & A721	Access only, no exit to A74 & A721
7	Access only, no exit	Exit only, no access
9	No access or exit	Exit only, no access
10	No restriction	Access only, no exit
11	Access only, no exit	Exit only, no access
12	Exit only, no access	Access only, no exit
18	Exit only, no access	Access only, no exit

M77 Glasgow - Kilmarnock

Junction	Northbound	Southbound
with M8 (jct 22)	No exit to M8 *(westbound)*	No access from M8 *(eastbound)*
4	Access only, no exit	Exit only, no access
6	Access only, no exit	Exit only, no access
7	Access only, no exit	No restriction
8	Exit only, no access	Exit only, no access

M80 Glasgow - Stirling

Junction	Northbound	Southbound
4A	Exit only, no access	Access only, no exit
6A	Access only, no exit	Exit only, no access
8	Exit only to M876 *(northeastbound)*	Access only from M876 *(southwestbound)*

M90 Edinburgh - Perth

Junction	Northbound	Southbound
1	No exit, access only	Exit only to A90 *(eastbound)*
2A	Exit only to A92 *(eastbound)*	Access only from A92 *(westbound)*
7	Access only, no exit	Exit only, no access
8	Exit only, no access	Access only, no exit
10	No access from A912. No exit to A912 *(southbound)*	No access from A912 *(northbound)* No exit to A912

M180 Doncaster - Grimsby

Junction	Westbound	Eastbound
1	Access only, no exit	Exit only, no access

M606 Bradford Spur

Junction	Northbound	Southbound
2	Exit only, no access	No restriction

M621 Leeds - M1

Junction	Clockwise	Anticlockwise
2A	Access only, no exit	Exit only, no access
4	No exit or access	No restriction
5	Access only, no exit	Exit only, no access
6	Exit only, no access	Access only, no exit
with M1 (jct 43)	Exit only to M1 *(southbound)*	Access only from M1 *(northbound)*

M876 Bonnybridge - Kincardine Bridge

Junction	Northeastbound	Southwestbound
with M80 (jct 5)	Access only from M80 *(northeastbound)*	Exit only to M80 *(southwestbound)*
with M9 (jct 8)	Exit only to M9 *(eastbound)*	Access only from M9 *(westbound)*

A1(M) South Mimms - Baldock

Junction	Northbound	Southbound
2	Exit only, no access	Access only, no exit
3	No restriction	Exit only, no access
5	Access only, no exit	No access or exit

A1(M) Pontefract - Bedale

Junction	Northbound	Southbound
41	No access to M62 *(eastbound)*	No restriction
43	Access only from M1 *(northbound)*	Exit only to M1 *(southbound)*

A1(M) Scotch Corner - Newcastle upon Tyne

Junction	Northbound	Southbound
57	Exit only to A66(M) *(eastbound)*	Access only from A66(M) *(westbound)*
65	No access Exit only to A194(M) & A1 *(northbound)*	No exit Access only from A194(M) & A1 *(southbound)*

A3(M) Horndean - Havant

Junction	Northbound	Southbound
1	Access only from A3	Exit only to A3
4	Exit only, no access	Access only, no exit

A38(M) Birmingham, Victoria Road (Park Circus)

Junction	Northbound	Southbound
with B4132	No exit	No access

A48(M) Cardiff Spur

Junction	Westbound	Eastbound
29	Access only from M4 *(westbound)*	Exit only to M4 *(eastbound)*
29A	Exit only to A48 *(westbound)*	Access only from A48 *(eastbound)*

A57(M) Manchester, Brook Street (A34)

Junction	Westbound	Eastbound
with A34	No exit	No access

A58(M) Leeds, Park Lane and Westgate

Junction	Northbound	Southbound
with A58	No restriction	No access

A64(M) Leeds, Clay Pit Lane (A58)

Junction	Westbound	Eastbound
with A58	No exit (to Clay Pit Lane)	No access (from Clay Pit Lane)

A66(M) Darlington Spur

Junction	Westbound	Eastbound
with A1(M) (jct 57)	Exit only to A1(M) *(southbound)*	Access only from A1(M) *(northbound)*

A74(M) Gretna - Abington

Junction	Northbound	Southbound
18	Exit only, no access	No exit

A194(M) Newcastle upon Tyne

Junction	Northbound	Southbound
with A1(M) (jct 65)	Access only from A1(M) *(northbound)*	Exit only to A1(M) *(southbound)*

A12 M25 - Ipswich

Junction	Northeastbound	Southwestbound
13	Access only, no exit	No restriction
14	Exit only, no access	Access only, no exit
20A	Exit only, no access	Access only, no exit
20B	Access only, no exit	Exit only, no access
21	No restriction	Access only, no exit
23	Exit only, no access	Access only, no exit
24	Access only, no exit	Exit only, no access
27	Exit only, no access	Access only, no exit
Dedham & Stratford St Mary (unnumbered)	Exit only	Access only

A14 M1 - Felixstowe

Junction	Westbound	Eastbound
with M1/M6 (jct19)	Exit only to M6 and M1 *(northbound)*	Access only from M6 and M1 *(southbound)*
4	Exit only, no access	Access only, no exit
31	Exit only to M11 *(for London)*	Access only, no exit
31A	Exit only to A14 *(northbound)*	Access only, no exit
34	Access only, no exit	Exit only, no access
36	Exit only to A11, access only from A1303	Access only from A11
38	Access only from A11	Exit only to A11
39	Exit only, no access	Access only, no exit
61	Access only, no exit	Exit only, no access

A55 Holyhead - Chester

Junction	Westbound	Eastbound
8A	Exit only, no access	Access only, no exit
23A	Access only, no exit	Exit only, no access
24A	Exit only, no access	No access or exit
27A	No restriction	No access or exit
33A	Exit only, no access	No access or exit
33B	Exit only, no access	Access only, no exit
36A	Exit only to A5104	Access only from A5104

Refer also to atlas pages 32–33

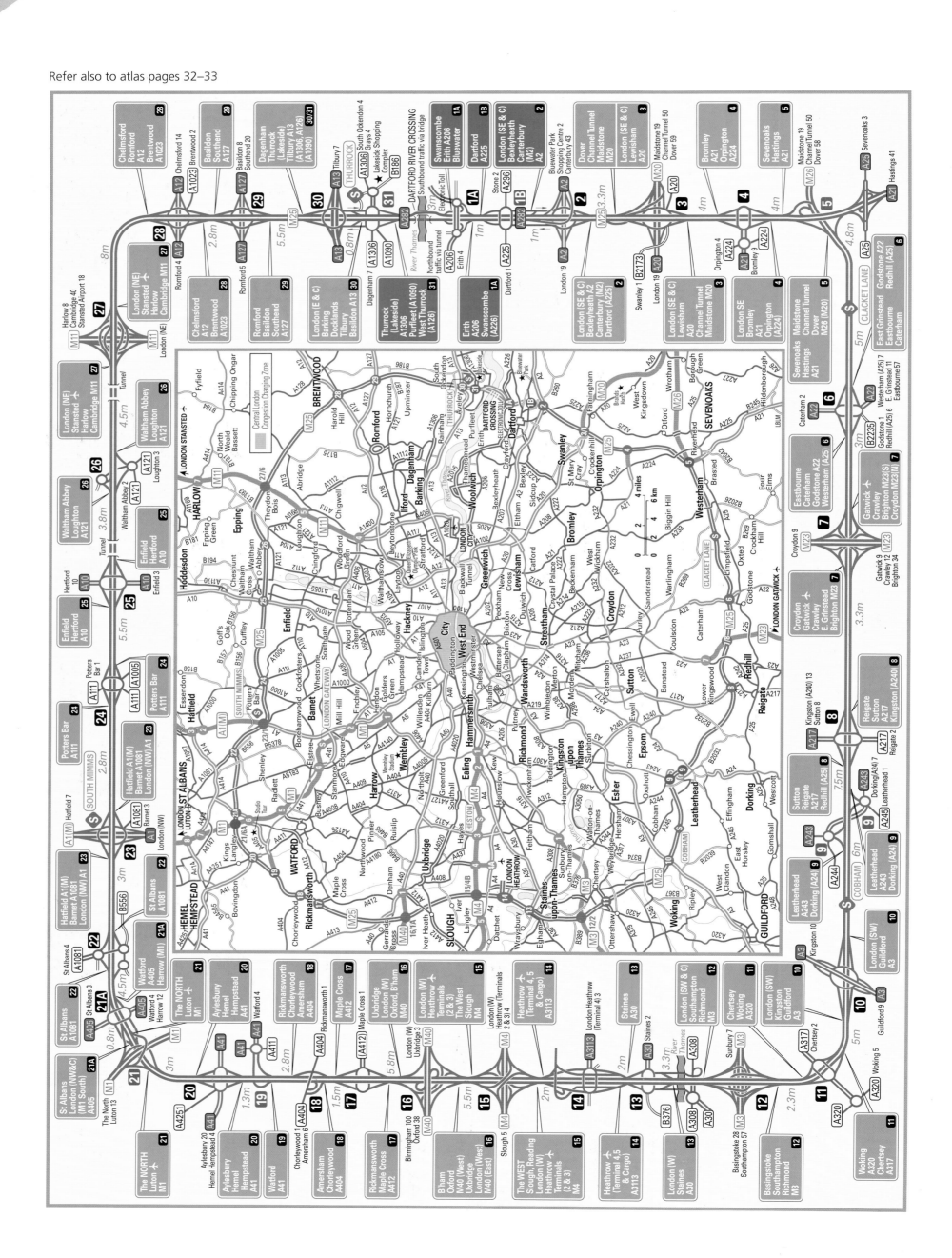

Refer also to atlas pages 53, 64–65

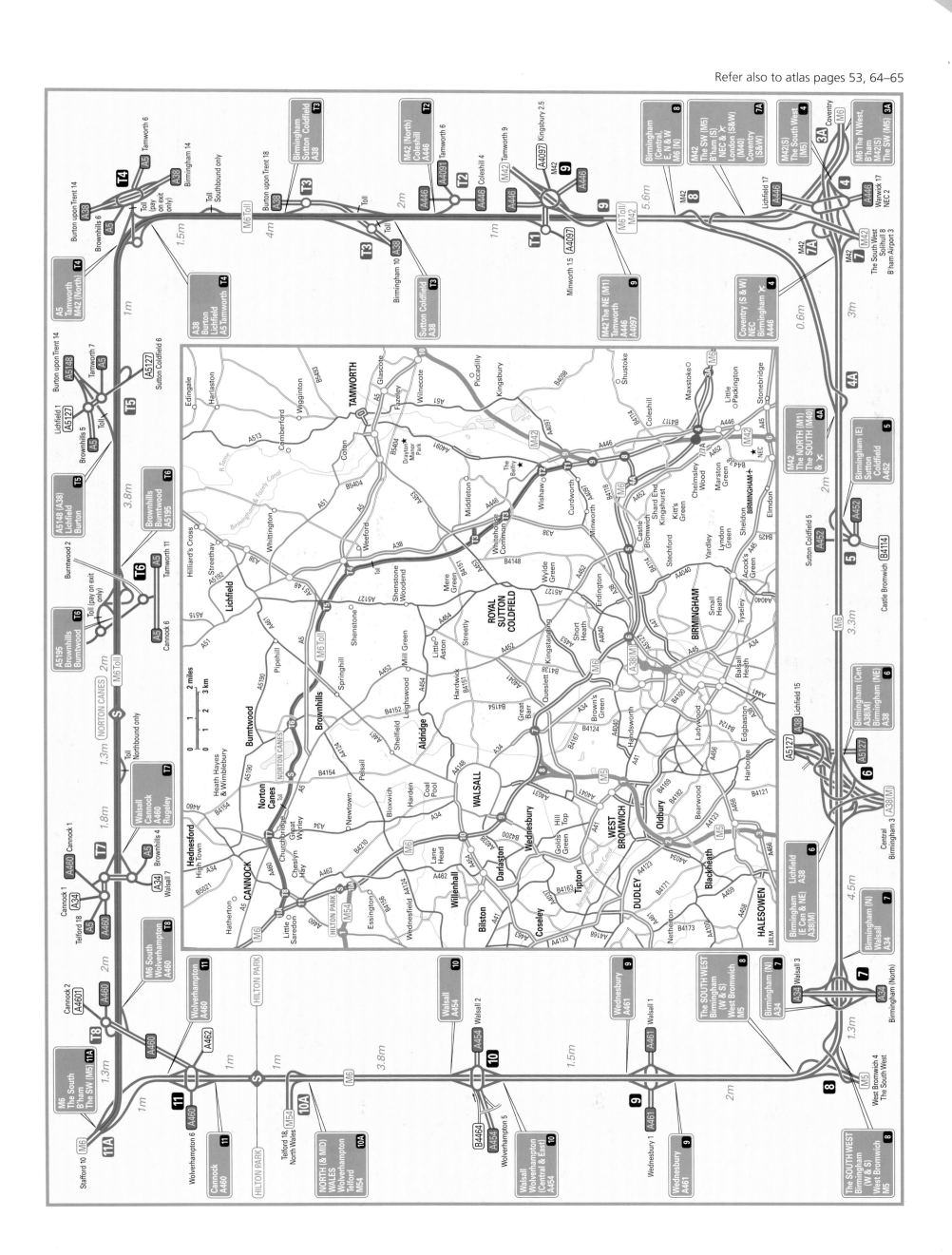

Smart motorways

Since Britain's first motorway (the Preston Bypass) opened in 1958, motorways have changed significantly. A vast increase in car journeys over the last 60 years has meant that motorways quickly filled to capacity. To combat this, the recent development of **smart motorways** uses technology to monitor and actively manage traffic flow and congestion.

How they work

Smart motorways utilise various active traffic management methods, monitored through a regional traffic control centre:

- Traffic flow is monitored using CCTV
- Speed limits are changed to smooth traffic flow and reduce stop-start driving
- Capacity of the motorway can be increased by either temporarily or permanently opening the hard shoulder to traffic
- Warning signs and messages alert drivers to hazards and traffic jams ahead
- Lanes can be closed in the case of an accident or emergency by displaying a red X sign

- Emergency refuge areas are located regularly along the motorway where there is no hard shoulder available

The map shows the main motorway network with the three different types of smart motorway in operation or planned to open over the next five years:

Controlled motorway
Variable speed limits without hard shoulder (the hard shoulder is used in emergencies only)

Hard shoulder running
Variable speed limits with part-time hard shoulder (the hard shoulder is open to traffic at busy times when signs permit)

All lane running
Variable speed limits with hard shoulder as permanent running lane (there is no hard shoulder); this is standard for all new motorway schemes since 2013

Standard motorway

Quick tips

- Never drive in a lane closed by a red X

- Keep to the speed limit shown on the gantries
- A solid white line indicates the hard shoulder – do not drive in it unless directed or in the case of an emergency
- A broken white line indicates a normal running lane
- Exit the smart motorway where possible if your vehicle is in difficulty. In an emergency, move onto the hard shoulder where there is one, or the nearest emergency refuge area
- Put on your hazard lights if you break down

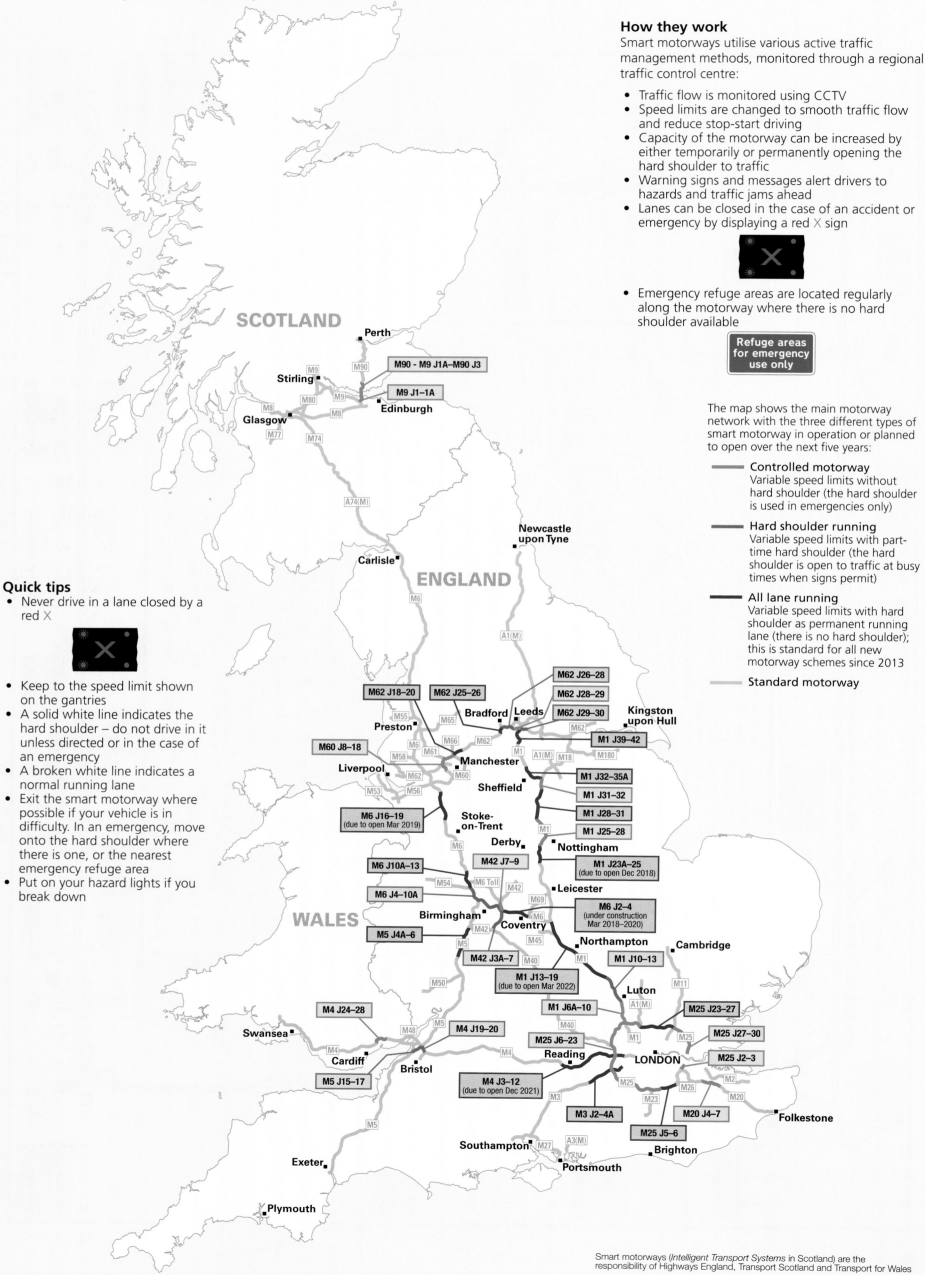

Smart motorways (*Intelligent Transport Systems* in Scotland) are the responsibility of Highways England, Transport Scotland and Transport for Wales

Motoring information

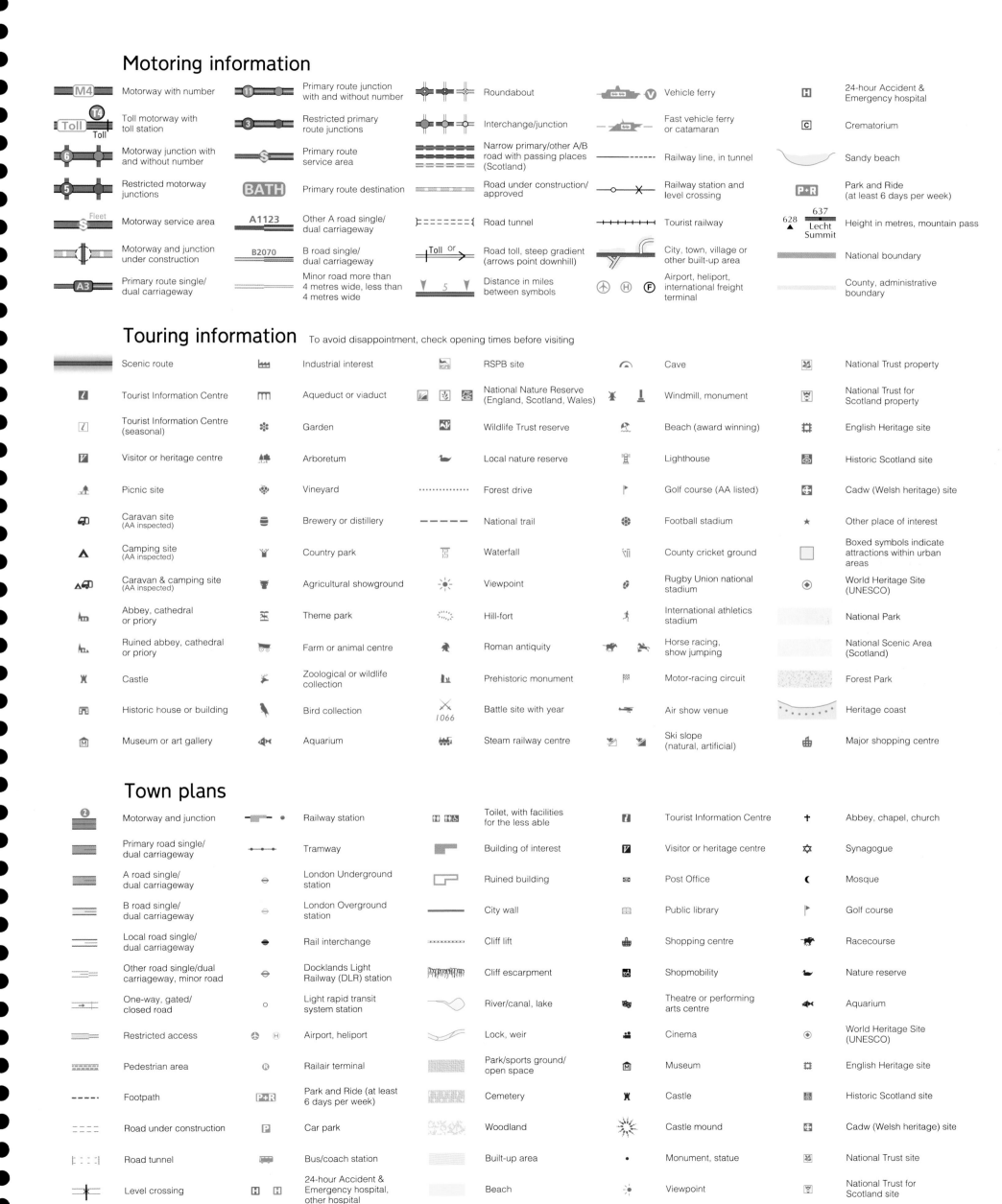

Touring information
To avoid disappointment, check opening times before visiting

Town plans

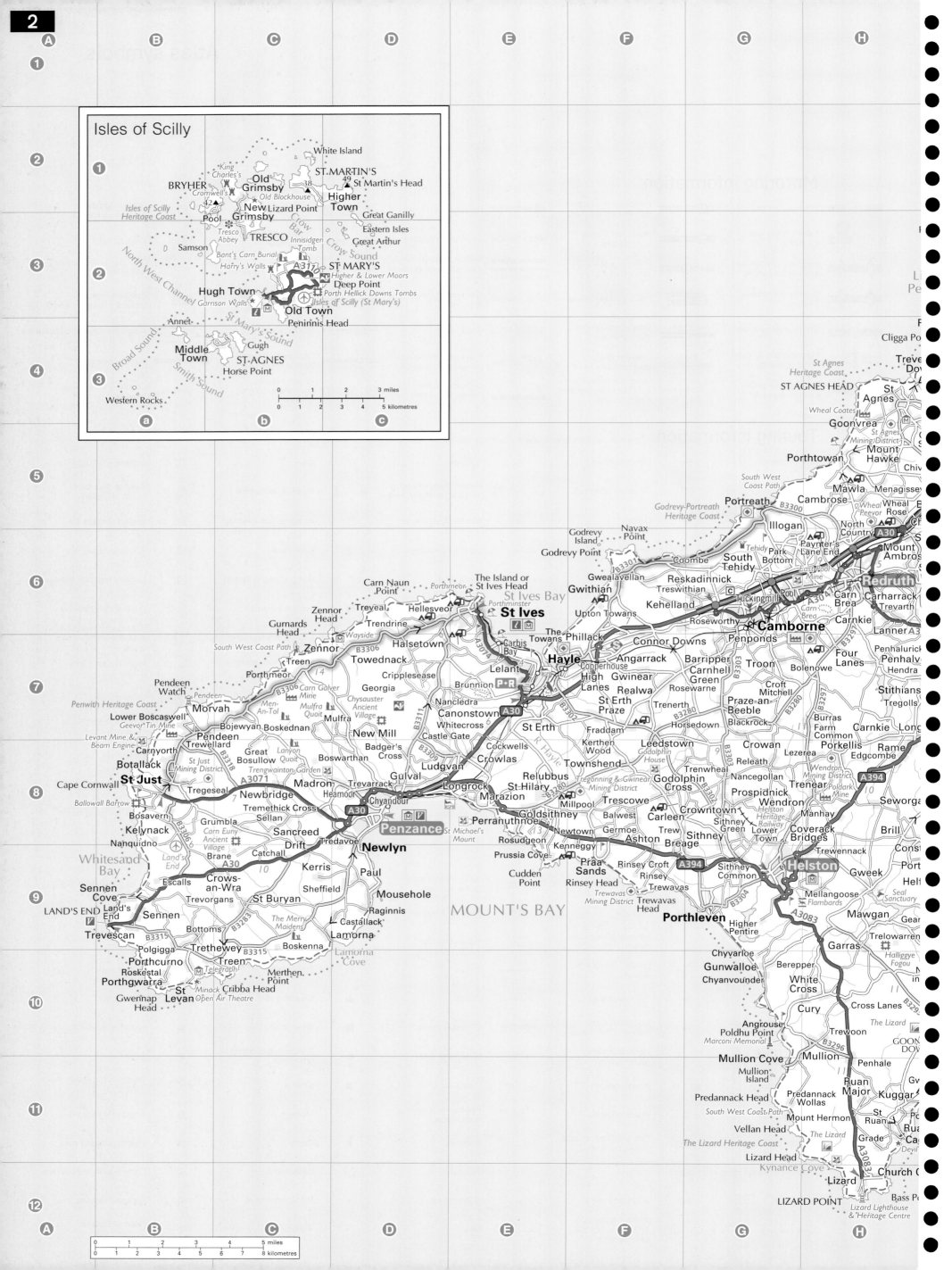

Newquay

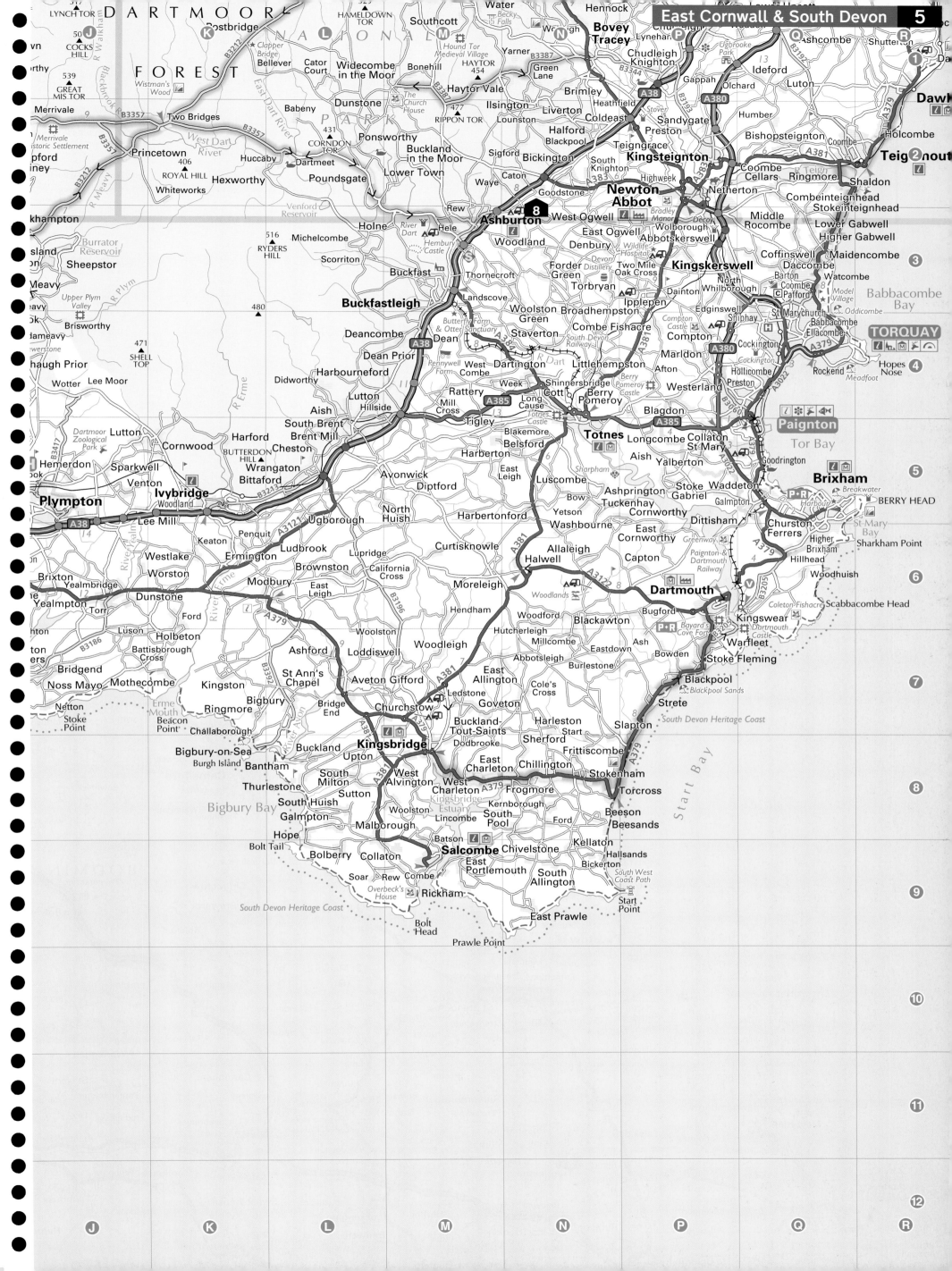

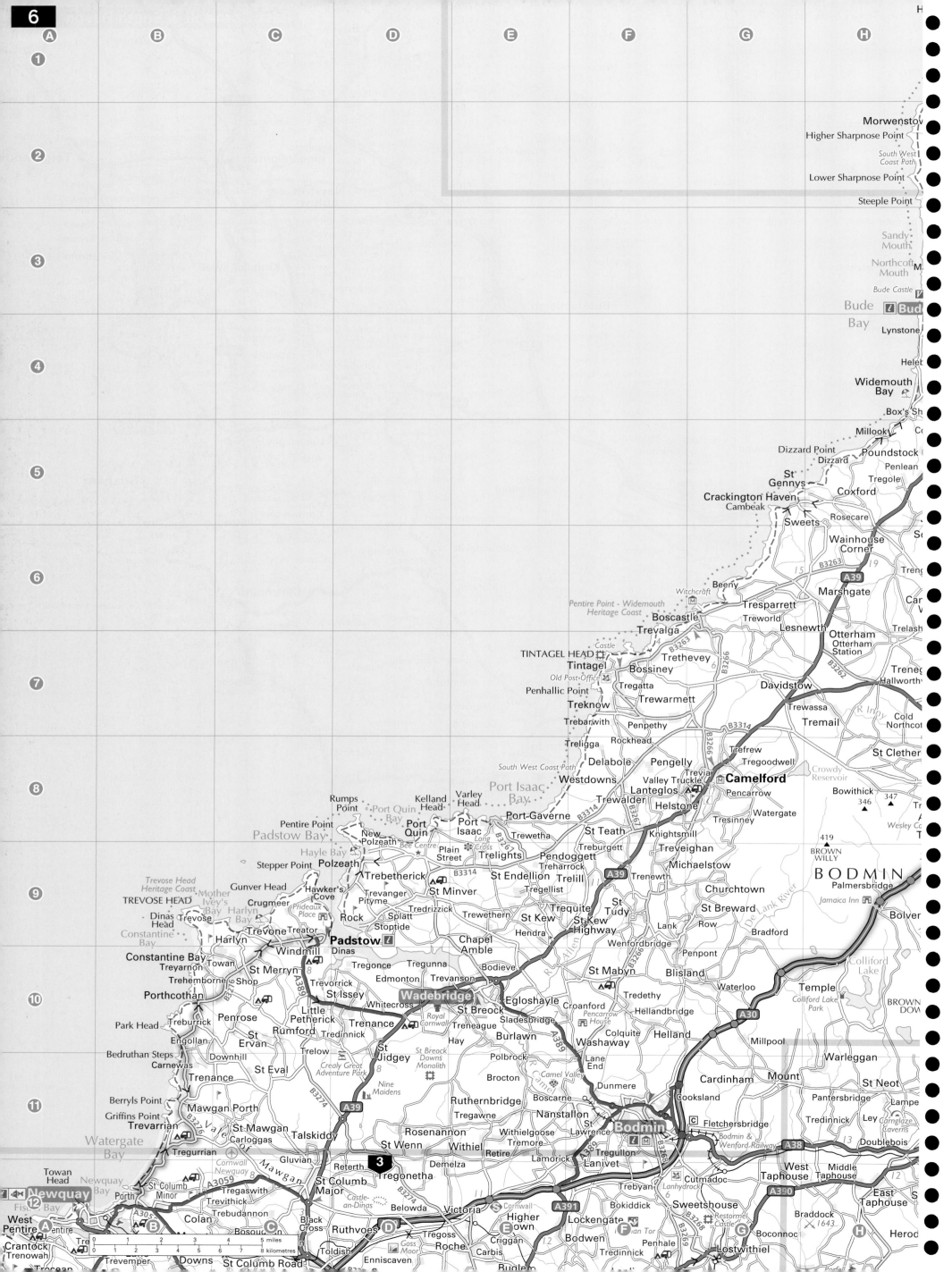

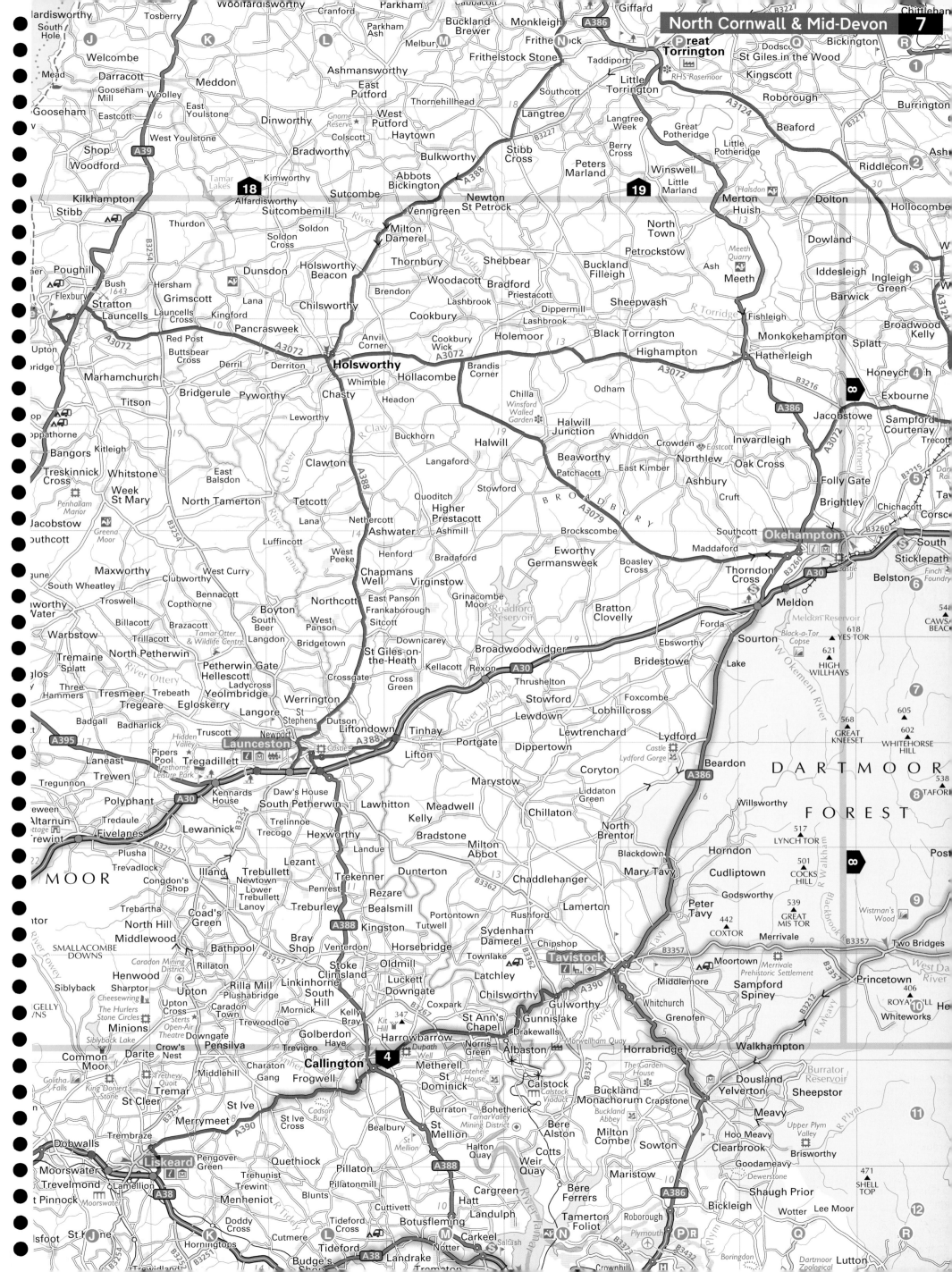

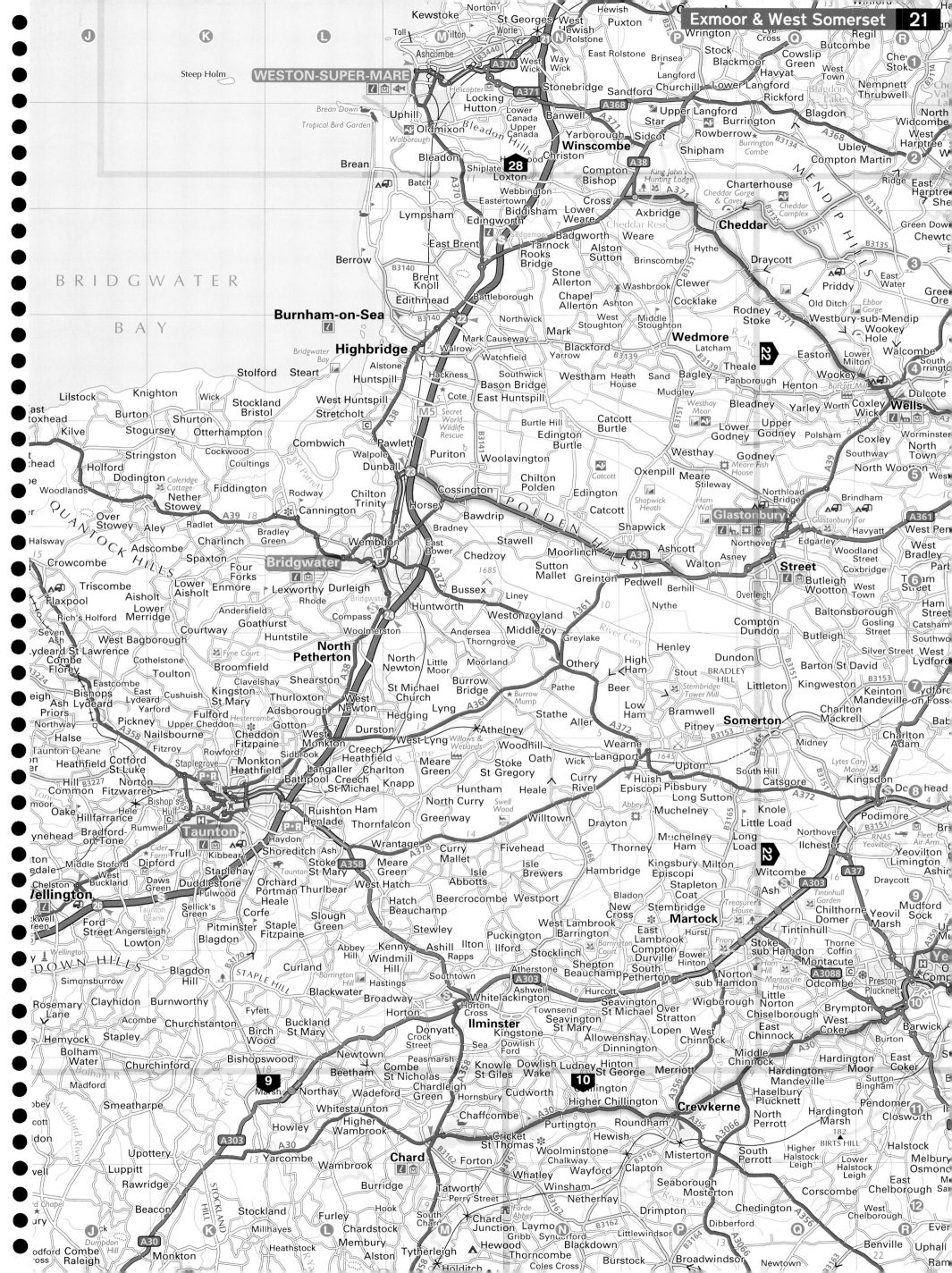

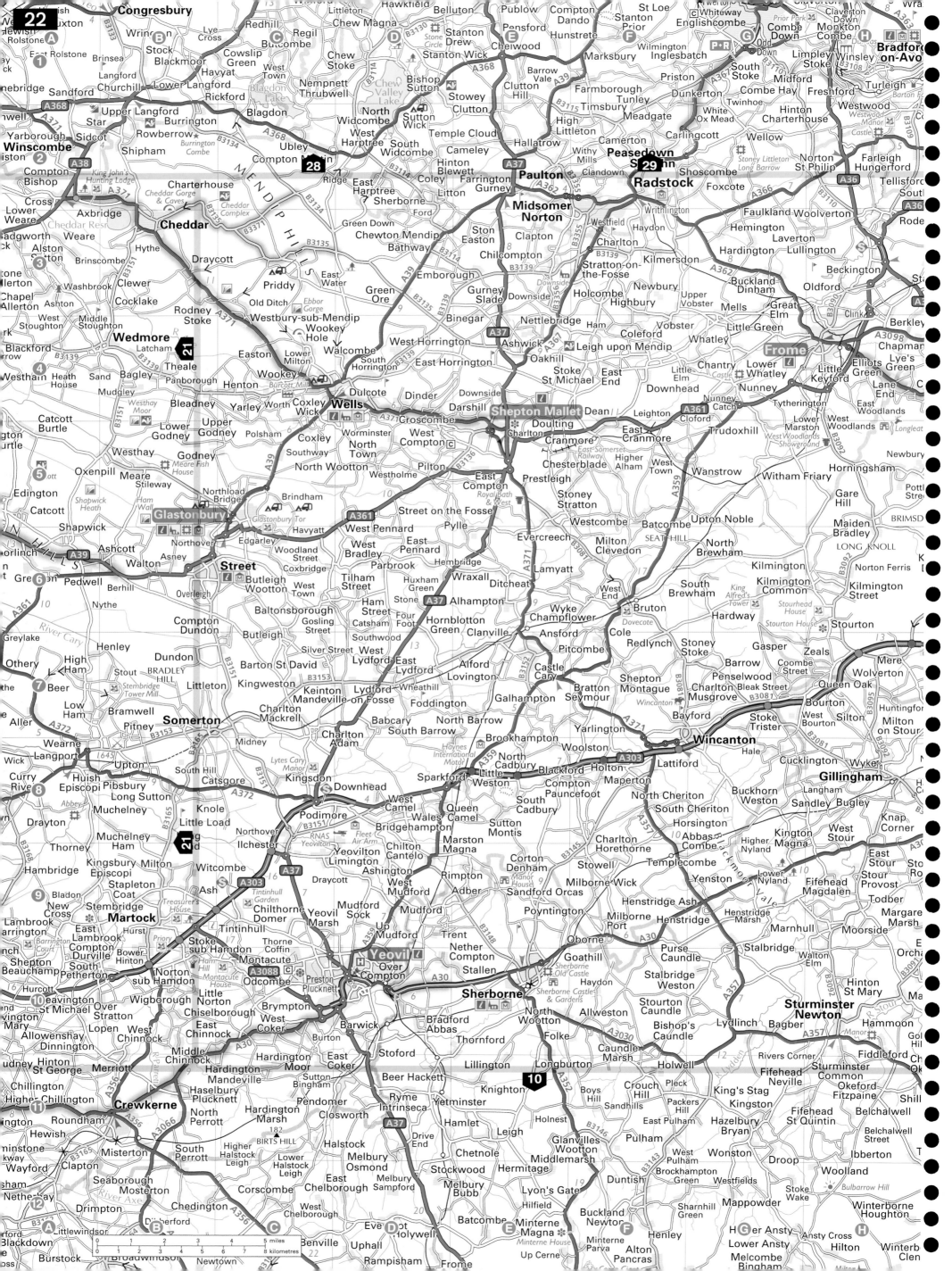

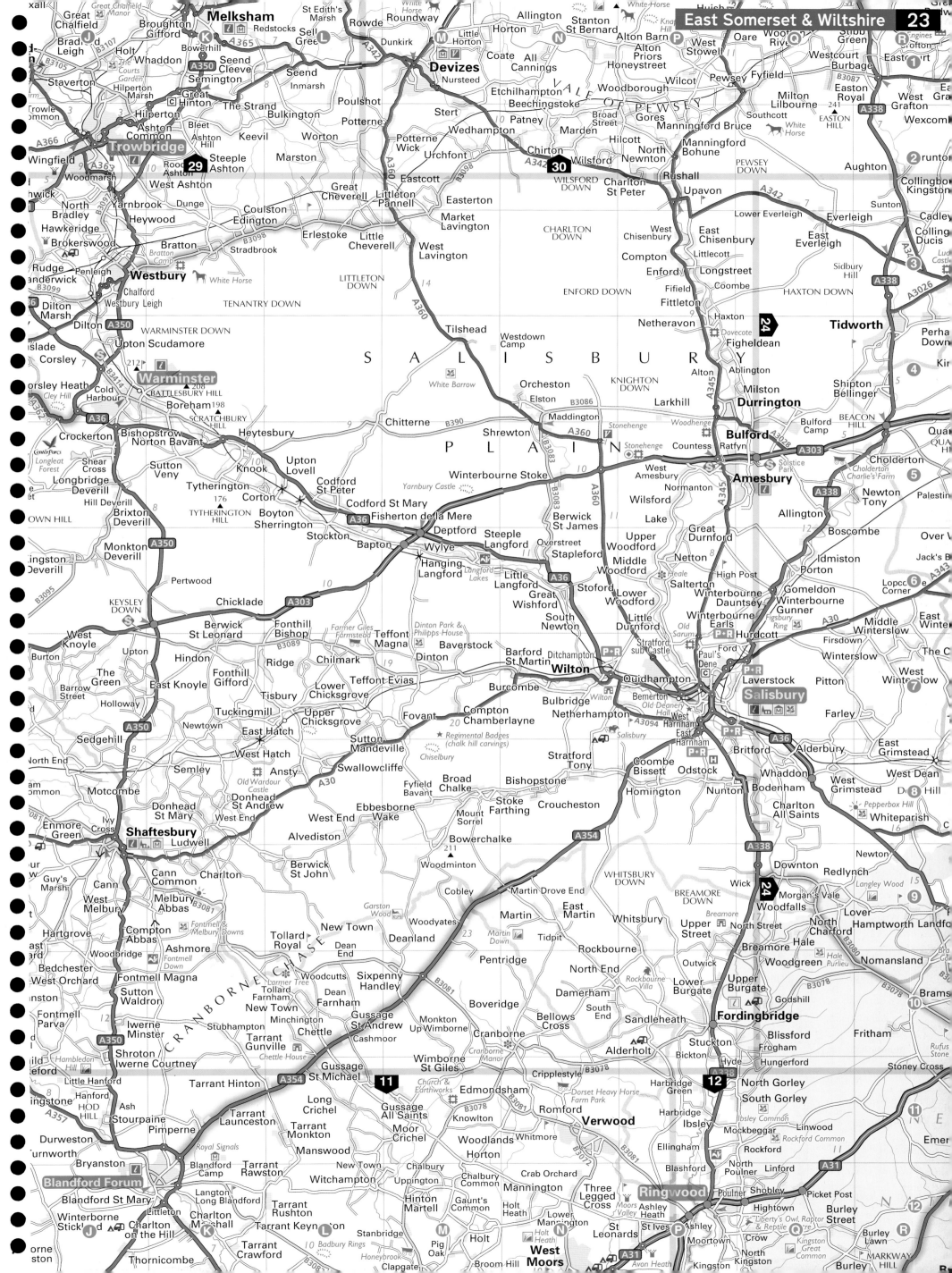

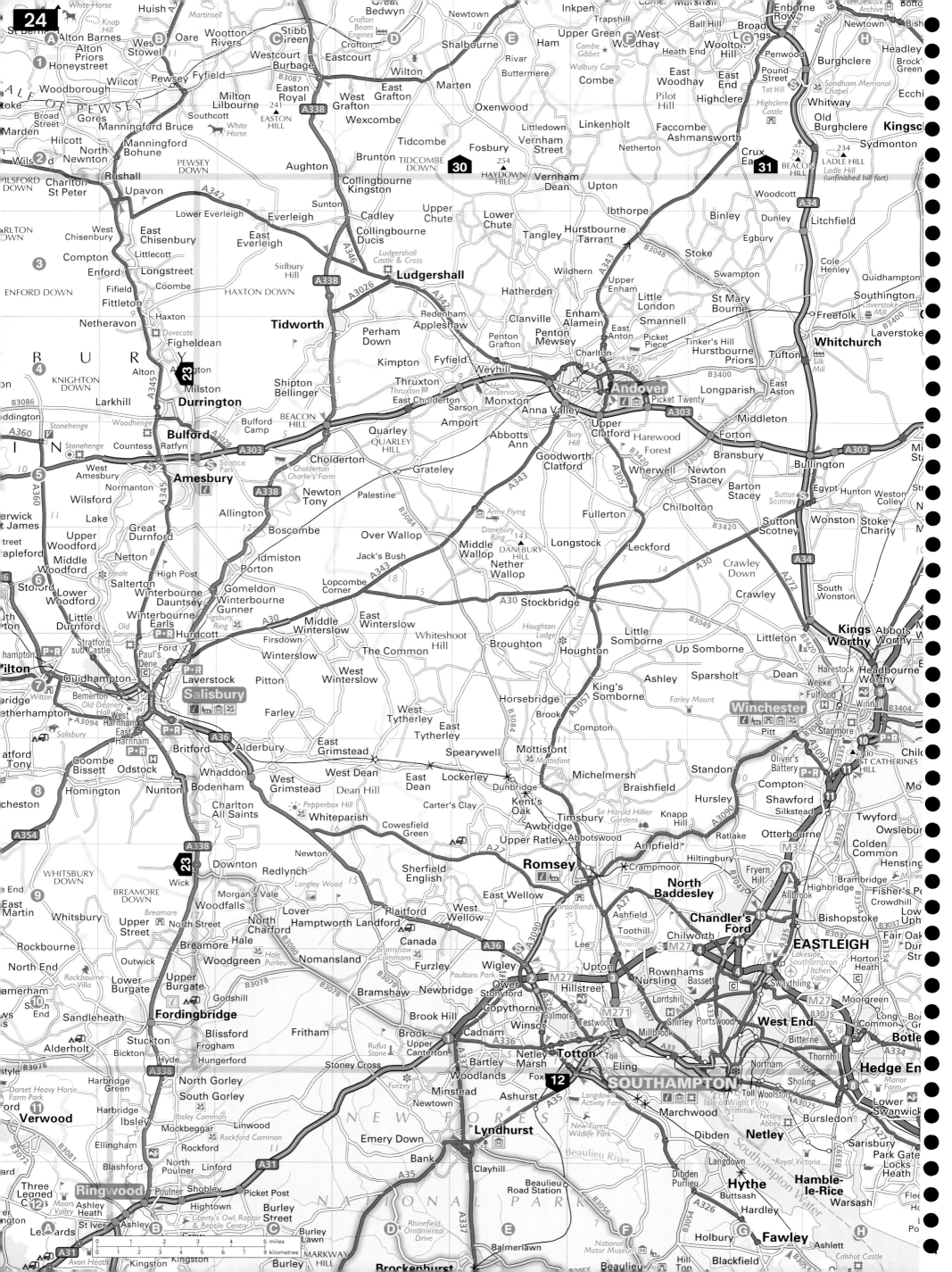

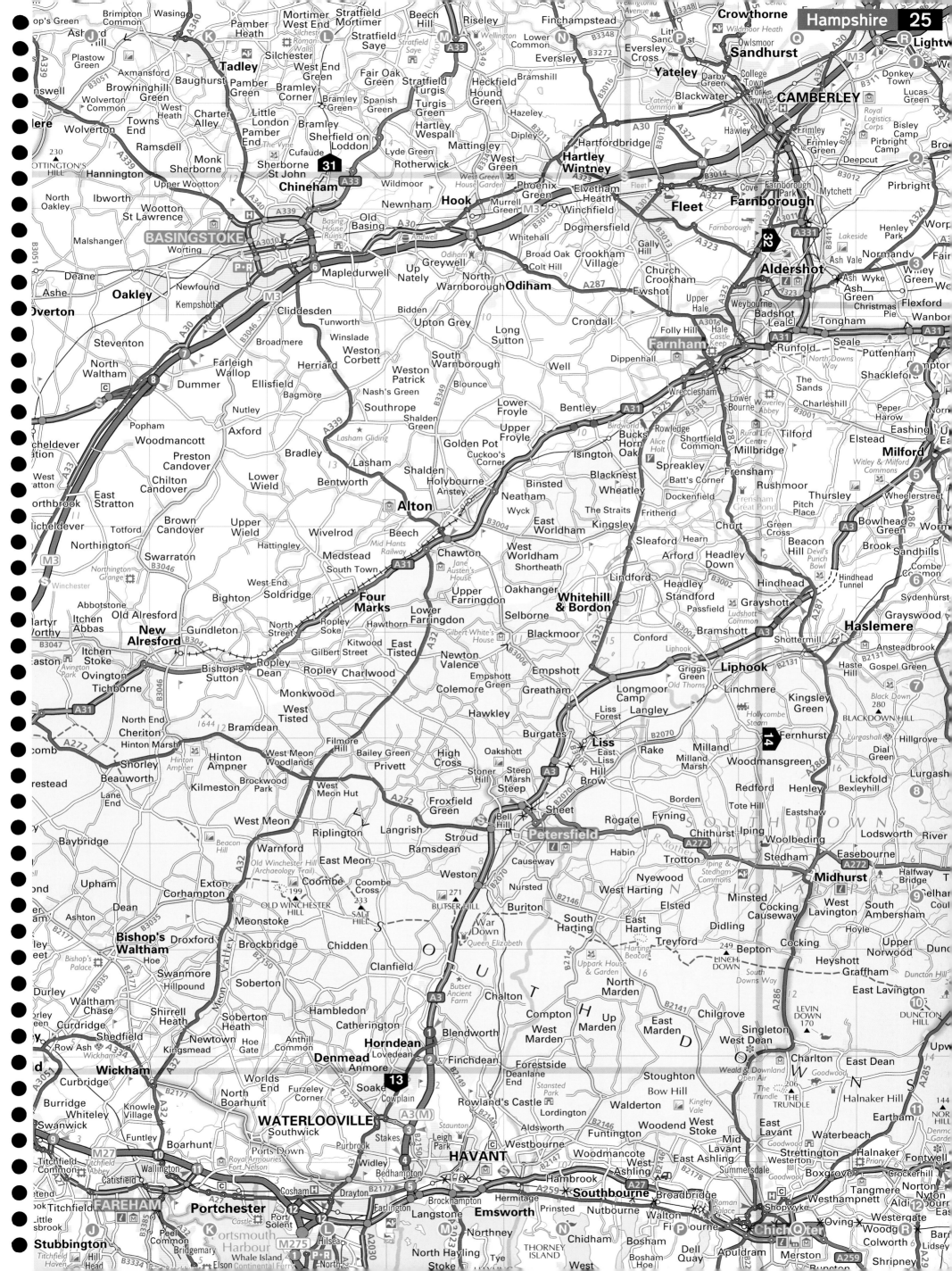

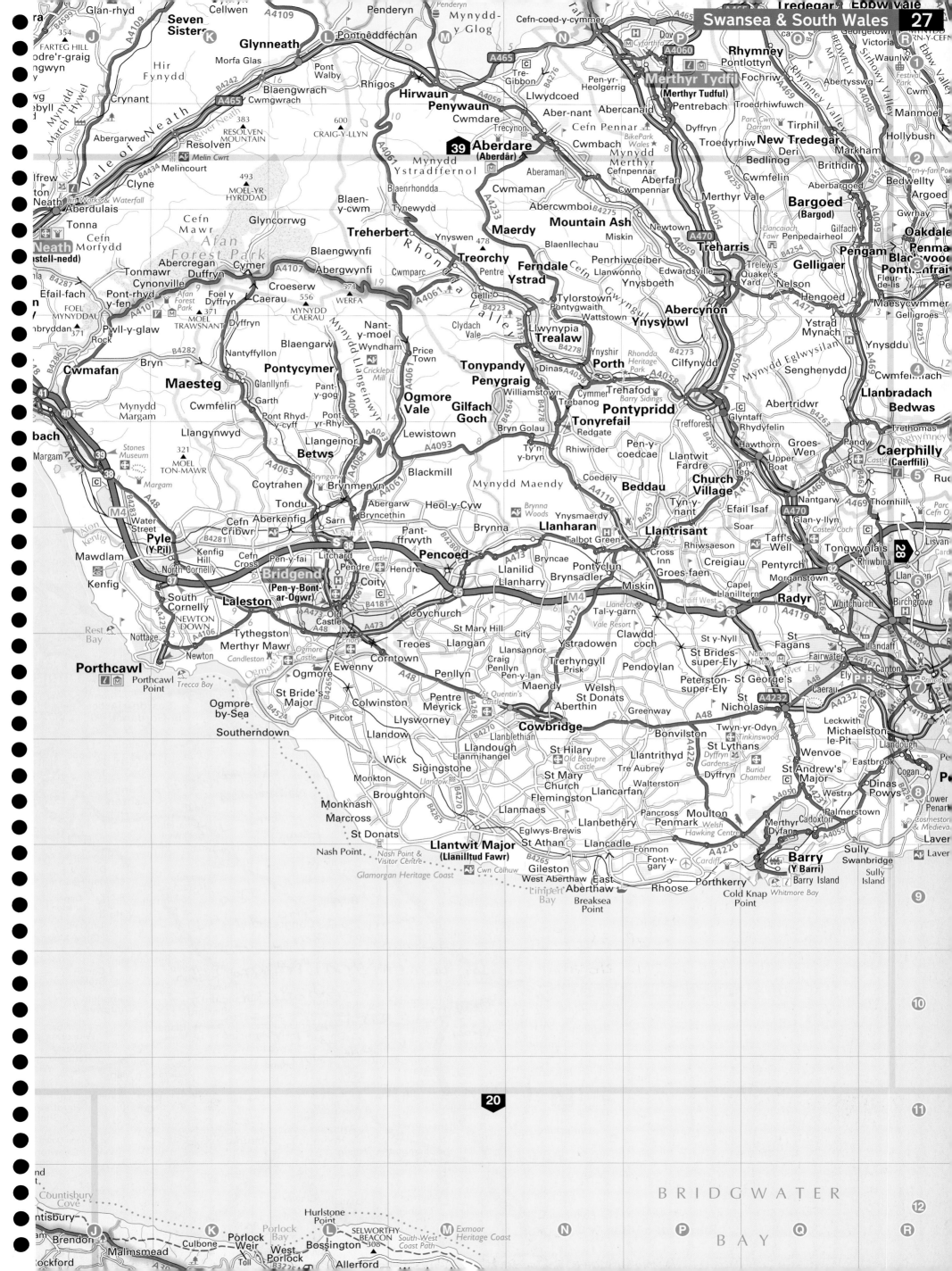

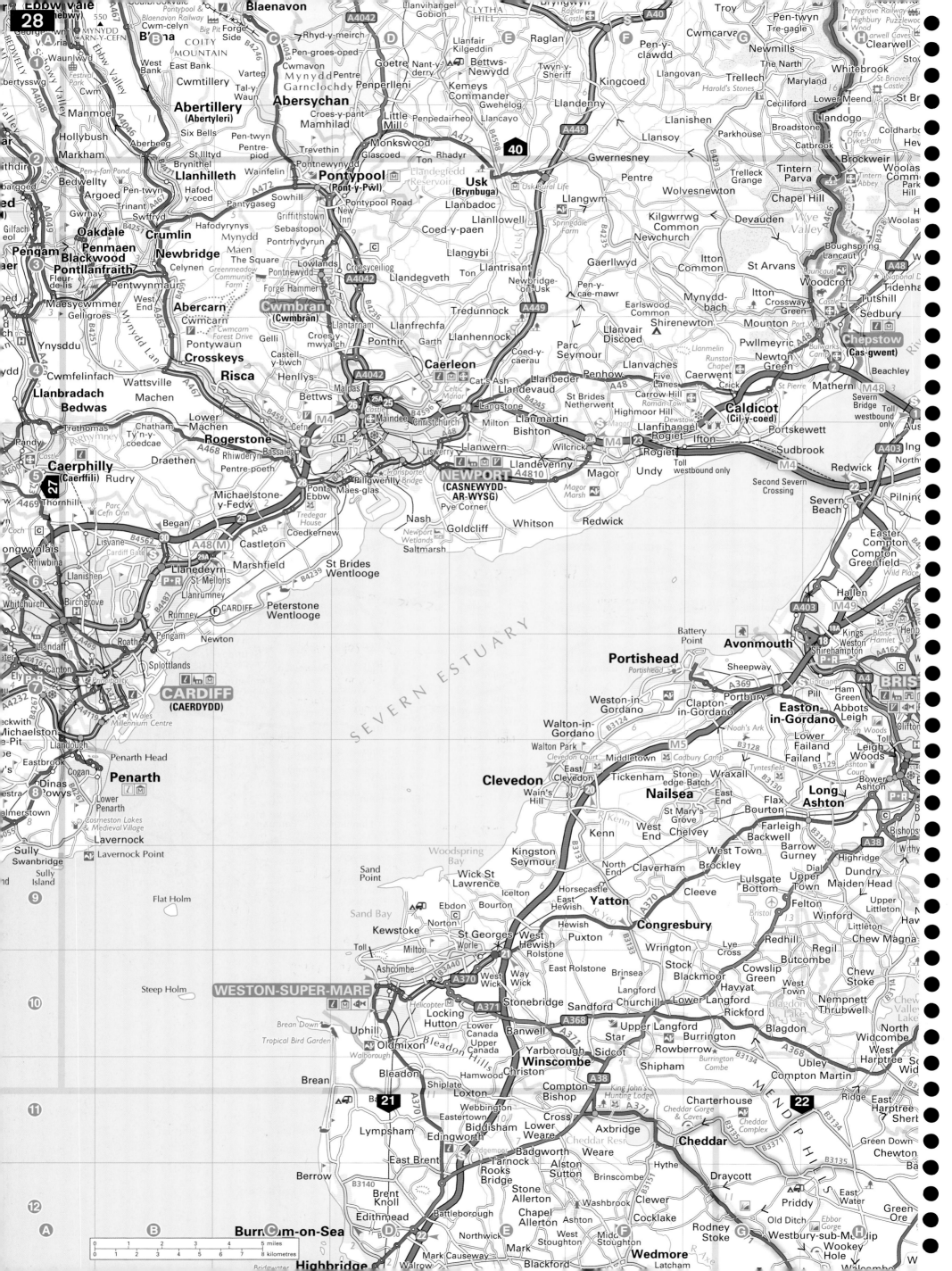

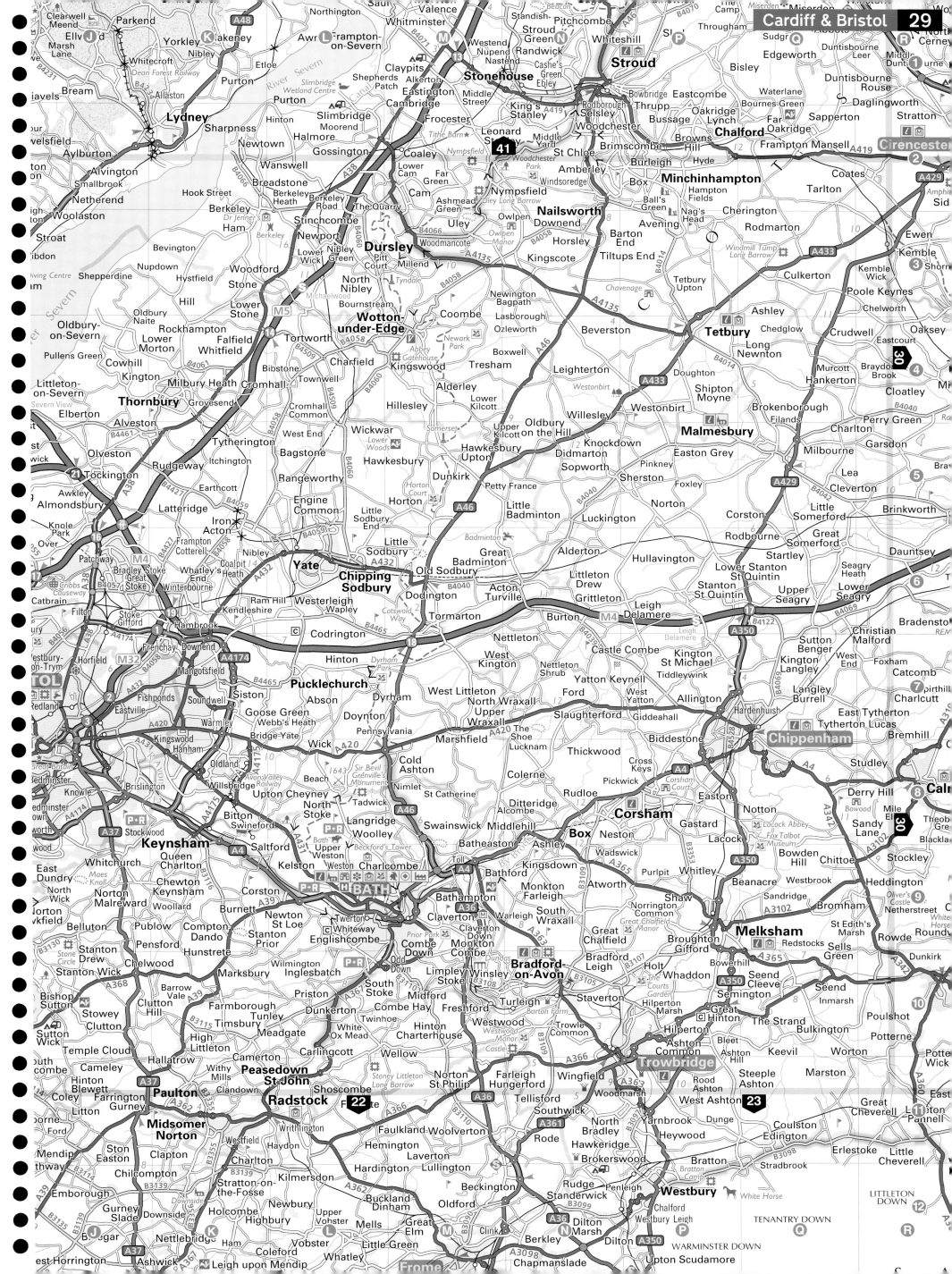

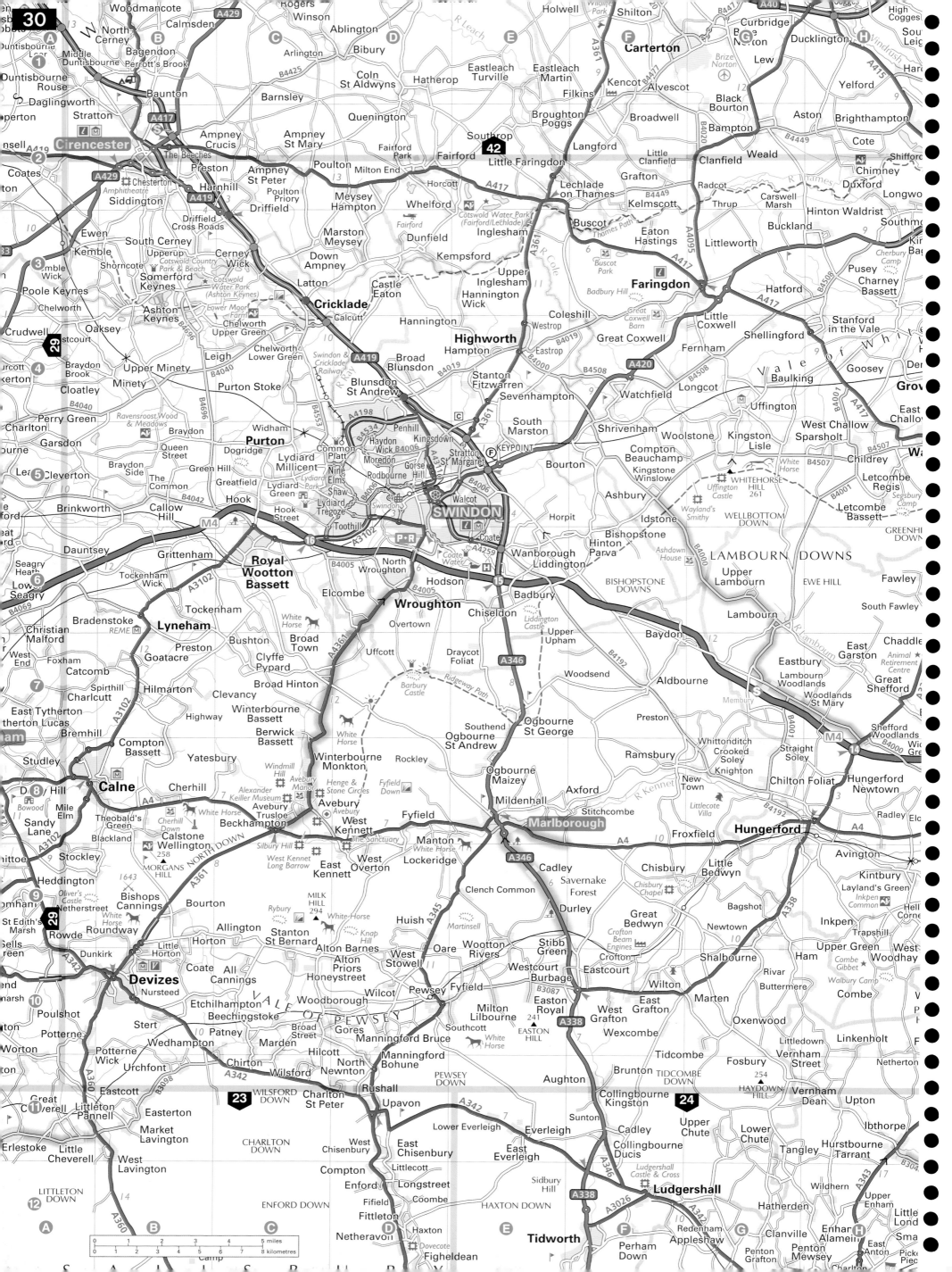

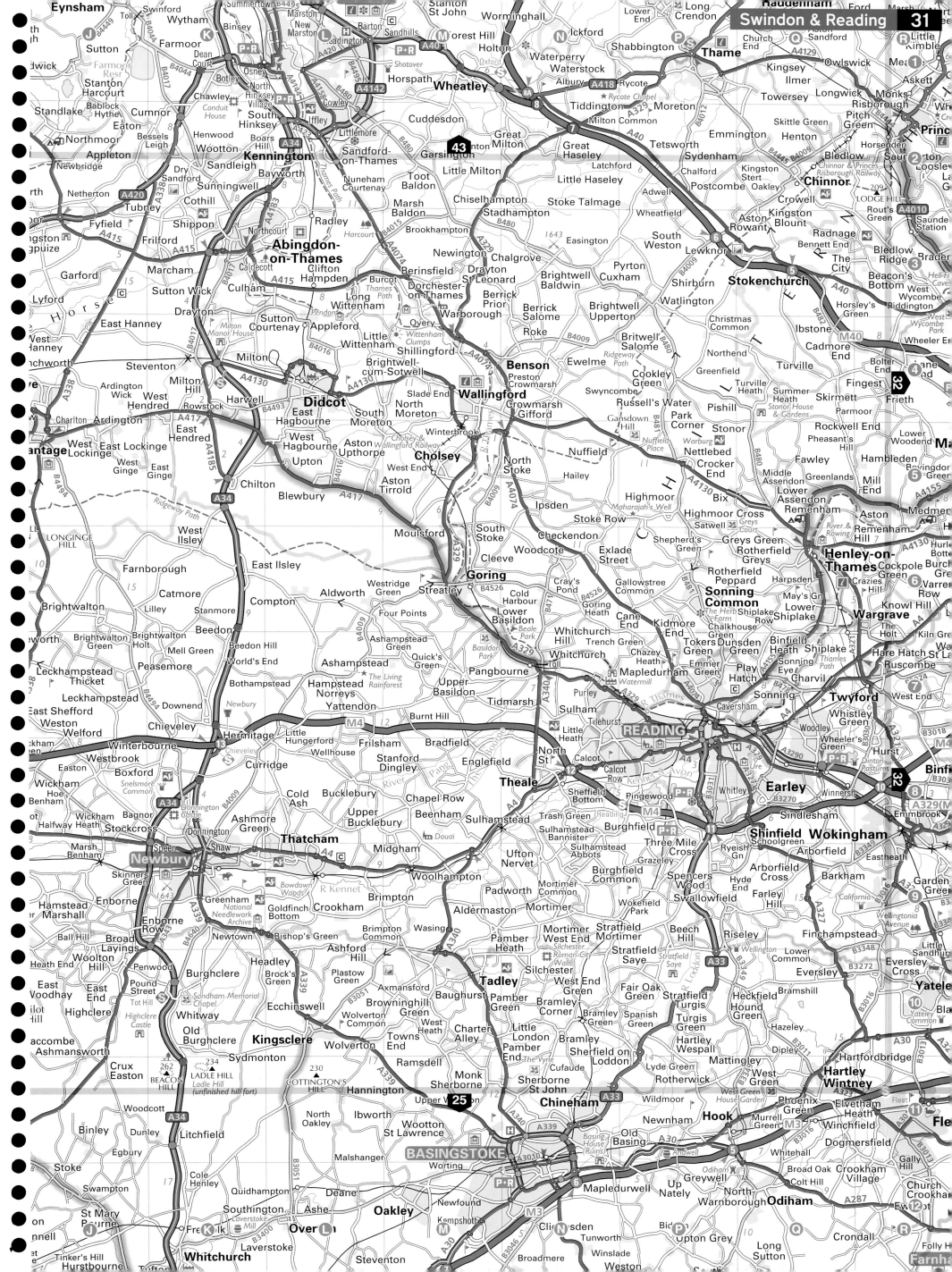

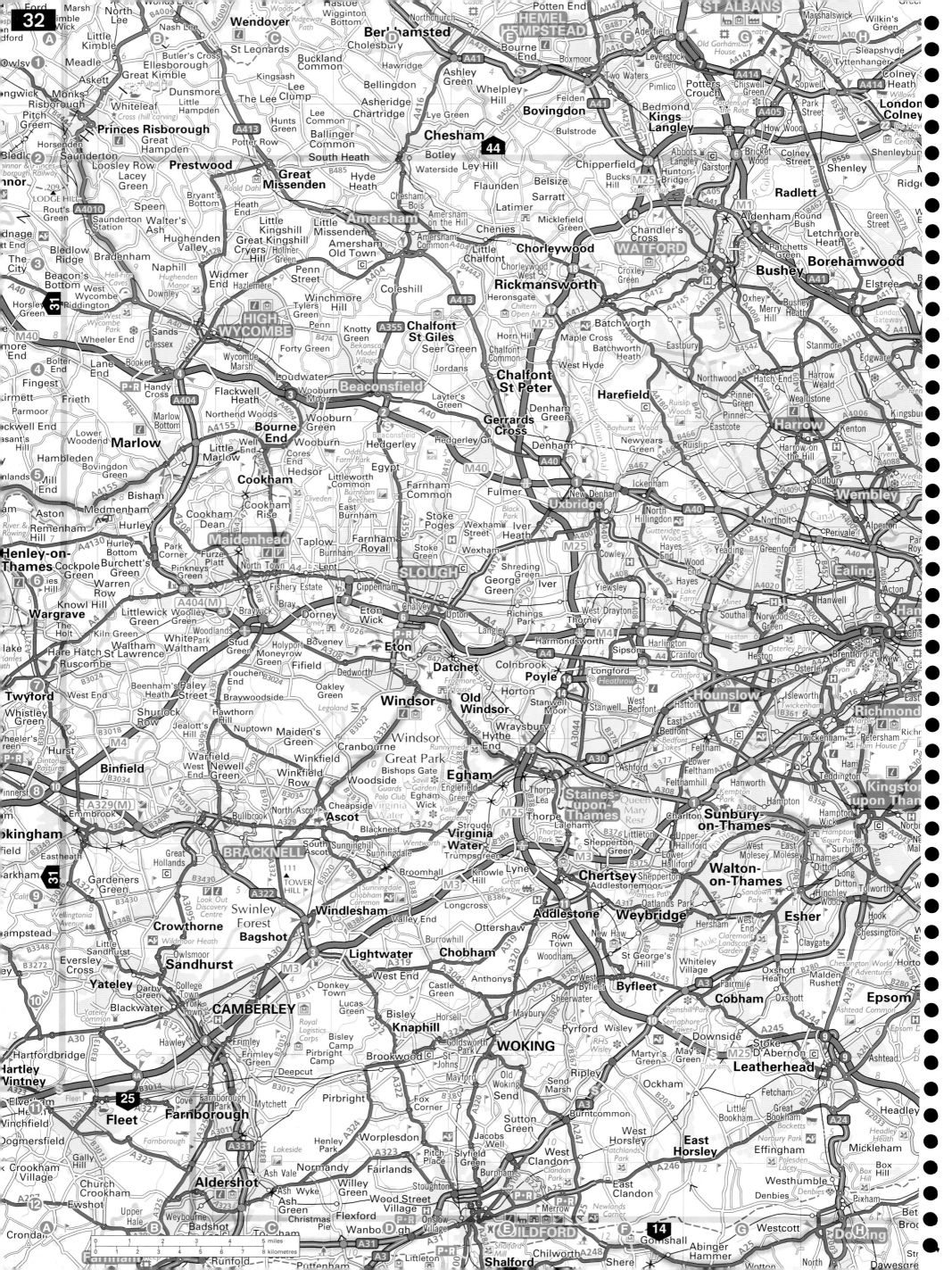

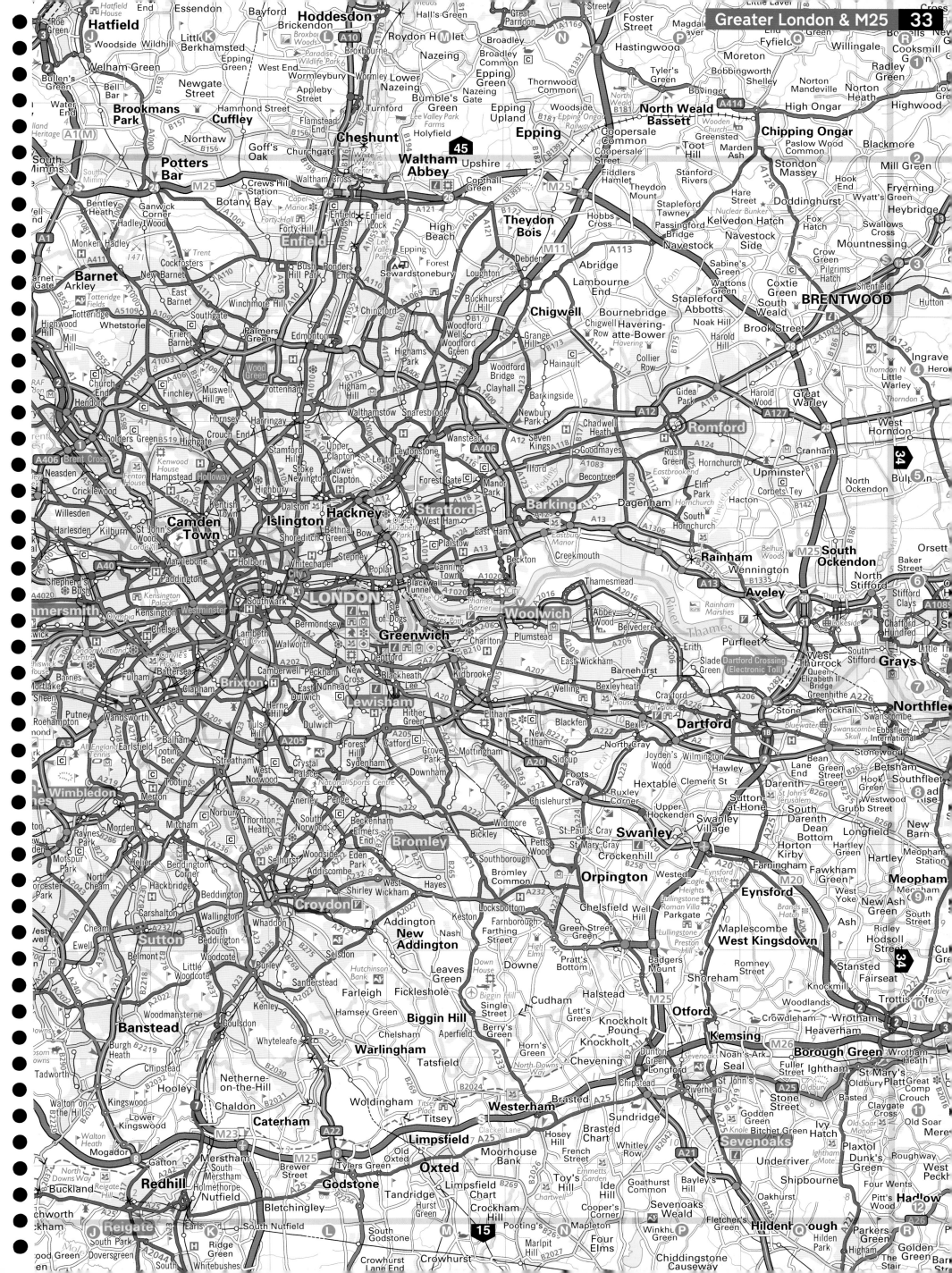

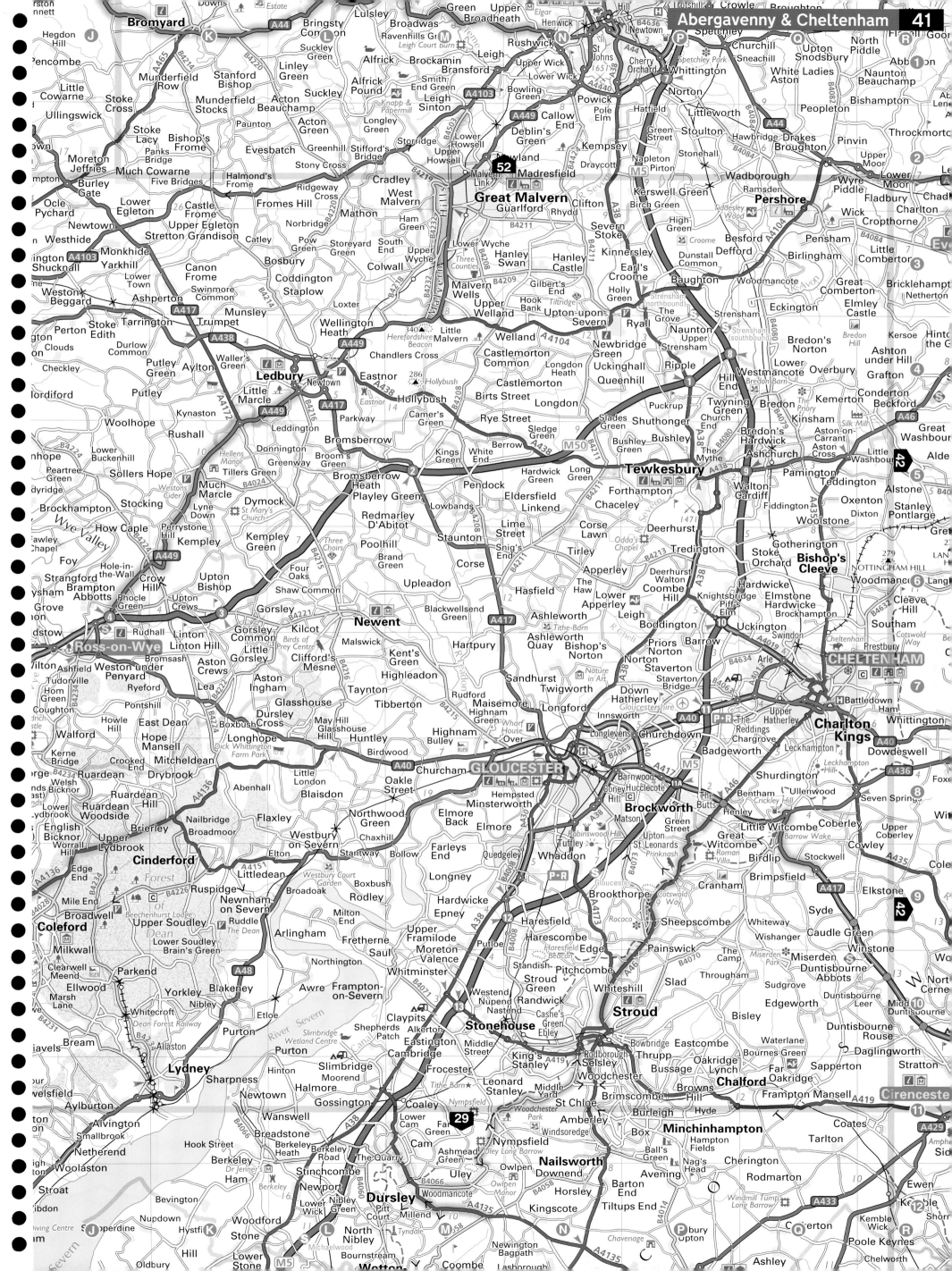

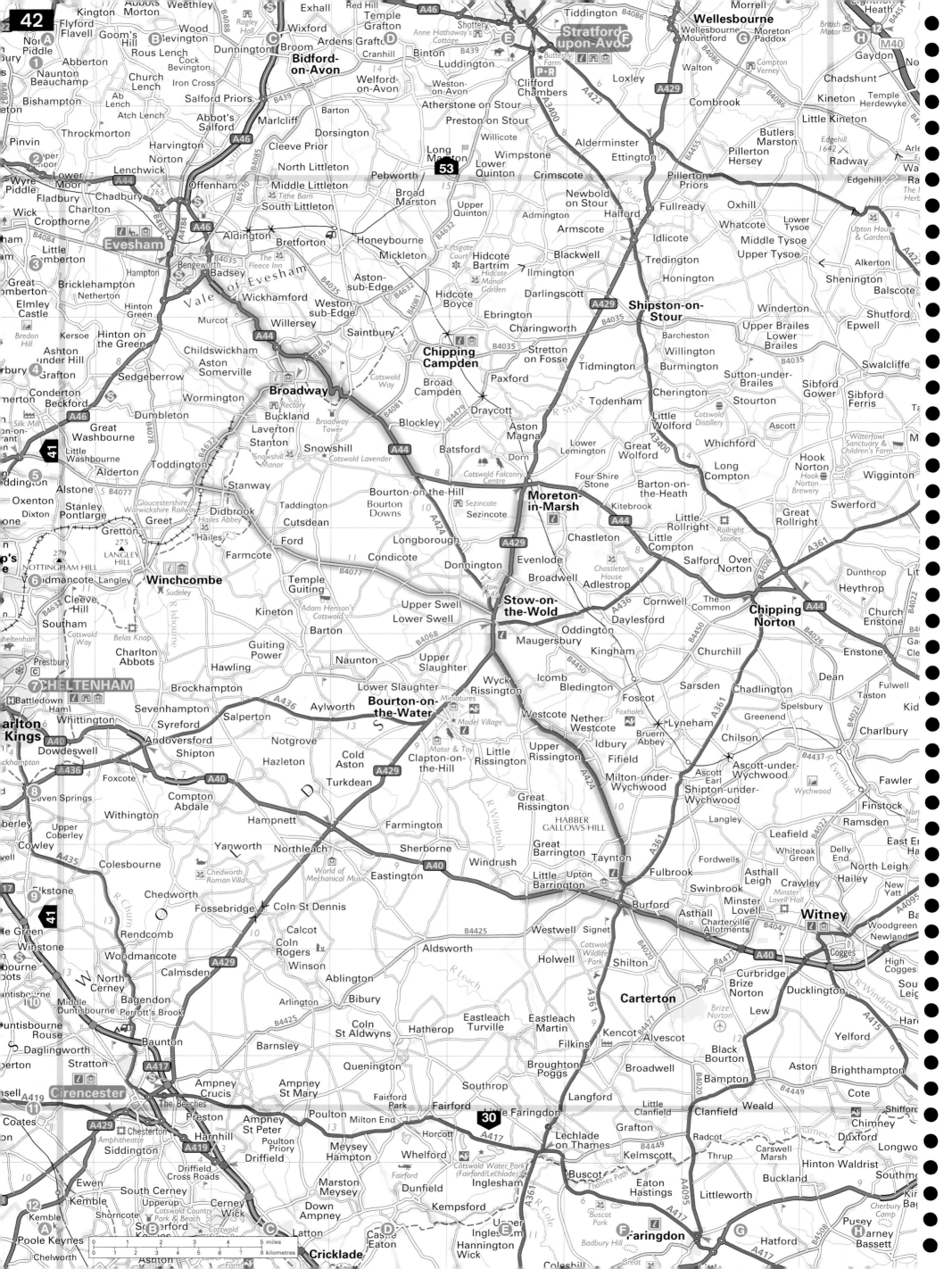

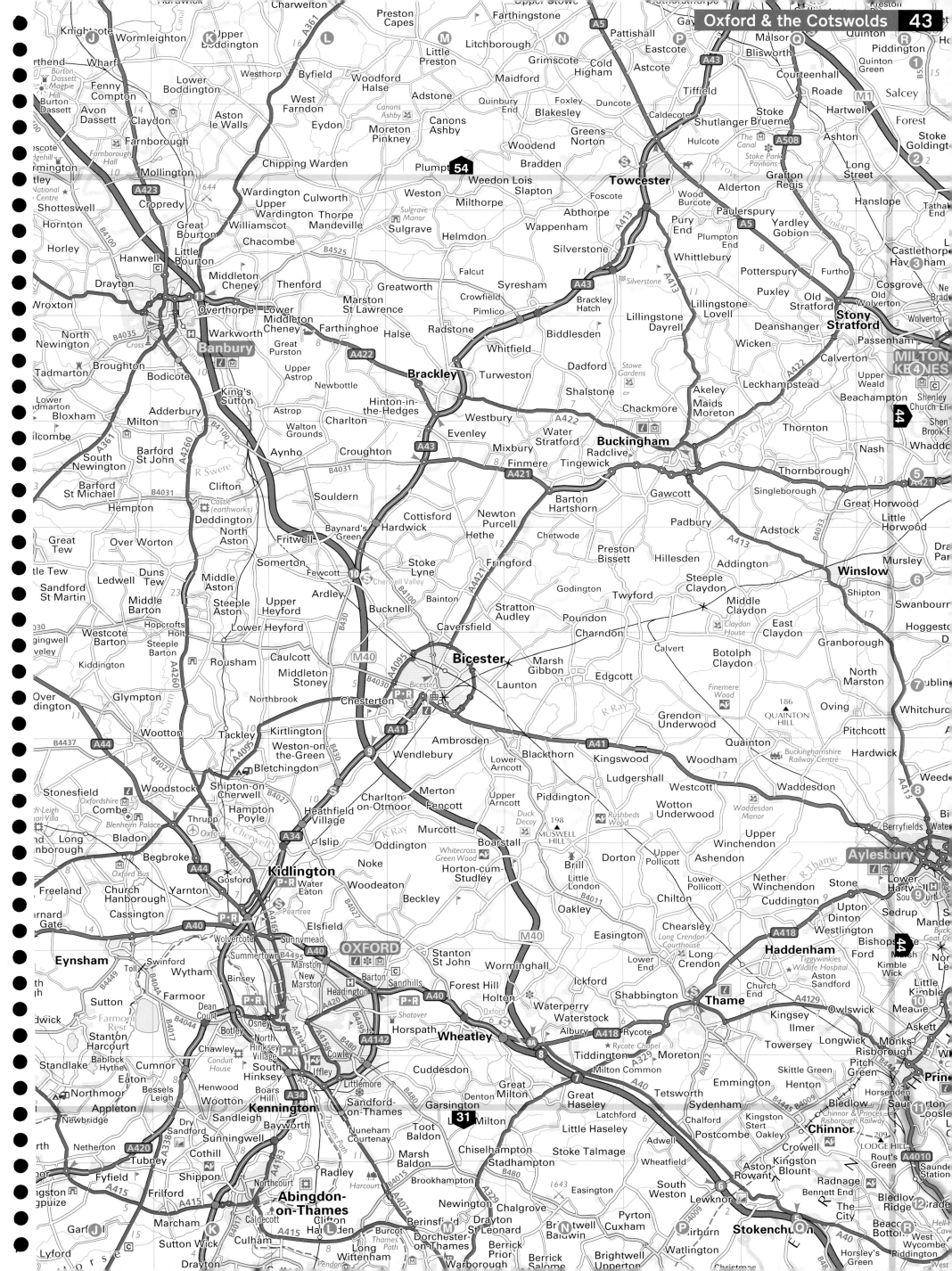

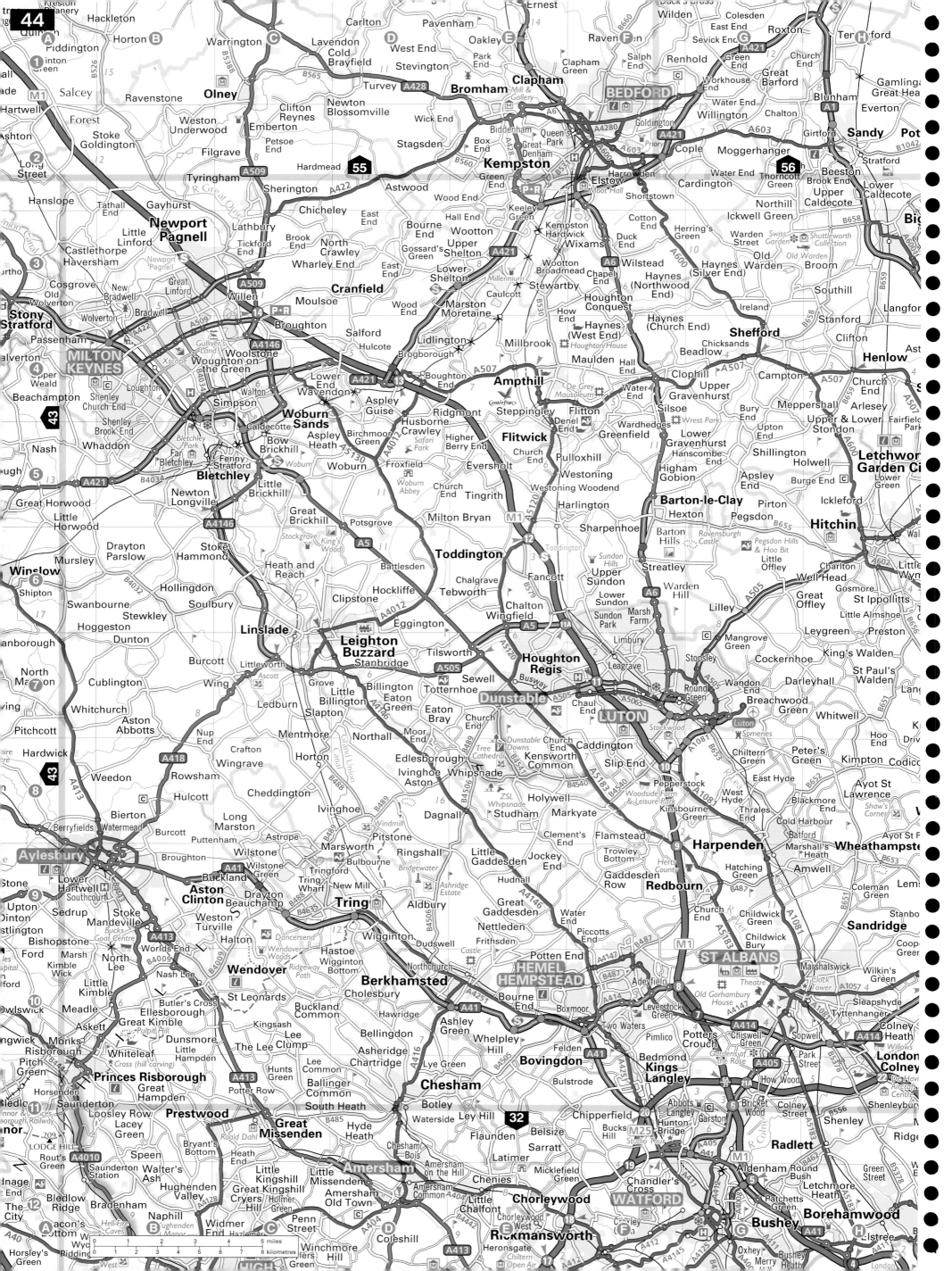

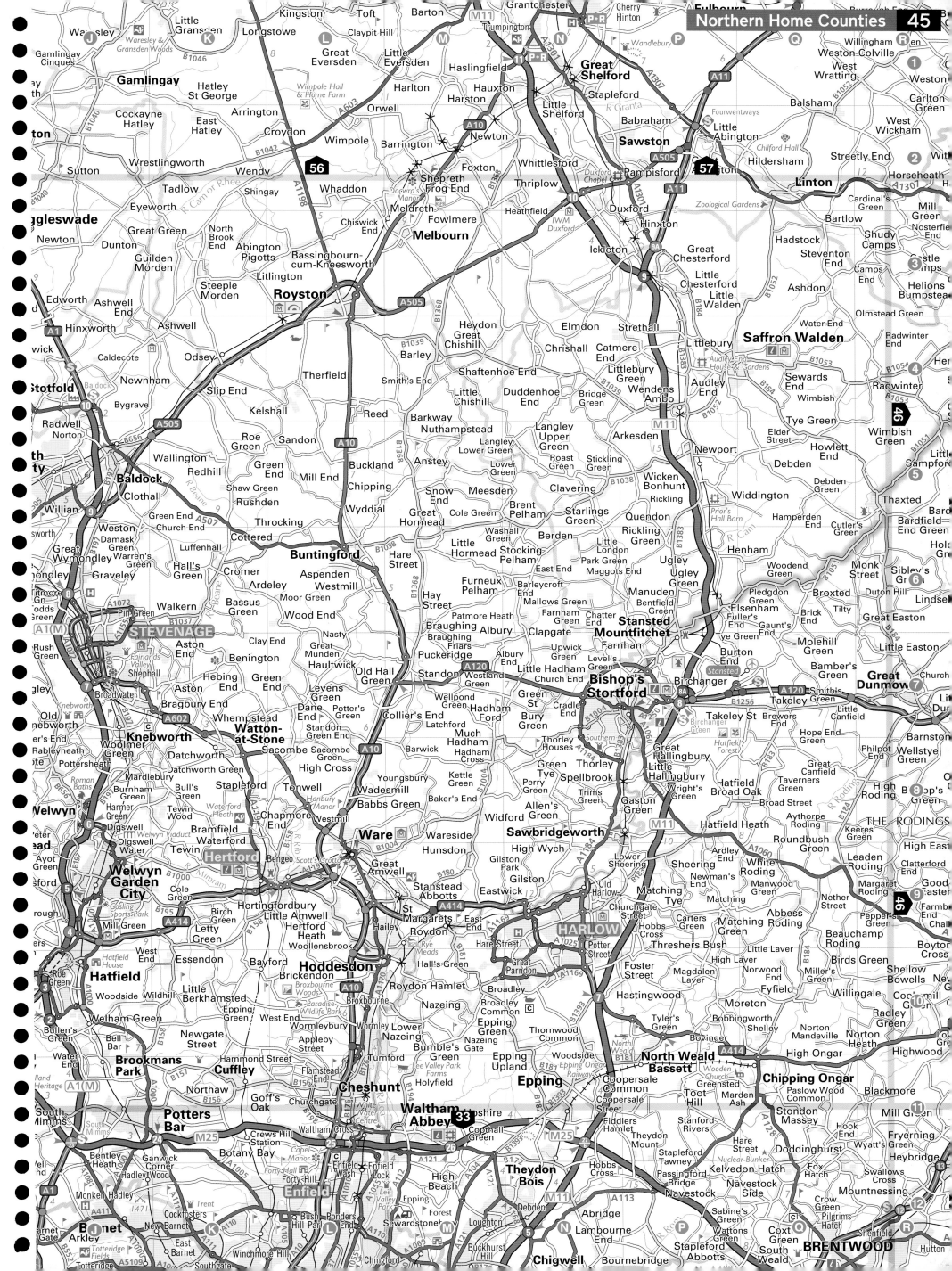

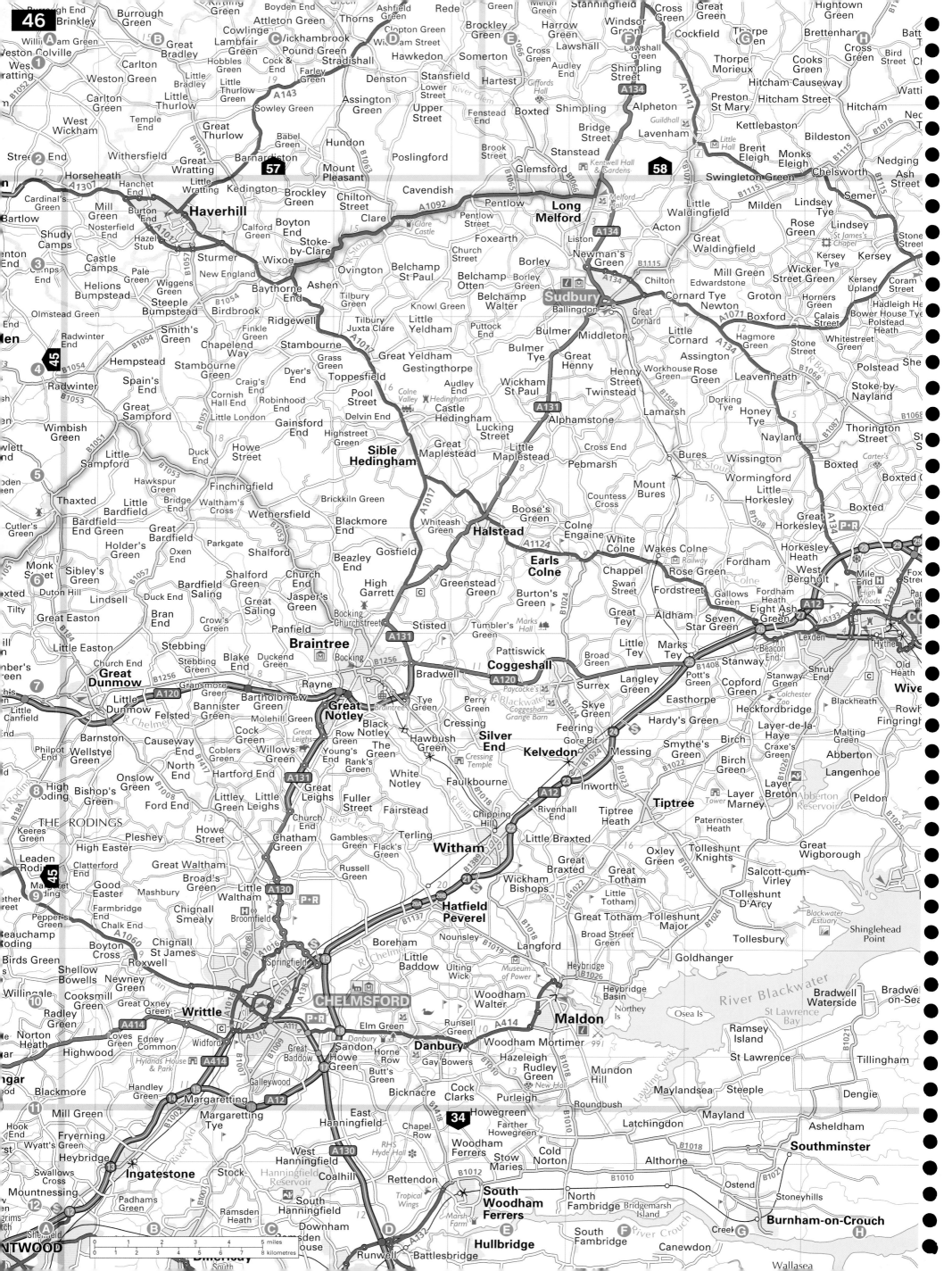

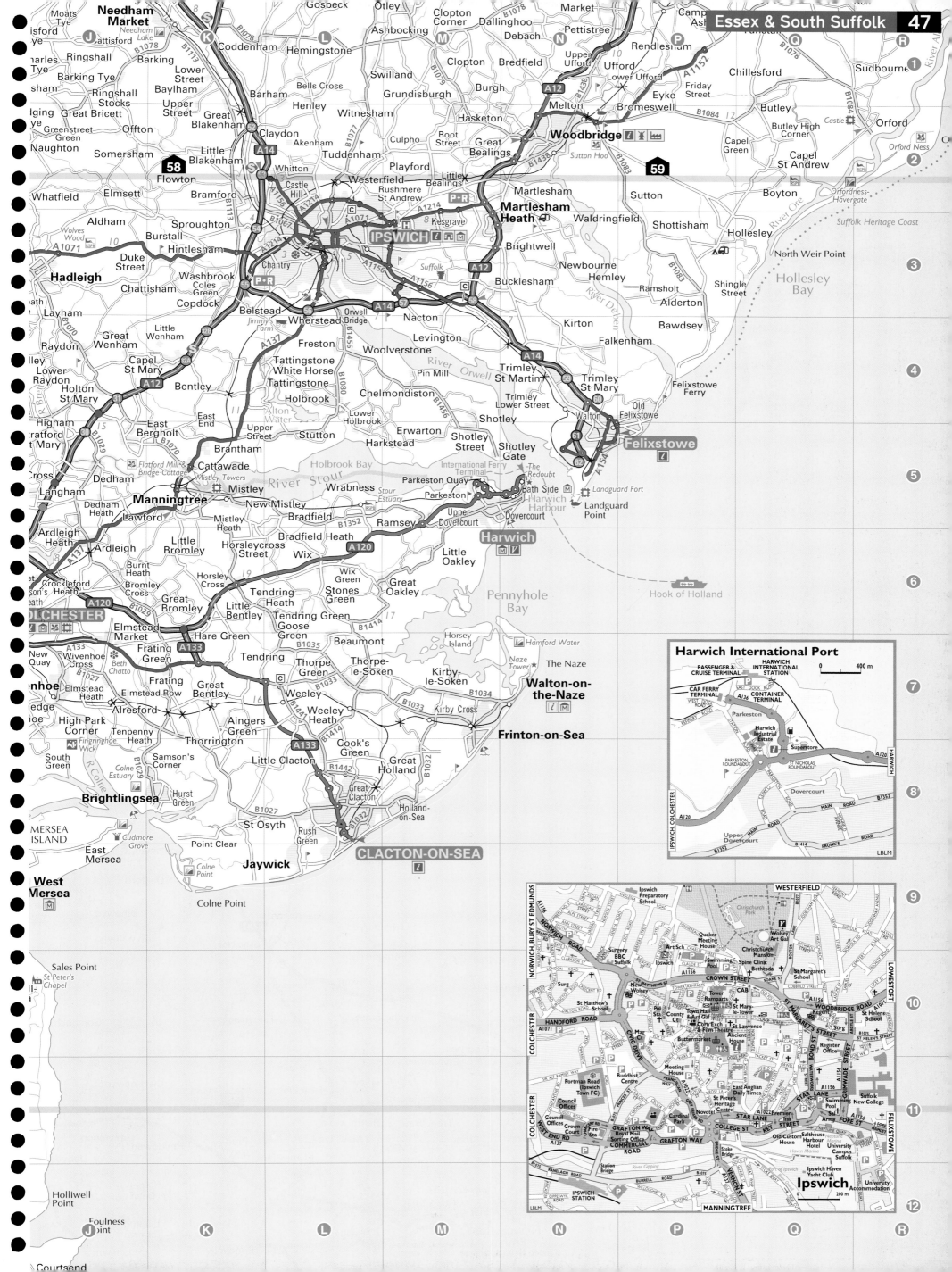

Harwich International Port

PASSENGER & CRUISE TERMINAL
HARWICH INTERNATIONAL STATION
CAR FERRY TERMINAL
CONTAINER TERMINAL
Parkeston
Harwich Industrial Estate
Superstore
PARKESTON ROUNDABOUT
ST NICHOLAS ROUNDABOUT
Dovercourt
Upper Dovercourt
IPSWICH, COLCHESTER
HARWICH
0   400 m
LBLM

Ipswich

WESTERFIELD
Ipswich Preparatory School
Christchurch Park
Wolsey Art Gal
Quaker Meeting House
Surgery BBC Suffolk
Art Sch
Ipswich
Christchurch Mansion
Spine Clinic
Bethesda
St Margaret's School
Swimming Pool
NORWICH, BURY ST EDMUNDS
NORWICH ROAD
New Wolsey
St Matthew's School
CROWN STREET
WOODBRIDGE ROAD
St Helens School
Tower Ramparts
CAB
St Mary-le-Tower
St Margaret's Street
BONDS
GRIMWADE STREET
LOWESTOFT
HANDFORD ROAD
County Ct
Town Hall & Art Gal
Corn Exch
St Lawrence
Ancient House
Register Office
Suffolk Swimming Pool
COLCHESTER
A1071
Surg
Buttermarket
Film Theatre
St Helens Street
Buddhist Centre
Meeting House
East Anglian Daily Times
Army
Suffolk New College
WEST END RD
Portman Road (Ipswich Town FC)
Council Offices
Council Offices
Crown Court
St Peter's Heritage Centre
Novotel
STAR LANE
Swimming Pool
KEY STREET
FORE ST
Cardinal Park
COLLEGE ST
FELIXSTOWE
A137
Royal Mail Sorting Office
Fire Sta
GRAFTON WAY
COMMERCIAL ROAD
GRAFTON WAY
Premier
Old Custom House
Salthouse Harbour Hotel
University Campus Suffolk
Stoke Bridge
River Gipping
Station Bridge
Ipswich Haven Yacht Club
Port of Ipswich
University Accommodation
RANELAGH ROAD
WILLOUGHBY ROAD
BURRELL RD
VERNON
IPSWICH STATION
Ipswich
MANNINGTREE
0   400 m
LBLM

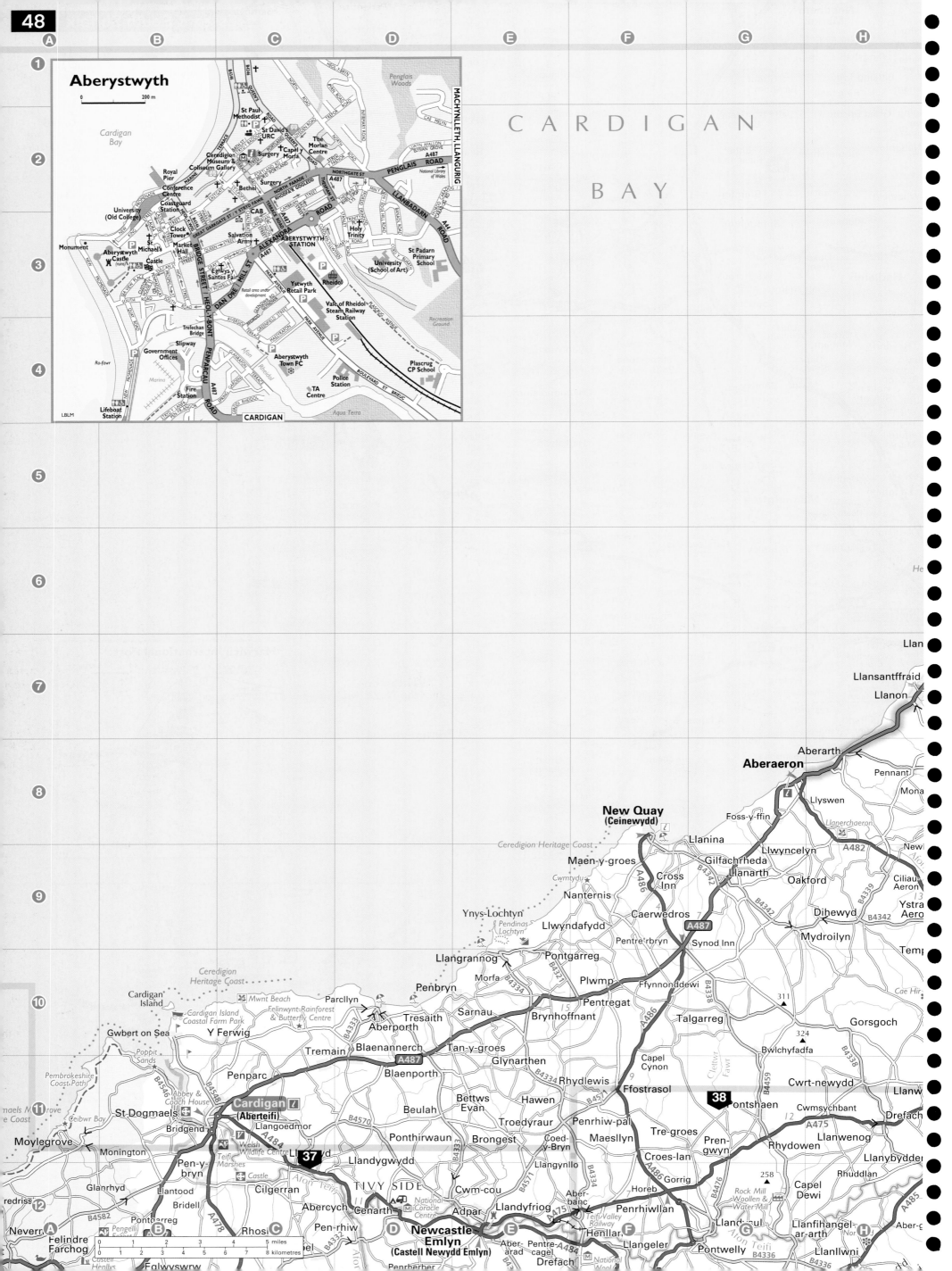

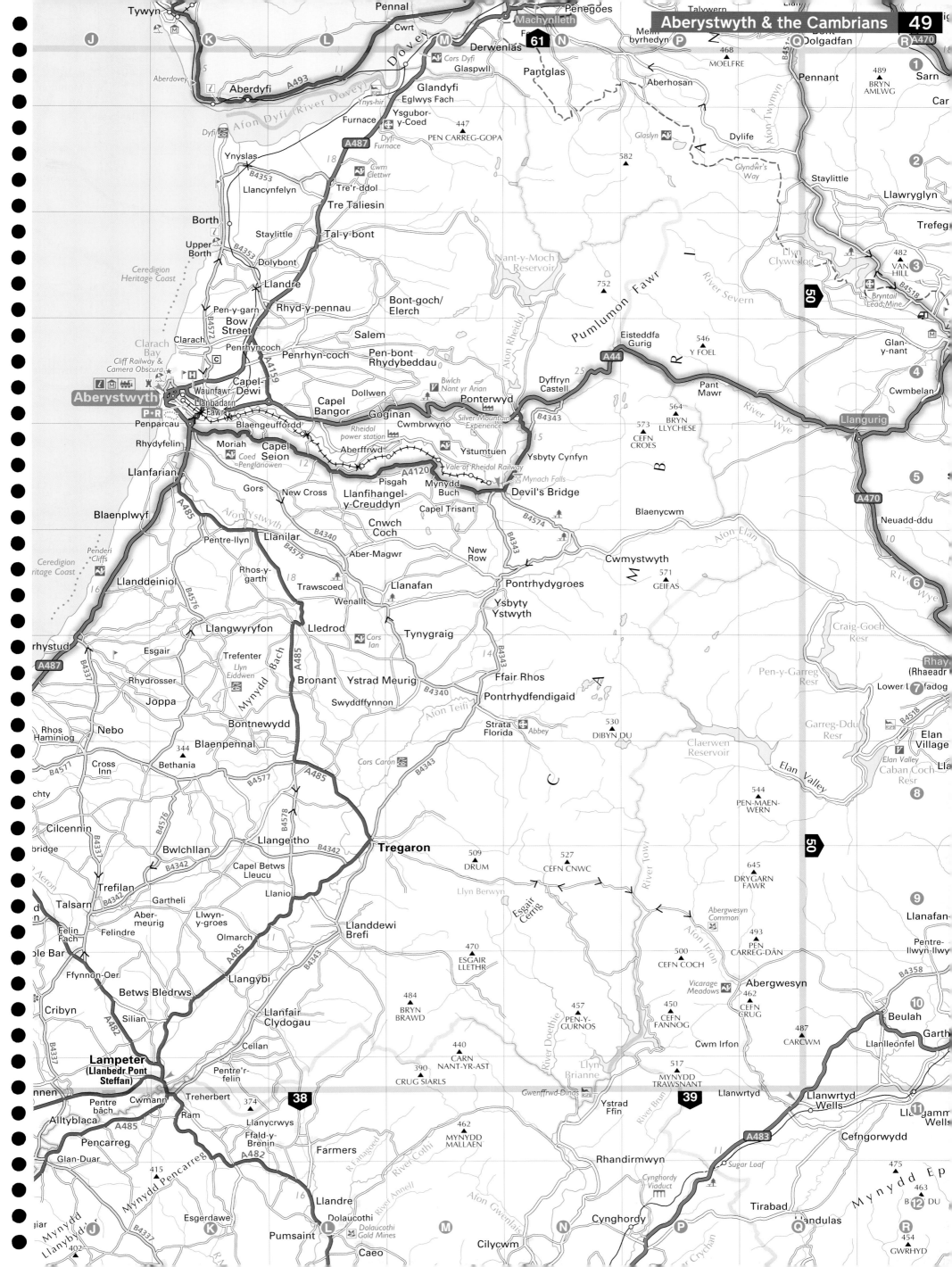

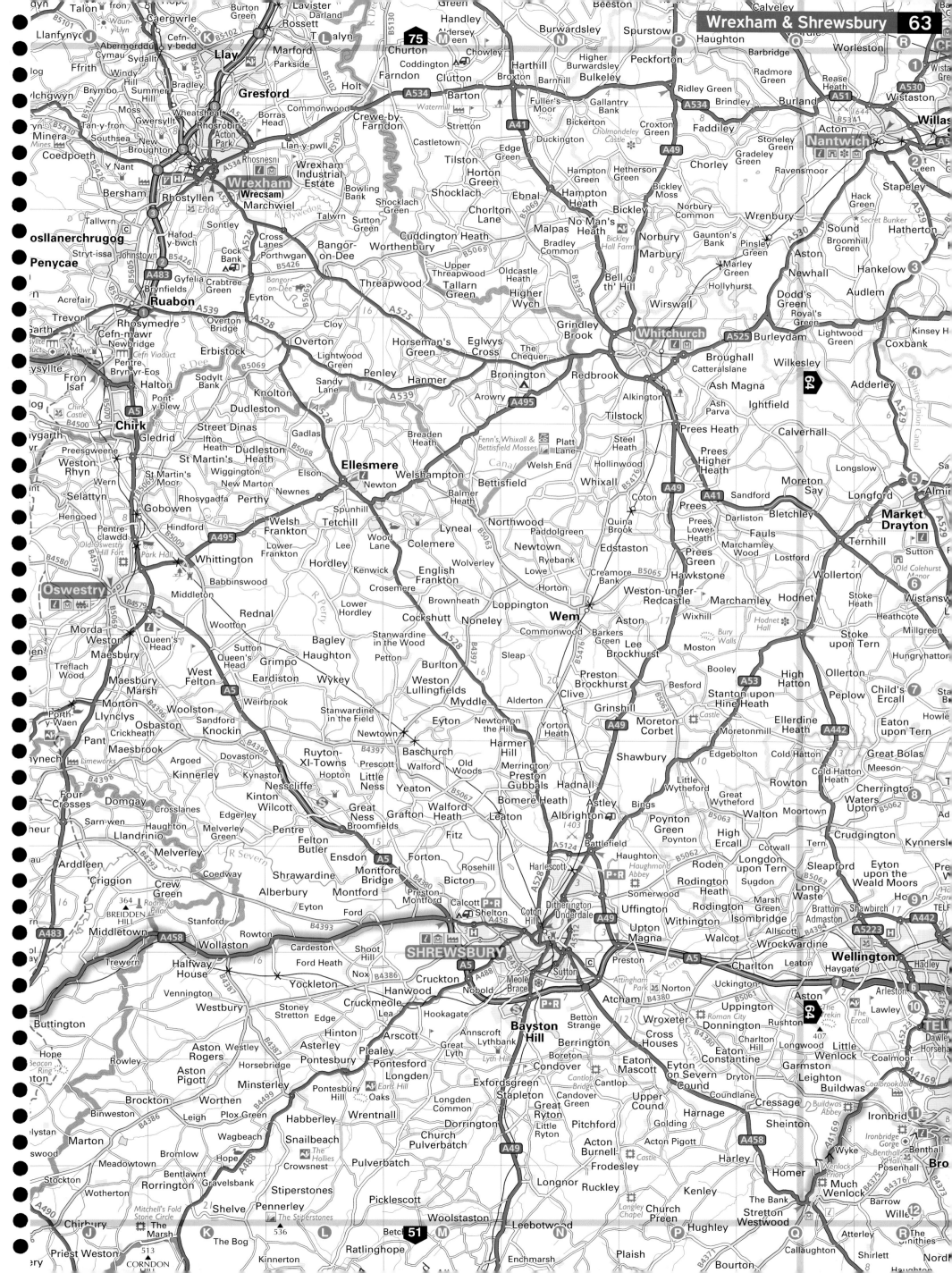

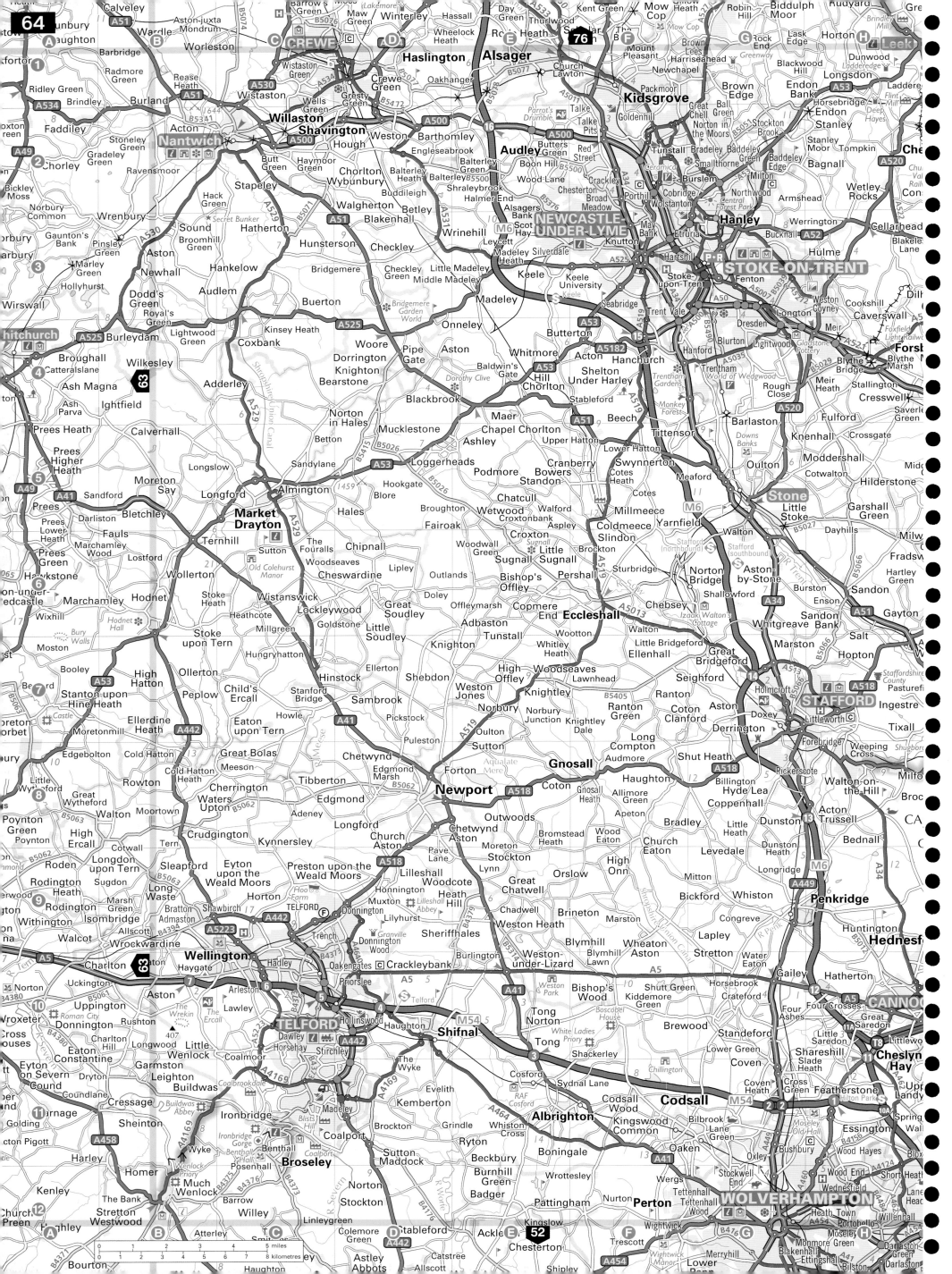

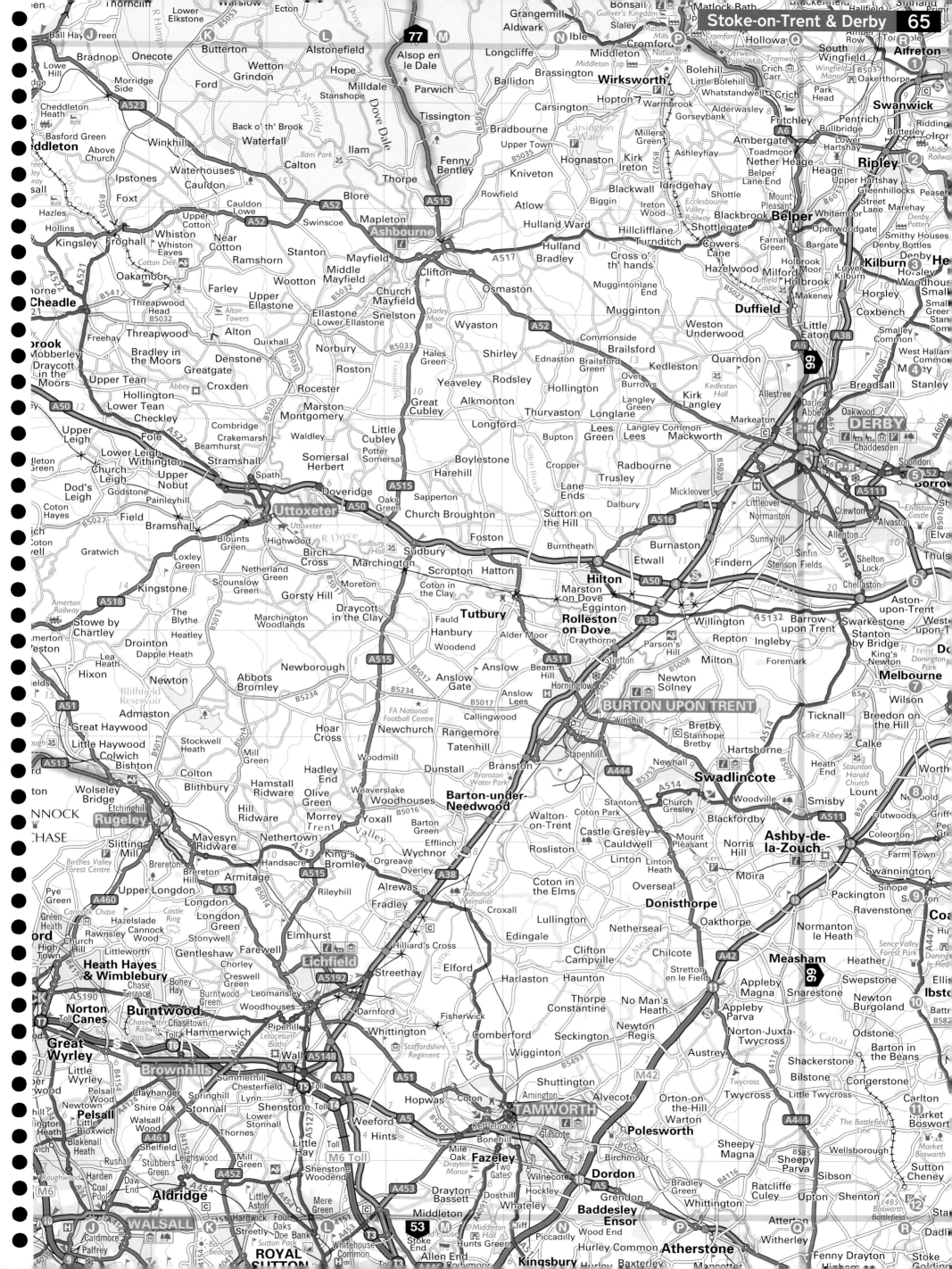

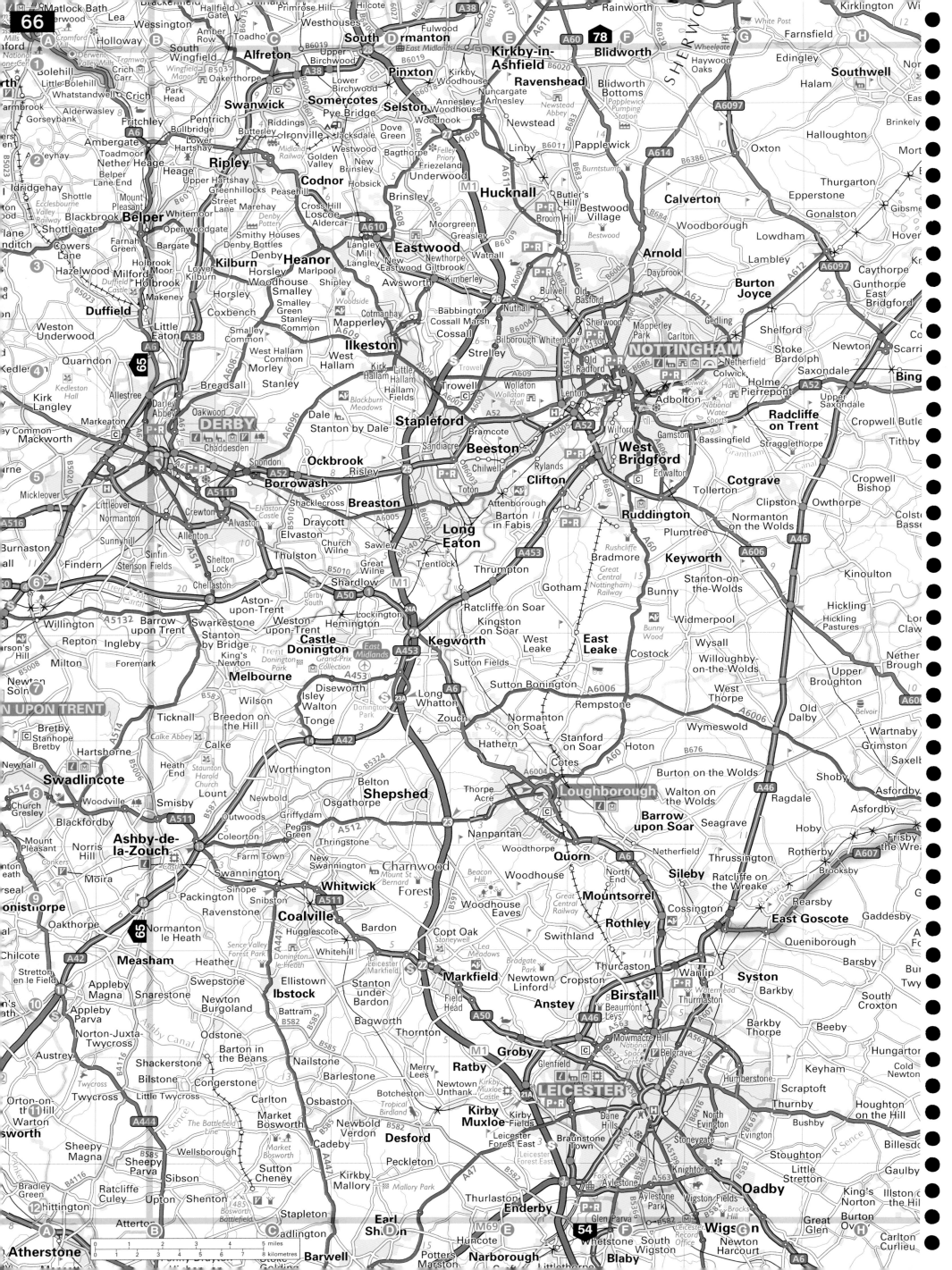

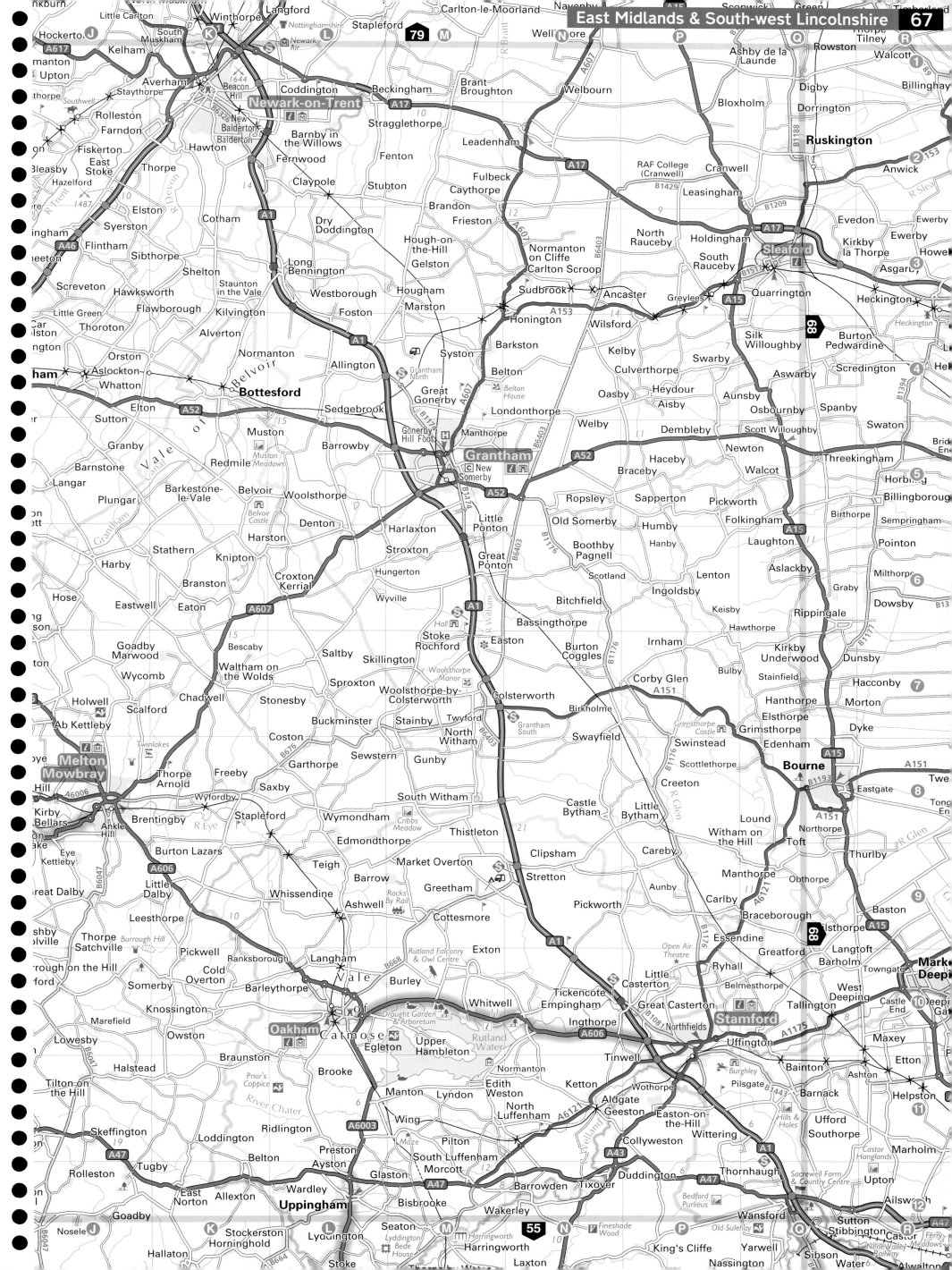

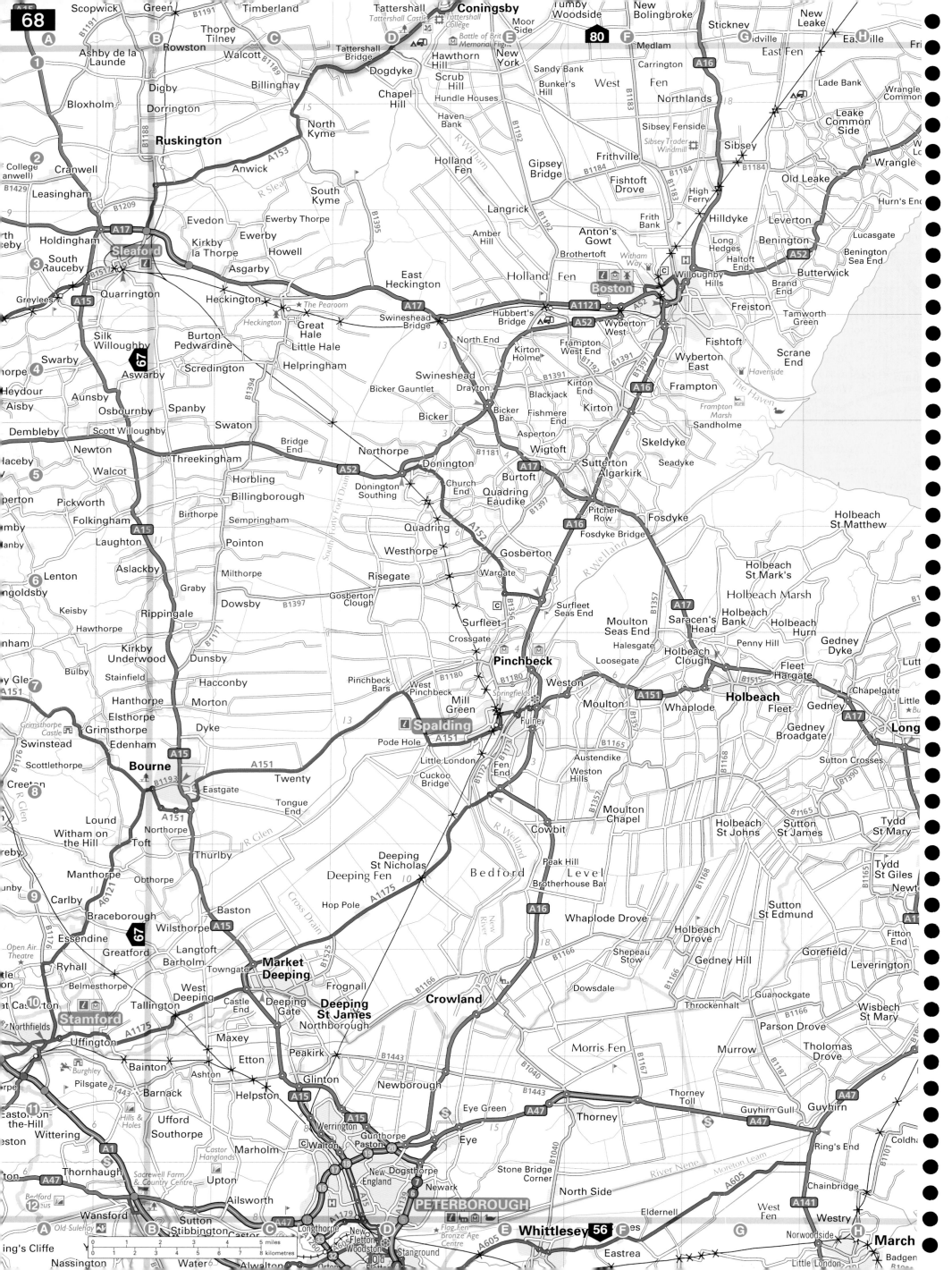

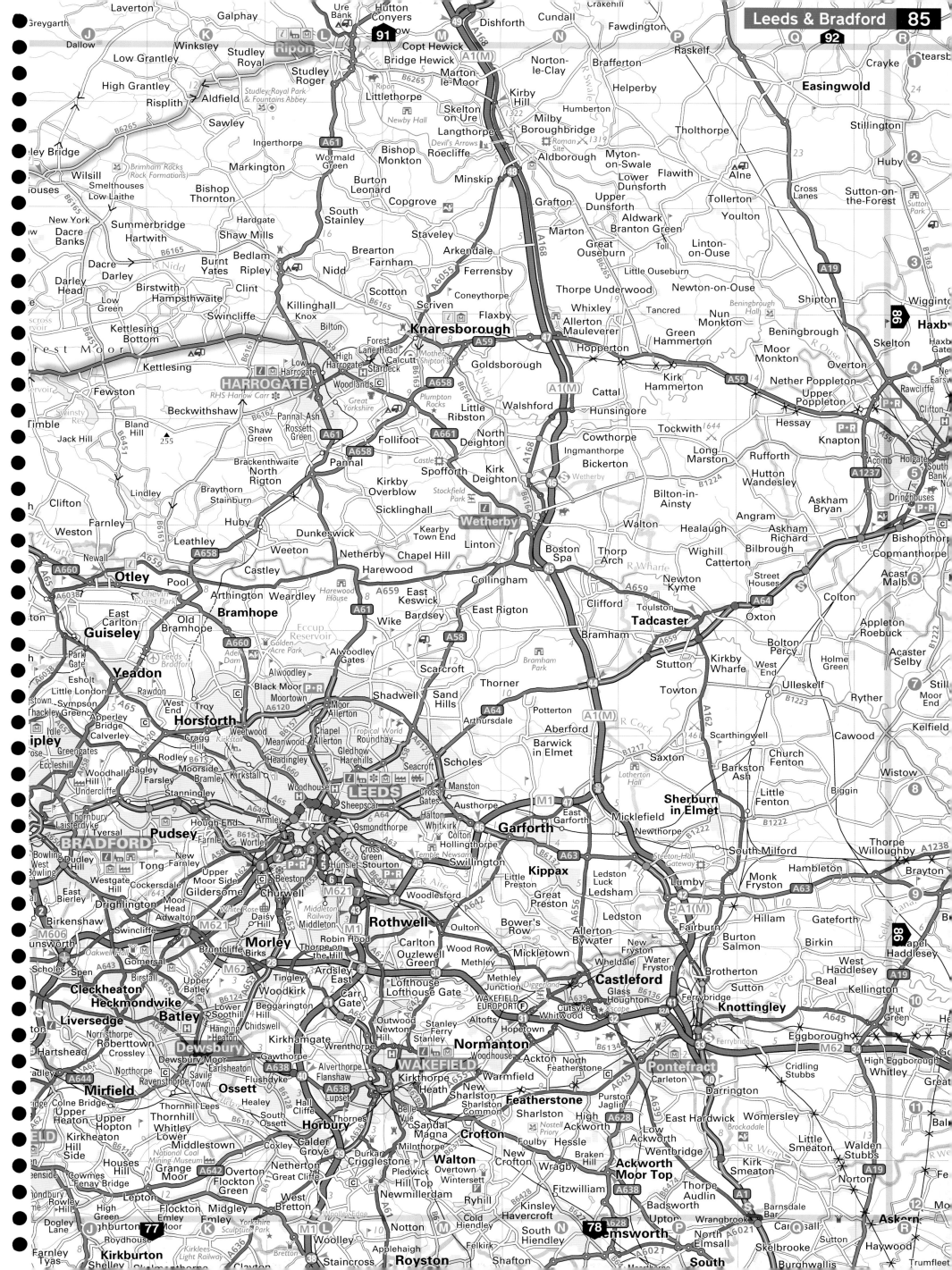

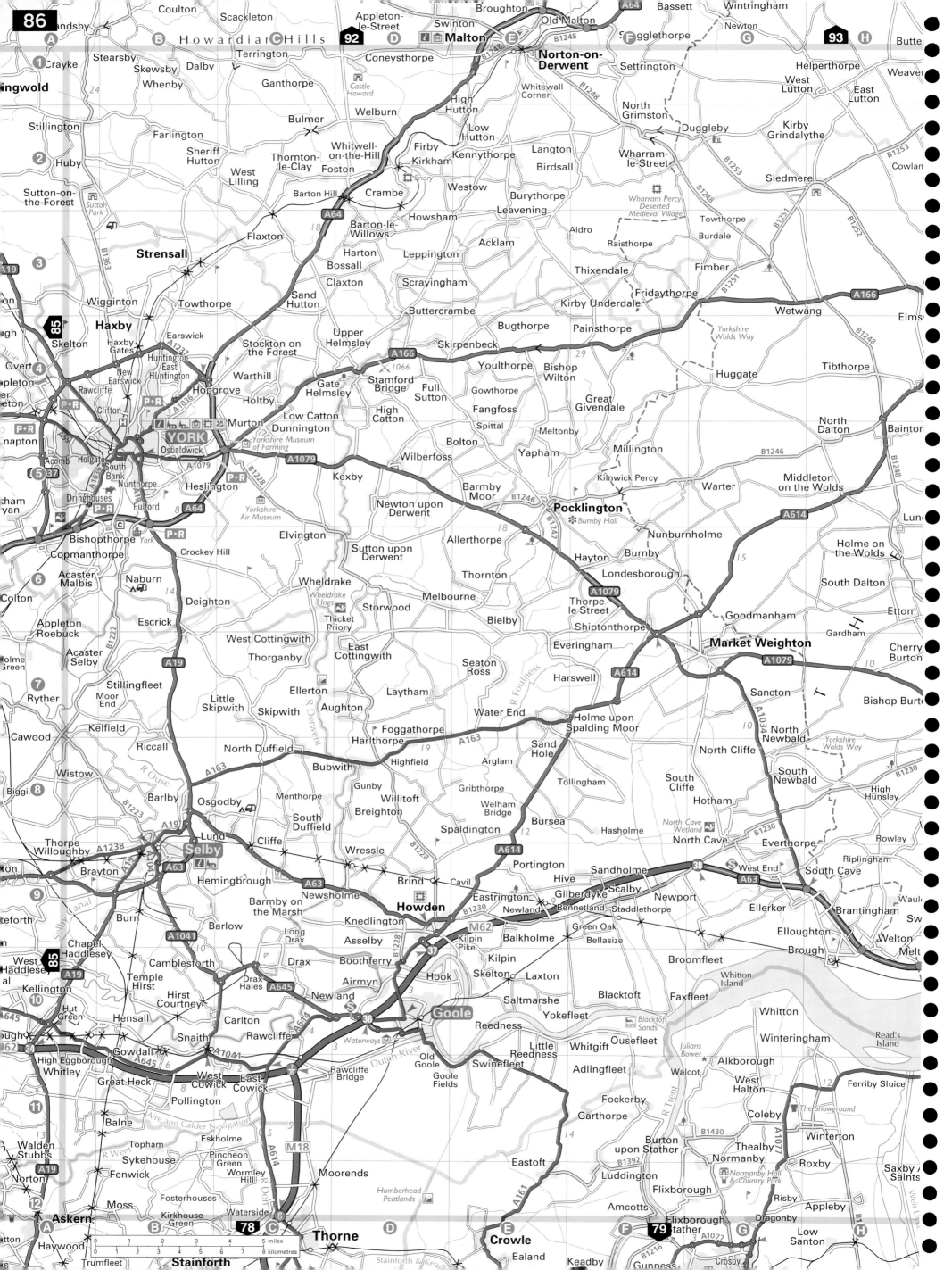

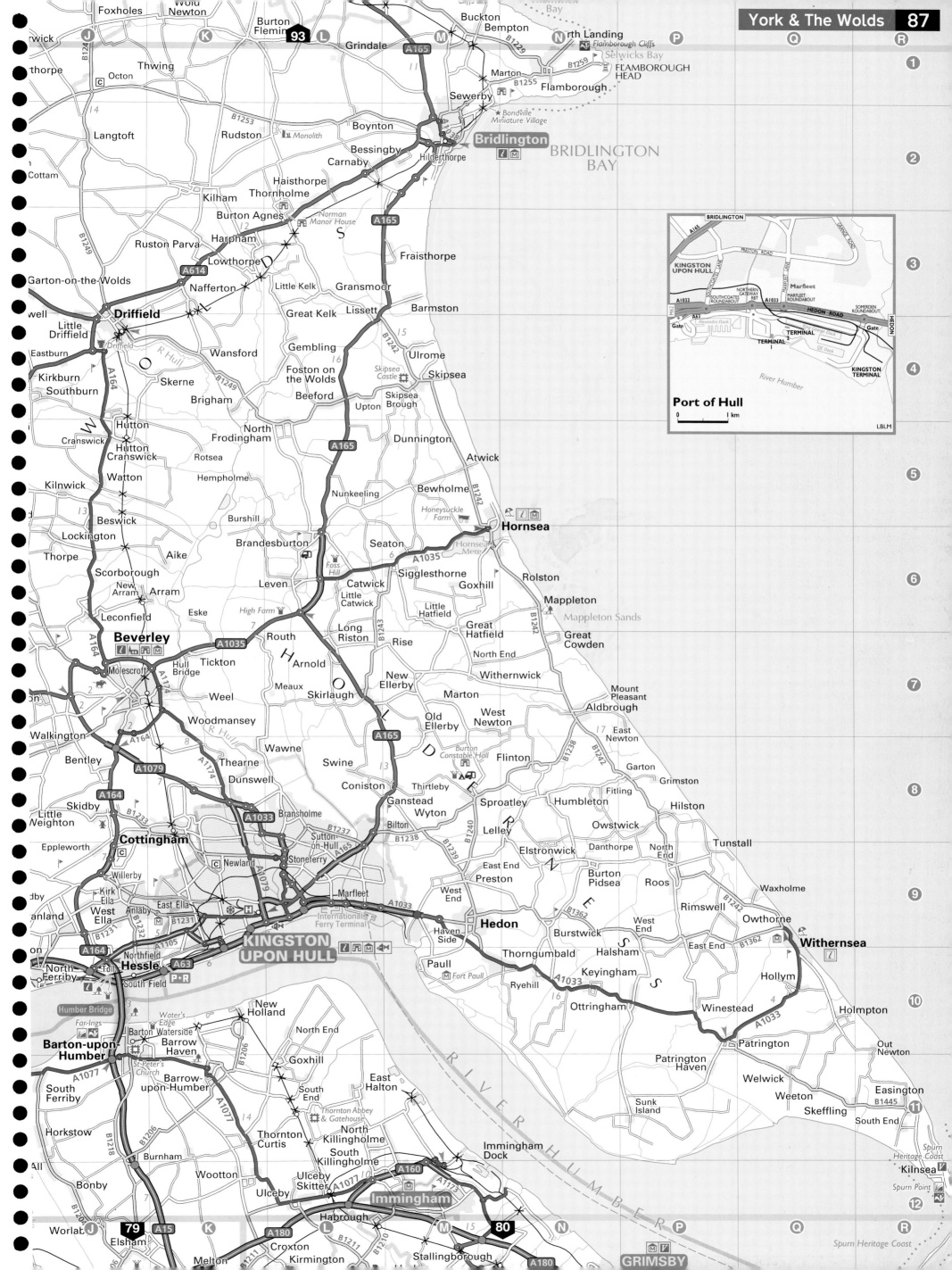

Port of Hull

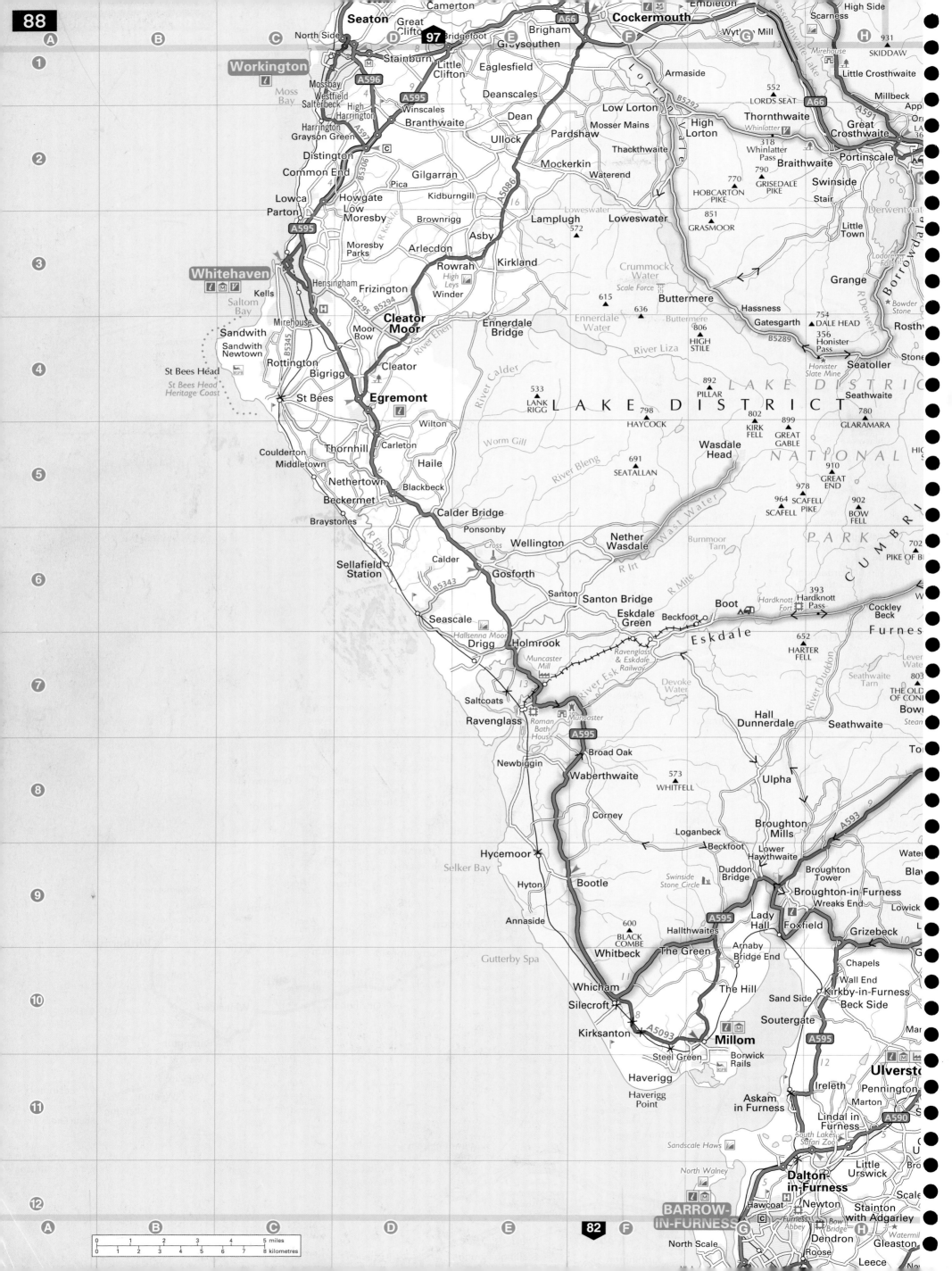

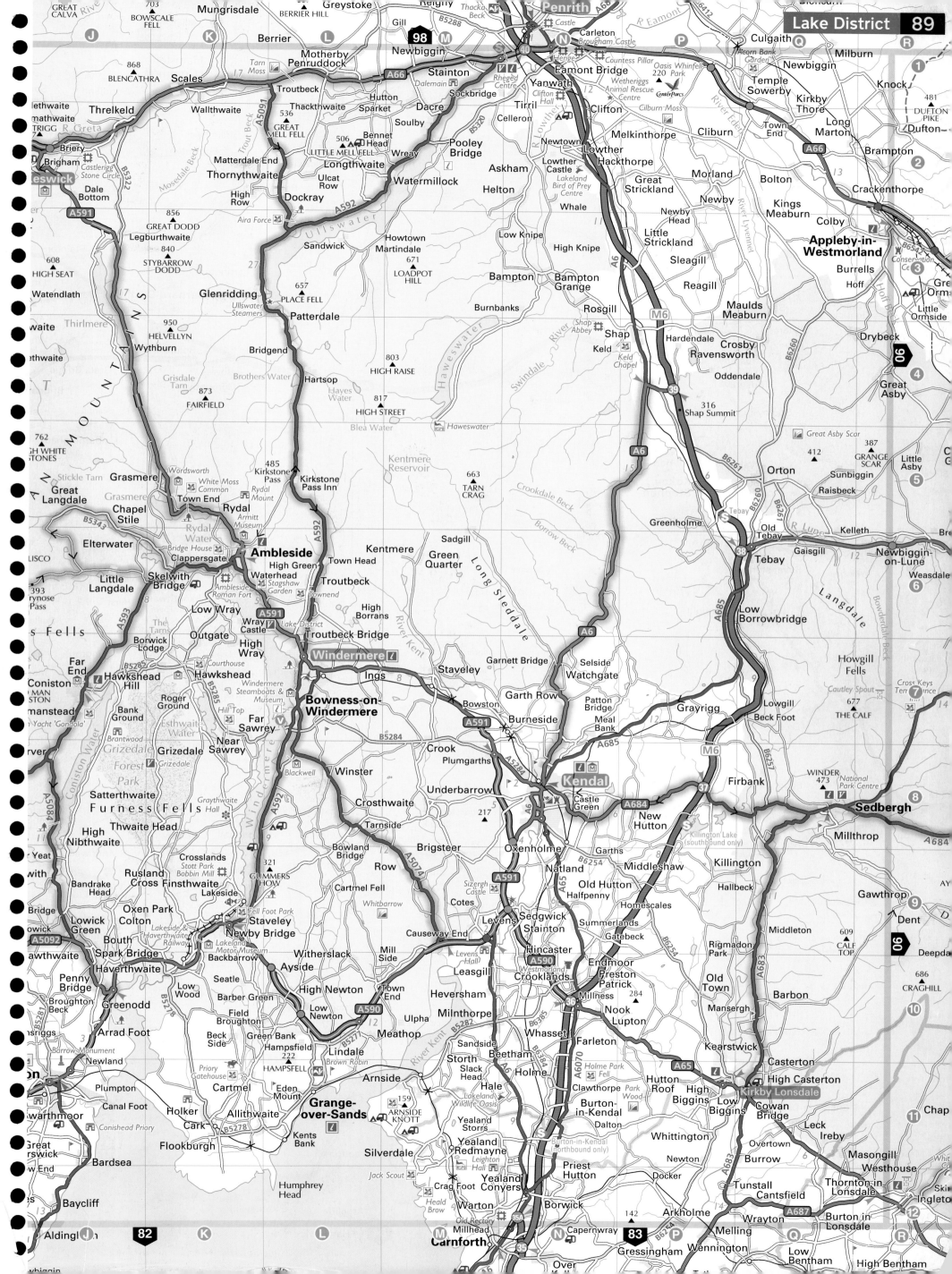

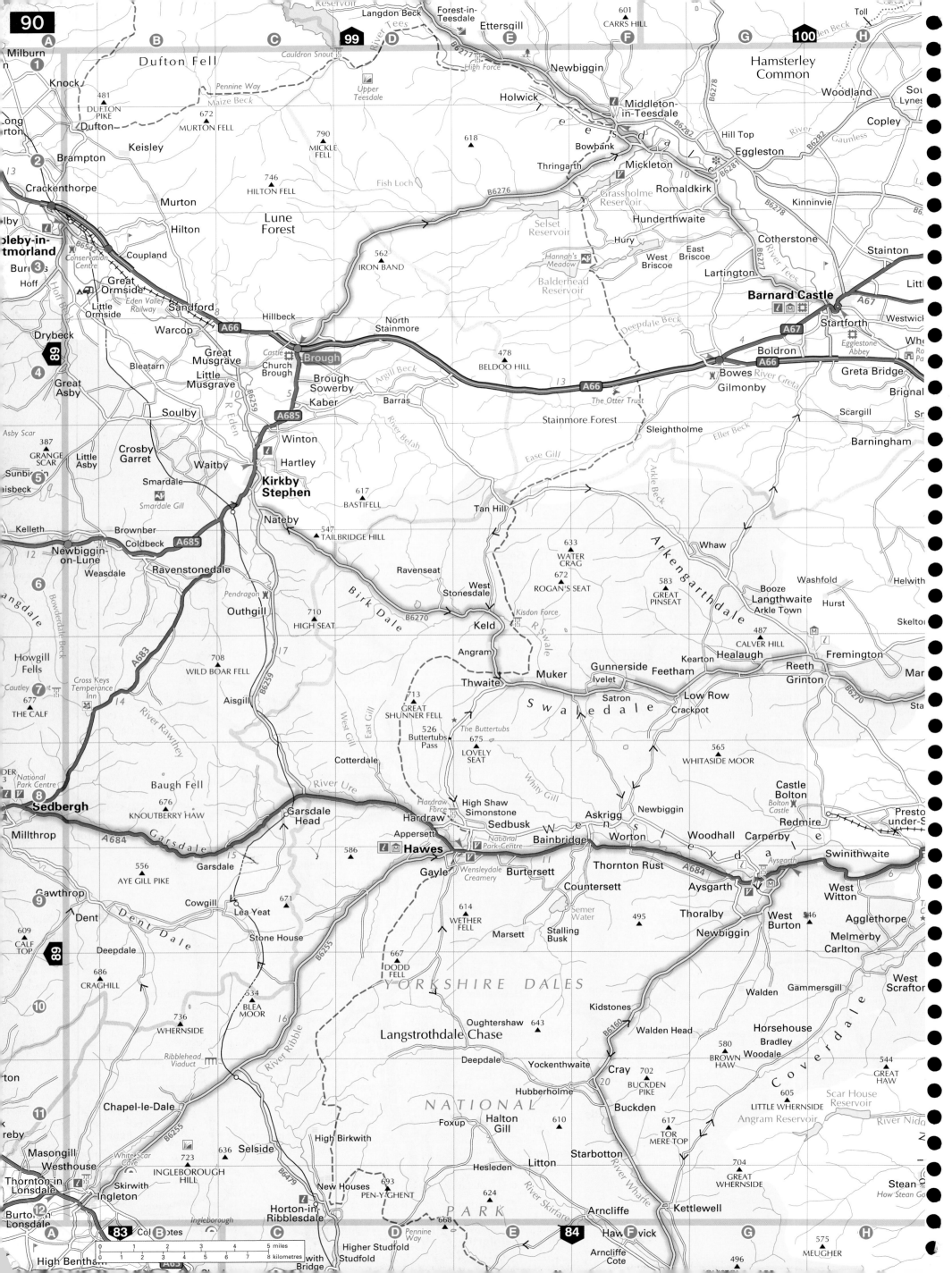

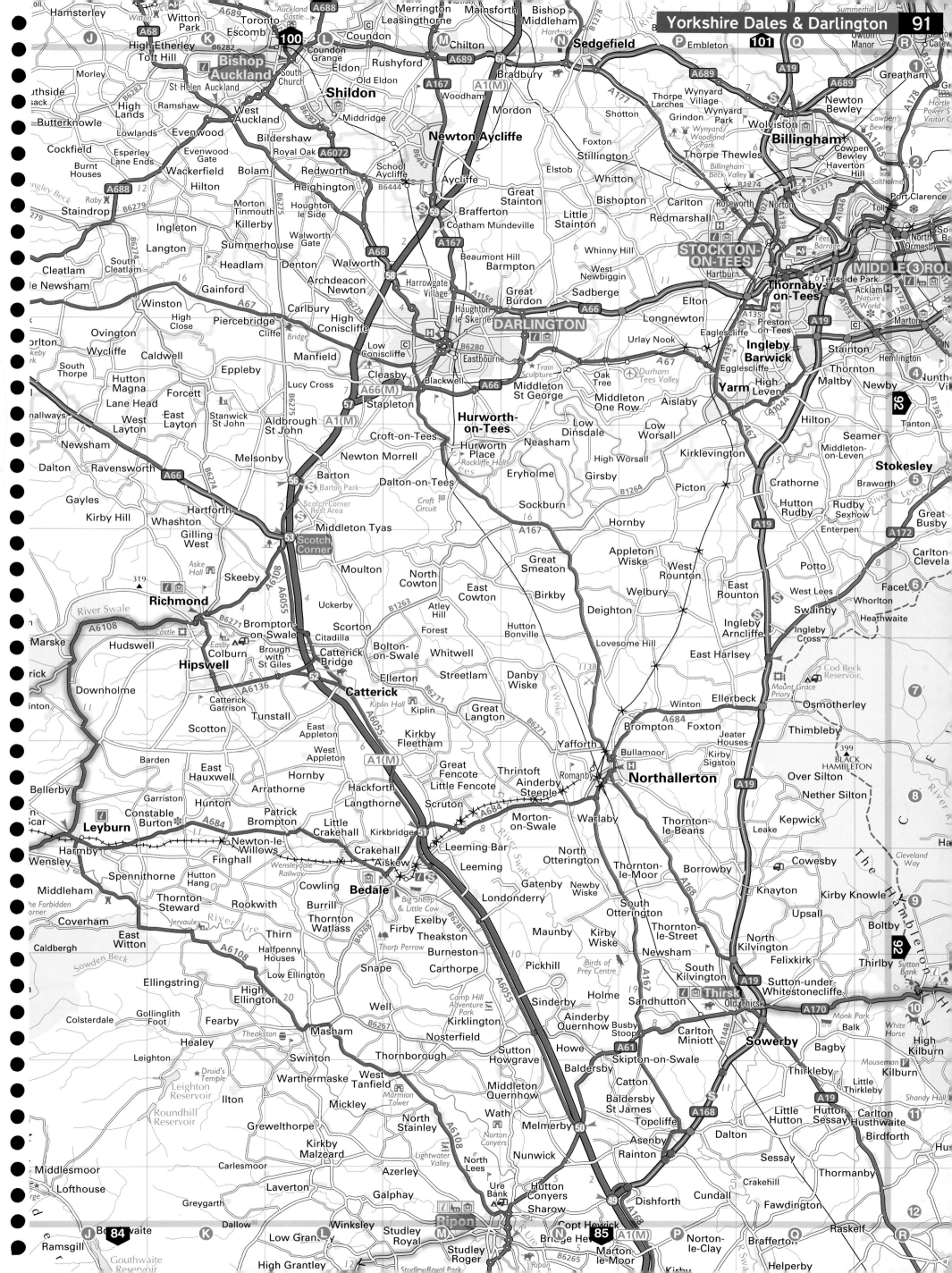

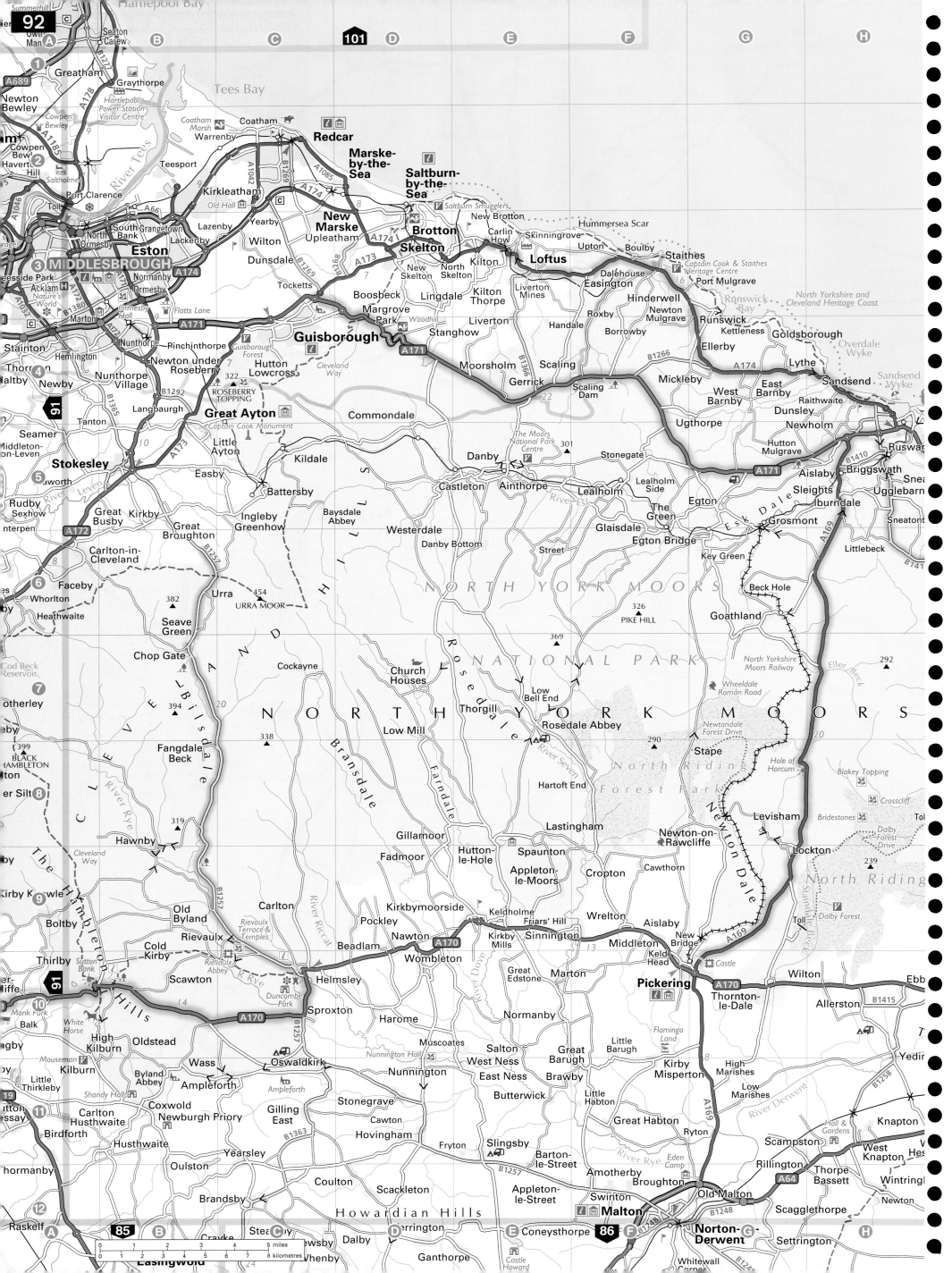

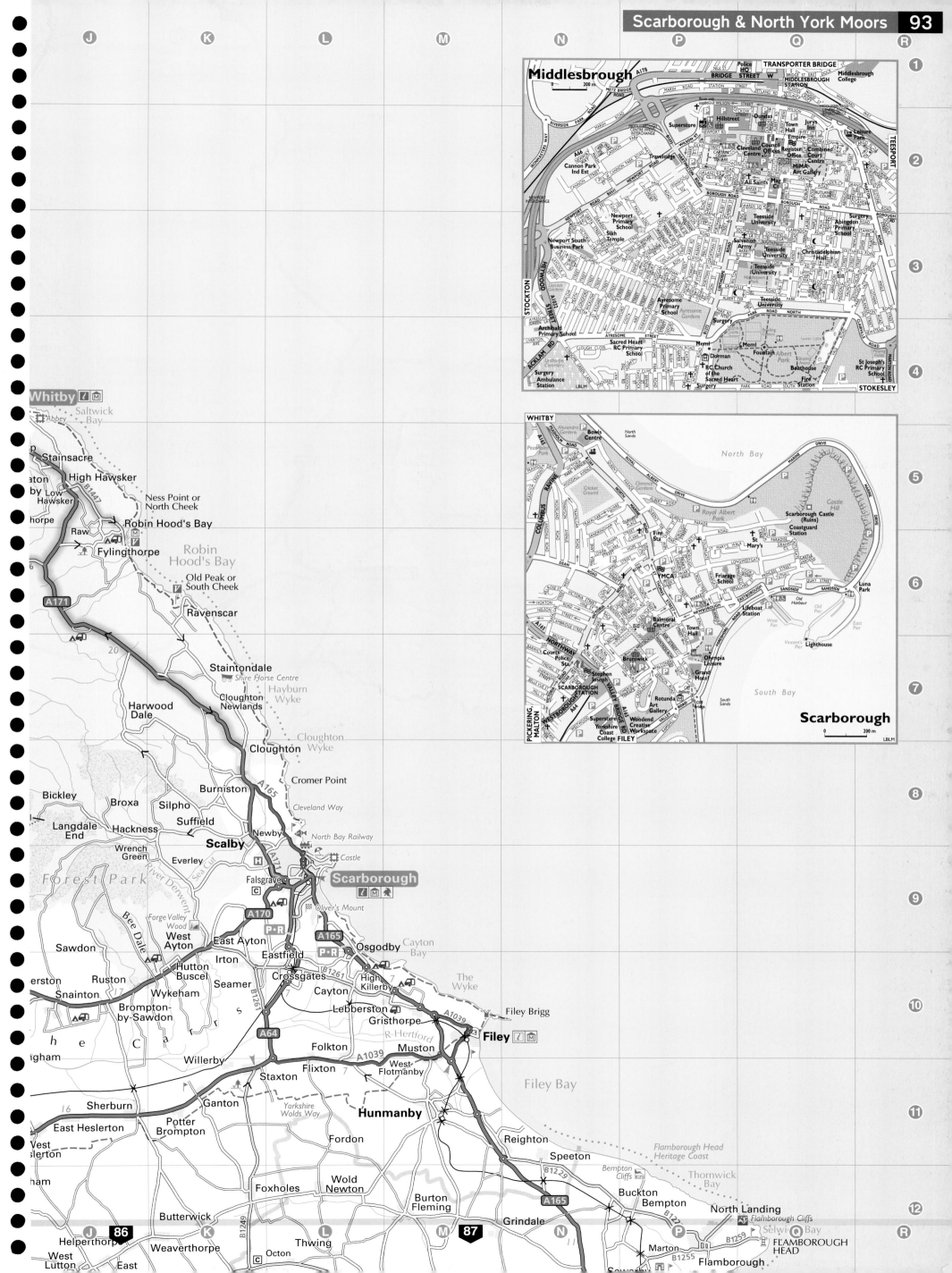

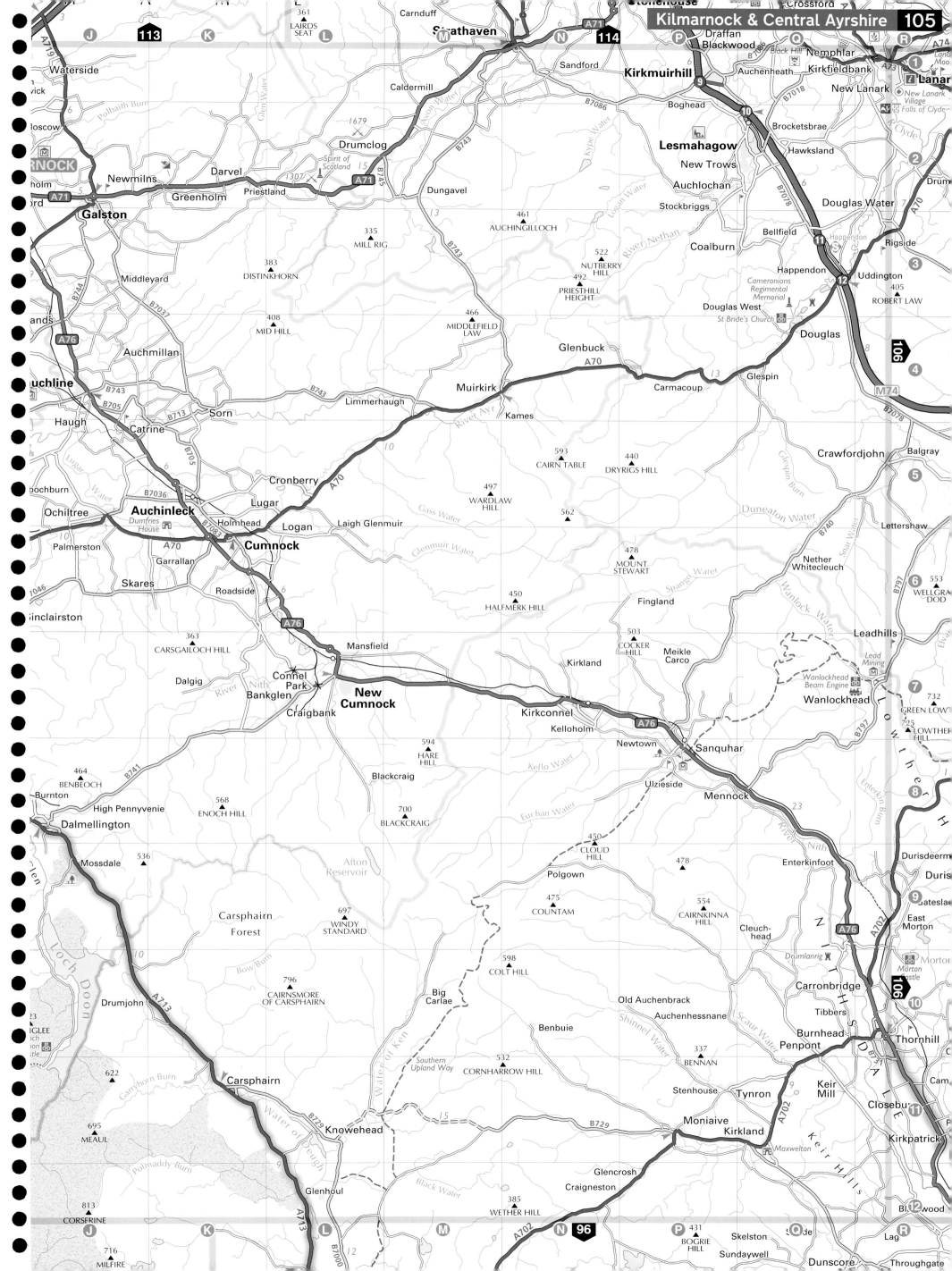

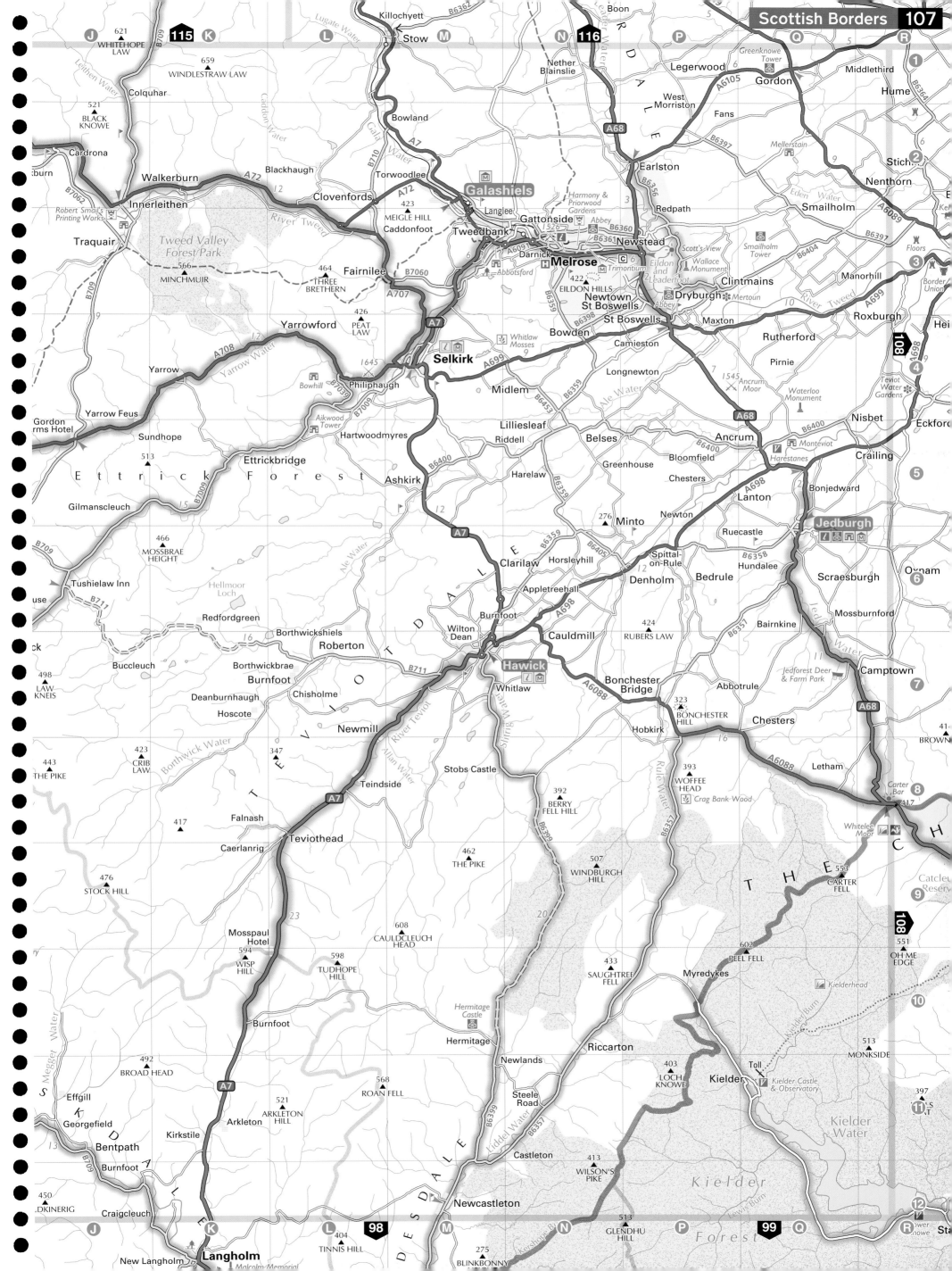

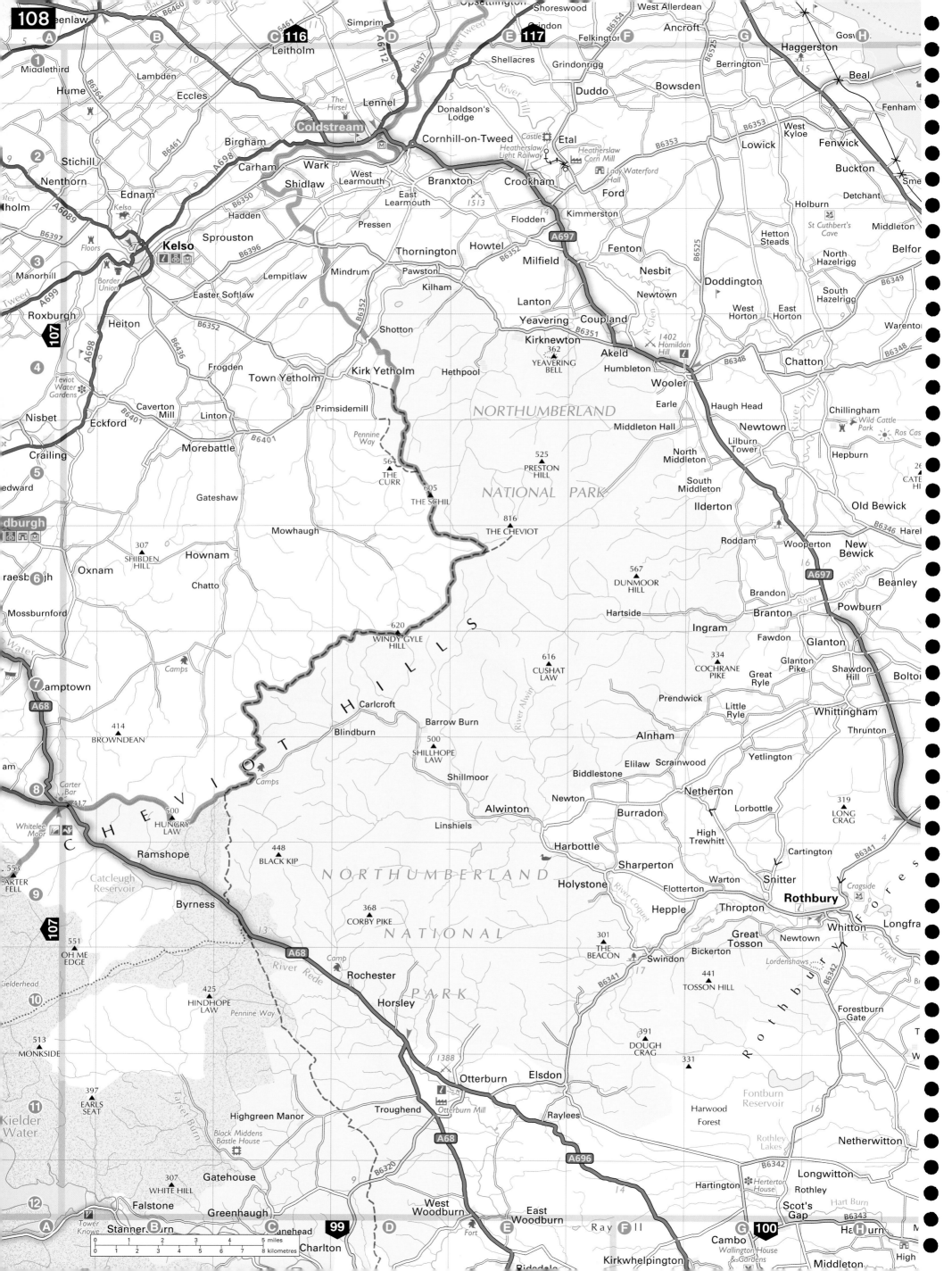

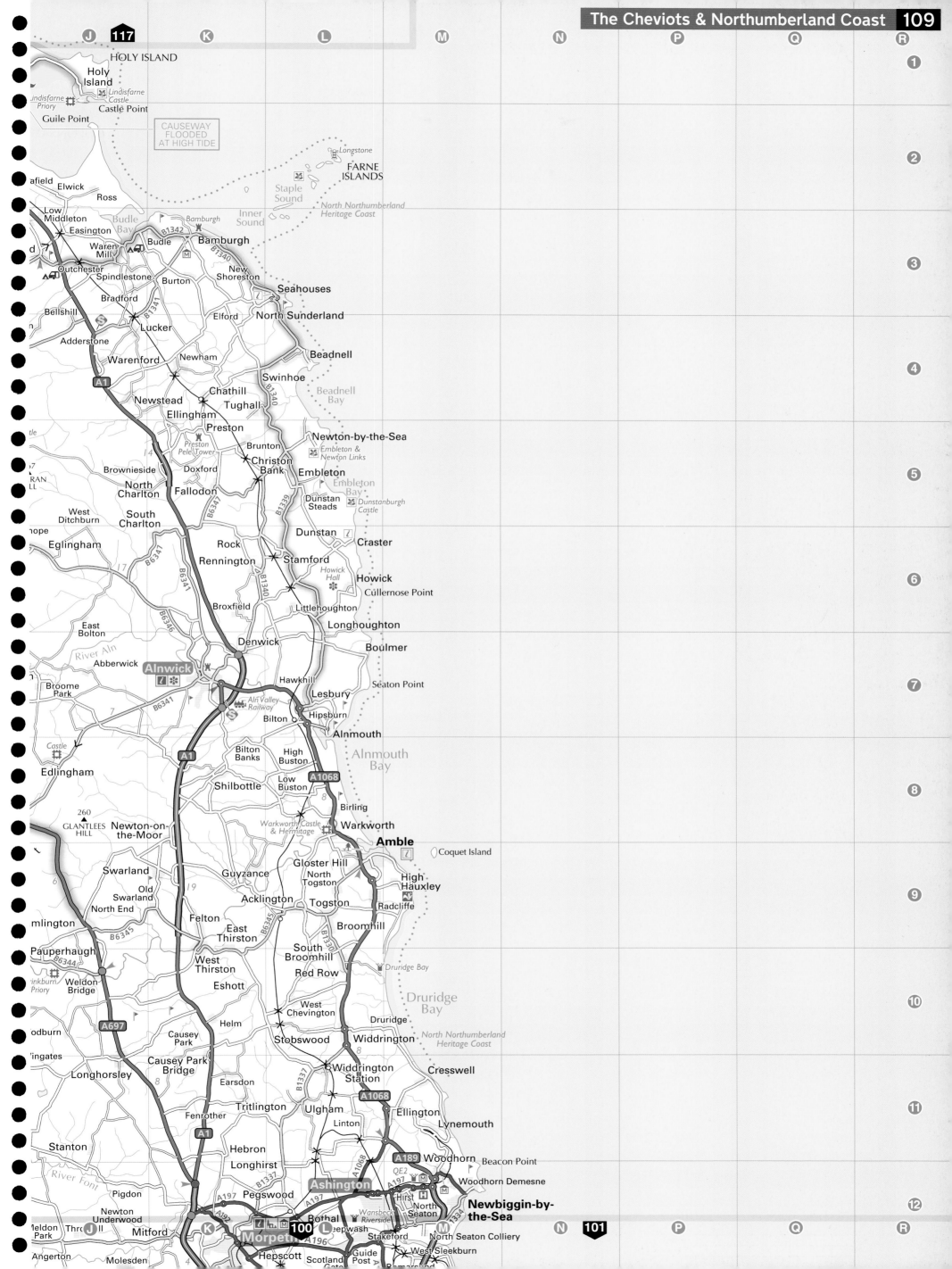

J   117   K   L   M   N   P   Q   R

1
2
3
4
5
6
7
8
9
10
11
12

HOLY ISLAND

Holy
Island

Lindisfarne
Castle

Lindisfarne
Priory

Castle Point
Guile Point

CAUSEWAY
FLOODED
AT HIGH TIDE

Longstone

FARNE
ISLANDS

Staple
Sound

Inner
Sound

North Northumberland
Heritage Coast

afield   Elwick
Low
Middleton   Ross

Budle
Bay

Bamburgh

Budle
Easington
Waren
Mill

Outchester   Spindlestone   Burton
New
Shoreston

Bradford

Bellshill   Seahouses

Lucker   Elford   North Sunderland

Adderstone

Warenford   Newham   Beadnell

Swinhoe

Newstead   Chathill   Tughall
Ellingham

Beadnell
Bay

Preston

Brownieside   Preston
Pele Tower   Brunton   Newton-by-the-Sea

Doxford   Christon
Bank   Embleton   Embleton
Bay   Embleton &
Newton Links

North
Charlton   Fallodon   Dunstan
Steads   Dunstanburgh
Castle

West
Ditchburn   South
Charlton

Eglingham   Rock   Dunstan   Craster
Rennington   Stamford

East
Bolton   Howick Hall   Howick
Cullernose Point

River Aln   Broxfield   Littlehoughton
Denwick   Longhoughton

Abberwick
Alnwick   Boulmer

Broome
Park   Hawkhill   Seaton Point
Lesbury

Aln Valley
Railway   Hipsburn
Bilton   Alnmouth

Castle   Bilton
Banks   High
Buston   Alnmouth
Bay

Edlingham   Shilbottle   Low
Buston

GLANTLEES
HILL   Newton-on-
the-Moor   Birling

Warkworth Castle
& Hermitage   Warkworth

Amble

Swarland   Gloster Hill   Coquet Island
Old
Swarland   Guyzance   North
Togston   High
Hauxley

North End   Acklington   Togston   Radcliffe

mlington   Felton   Broomhill

Pauperhaugh   East
Thirston

West
Thirston   South
Broomhill

inkburn
Priory   Weldon
Bridge   Eshott   Red Row   Druridge Bay

odburn   Helm   West
Chevington   Druridge   North Northumberland
Heritage Coast

ingates   Causey
Park   Stobswood   Widdrington
Longhorsley   Causey Park
Bridge   Druridge
Bay

Earsdon   Widdrington
Station   Cresswell
Stanton   Tritlington   Ulgham
Fenrother   Linton   Ellington
Hebron   Lynemouth

Woodhorn   Beacon Point
River Font   Longhirst

Pigdon   Pegswood   Woodhorn Demesne
Newton
Underwood   Ashington

Bothal   Hirst
North   Newbiggin-by-
Seaton   the-Sea

eldon
Park   Mitford   Sleepwash   Stakeford   North Seaton Colliery
Throp   Morpeth   100   Guide   West Sleekburn
Angerton   Hepscott   Post

A B C D E F G H

1
2
3
4
5
6
7
8
9
10
11
12

A B C D E F G H

COLONSAY

Kilchattan

Colonsay

Garvard

Oronsay

Dubh Eilean

ORONSAY

ISLAY

Nave Island

Ardnave
Point

Gortantaoid
Point

Ton Mhòr

Kilnave

Eilean Mòr

Sanaigmore

Loch Gruinart

Rudha Lamanais

Loch
Gòrr

Lecht Gruinart

B8018

B8017

Fir

Saligo Bay

Loch
Gorm

Gruinart

Gleann Mòr

Coul Point

B8018

Sunderland

Machir
Bay

Kilchoman

A847

Bridgend

Gartacho

Bruichladdich

Loch
Indaal

Kilchiaran Bay

Bowmore

3

RHINNS OF ISLAY

River Laggan

231

Port
Charlotte

BEINN TART A'MHILL

Laggan
Point

Duich R.

A846

B8016

Lossit Bay

Nereabolls

Rudha na
Faing

A847

Glenegedale

Portnahaven

Port Wemyss

Orsay

Islay

Laggan

RHINNS
POINT

Bay

Rudha Mòr

Kintra

165

MAOL BUIDHE

Kilnaughton Bay

THE OA

Lov
Killeyan

Risabus

Kinnabus

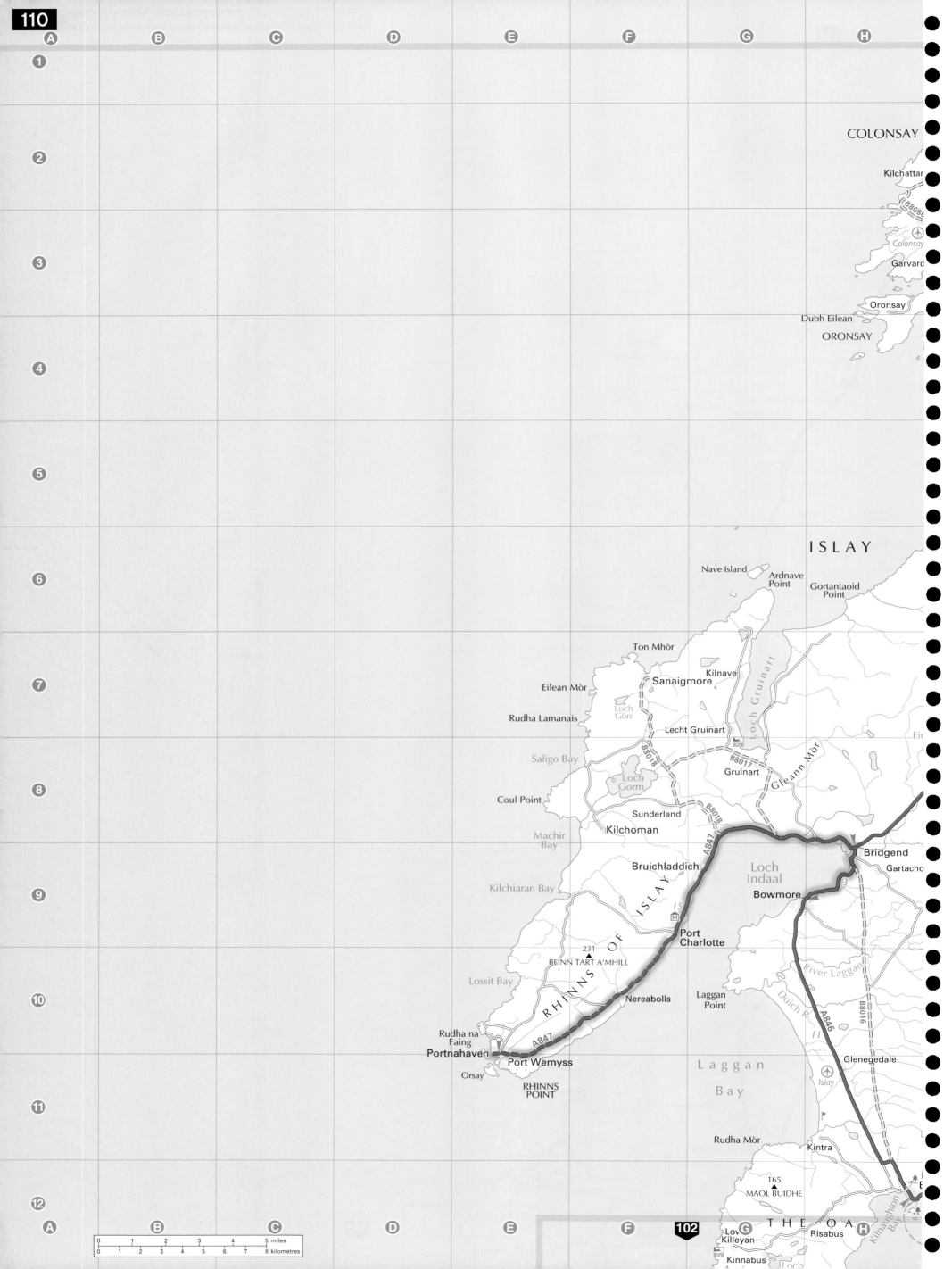

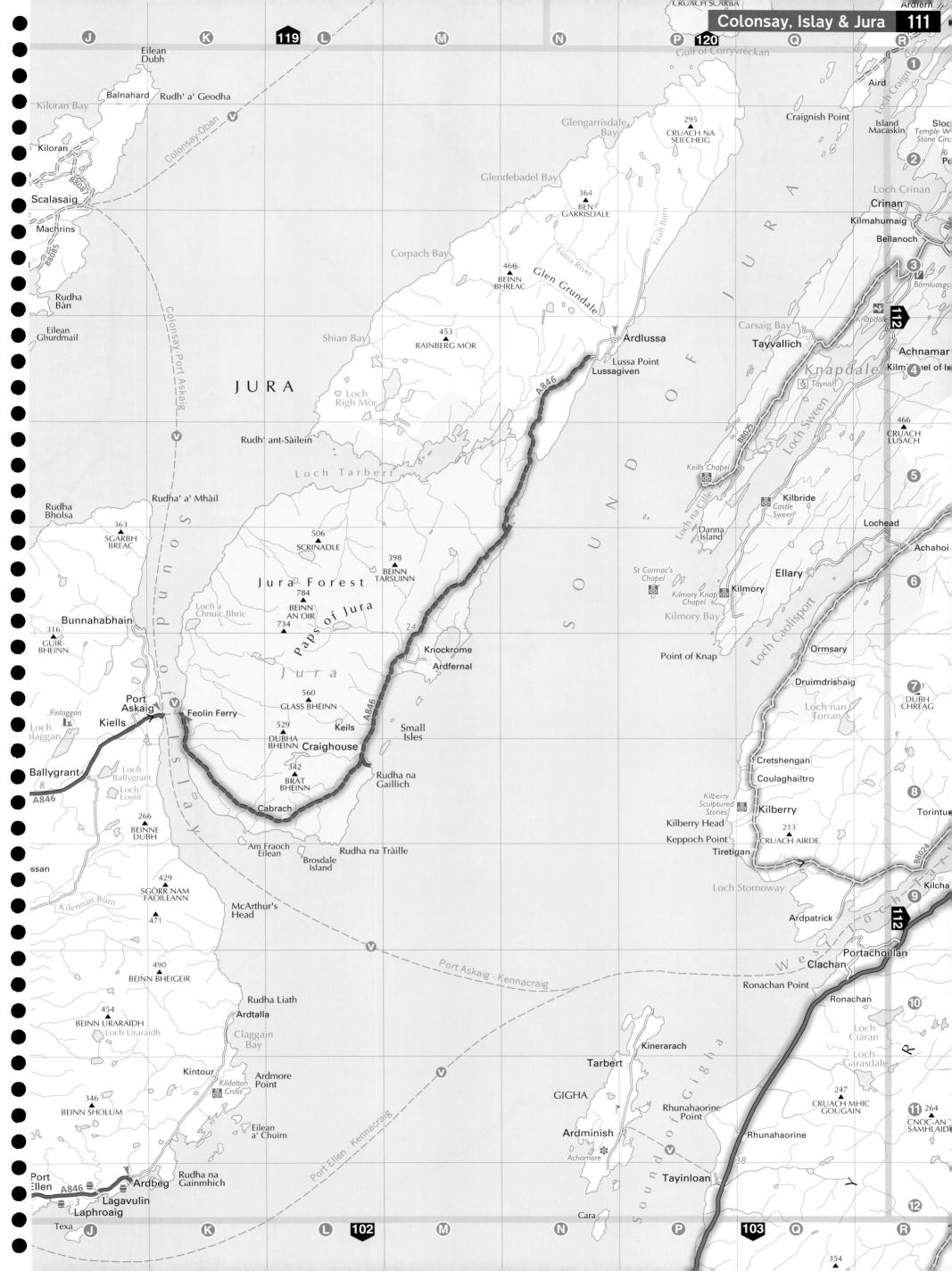

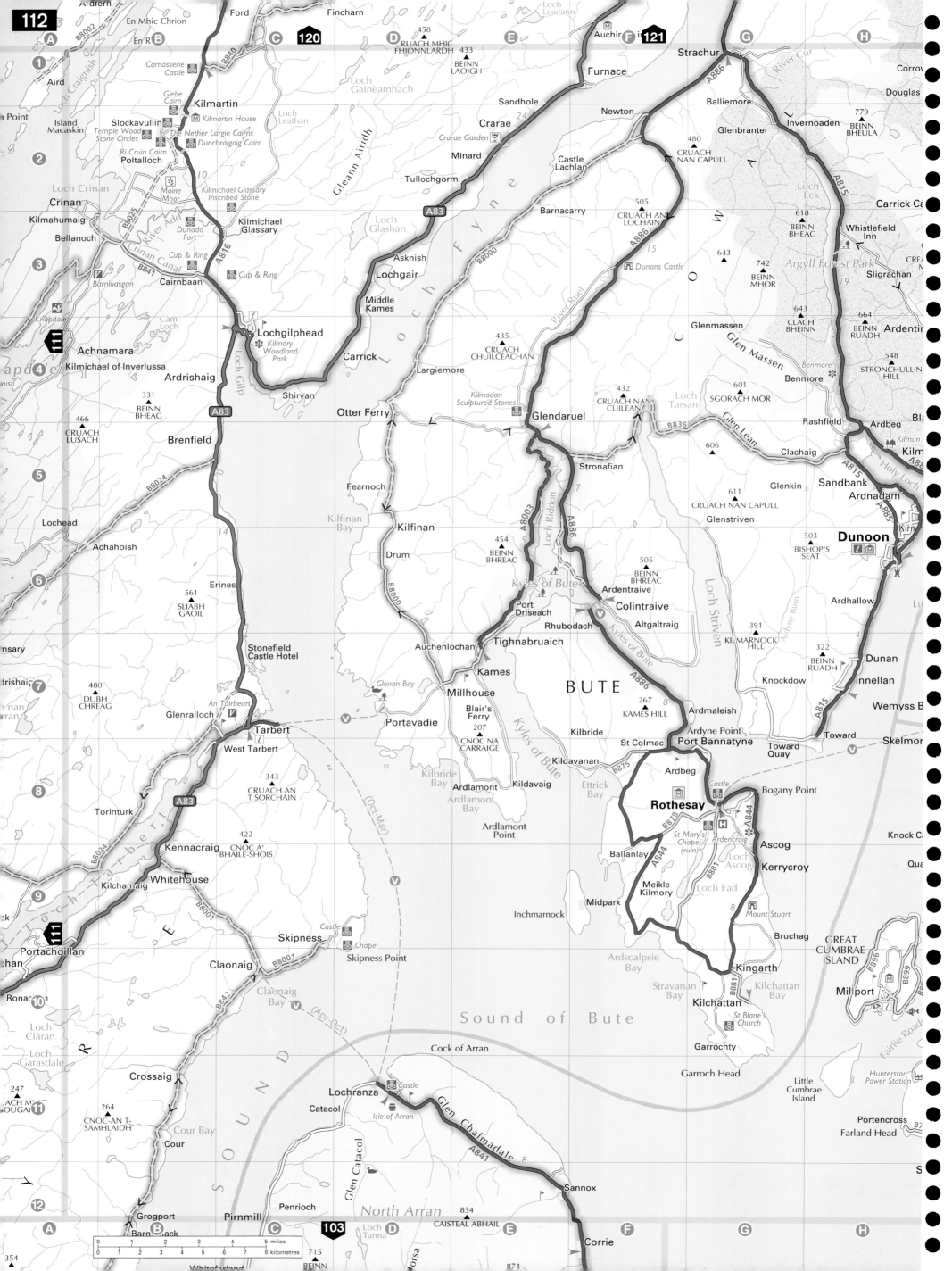

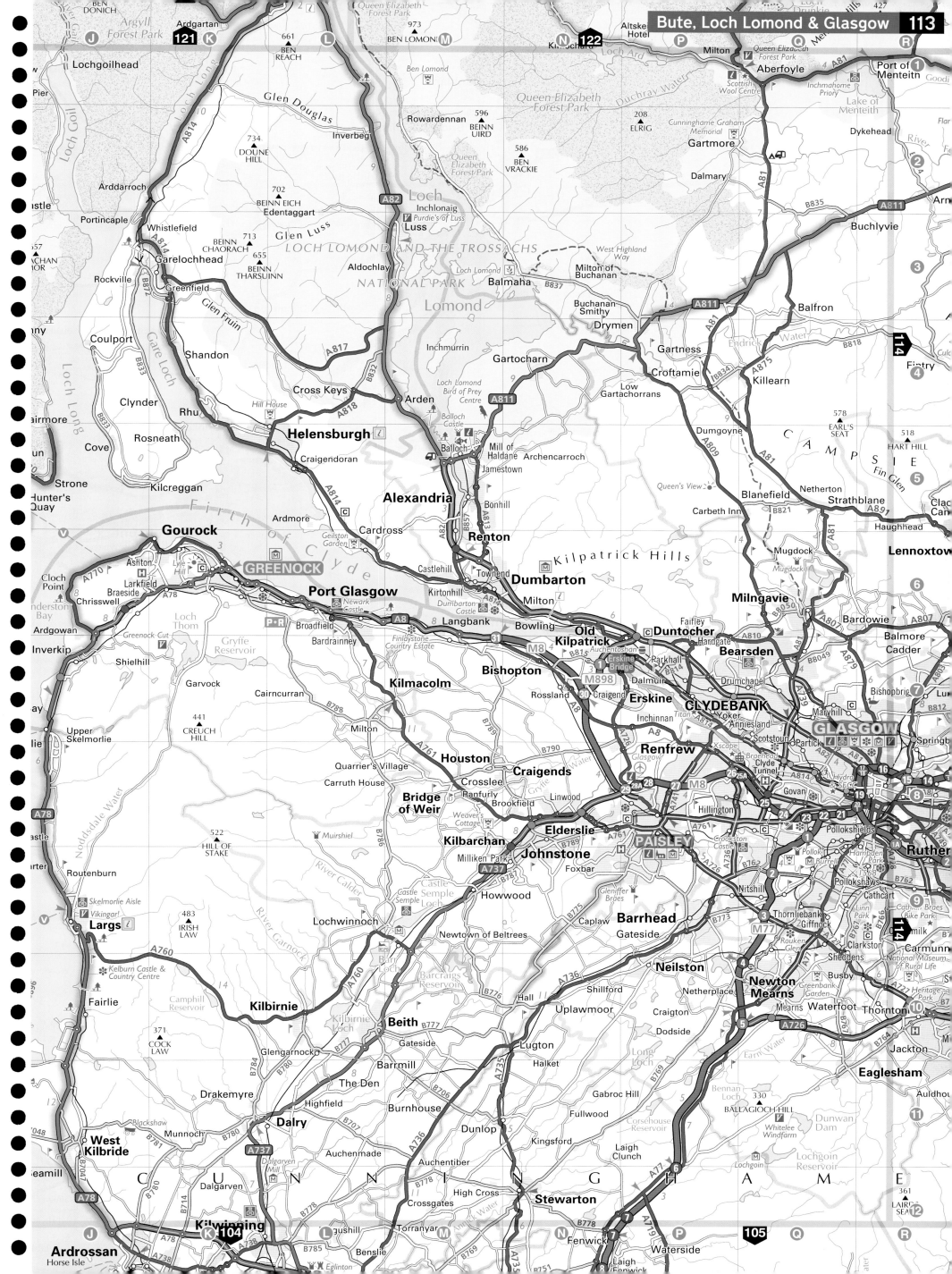

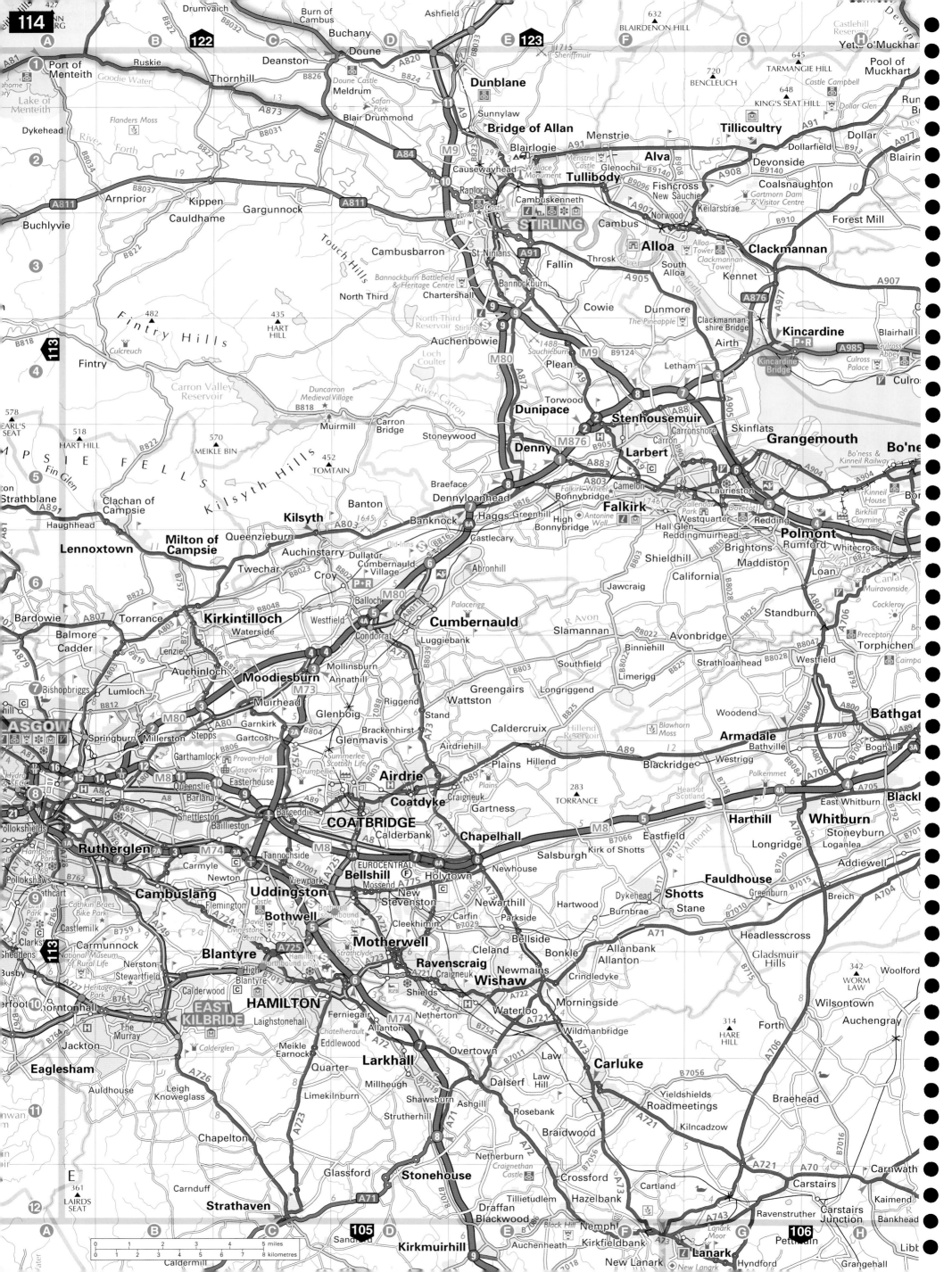

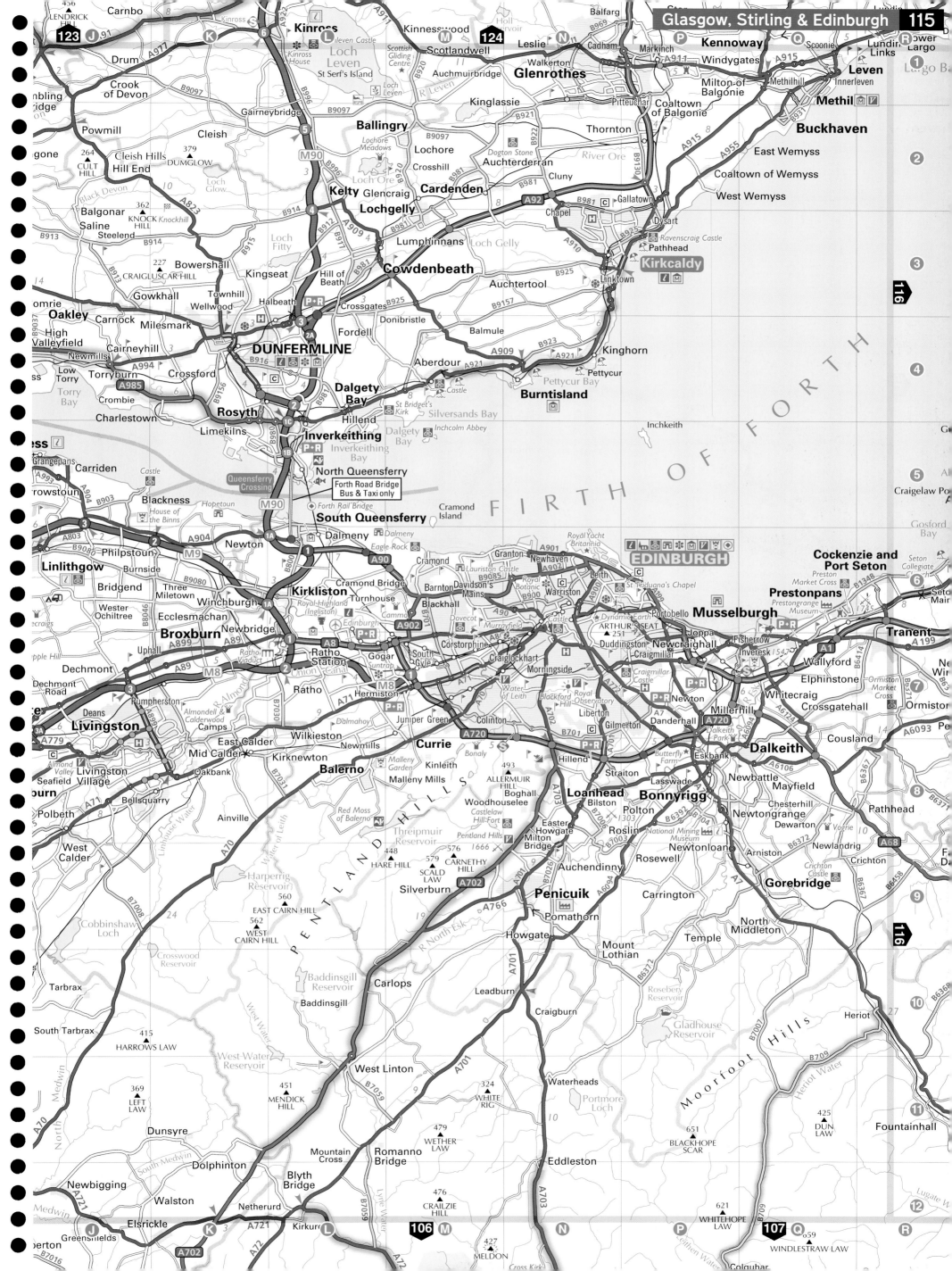

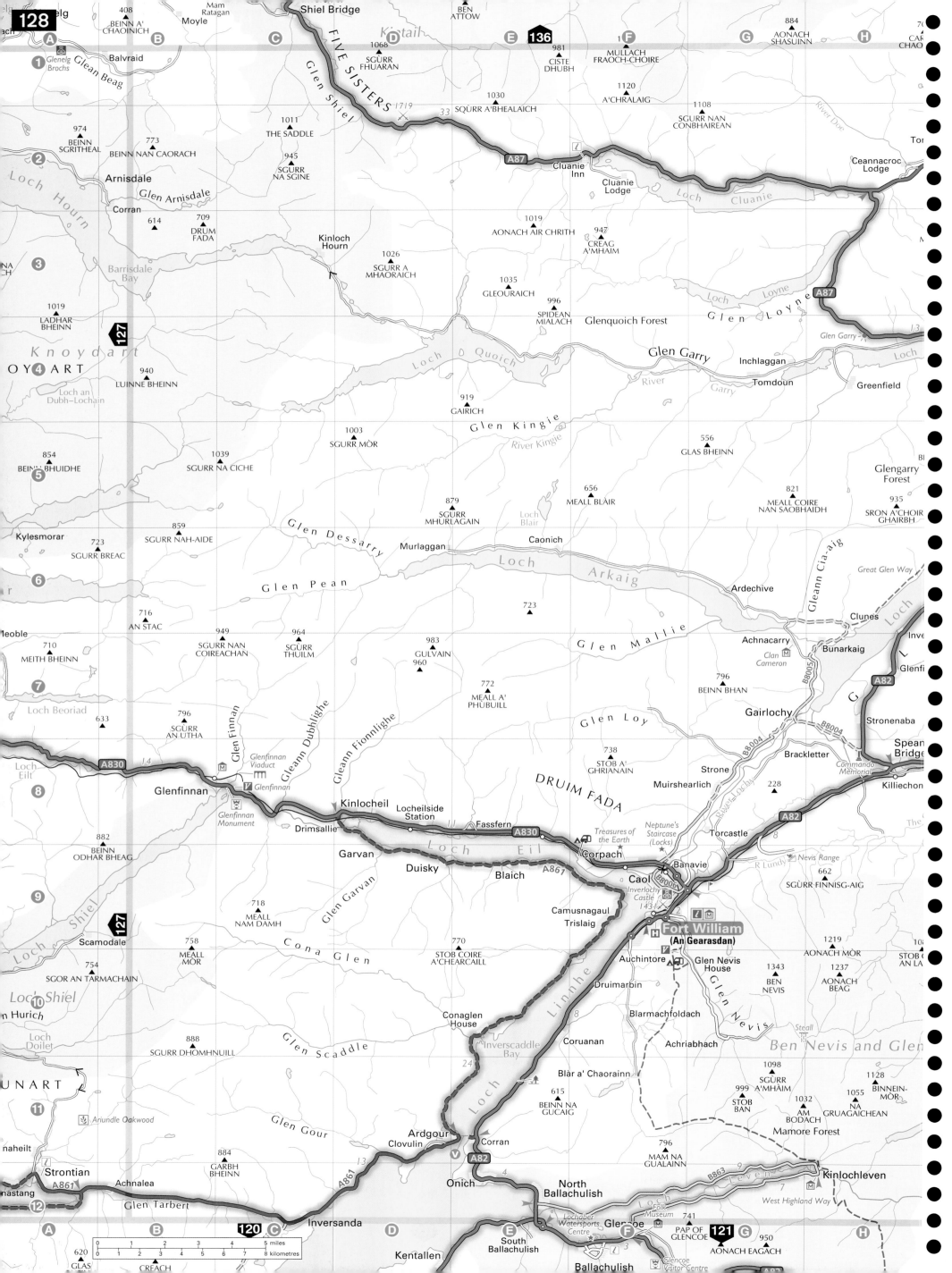

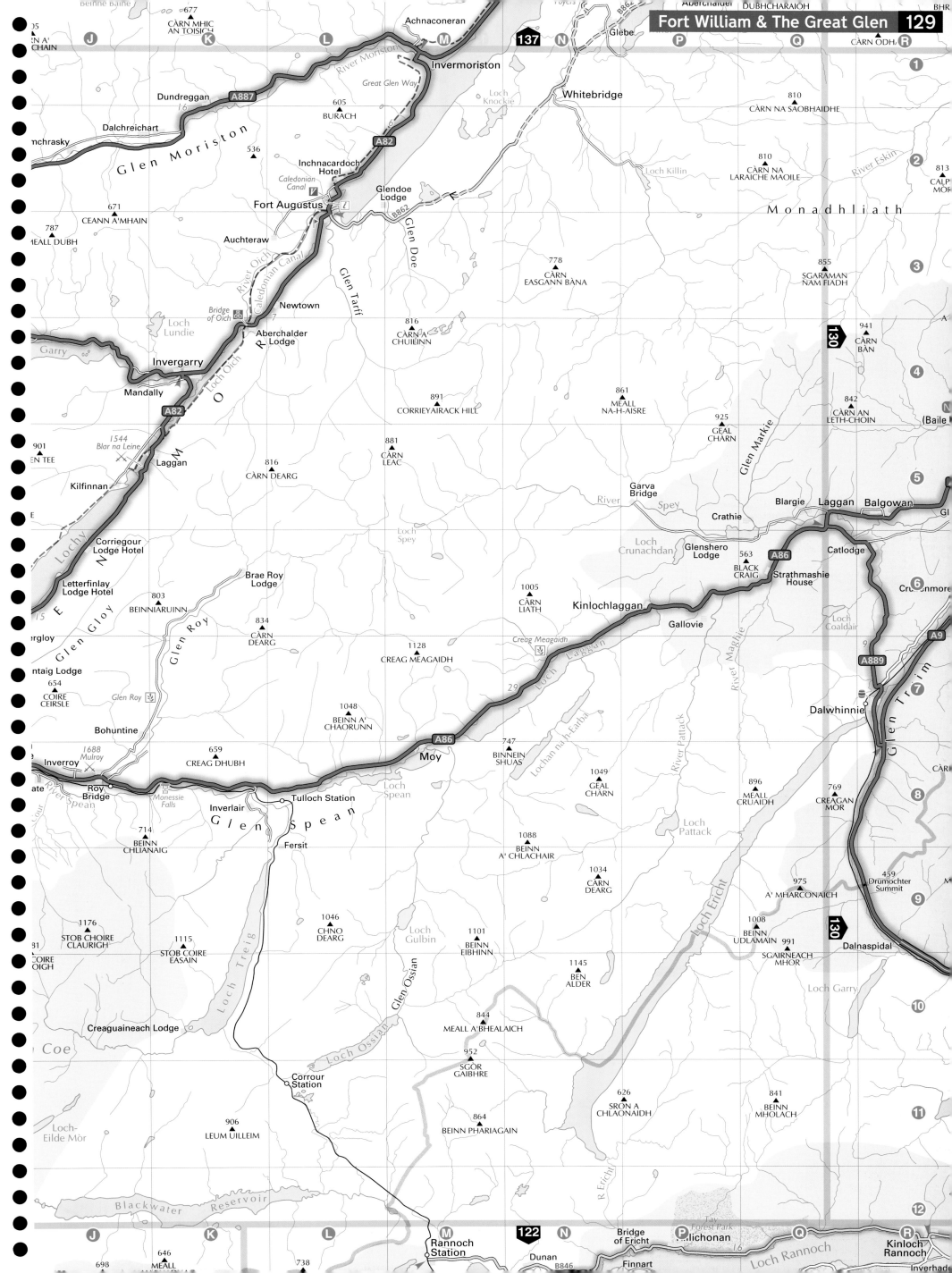

J K L M 137 N P Q R

1

Aberchalder DUBHCHARAIOH BHR

Achnaconeran Toyers B862 Glebe CÀRN ODHA

677 CÀRN MHIC AN TOISICH

River Moriston

Invermoriston

Great Glen Way

Whitebridge

810 CÀRN NA SAOBHAIDHE

Dundreggan A887 16 Loch Knockie

605 BURACH

Dalchreichart A82 2

nchrasky 536 Loch Killin 810 CÀRN NA LARAICHE MAOILE River Eskin 813 CALP MÒR

Glen Moriston Inchnacardoch Hotel

Caledonian Canal

Glendoe Lodge

671 CEANN A'MHAIN Fort Augustus Glen Doe M o n a d h l i a t h 3

787 MEALL DUBH Auchteraw B862

778 CÀRN EASGANN BÀNA

855 SGARAMAN NAM FIADH

River Oich Glen Tarff 130 941 CÀRN BÀN

Newtown Caledonian Canal

Bridge of Oich Aberchalder Lodge

816 CÀRN A CHUILINN

842 CÀRN AN LETH-CHOIN 4

Loch Lundie Garry

Invergarry Loch Oich

891 CORRIEYAIRACK HILL 861 MEALL NA-H-AISRE

925 GEAL CHÀRN (Baile

Mandally A82

901 N TEE 1544 Blar na Leine

816 CÀRN DEARG 881 CÀRN LEAC

Glen Markie 5

Laggan River Spey Blargie Laggan Balgowan

Kilfinnan Garva Bridge Crathie GI

Corriegour Lodge Hotel Loch Spey Loch Crunachdan Glenshero Lodge 563 BLACK CRAIG A86 Catlodge 6

Lochy Letterfinlay Lodge Hotel 803 BEINNIARUINN Brae Roy Lodge Strathmashie House Cru nmore

15 E Glen Gloy Glen Roy 834 CÀRN DEARG 1005 CÀRN LIATH Kinlochlaggan Gallovie Loch Coaldair A9

ergloy 1128 CREAG MEAGAIDH Creag Meagaidh A889 7

ntaig Lodge River Maghie

654 COIRE CEIRSLE Glen Roy 1048 BEINN A' CHAORUNN Loch Laggan 29 River Pattack Dalwhinnie Glen Truim

Bohuntine 747 BINNEIN SHUAS Lochan na h-Earba CÀR

1688 Mulroy 659 CREAG DHUBH A86 Moy 9 8

Inverroy 1049 GEAL CHÀRN 896 MEALL CRUAIDH 769 CREAGAN MÒR

ate Roy Bridge Monessie Falls Inverlair Tulloch Station Loch Spean Loch Pattack 975 A' MHARCONAICH 459 Drumochter Summit 9

River Spean 714 BEINN CHLIANAIG Fersit 1088 BEINN A' CHLACHAIR 130

Glen Spean 1034 CÀRN DEARG 1008 BEINN UDLAMAIN 991 SGAIRNEACH MHOR Dalnaspidal

1176 STOB CHOIRE CLAURIGH 1115 STOB COIRE EASAIN Loch Treig 1046 CHNO DEARG Loch Gulbin 1101 BEINN EIBHINN Loch Ericht

1 COIRE OIGH 1145 BEN ALDER Loch Garry 10

Coe Creaguaineach Lodge Glen Ossian 844 MEALL A'BHEALAICH

Loch Eilde Mòr Loch Ossian 952 SGÒR GAIBHRE Tay Forest Park 11

Corrour Station 626 SRON A CHLAONAIDH 841 BEINN MHOLACH

906 LEUM UILLEIM 864 BEINN PHARIAGAIN

Blackwater Reservoir Loch Rannoch 12

J K L M 122 N P lichonan Q R Kinloch Rannoch

698 646 MEALL 738 Rannoch Station Dunan Bridge of Ericht Finnart Inverhaı B846 Loch Rannoch

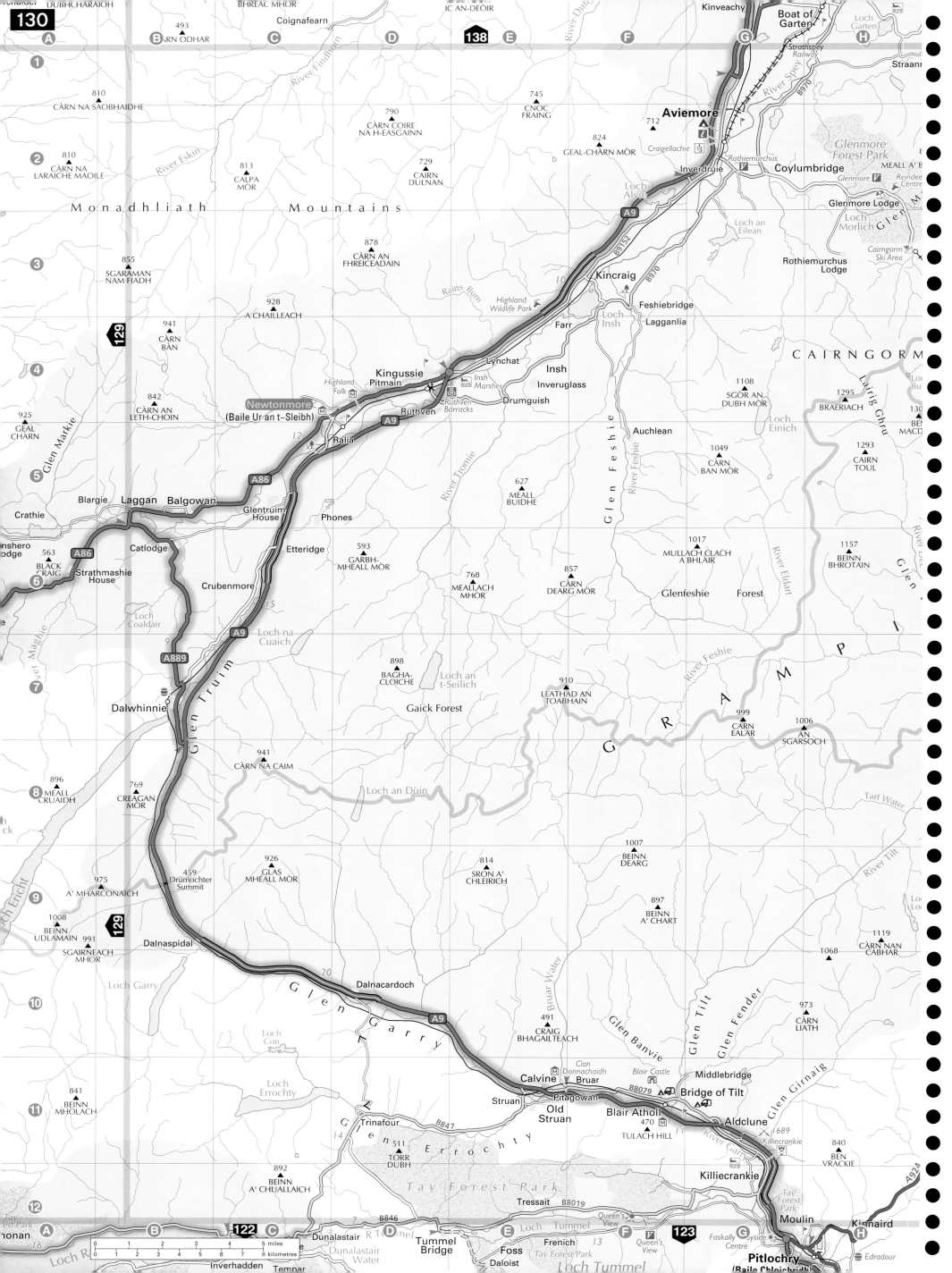

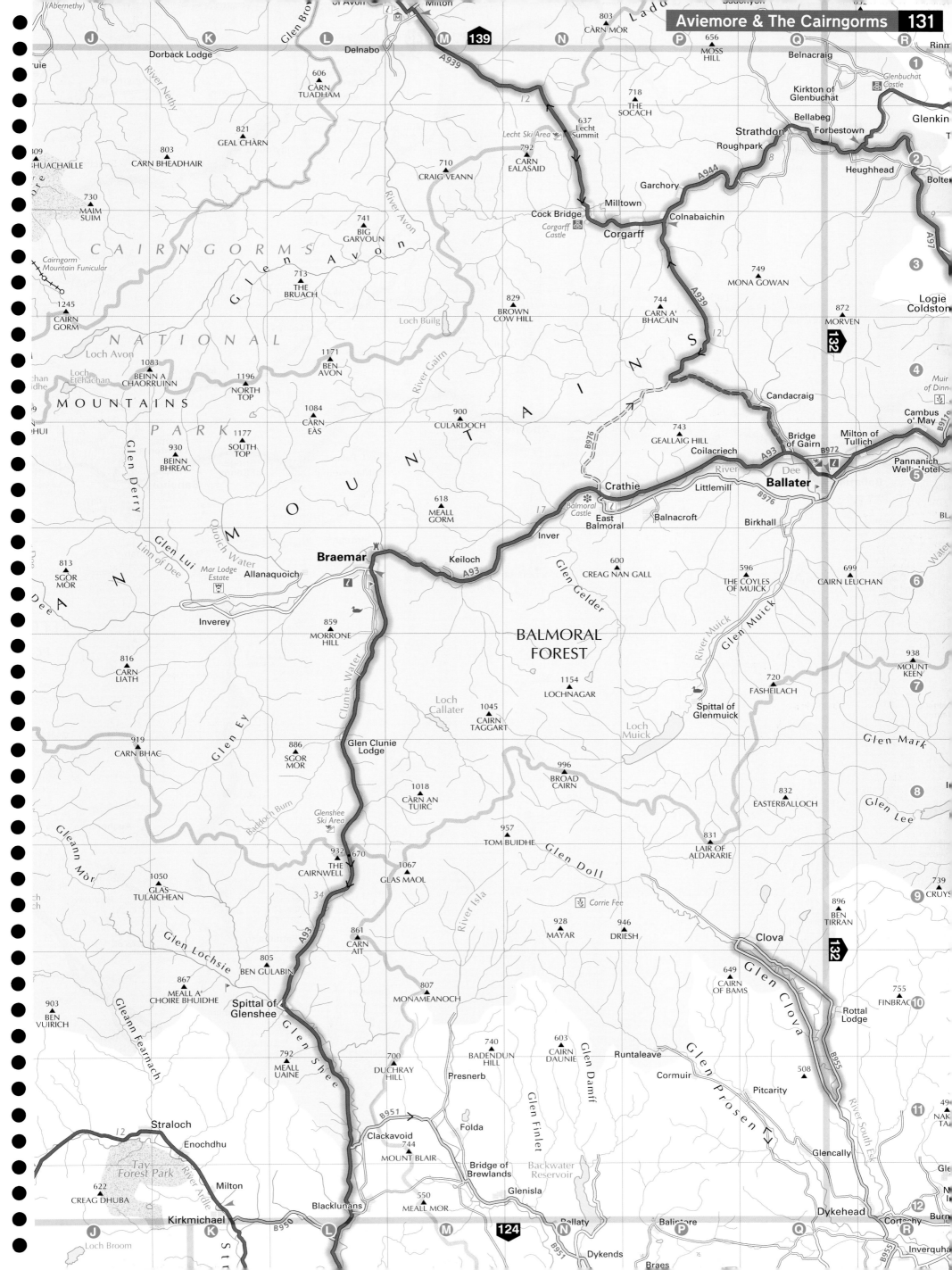

(Abernethy)
St Avon
Milton
Delnabo
Dorback Lodge
J
K
L
M
139
N
803
CÀRN MÒR
P
656
MOSS HILL
Q
Belnacraig
R
Rinm
1
Glenbuchat Castle
606
CARN TUADHAM
718
THE SOCACH
Kirkton of Glenbuchat
Bellabeg
Forbestown
Glenkin
821
GEAL CHÀRN
792
CARN EALASAID
637
Lecht Summit
Lecht Ski Area
Strathdon
Roughpark
Heughhead
Bolte
803
CARN BHEADHAIR
710
CRAIG VEANN
Milltown
Garchory
Colnabaichin
A944
2
A97
809
SHUACHAILLE
re
730
MAIM SUIM
Cock Bridge
Corgarff Castle
Corgarff
749
MONA GOWAN
3
741
BIG GARVOUN
744
CARN A' BHACAIN
A939
872
MORVEN
132
Logie Coldston
CAIRNGORMS
713
THE BRUACH
829
BROWN COW HILL
12
1245
CAIRN GORM
Loch Builg
Candacraig
4
Muir of Dinn
Cairngorm Mountain Funicular
NATIONAL
Loch Avon
1171
BEN AVON
900
CULARDOCH
743
GEALLAIG HILL
Cambus o' May
B9170
Loch Etchachan
1083
BEINN A CHAORRUINN
1196
NORTH TOP
River Cairn
B976
Coilacriech
Bridge of Gairn
Milton of Tullich
MOUNTAINS
1084
CÀRN EÀS
Crathie
Littlemill
A93
Ballater
B976
Pannanich Wells Hotel
PARK
1177
SOUTH TOP
930
BEINN BHREAC
618
MEALL GORM
Balmoral Castle
East Balmoral
Balnacroft
Birkhall
River Dee
5
HUI
Glen Derry
Braemar
Keiloch
A93
Inver
600
CREAG NAN GALL
596
THE COYLES OF MUICK
699
CAIRN LEUCHAN
6
813
SGOR MOR
Mar Lodge Estate
Allanaquoich
Glen Lui
Quoich Water
Linn of Dee
Glen Gelder
BALMORAL FOREST
Dee
816
CARN LIATH
Inverey
859
MORRONE HILL
Glen Ey
1154
LOCHNAGAR
720
FASHEILACH
938
MOUNT KEEN
7
Clunie Water
1045
CAIRN TAGGART
Loch Callater
Spittal of Glenmuick
919
CARN BHAC
886
SGOR MOR
Glen Clunie Lodge
Loch Muick
Glen Mark
996
BROAD CAIRN
832
EASTERBALLOCH
Glen Lee
8
Baddoch Burn
1018
CÀRN AN TUIRC
Glenshee Ski Area
957
TOM BUIDHE
Glen Doll
831
LAIR OF ALDARARIE
Gleann Mòr
932
670
THE CAIRNWELL
1067
GLAS MAOL
River Isla
Corrie Fee
739
CRUYS
9
1050
GLAS TULAICHEAN
34
896
BEN TIRRAN
ch
A93
861
CARN AIT
928
MAYAR
946
DRIESH
Clova
132
Glen Lochsie
805
BEN GULABIN
807
MONAMEANOCH
649
CAIRN OF BAMS
Glen Clova
755
FINBRAC
10
867
MEALL A' CHOIRE BHUIDHE
Rottal Lodge
903
BEN VUIRICH
Glen Shee
792
MEALL UAINE
Spittal of Glenshee
700
DUCHRAY HILL
740
BADENDUN HILL
603
CAIRN DAUNIE
Runtaleave
Glen Prosen
508
Gleann Fearnach
Presnerb
Cormuir
Pitcarity
River South Esk
11
NAK TA
Stralloch
Enochdhu
B951
Clackavoid
744
MOUNT BLAIR
Folda
Bridge of Brewlands
Glen Finlet
Glencally
Gle
12
Tay Forest Park
River Ardle
Milton
622
CREAG DHUBA
Blacklunans
B950
550
MEALL MOR
Glenisla
Backwater Reservoir
Ballaty
Balintore
Dykehead
Cortachy
Kirkmichael
J
K
L
M
124
N
Braes
P
Q
Interquha
R
Loch Broom
Dykends
B951
B955

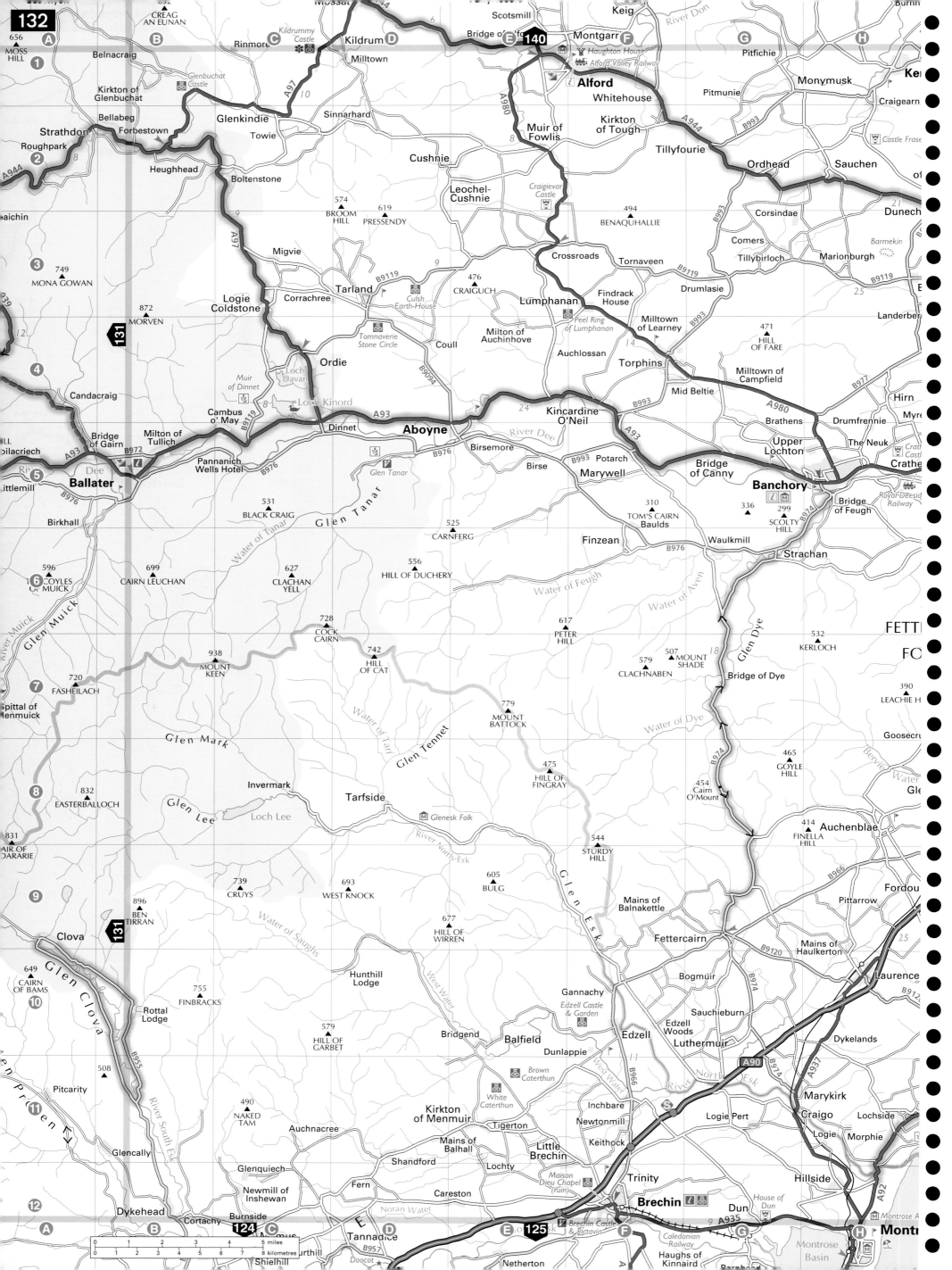

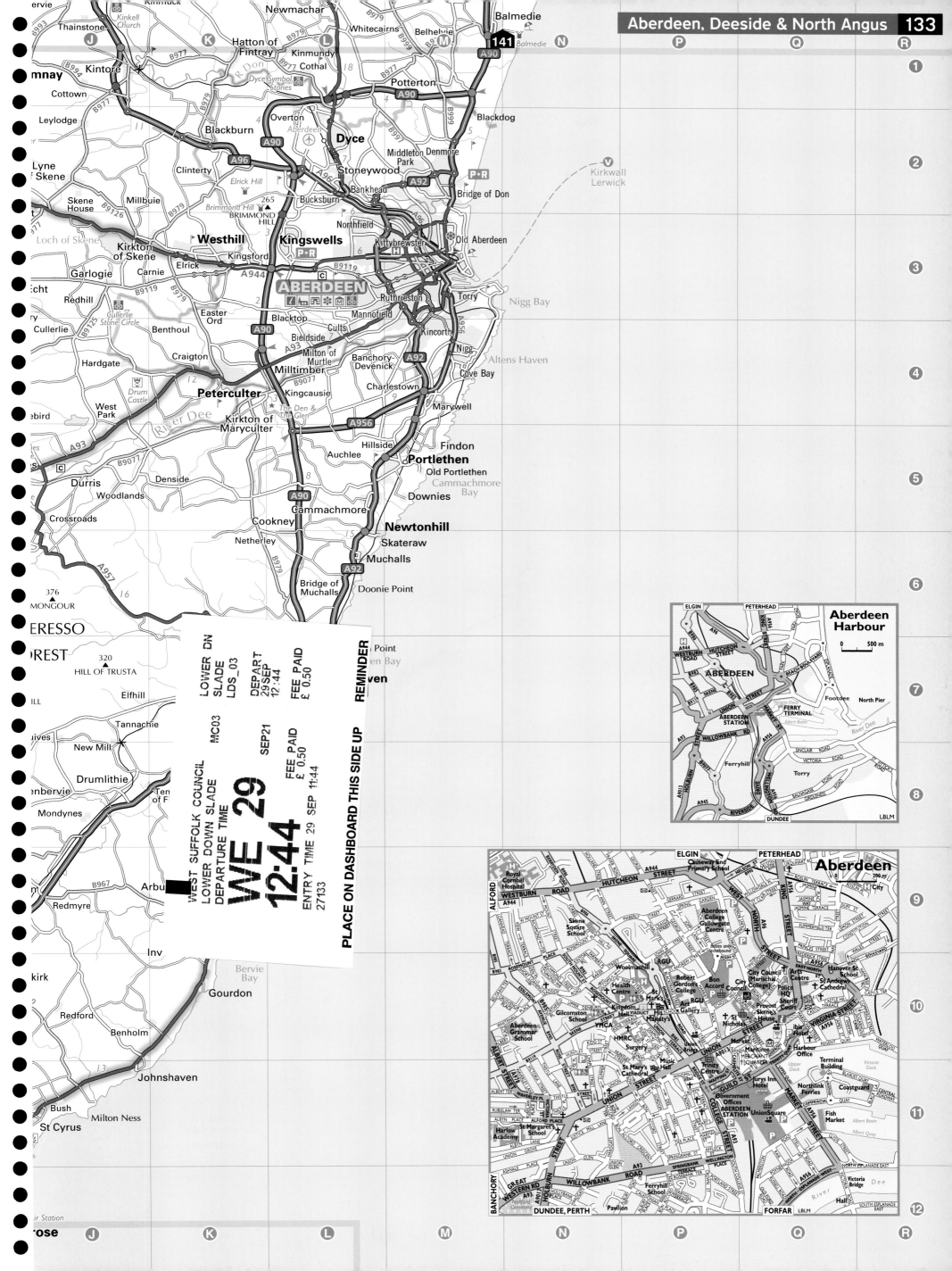

Aberdeen Harbour

Aberdeen

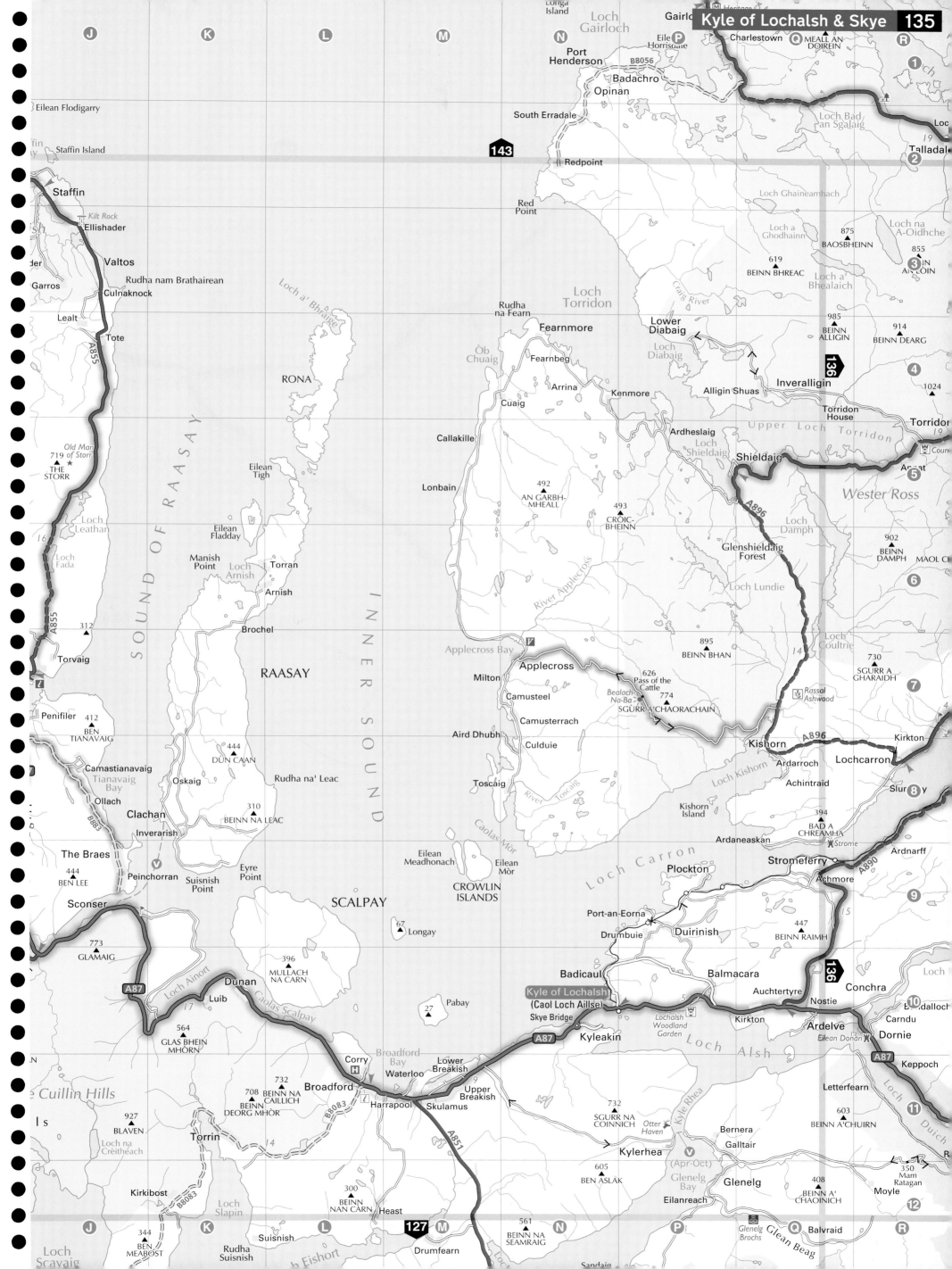

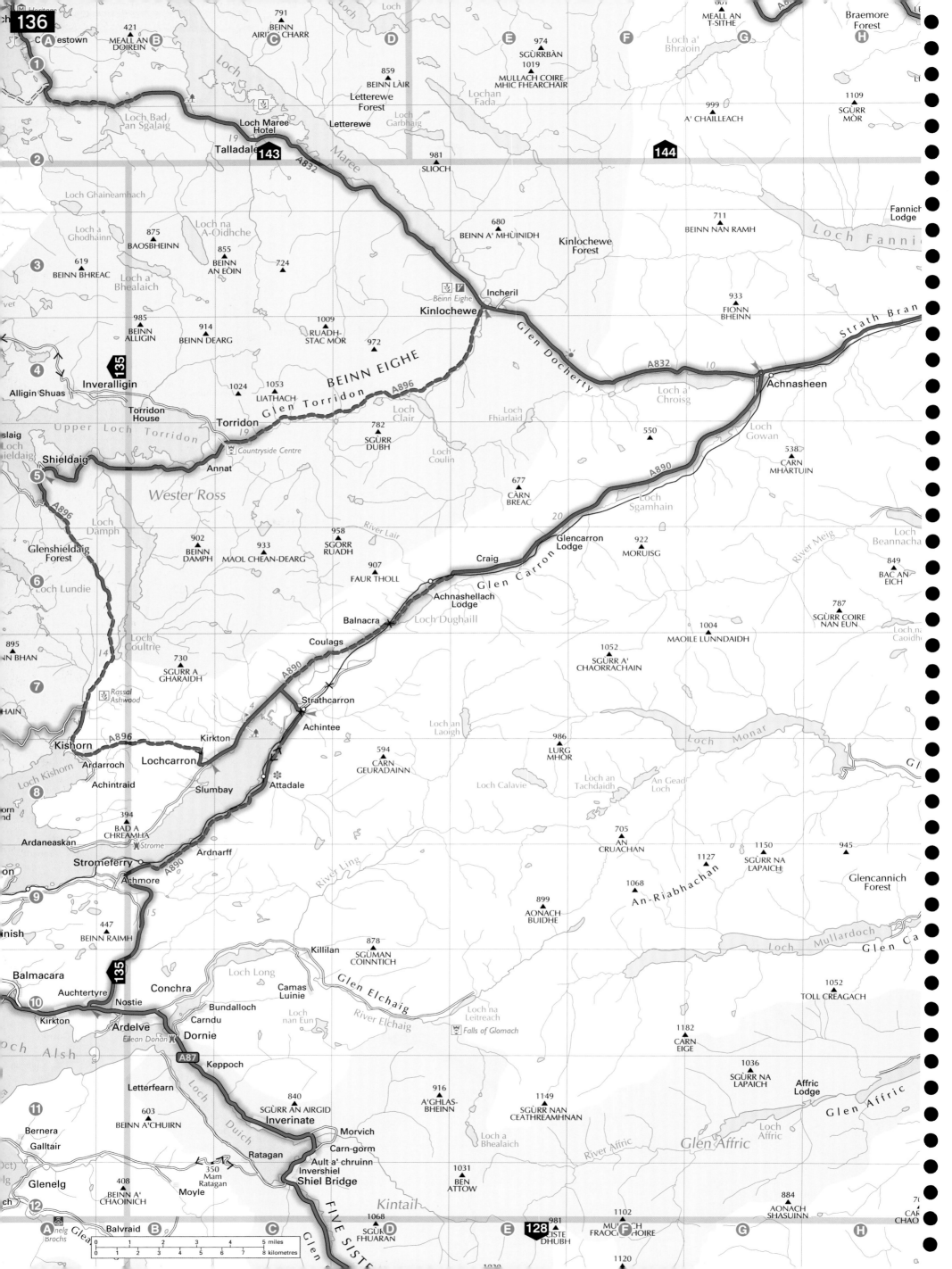

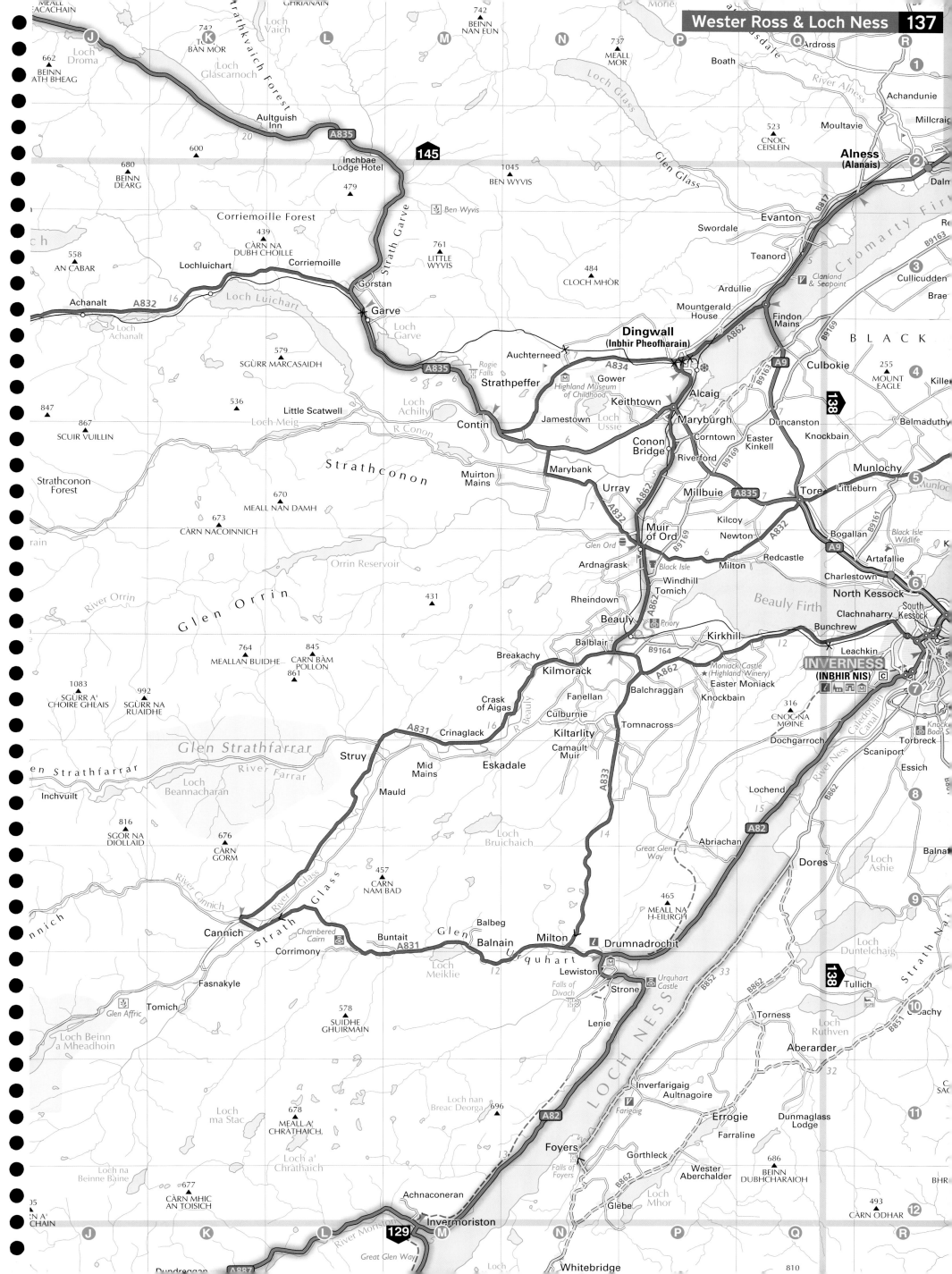

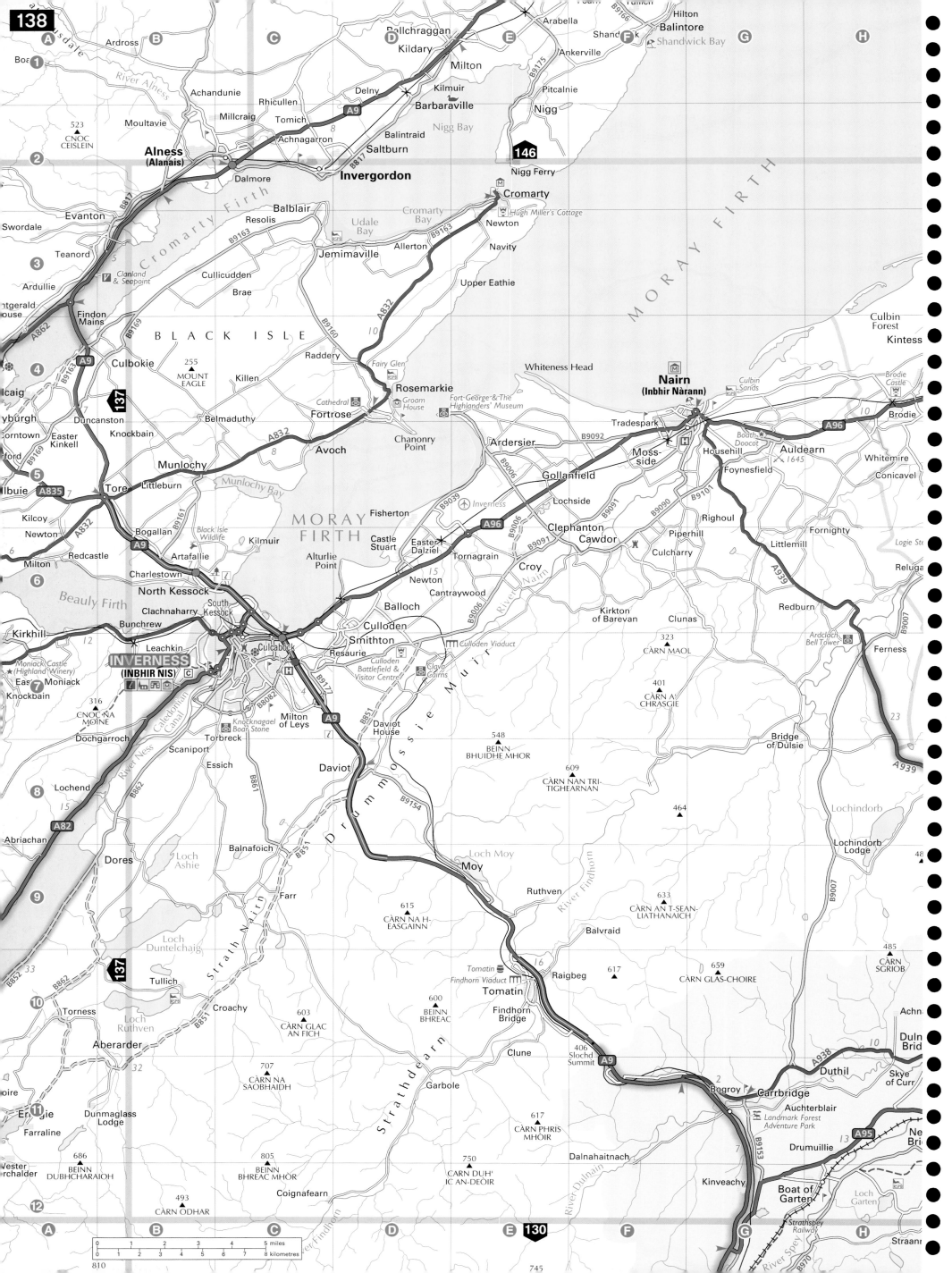

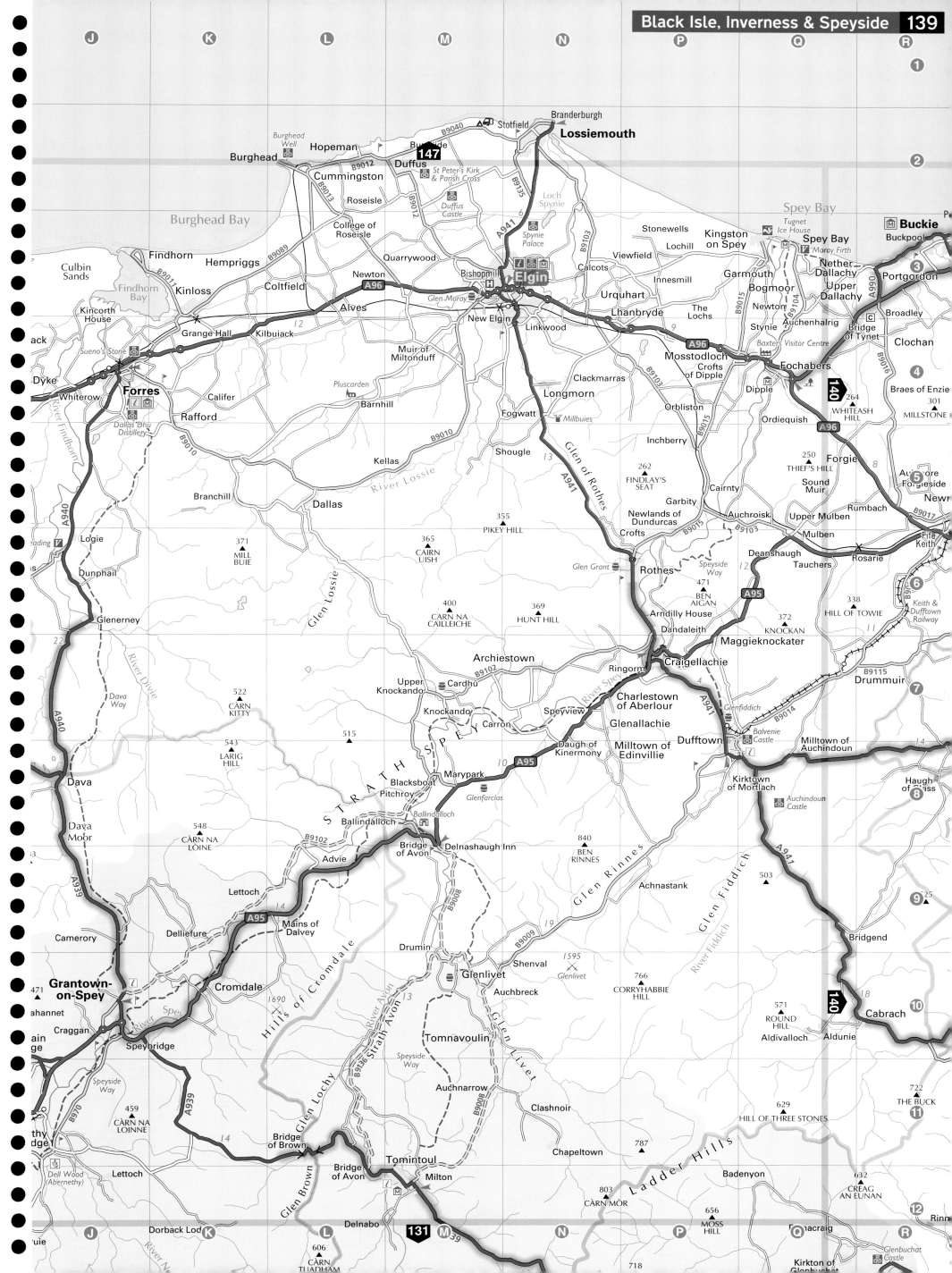

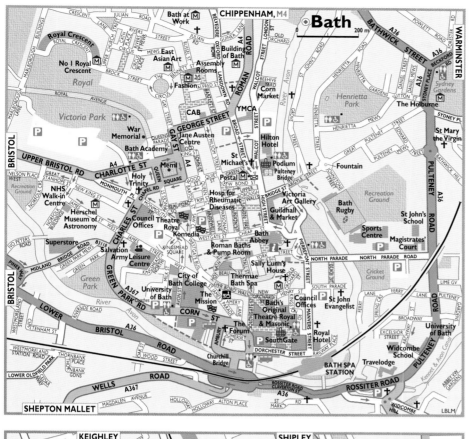

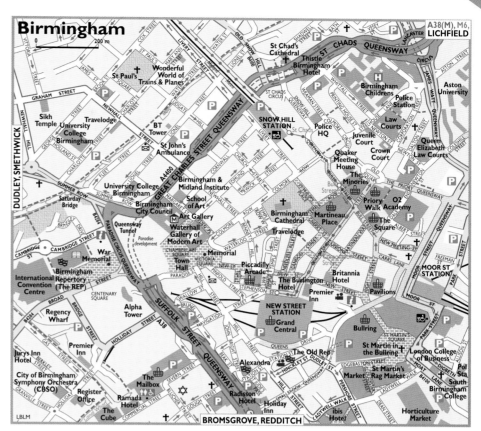

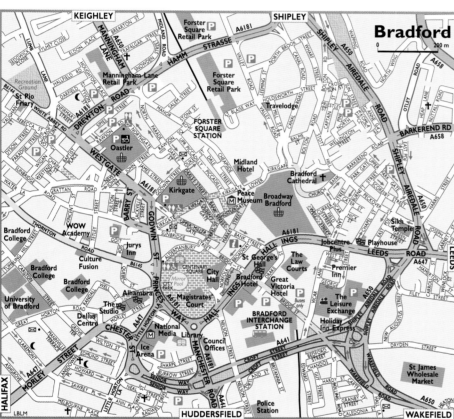

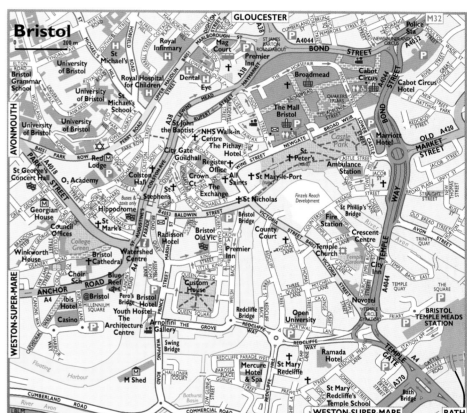

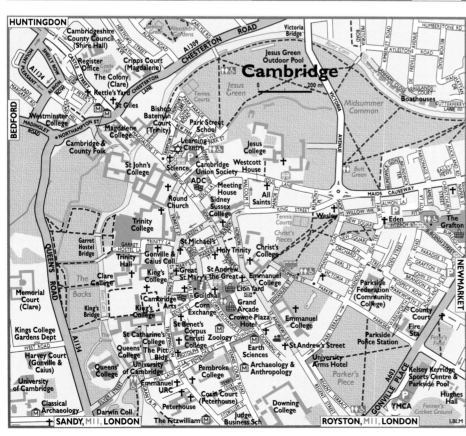

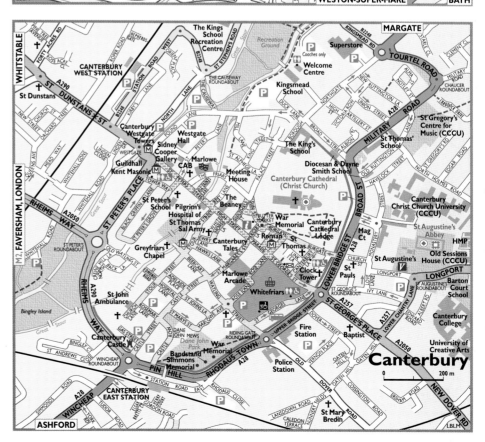

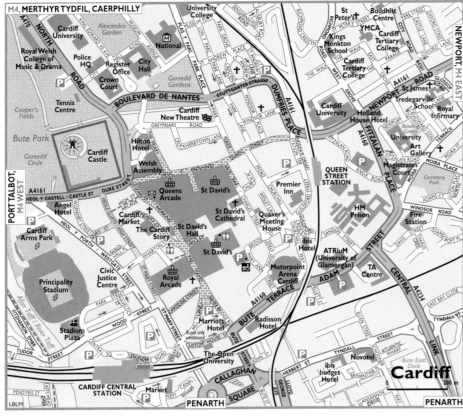

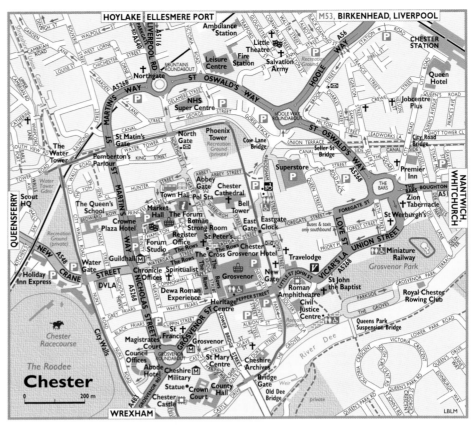

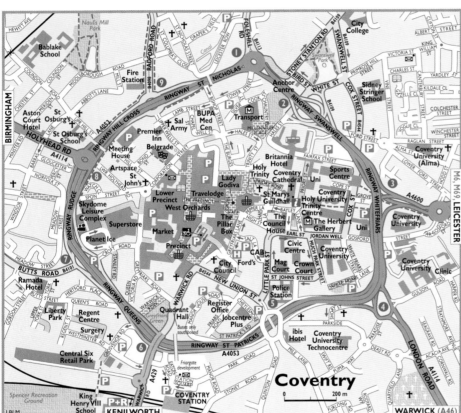

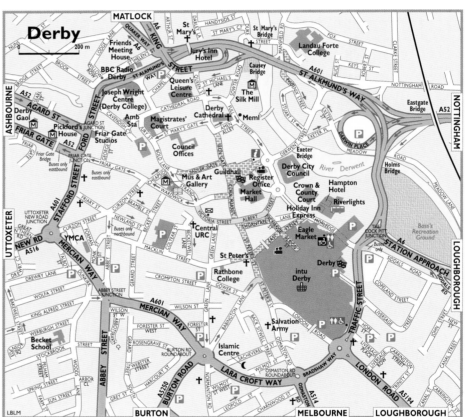

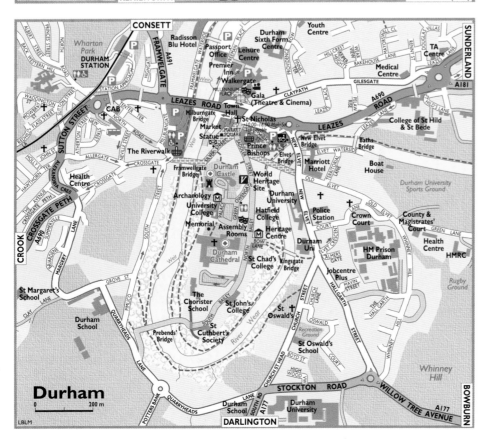

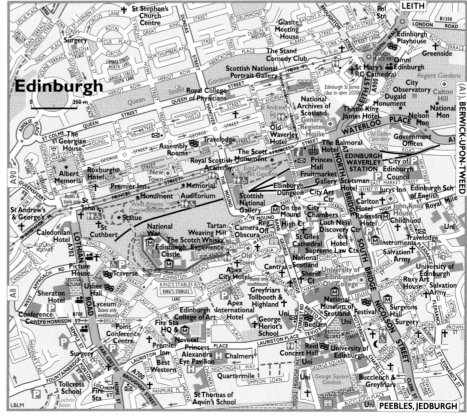

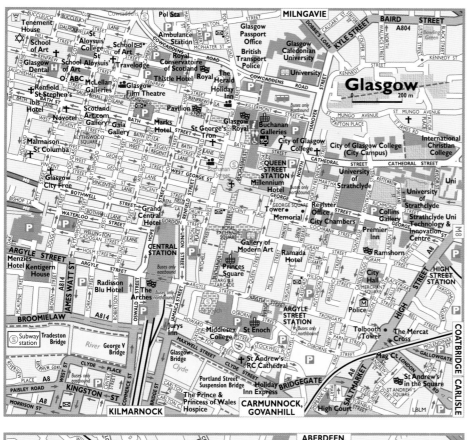

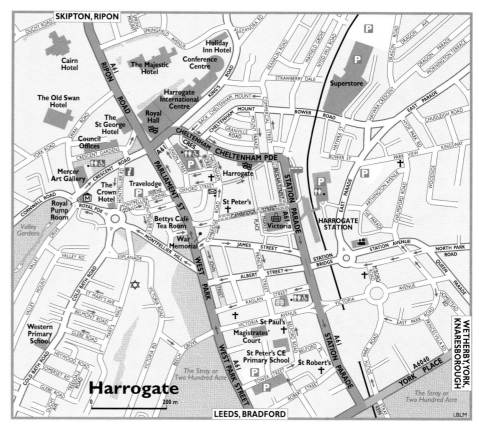

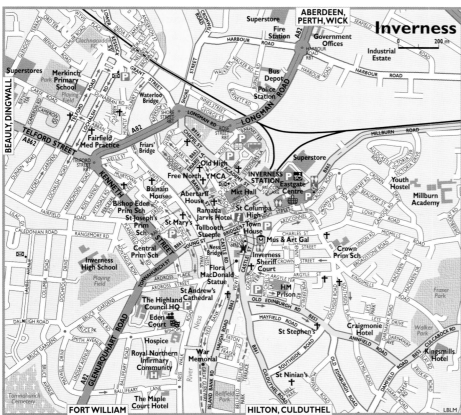

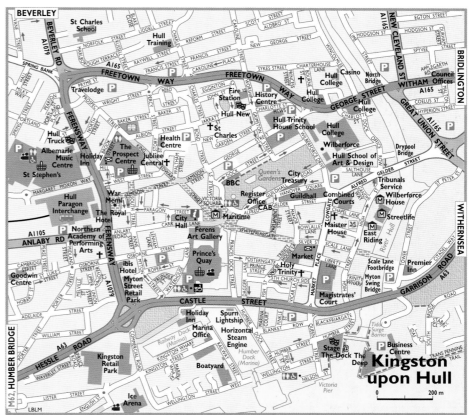

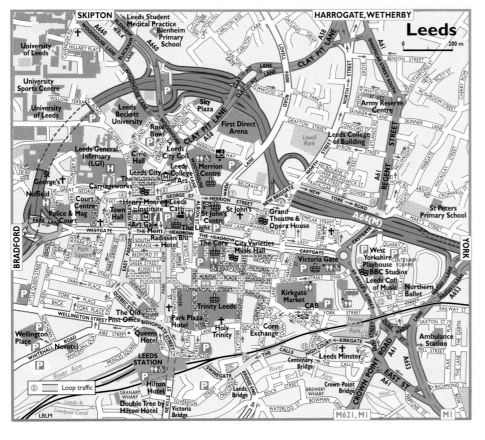

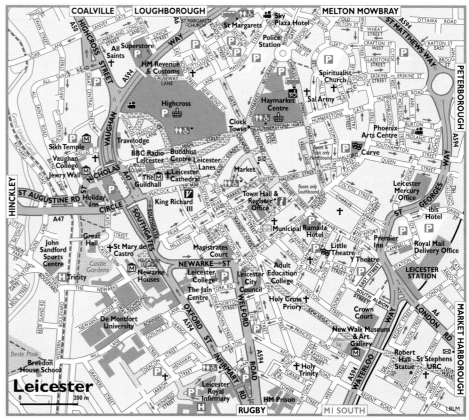

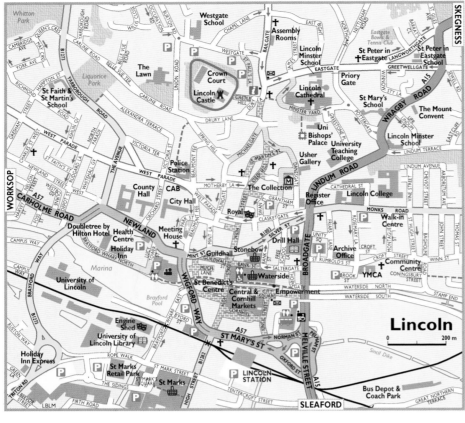

Lincoln

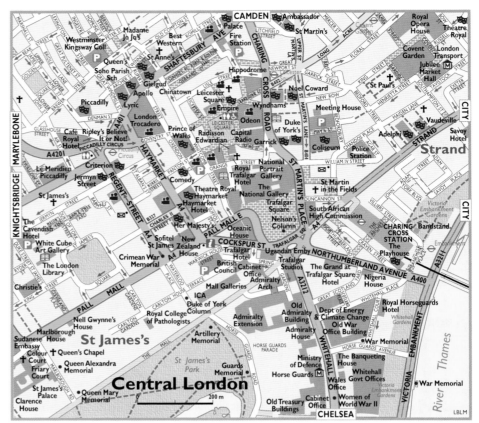

Central London

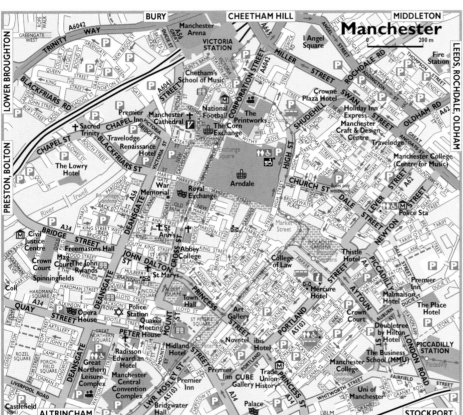

Manchester

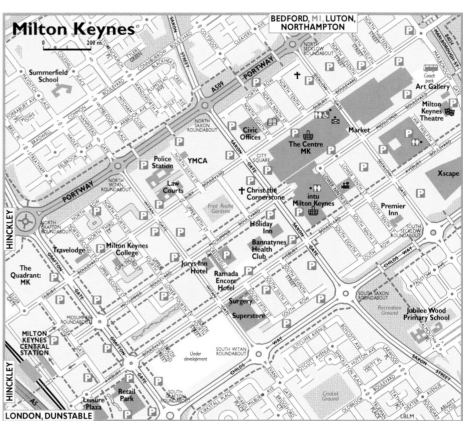

Milton Keynes

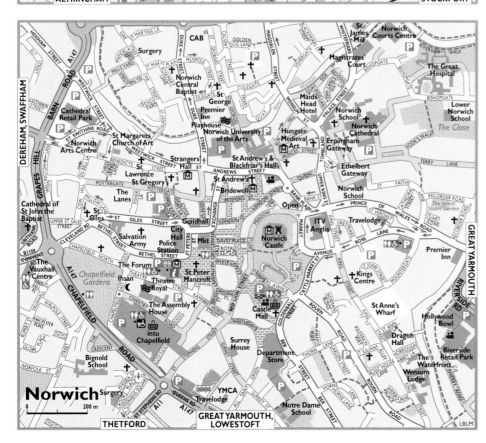

Norwich

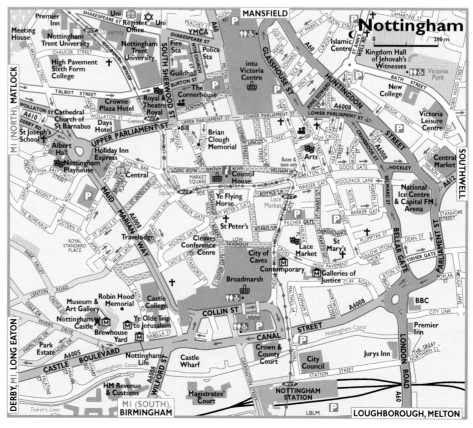

Nottingham

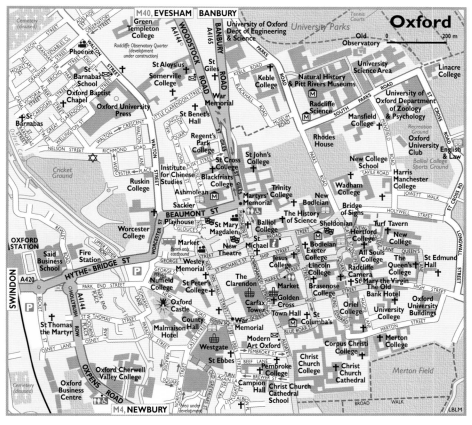

Oxford

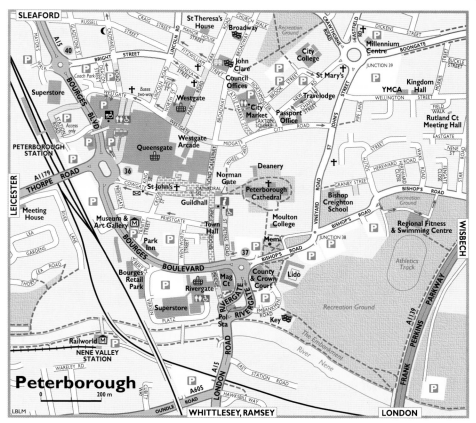

Peterborough

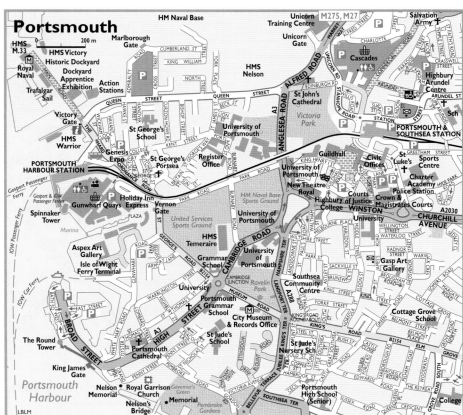

Portsmouth

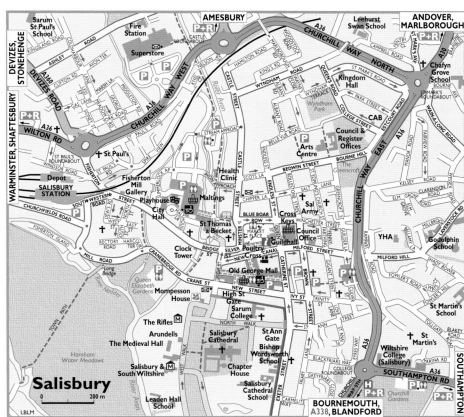

Salisbury

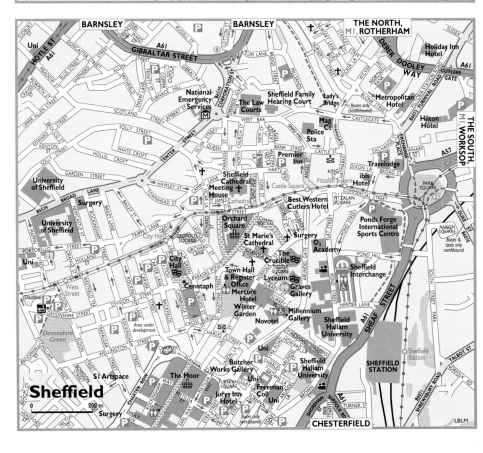

Sheffield

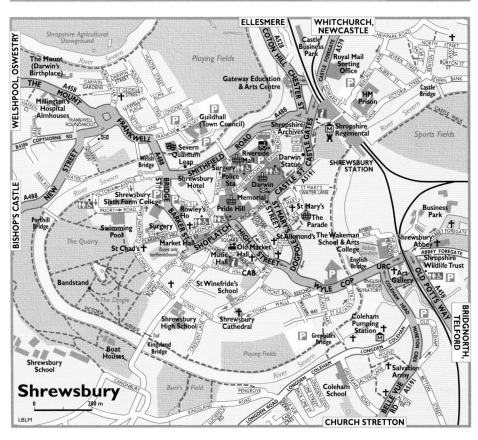

Shrewsbury

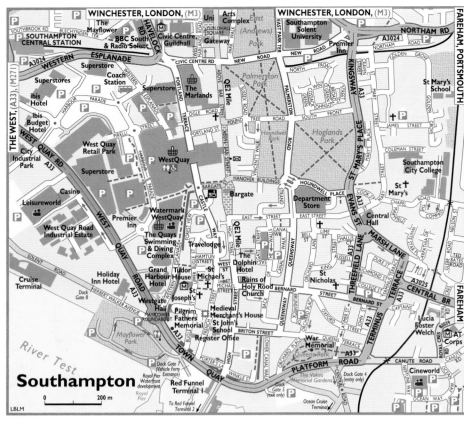

Southampton

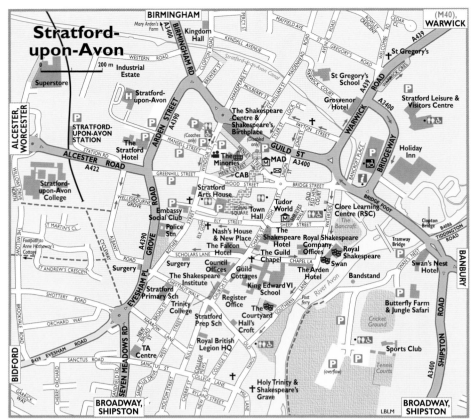

Stratford-upon-Avon

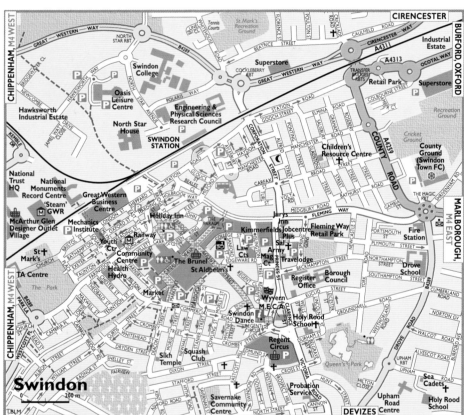

Swindon

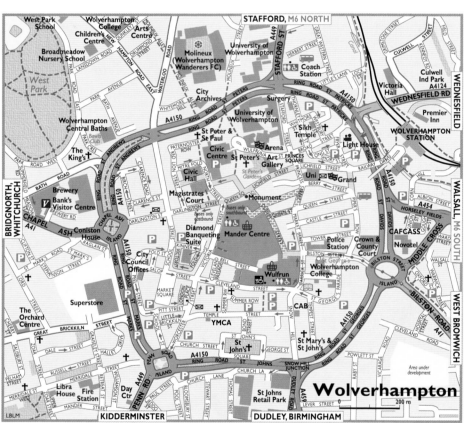

Wolverhampton

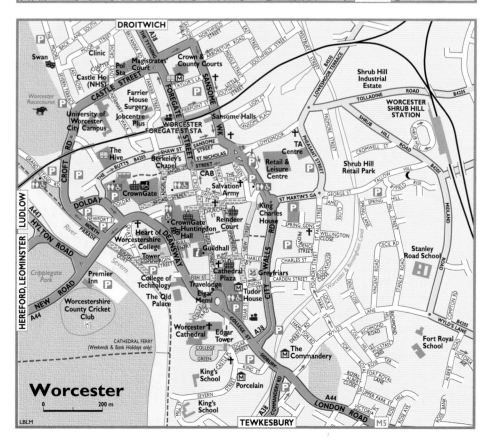

Worcester

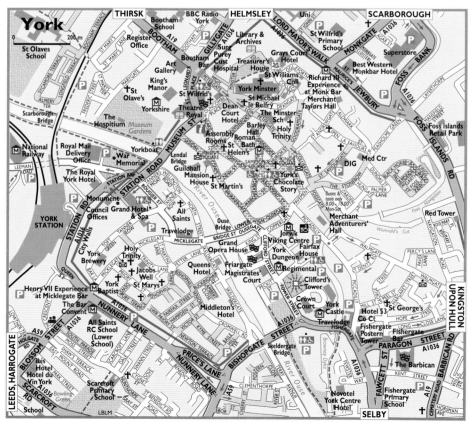

York

Heathfield – Hornsby 175

Heathfield Cambs 45 N2
Heathfield Devon 8 F9
Heathfield E Susx 15 Q6
Heathfield N York 84 H2
Heathfield Somset 21 J8
Heathfield Village Oxon 43 L8
Heath Green Worcs 53 K6
Heath Hall D & G 97 K2
Heath Hayes & Wimblebury Staffs 65 J10
Heath Hill Shrops 64 E9
Heath House Somset 21 P4
Heathrow Airport Gt Lon 32 F7
Heathstock Devon 9 N4
Heathton Shrops 52 E2
Heath Town Wolves 64 H12
Heathwaite N York 91 R6
Heatley Staffs 65 K7
Heatley Warrtn 76 C6
Heaton Bolton 76 C2
Heaton C Brad 84 H8
Heaton Lancs 83 K3
Heaton N u Ty 100 H5
Heaton Staffs 76 H11
Heaton Chapel Stockp 76 G5
Heaton Mersey Stockp 76 F5
Heaton Norris Stockp 76 G5
Heaton's Bridge Lancs 75 L1
Heaverham Kent 33 Q10
Heaviley Stockp 76 G6
Heavitree Devon 8 H6
Hebburn S Tyne 101 J5
Hebden N York 84 F3
Hebden Bridge Calder 84 E9
Hebden Green Ches W 76 B10
Hebing End Herts 45 K7
Hebron Carmth 37 N5
Hebron IoA 72 G7
Hebron Nthumb 109 K11
Heckfield Hants 31 P10
Heckfield Green Suffk 59 J5
Heckfordbridge Essex 46 G7
Heckington Lincs 68 C3
Heckmondwike Kirk 85 J10
Heddington Wilts 30 A9
Heddon-on-the-Wall Nthumb 100 E5
Hedenham Norfk 59 L2
Hedge End Hants 24 H10
Hedgerley Bucks 32 D5
Hedgerley Green Bucks 32 D5
Hedging Somset 21 L7
Hedley on the Hill Nthumb 100 D6
Hednesford Staffs 65 J9
Hedon E R Yk 87 M9
Hedsor Bucks 32 C5
Heeley Sheff 78 B7
Hegdon Hill Herefs 51 Q10
Heglibister Shet 147 i6
Heighington Darltn 91 L2
Heighington Lincs 79 P10
Heightington Worcs 52 E6
Heiton Border 108 B4
Hele Devon 5 M3
Hele Devon 9 J4
Hele Devon 19 K4
Hele Somset 21 J8
Helebridge Cnwll 7 J4
Hele Lane Devon 8 E3
Helensburgh Ag & B 113 K5
Helenton S Ayrs 104 G4
Helford Cnwll 3 J9
Helford Passage Cnwll 3 J9
Helhoughton Norfk 70 C7
Helions Bumpstead Essex 46 B3
Hellaby Rothm 78 E5
Helland Cnwll 6 F10
Hellandbridge Cnwll 6 F10
Hell Corner W Berk 30 H9
Hellescott Cnwll 7 K7
Hellesdon Norfk 71 J9
Hellesveor Cnwll 2 D6
Hellidon Nhants 54 E9
Hellifield N York 84 C4
Hellingly E Susx 15 Q8
Hellington Norfk 71 L11
Helm Nthumb 109 K10
Helmdon Nhants 43 M3
Helme Kirk 77 L1
Helmingham Suffk 59 J9
Helmington Row Dur 100 F11
Helmsdale Highld 147 J2
Helmshore Lancs 84 B11
Helmsley N York 92 C10
Helperby N York 85 N1
Helperthorpe N York 86 H1
Helpringham Lincs 68 C4
Helpston C Pete 68 C11
Helsby Ches W 75 N8
Helsey Lincs 81 K9
Helston Cnwll 2 G9
Helstone Cnwll 6 F8
Helton Cumb 89 N2
Helwith N York 90 H6
Helwith Bridge N York 84 B1
Hemblington Norfk 71 L10
Hembridge Somset 22 D6
Hemel Hempstead Herts 44 F10
Hemerdon Devon 5 J5
Hemingbrough N York 86 C9
Hemingby Lincs 80 E9
Hemingfield Barns 78 C3
Hemingford Abbots Cambs 56 F6
Hemingford Grey Cambs 56 F6
Hemingstone Suffk 58 H10
Hemington Leics 66 D6
Hemington Nhants 56 B4
Hemington Somset 22 G3
Hemley Suffk 47 N3
Hemlington Middsb 92 A4
Hempholme E R Yk 87 K5
Hempnall Norfk 59 K2
Hempnall Green Norfk 59 K2
Hempriggs Moray 139 K3
Hempstead Essex 46 B4
Hempstead Medway 34 D9
Hempstead Norfk 70 G5
Hempstead Norfk 71 N6
Hempsted Gloucs 41 N8
Hempton Norfk 70 D6
Hempton Oxon 43 J5
Hemsby Norfk 71 P8
Hemswell Lincs 79 M5
Hemswell Cliff Lincs 79 N6
Hemsworth Wakefd 78 C1
Hemyock Devon 21 J10
Henbury Bristl 28 H6
Henbury Ches E 76 G9
Hendham Devon 5 M6
Hendomen Powys 50 H1
Hendon Gt Lon 33 J4
Hendon Sundld 101 K7
Hendon Crematorium Gt Lon 33 J4
Hendra Cnwll 2 H7
Hendra Cnwll 6 E9
Hendre Brdgnd 27 M6
Hendre Flints 74 G10
Hendre Mons 40 F9
Hendy Carmth 38 E11
Heneglwys IoA 72 G8
Henfield W Susx 15 J7
Henford Devon 7 M6
Henghurst Kent 16 G3
Hengoed Caerph 27 R3
Hengoed Powys 50 H10
Hengoed Shrops 63 J5
Hengrave Suffk 58 B7
Henham Essex 45 Q6
Heniarth Powys 62 F10
Henlade Somset 21 L8
Henley Dorset 10 H4
Henley Gloucs 41 P8
Henley Shrops 51 M3
Henley Shrops 51 P5
Henley Somset 21 P7
Henley Suffk 58 H10
Henley W Susx 14 C6
Henley Green Covtry 54 B4
Henley-in-Arden Warwks 53 M7
Henley-on-Thames Oxon 31 Q6
Henley Park Surrey 32 D11
Henley's Down E Susx 16 C8
Henley Street Kent 34 B9
Henllan Cerdgn 38 A4
Henllan Denbgs 74 D10
Henllan Amgoed Carmth 37 N6
Henllys Torfn 28 C4
Henlow C Beds 44 H4
Hennock Devon 8 F8
Henny Street Essex 46 F4
Henryd Conwy 73 N9
Henry's Moat (Castell Hendre) Pembks 37 K5
Hensall N York 86 B10
Henshaw Nthumb 99 L5
Hensingham Cumb 88 C3
Henstead Suffk 59 P3
Hensting Hants 24 H9
Henstridge Somset 22 G9
Henstridge Ash Somset 22 G9
Henstridge Marsh Somset 22 G9
Henton Oxon 43 Q11
Henton Somset 22 C4
Henwick Worcs 52 F9
Henwood Cnwll 7 K10
Henwood Oxon 43 K11
Heol-las Swans 26 G3
Heol Senni Powys 39 L7
Heol-y-Cyw Brdgnd 27 M5
Hepburn Nthumb 108 H5
Hepple Nthumb 108 G9
Hepscott Nthumb 100 G1
Heptonstall Calder 84 E9
Hepworth Kirk 77 M2
Hepworth Suffk 58 E6
Herbrandston Pembks 36 G9
Hereford Herefs 40 G4
Hereford Crematorium Herefs 40 G4
Hereson Kent 35 Q9
Heribusta Highld 142 D11
Heriot Border 115 R10
Hermiston C Edin 115 M7
Hermitage Border 107 M10
Hermitage Dorset 10 G3
Hermitage W Berk 31 L8
Hermitage W Susx 13 N4
Hermit Hill Barns 77 Q3
Hermon Carmth 38 A5
Hermon IoA 72 F10
Hermon Pembks 37 N4
Herne Kent 35 L9
Herne Bay Kent 35 L8
Herne Common Kent 35 L9
Herne Hill Gt Lon 33 L7
Herne Pound Kent 34 B11
Herner Devon 19 L8
Hernhill Kent 35 J10
Herodsfoot Cnwll 4 C4
Heronden Kent 35 N11
Herongate Essex 34 A4
Heronsford S Ayrs 94 G2
Heronsgate Herts 32 E3
Herriard Hants 25 L4
Herringfleet Suffk 59 P1
Herring's Green Bed 44 F3
Herringswell Suffk 57 N6
Herringthorpe Rothm 78 D5
Herrington Sundld 101 J7
Hersden Kent 35 M10
Hersham Cnwll 7 K3
Hersham Surrey 32 G9
Herstmonceux E Susx 16 B8
Herston Dorset 11 N9
Herston Ork 147 c6
Hertford Herts 45 L9
Hertford Heath Herts 45 L9
Hertingfordbury Herts 45 K9
Hesketh Bank Lancs 83 K10
Hesketh Lane Lancs 83 N7
Hesket Newmarket Cumb 98 D10
Heskin Green Lancs 83 M12
Hesleden Dur 101 L10
Hesleden N York 90 E11
Hesley Donc 78 G5
Hesleyside Nthumb 99 M2
Heslington C York 86 B5
Hessay C York 85 Q4
Hessenford Cnwll 4 D5
Hessett Suffk 58 D8
Hessle E R Yk 87 J10
Hessle Wakefd 85 N11
Hest Bank Lancs 83 L2
Hestley Green Suffk 58 H7
Heston Gt Lon 32 G7
Heston Services Gt Lon 32 G7
Hestwall Ork 147 b4
Heswall Wirral 75 J7
Hethe Oxon 43 M6
Hethersett Norfk 70 H11
Hethersgill Cumb 98 F5
Hetherside Cumb 98 E5
Hetherson Green Ches W 63 N2
Hethpool Nthumb 108 E4
Hett Dur 100 H11
Hetton N York 84 E3
Hetton-le-Hole Sundld 101 J8
Hetton Steads Nthumb 108 G3
Heugh Nthumb 100 E4
Heughhead Abers 132 B2
Heugh Head Border 117 K9
Heveningham Suffk 59 L6
Hever Kent 15 N2
Heversham Cumb 89 M10
Hevingham Norfk 71 J8
Hewas Water Cnwll 3 N4
Hewelsfield Gloucs 40 H11
Hewenden C Brad 84 G8
Hewish N Som 28 E9
Hewish Somset 10 C3
Hewood Dorset 9 Q4
Hexham Nthumb 99 P5
Hextable Kent 33 P8
Hexthorpe Donc 78 F3
Hexton Herts 44 G5
Hexworthy Cnwll 7 L8
Hexworthy Devon 8 C10
Hey Lancs 84 C6
Heybridge Essex 34 B3
Heybridge Essex 46 E10
Heybridge Basin Essex 46 F10
Heybrook Bay Devon 4 H7
Heydon Cambs 45 N4
Heydon Norfk 70 G7
Heydour Lincs 67 P4
Heyhead Manch 76 F6
Hey Houses Lancs 82 H9
Heylipoll Ag & B 118 D4
Heylor Shet 147 h4
Heyrod Tamesd 76 H4
Heysham Lancs 83 K3
Heyshaw N York 85 J3
Heyshott W Susx 14 C7
Heyside Oldham 76 H2
Heytesbury Wilts 23 K5
Heythrop Oxon 42 H6
Heywood Rochdl 76 F2
Heywood Wilts 23 J3
Hibaldstow N Linc 79 N3
Hickleton Donc 78 D3
Hickling Norfk 71 N7
Hickling Notts 66 H6
Hickling Green Norfk 71 N7
Hickling Heath Norfk 71 M7
Hickling Pastures Notts 66 H6
Hickmans Green Kent 35 J10
Hicks Forstal Kent 35 L9
Hickstead W Susx 15 K7
Hidcote Bartrim Gloucs 42 E3
Hidcote Boyce Gloucs 42 E3
High Ackworth Wakefd 85 N11
Higham Barns 77 P2
Higham Derbys 78 C12
Higham Kent 15 R1
Higham Kent 34 C8
Higham Lancs 84 B8
Higham Suffk 47 J4
Higham Suffk 57 P7
Higham Dykes Nthumb 100 E3
Higham Ferrers Nhants 55 N7
Higham Gobion C Beds 44 G5
Higham Hill Gt Lon 33 L4
Higham on the Hill Leics 54 C2
Highampton Devon 7 P4
Highams Park Gt Lon 33 M4
High Angerton Nthumb 100 E1
High Ardwell D & G 94 F9
High Auldgirth D & G 106 B12
High Bankhill Cumb 98 H10
High Beach Essex 33 M3
High Bentham N York 83 P1
High Bewaldeth Cumb 97 P11
High Bickington Devon 19 L9
High Biggins Cumb 89 P11
High Birkwith N York 90 C11
High Blantyre S Lans 114 C10
High Bonnybridge Falk 114 E5
High Borrans Cumb 89 L6
High Bradley N York 84 F5
High Bray Devon 19 N6
Highbridge Hants 24 H9
Highbridge Somset 21 M4
Highbrook W Susx 15 L5
High Brooms Kent 15 Q2
High Bullen Devon 19 K9
Highburton Kirk 77 M1
Highbury Gt Lon 33 K5
Highbury Somset 22 F3
High Buston Nthumb 109 L8
High Callerton Nthumb 100 F4
High Casterton Cumb 89 Q11
High Catton E R Yk 86 D4
Highclere Hants 31 J10
Highcliffe Dorset 12 C6
High Close Dur 91 K4
High Cogges Oxon 42 H10
High Common Norfk 70 E11
High Coniscliffe Darltn 91 L4
High Crosby Cumb 98 F6
High Cross Cnwll 3 J8
High Cross E Ayrs 113 M12
High Cross Hants 25 M8
High Cross Herts 45 L8
Highcross Lancs 82 H7
High Cross W Susx 15 J7
High Cross Warwks 53 M7
High Drummore D & G 94 G11
High Dubmire Sundld 101 J8
High Easter Essex 46 A8
High Eggborough N York 86 A11
High Ellington N York 91 K10
Higher Alham Somset 22 F5
Higher Ansty Dorset 11 J4
Higher Ballam Lancs 83 J9
Higher Bartle Lancs 83 L8
Higher Berry End C Beds 44 D5
Higher Bockhampton Dorset 10 H6
Higher Brixham Torbay 5 Q6
Higher Burrowton Devon 9 J5
Higher Burwardsley Ches W 75 N12
High Ercall Wrekin 63 Q8
Higher Chillington Somset 10 B3
Higher Clovelly Devon 18 F8
Highercombe Somset 20 D7
Higher Coombe Dorset 10 E6
Higher Disley Ches E 76 H7
Higher Folds Wigan 76 C4
Higherford Lancs 84 C7
Higher Gabwell Devon 5 Q3
Higher Halstock Leigh Dorset 10 D3
Higher Harpers Lancs 84 B7
Higher Heysham Lancs 83 K3
Higher Hurdsfield Ches E 76 H8
Higher Irlam Salfd 76 D5
Higher Kingcombe Dorset 10 E5
Higher Kinnerton Flints 75 K11
Higher Marston Ches W 76 C8
Higher Muddiford Devon 19 L6
Higher Nyland Dorset 22 G9
Higher Ogden Rochdl 76 H1
Higher Pentire Cnwll 2 G9
Higher Penwortham Lancs 83 L9
Higher Prestacott Devon 7 M5
Higher Studfold N York 84 B1
Higher Town Cnwll 3 K5
Higher Town Cnwll 3 N2
Higher Town IoS 2 b1
Higher Tregantle Cnwll 4 F6
Higher Walton Lancs 83 N9
Higher Walton Warrtn 75 Q6
Higher Wambrook Somset 9 P3
Higher Waterston Dorset 10 H5
Higher Whatcombe Dorset 11 K4
Higher Wheelton Lancs 83 N10
Higher Whitley Ches W 76 B7
Higher Wincham Ches W 76 C8
Higher Wraxhall Dorset 10 E4
Higher Wych Ches W 63 N3
High Etherley Dur 91 K1
High Ferry Lincs 68 G2
Highfield E R Yk 86 D8
Highfield Gatesd 100 F6
Highfield N Ayrs 113 L11
Highfields Donc 78 E2
High Flats Kirk 77 N2
High Garrett Essex 46 D6
Highgate E Susx 15 M4
Highgate Gt Lon 33 K5
Highgate Kent 16 D5
High Grange Dur 100 F12
High Grantley N York 85 K1
High Green Cumb 89 L6
High Green Kirk 85 J12
High Green Norfk 58 H3
High Green Norfk 70 H11
High Green Sheff 77 Q4
High Green Shrops 52 C4
High Green Suffk 58 C8
High Green Worcs 41 P3
Highgreen Manor Nthumb 108 C11
High Halden Kent 16 F3
High Halstow Medway 34 D7
High Ham Somset 21 P7
High Harrington Cumb 88 D2
High Harrogate N York 85 L4
High Haswell Dur 101 K9
High Hatton Shrops 63 Q7
High Hauxley Nthumb 109 M9
High Hawsker N York 93 J5
High Hesket Cumb 98 F9
High Hoyland Barns 77 P2
High Hunsley E R Yk 86 H8
High Hurstwood E Susx 15 P5
High Hutton N York 86 D2
High Ireby Cumb 97 P10
High Kelling Norfk 70 G4
High Kilburn N York 92 B10
High Killerby N York 93 L10
High Knipe Cumb 89 N3
High Lands Dur 91 J2
Highlane Ches E 76 G10
Highlane Derbys 78 C7
High Lane Stockp 76 H6
High Lanes Cnwll 2 F7
High Laver Essex 45 P10
Highlaws Cumb 97 N8
Highleadon Gloucs 41 M7
High Legh Ches E 76 C7
Highleigh W Susx 13 P5
High Leven S on T 91 Q4
Highley Shrops 52 D4
High Littleton BaNES 29 K10
High Lorton Cumb 88 F2
High Marishes N York 92 G11
High Marnham Notts 79 K9
High Melton Donc 78 E3
High Mickley Nthumb 100 D6
Highmoor Cumb 98 B8
Highmoor Oxon 31 P5
Highmoor Cross Oxon 31 P5
Highmoor Hill Mons 28 F4
High Moorsley Sundld 101 J9
Highnam Gloucs 41 M8
Highnam Green Gloucs 41 M7
High Newport Sundld 101 K7
High Newton Cumb 89 L10
High Nibthwaite Cumb 89 J9
High Offley Staffs 64 E7
High Ongar Essex 45 Q11
High Onn Staffs 64 F9
High Park Corner Essex 47 J7
High Pennyvenie E Ayrs 105 J8
High Post Wilts 23 P6
Highridge N Som 28 H9
High Roding Essex 45 R8
High Row Cumb 89 K2
High Row Cumb 98 D11
High Salter Lancs 83 N3
High Salvington W Susx 14 G9
High Scales Cumb 97 N9
High Seaton Cumb 97 L12
High Shaw N York 90 E8
High Side Cumb 97 P12
High Spen Gatesd 100 E6
Highstead Kent 35 M9
Highsted Kent 34 F10
High Stoop Dur 100 E10
High Street Cnwll 3 N4
High Street Kent 16 D5
Highstreet Kent 35 K10
High Street Suffk 59 N6
High Street Suffk 59 N9
Highstreet Green Essex 46 D5
Highstreet Green Surrey 14 D4
Hightae D & G 97 M2
Highter's Heath Birm 53 K5
High Throston Hartpl 101 M11
Hightown Ches E 76 G11
Hightown Hants 12 B4
Hightown Sefton 75 J3
High Town Staffs 65 J9
Hightown Green Suffk 58 E9
High Toynton Lincs 80 F9
High Trewhitt Nthumb 108 G8
High Urpeth Dur 100 G7
High Valleyfield Fife 114 H4
High Warden Nthumb 99 P5
Highway Herefs 51 M10
Highway Wilts 30 B7
Highweek Devon 8 F10
High Westwood Dur 100 E7
Highwood Essex 46 B11
Highwood Staffs 65 L6
Highwood Hill Gt Lon 33 J4
High Woolaston Gloucs 29 J2
High Worsall N York 91 P5
Highworth Swindn 30 E4
High Wray Cumb 89 K7
High Wych Herts 45 N9
High Wycombe Bucks 32 B4
Hilborough Norfk 70 B12
Hilcote Derbys 78 D12
Hilcott Wilts 30 C10
Hildenborough Kent 15 Q1
Hilden Park Kent 15 Q1
Hildersham Cambs 57 K11
Hilderstone Staffs 64 H5
Hilderthorpe E R Yk 87 M2
Hilfield Dorset 10 G4
Hilgay Norfk 57 M1
Hill S Glos 29 K3
Hill Warwks 54 D7
Hillam N York 85 Q9
Hillbeck Cumb 90 C4
Hillborough Kent 35 M8
Hill Brow Hants 25 N8
Hillbutts Dorset 11 N4
Hill Chorlton Staffs 64 E4
Hillcliffane Derbys 65 P3
Hill Common Norfk 71 N7
Hill Common Somset 21 J8
Hill Deverill Wilts 23 J5
Hilldyke Lincs 68 G3
Hill End Dur 100 C11
Hill End Fife 115 J2
Hillend Fife 115 L4
Hill End Gloucs 41 P4
Hillend Mdloth 115 N8
Hillend N Lans 114 E8
Hillend Swans 26 B4
Hillersland Gloucs 40 H9
Hillerton Devon 8 D5
Hillesden Bucks 43 P6
Hillesley Gloucs 29 M4
Hillfarrance Somset 21 J8
Hill Green Kent 34 E10
Hillgrove W Susx 14 D5
Hillhampton Herefs 41 J2
Hillhead Abers 140 F8
Hillhead Devon 5 Q6
Hill Head Hants 13 J4
Hillhead S Lans 106 C2
Hillhead of Cocklaw Abers 141 Q7
Hilliard's Cross Staffs 65 M10
Hilliclay Highld 151 L4
Hillingdon Gt Lon 32 F6
Hillington C Glas 113 P8
Hillington Norfk 69 N7
Hillis Corner IoW 12 H6
Hillmorton Warwks 54 E6
Hillock Vale Lancs 84 A9
Hill of Beath Fife 115 L3
Hill of Fearn Highld 146 E9
Hillowton D & G 96 F5
Hillpool Worcs 52 G5
Hillpound Hants 25 K10
Hill Ridware Staffs 65 K8
Hillside Abers 133 M5
Hillside Angus 132 H12
Hillside Devon 5 L4
Hill Side Kirk 85 J11
Hill Side Worcs 52 D8
Hills Town Derbys 78 D9
Hillstreet Hants 24 E10
Hillswick Shet 147 h4
Hill Top Dur 90 G2
Hill Top Hants 12 F4
Hill Top Kirk 77 K1
Hill Top Rothm 78 C5
Hill Top Sandw 53 J2
Hill Top Wakefd 85 M12
Hillwell Shet 147 i9
Hilmarton Wilts 30 B7
Hilperton Wilts 29 P10
Hilperton Marsh Wilts 29 P10
Hilsea C Port 13 L4
Hilston E R Yk 87 P8
Hiltingbury Hants 24 G9
Hilton Border 117 K11
Hilton Cambs 56 F7
Hilton Cumb 90 B3
Hilton Derbys 65 N6
Hilton Dorset 11 J4
Hilton Dur 91 K2
Hilton Highld 146 F10
Hilton S on T 91 Q4
Hilton Shrops 52 E2
Hilton Park Services Staffs 64 H11
Himbleton Worcs 52 H9
Himley Staffs 52 G2
Hincaster Cumb 89 N10
Hinchley Wood Surrey 32 H9
Hinckley Leics 54 C2
Hinderclay Suffk 58 F5
Hinderwell N York 92 F3
Hindford Shrops 63 K5
Hindhead Surrey 14 C4
Hindhead Tunnel Surrey 14 C4
Hindle Fold Lancs 83 Q8
Hindley Nthumb 100 D6
Hindley Wigan 76 B3
Hindley Green Wigan 76 B3
Hindlip Worcs 52 G9
Hindolveston Norfk 70 F6
Hindon Wilts 23 K7
Hindringham Norfk 70 E5
Hingham Norfk 70 F11
Hinksford Staffs 52 F3
Hinstock Shrops 64 C7
Hintlesham Suffk 47 K3
Hinton Gloucs 41 K11
Hinton Hants 12 C6
Hinton Herefs 40 D4
Hinton S Glos 29 L7
Hinton Shrops 52 C4
Hinton Shrops 63 L10
Hinton Admiral Hants 12 C5
Hinton Ampner Hants 25 K8
Hinton Blewett BaNES 29 J11
Hinton Charterhouse BaNES 29 M10
Hinton Green Worcs 42 B4
Hinton-in-the-Hedges Nhants 43 M4
Hinton Marsh Hants 25 K8
Hinton Martell Dorset 11 N3
Hinton on the Green Worcs 42 B4
Hinton Parva Swindn 30 F6
Hinton St George Somset 21 P11
Hinton St Mary Dorset 22 H10
Hinton Waldrist Oxon 30 H2
Hints Shrops 51 Q6
Hints Staffs 65 M11
Hinwick Bed 55 M8
Hinxhill Kent 17 J2
Hinxton Cambs 45 P3
Hinxworth Herts 45 J4
Hipperholme Calder 84 H10
Hipsburn Nthumb 109 L7
Hipswell N York 91 K7
Hirn Abers 132 H4
Hirnant Powys 62 E7
Hirst Nthumb 109 M12
Hirst Courtney N York 86 B10
Hirwaen Denbgs 74 F11
Hirwaun Rhondd 39 M10
Hiscott Devon 19 K8
Histon Cambs 56 H8
Hitcham Suffk 58 E10
Hitcham Causeway Suffk 58 E10
Hitcham Street Suffk 58 E10
Hitchin Herts 44 H6
Hither Green Gt Lon 33 M7
Hittisleigh Devon 8 D5
Hive E R Yk 86 F9
Hixon Staffs 65 J7
Hoaden Kent 35 N10
Hoar Cross Staffs 65 L7
Hoarwithy Herefs 40 H6
Hoath Kent 35 M9
Hoathly Kent 16 B3
Hobarris Shrops 51 K5
Hobbles Green Suffk 57 N10
Hobbs Cross Essex 33 N2
Hobbs Cross Essex 45 P9
Hobkirk Border 107 P7
Hobland Hall Norfk 71 P11
Hobsick Notts 66 D2
Hobson Dur 100 F7
Hoby Leics 66 H8
Hoccombe Somset 20 H7
Hockering Norfk 70 G9
Hockerton Notts 79 J12
Hockley Ches E 76 H7
Hockley Covtry 53 P5
Hockley Essex 34 E4
Hockley Staffs 65 N12
Hockley Heath Solhll 53 M6
Hockliffe C Beds 44 D6
Hockwold cum Wilton Norfk 57 P3
Hockworthy Devon 20 G9
Hoddesdon Herts 45 L10
Hoddlesden Bl w D 83 Q10
Hoddom Cross D & G 97 N3
Hoddom Mains D & G 97 N4
Hodgehill Ches E 76 F9
Hodgeston Pembks 37 K10
Hodnet Shrops 63 Q6
Hodsock Notts 78 G6
Hodsoll Street Kent 34 A9
Hodson Swindn 30 E6
Hodthorpe Derbys 78 E8
Hoe Hants 25 J10
Hoe Norfk 70 E9
Hoe Benham W Berk 31 J8
Hoe Gate Hants 25 K10
Hoff Cumb 89 R3
Hogben's Hill Kent 35 J11
Hoggards Green Suffk 58 C9
Hoggeston Bucks 44 A7
Hoggrill's End Warwks 53 N2
Hog Hill E Susx 16 F7
Hoghton Lancs 83 N9
Hoghton Bottoms Lancs 83 N10
Hognaston Derbys 65 N2
Hogsthorpe Lincs 81 K9
Holbeach Lincs 68 G7
Holbeach Bank Lincs 68 G7
Holbeach Clough Lincs 68 G7
Holbeach Drove Lincs 68 F9
Holbeach Hurn Lincs 68 G7
Holbeach St Johns Lincs 68 G8
Holbeach St Mark's Lincs 68 G6
Holbeach St Matthew Lincs 68 H6
Holbeck Notts 78 E9
Holbeck Woodhouse Notts 78 F9
Holberrow Green Worcs 53 J9
Holbeton Devon 5 K6
Holborn Gt Lon 33 K6
Holborough Kent 34 C9
Holbrook Derbys 66 B3
Holbrook Sheff 78 D7
Holbrook Suffk 47 L4
Holbrook Moor Derbys 66 B3
Holbrooks Covtry 53 Q4
Holburn Nthumb 108 G3
Holbury Hants 12 G4
Holcombe Devon 8 H9
Holcombe Somset 22 F3
Holcombe Rogus Devon 20 G9
Holcot Nhants 55 K7
Holden Lancs 84 B5
Holdenby Nhants 54 H7
Holden Gate Calder 84 D10
Holder's Green Essex 46 B6
Holdgate Shrops 51 P3
Holdingham Lincs 67 Q3
Holditch Dorset 9 Q4
Holdsworth Calder 84 G9
Holehouse Derbys 77 J5
Hole-in-the-Wall Herefs 41 J6
Holemoor Devon 7 M4
Hole Street W Susx 14 G8
Holford Somset 21 J5
Holgate C York 86 A5
Holker Cumb 89 K11
Holkham Norfk 70 C3
Hollacombe Devon 7 M4
Holland Fen Lincs 68 E2
Holland Lees Lancs 75 N2
Holland-on-Sea Essex 47 M8
Hollandstoun Ork 147 f1
Hollee D & G 98 B4
Hollesley Suffk 47 P3
Hollicombe Torbay 5 Q4
Hollingbourne Kent 34 E11
Hollingbury Br & H 15 K9
Hollingdon Bucks 44 C6
Hollingthorpe Leeds 85 M9
Hollington Derbys 65 N4
Hollington Staffs 65 K4
Hollingworth Tamesd 77 J4
Hollinlane Ches E 76 F7
Hollins Bury 76 E2
Hollins Derbys 77 Q9
Hollins Staffs 65 J3
Hollinsclough Staffs 77 K10
Hollins End Sheff 78 C7
Hollins Green Warrtn 76 C5
Hollins Lane Lancs 83 L5
Hollinswood Wrekin 64 D10
Hollinwood Shrops 63 N5
Hollingrove E Susx 16 C6
Hollocombe Devon 8 B2
Holloway Derbys 77 Q12
Holloway Gt Lon 33 K5
Holloway Wilts 23 J7
Hollowell Nhants 54 H6
Hollowmoor Heath Ches W 75 N10
Hollows D & G 98 E3
Hollybush Caerph 39 R11
Hollybush E Ayrs 104 G7
Hollybush Herefs 41 M4
Holly End Norfk 69 J11
Holly Green Worcs 41 P3
Hollyhurst Ches E 63 P3
Hollym E R Yk 87 Q10
Hollywood Worcs 53 K5
Holmbridge Kirk 77 L2
Holmbury St Mary Surrey 14 G2
Holmbush Cnwll 3 P4
Holmcroft Staffs 64 G7
Holme Cambs 56 D3
Holme Cumb 89 N11
Holme Kirk 77 L2
Holme N Linc 79 M2
Holme N York 91 N10
Holme Notts 79 K11
Holme Chapel Lancs 84 C9
Holme Green N York 85 Q7
Holme Hale Norfk 70 C10
Holme Lacy Herefs 40 H5
Holme Marsh Herefs 51 K9
Holme next the Sea Norfk 69 N3
Holme on the Wolds E R Yk 86 H6
Holme Pierrepont Notts 66 G4
Holmer Herefs 40 G3
Holmer Green Bucks 32 C3
Holme St Cuthbert Cumb 97 M9
Holmes Chapel Ches E 76 E10
Holmesfield Derbys 77 Q8
Holmes Hill E Susx 15 P8
Holmeswood Lancs 83 K12
Holmethorpe Surrey 33 K12
Holme upon Spalding Moor E R Yk 86 E7
Holmewood Derbys 78 C10
Holmfield Calder 84 G9
Holmfirth Kirk 77 L2
Holmhead E Ayrs 105 K6
Holmpton E R Yk 87 Q10
Holmrook Cumb 88 E7
Holmsford Bridge Crematorium N Ayrs 104 G2
Holmshurst E Susx 16 B6
Holmside Dur 100 G8
Holmwrangle Cumb 98 G8
Holne Devon 5 L3
Holnest Dorset 10 G3
Holnicote Somset 20 E4
Holsworthy Devon 7 L4
Holsworthy Beacon Devon 7 L3
Holt Dorset 11 P4
Holt Norfk 70 G4
Holt Wilts 29 P10
Holt Worcs 52 F8
Holt Wrexhm 63 L1
Holtby C York 86 C4
Holt End Worcs 53 K7
Holt Fleet Worcs 52 F8
Holt Green Lancs 75 L3
Holt Heath Dorset 11 P4
Holt Heath Worcs 52 F8
Holton Oxon 43 M10
Holton Somset 22 F8
Holton Suffk 59 M5
Holton cum Beckering Lincs 80 C7
Holton Heath Dorset 11 M6
Holton Hill E Susx 16 B6
Holton le Clay Lincs 80 F3
Holton le Moor Lincs 79 Q4
Holton St Mary Suffk 47 J4
Holt Street Kent 35 N12
Holtye E Susx 15 N3
Holway Flints 74 G8
Holwell Dorset 10 H2
Holwell Herts 44 H5
Holwell Leics 67 J7
Holwell Oxon 42 F10
Holwick Dur 90 E1
Holworth Dorset 11 J8
Holybourne Hants 25 M5
Holy Cross Worcs 52 G5
Holyfield Essex 45 M11
Holyhead IoA 72 D7
Holy Island IoA 72 D7
Holy Island Nthumb 109 J1
Holy Island Nthumb 109 J1
Holymoorside Derbys 77 Q10
Holyport W & M 32 C7
Holystone Nthumb 108 F9
Holytown N Lans 114 D9
Holytown Crematorium N Lans 114 D9
Holywell C Beds 44 E8
Holywell Cambs 56 G6
Holywell Cnwll 3 J3
Holywell Dorset 10 F4
Holywell Flints 74 G8
Holywell Nthumb 101 J3
Holywell Warwks 53 M7
Holywell Green Calder 84 G11
Holywell Lake Somset 20 H9
Holywell Row Suffk 57 N5
Holywood D & G 97 J2
Holywood Village D & G 97 J2
Homer Shrops 64 B12
Homer Green Sefton 75 K3
Homersfield Suffk 59 K3
Homescales Cumb 89 N9
Hom Green Herefs 41 J7
Homington Wilts 23 P8
Honeyborough Pembks 37 J9
Honeybourne Worcs 42 D3
Honeychurch Devon 8 B4
Honey Hill Kent 35 K10
Honeystreet Wilts 30 C10
Honey Tye Suffk 46 G4
Honiley Warwks 53 N6
Honing Norfk 71 L6
Honingham Norfk 70 G10
Honington Lincs 67 N3
Honington Suffk 58 D6
Honington Warwks 42 F3
Honiton Devon 9 M5
Honley Kirk 77 L1
Honnington Wrekin 64 D9
Honor Oak Crematorium Gt Lon 33 L7
Hoo Kent 35 N9
Hoobrook Worcs 52 F6
Hood Green Barns 77 P3
Hood Hill Rothm 78 B4
Hooe C Plym 4 H6
Hooe E Susx 16 C8
Hoo End Herts 44 H7
Hoo Green Ches E 76 D7
Hoohill Bpool 82 H7
Hook Cambs 56 H2
Hook Devon 9 Q4
Hook E R Yk 86 E10
Hook Gt Lon 32 H9
Hook Hants 12 H4
Hook Hants 25 M3
Hook Pembks 37 J8
Hook Wilts 30 C5
Hookagate Shrops 63 M10
Hook Bank Worcs 41 N3
Hooke Dorset 10 E5
Hook End Essex 33 Q2
Hookgate Staffs 64 D5
Hook Green Kent 16 B4
Hook Green Kent 33 R8
Hook Norton Oxon 42 H5
Hook Street Gloucs 29 K2
Hook Street Wilts 30 C5
Hookway Devon 8 F5
Hookwood Surrey 15 J2
Hooley Surrey 33 K11
Hooley Bridge Rochdl 76 F1
Hoo Meavy Devon 4 H3
Hoo St Werburgh Medway 34 D8
Hooton Ches W 75 L8
Hooton Levitt Rothm 78 E5
Hooton Pagnell Donc 78 D2
Hooton Roberts Rothm 78 D4
Hopcrofts Holt Oxon 43 K7
Hope Derbys 77 M7
Hope Devon 5 L8
Hope Flints 75 K12
Hope Powys 63 J10
Hope Shrops 63 K12
Hope Staffs 65 L1
Hope Bagot Shrops 51 Q6
Hope Bowdler Shrops 51 N2
Hope End Green Essex 45 Q7
Hopehouse Border 107 J6
Hopeman Moray 147 L11
Hope Mansell Herefs 41 J8
Hopesay Shrops 51 L4
Hopetown Wakefd 85 N10
Hope under Dinmore Herefs 51 N10
Hopgrove C York 86 B4
Hopperton N York 85 N4
Hop Pole Lincs 68 D9
Hopsford Warwks 54 C4
Hopstone Shrops 52 E2
Hopton Derbys 65 N2
Hopton Shrops 63 L8
Hopton Staffs 64 H7
Hopton Suffk 58 E5
Hopton Cangeford Shrops 51 P4
Hopton Castle Shrops 51 L5
Hoptonheath Shrops 51 L5
Hopton on Sea Norfk 71 Q12
Hopton Wafers Shrops 52 B5
Hopwas Staffs 65 M11
Hopwood Rochdl 76 F2
Hopwood Worcs 53 J5
Hopwood Park Services Worcs 53 J6
Horam E Susx 15 Q7
Horbling Lincs 68 C5
Horbury Wakefd 85 L11
Horcott Gloucs 30 D2
Horden Dur 101 L10
Horderley Shrops 51 L3
Hordle Hants 12 D6
Hordley Shrops 63 L6
Horeb Carmth 38 D10
Horeb Cerdgn 38 B3
Horfield Bristl 29 J7
Horham Suffk 59 J6
Horkesley Heath Essex 46 H6
Horkstow N Linc 87 J11
Horley Oxon 43 J3
Horley Surrey 15 K2
Hornblotton Green Somset 22 D6
Hornby Lancs 83 N2
Hornby N York 91 L8
Hornby N York 91 N5
Horncastle Lincs 80 E10
Hornchurch Gt Lon 33 P5
Horncliffe Nthumb 117 K11
Horndean Border 117 K11
Horndean Hants 25 M10
Horndon Devon 7 P8
Horndon on the Hill Thurr 34 B6
Horne Surrey 15 L2
Horner Somset 20 D4
Horne Row Essex 46 D10
Horners Green Suffk 46 G3
Horney Common E Susx 15 N6
Horn Hill Bucks 32 E4
Horning Norfk 71 L8
Horninghold Leics 55 K1
Horninglow Staffs 65 N7
Horningsea Cambs 57 J8
Horningsham Wilts 22 H5
Horningtoft Norfk 70 D7
Horningtops Cnwll 4 D4
Hornsbury Somset 9 Q3
Hornsby Cumb 98 G8

Kildavanan – Lealholm Side

177

Kildavanan Ag & B 112 F8
Kildonan Highld 146 G1
Kildonan N Ayrs 103 Q5
Kildonan Lodge Highld 150 G12
Kildonnan Highld 127 J7
Kildrochet House D & G 94 F7
Kildrummy Abers 140 D12
Kildwick N York 84 F6
Kilfinan Ag & B 112 D5
Kilfinnan Highld 129 J5
Kilford Denbgs 74 E10
Kilgetty Pembks 37 M9
Kilgrammie S Ayrs 104 E9
Kilgwrrwg Common Mons 28 G3
Kilham E R Yk 87 K2
Kilham Nthumb 108 E3
Kilkenneth Ag & B 118 C4
Kilkenzie Ag & B 103 J5
Kilkerran Ag & B 103 K6
Kilkhampton Cnwll 7 J2
Killamarsh Derbys 78 D7
Killay Swans 26 F4
Killearn Stirlg 113 Q4
Killen Highld 138 C4
Killerby Darltn 91 K3
Killerton Devon 9 J5
Killichonan P & K 122 F1
Killiechonate Highld 129 J8
Killiechronan Ag & B 119 P4
Killiecrankie P & K 130 G11
Killilan Highld 136 C10
Killimster Highld 151 P5
Killin Stirlg 122 F6
Killinghall N York 85 L3
Killington Cumb 89 Q9
Killington Devon 19 N4
Killington Lake Services Cumb 89 P8
Killingworth N Tyne 100 H4
Killiow Cnwll 3 K6
Killochyett Border 116 B12
Kilmacolm Inver 113 M7
Kilmahog Stirlg 122 G11
Kilmahumaig Ag & B 112 A3
Kilmaluag Highld 142 E10
Kilmany Fife 124 H8
Kilmarnock E Ayrs 104 H2
Kilmartin Ag & B 112 B2
Kilmaurs E Ayrs 104 G2
Kilmelford Ag & B 120 F10
Kilmersdon Somset 22 F3
Kilmeston Hants 25 K8
Kilmichael Ag & B 103 J5
Kilmichael Glassary Ag & B 112 C3
Kilmichael of Inverlussa Ag & B 112 A4
Kilmington Devon 9 P5
Kilmington Wilts 22 H6
Kilmington Common Wilts 22 H6
Kilmington Street Wilts 22 H6
Kilmorack Highld 137 N7
Kilmore Ag & B 120 G8
Kilmore Highld 127 M3
Kilmory Ag & B 111 P6
Kilmory Highld 127 J10
Kilmory N Ayrs 103 P5
Kilmuir Highld 134 D6
Kilmuir Highld 138 C6
Kilmuir Highld 142 D11
Kilmuir Highld 146 D10
Kilmun Ag & B 112 H5
Kilnave Ag & B 110 G7
Kilncadzow S Lans 114 F11
Kilndown Kent 16 C4
Kiln Green Wokham 32 A6
Kilnhill Cumb 97 P11
Kilnhouses Ches W 76 B10
Kilnhurst Rothm 78 D4
Kilninver Ag & B 120 F8
Kiln Pit Hill Nthumb 100 D7
Kilnsea E R Yk 87 R12
Kilnsey N York 84 E2
Kilnwick E R Yk 87 J5
Kilnwick Percy E R Yk 86 F5
Kiloran Ag & B 111 J2
Kilpatrick N Ayrs 103 N4
Kilpeck Herefs 40 F5
Kilpin E R Yk 86 E10
Kilpin Pike E R Yk 86 E10
Kilrenny Fife 125 L11
Kilsby Nhants 54 F6
Kilspindie P & K 124 E7
Kilstay D & G 94 G10
Kilsyth N Lans 114 C6
Kiltarlity Highld 137 N7
Kilton R & Cl 92 E3
Kilton Thorpe R & Cl 92 E3
Kilvaxter Highld 142 D11
Kilve Somset 21 J5
Kilvington Notts 67 K4
Kilwinning N Ayrs 104 E1
Kimberley Norfk 70 G11
Kimberley Notts 66 E3
Kimberworth Rothm 78 C5
Kimblesworth Dur 100 H8
Kimble Wick Bucks 44 A10
Kimbolton Cambs 56 B7
Kimbolton Herefs 51 N8
Kimcote Leics 54 F3
Kimmeridge Dorset 11 M9
Kimmerston Nthumb 108 F3
Kimpton Hants 24 D4
Kimpton Herts 44 H8
Kimworthy Devon 18 F10
Kinbrace Highld 150 F10
Kinbuck Stirlg 123 K11
Kincaple Fife 125 J9
Kincardine Fife 114 G4
Kincardine Highld 145 N7
Kincardine Bridge Fife 114 G4
Kincardine O'Neil Abers 132 F4
Kinclaven P & K 124 C5
Kincorth C Aber 133 M4
Kincorth House Moray 139 J3
Kincraig Highld 130 F3
Kincraigie P & K 123 P3
Kindallachan P & K 123 P3
Kinerarach Ag & B 111 P10
Kineton Gloucs 42 C6
Kineton Warwks 53 Q10
Kinfauns P & K 124 D8
Kingarth Ag & B 112 G10
Kingcausie Abers 133 L4
Kingcoed Mons 40 F10
Kingerby Lincs 79 Q5
Kingford Devon 7 K3
Kingham Oxon 42 F7
Kingholm Quay D & G 97 K3
Kinghorn Fife 115 N4
Kinglassie Fife 115 N2
Kingoldrum Angus 124 G2
Kingoodie P & K 124 G7
King's Acre Herefs 40 G3
Kingsand Cnwll 4 G6
Kingsash Bucks 44 C10
Kingsbarns Fife 125 L10
Kingsbridge Devon 5 M8
Kingsbridge Somset 20 F6
Kings Bridge Swans 26 E3
King's Bromley Staffs 65 L9
Kingsburgh Highld 134 G5
Kingsbury Gt Lon 32 H5
Kingsbury Warwks 53 N1
Kingsbury Episcopi Somset 21 P9
King's Caple Herefs 40 H6
Kingsclere Hants 31 L10
King's Cliffe Nhants 55 P1
Kings Clipstone Notts 78 G10
Kingscote Gloucs 29 N3
Kingscott Devon 19 K9
King's Coughton Warwks 53 K9
Kingscross N Ayrs 103 R4
Kingsdon Somset 22 C8
Kingsdown Kent 17 Q1
Kingsdown Swindn 30 D5
Kingsdown Wilts 29 N9
Kingsdown Crematorium Swindn 30 E4
Kingseat Fife 115 L3
Kingsey Bucks 43 Q10
Kingsfold W Susx 14 H4
Kingsford C Aber 133 K3
Kingsford E Ayrs 113 N11
Kingsford Worcs 52 F4
Kingsgate Kent 35 Q8
Kings Green Gloucs 41 M5
Kingshall Street Suffk 58 D8
Kingsheanton Devon 19 L6
King's Heath Birm 53 K4
Kings Hill Kent 34 B11
King's Hill Wsall 52 H1
Kings House Hotel Highld 121 P2
Kingshouse Hotel Stirlg 122 F8
Kingshurst Solhll 53 M3
Kingside Hill Cumb 97 N8
Kingskerswell Devon 5 P3
Kingskettle Fife 124 F11
Kingsland Dorset 10 C5
Kingsland Herefs 51 M8
Kingsland IoA 72 D7
Kings Langley Herts 44 F11
Kingsley Ches W 75 P9
Kingsley Hants 25 N6
Kingsley Staffs 65 J3
Kingsley Green W Susx 14 C5
Kingsley Park Nhants 55 J8
Kingslow Shrops 52 E1
King's Lynn Norfk 69 M8
Kings Meaburn Cumb 89 Q2
Kingsmead Hants 25 K10
King's Mills Guern 12 b2
Kings Moss St Hel 75 N3
Kingsmuir Angus 125 J3
Kings Muir Border 106 H2
Kingsmuir Fife 125 K11
Kings Newnham Warwks 54 D5
King's Newton Derbys 66 C7
Kingsnorth Kent 16 H3
King's Norton Birm 53 K5
King's Norton Leics 66 H12
Kings Nympton Devon 19 N9
King's Pyon Herefs 51 M10
Kings Ripton Cambs 56 E5
King's Somborne Hants 24 F7
King's Stag Dorset 10 H3
King's Stanley Gloucs 41 N11
King's Sutton Nhants 43 K4
Kingstanding Birm 53 K2
Kingsteignton Devon 8 G10
King Sterndale Derbys 77 K9
Kingsthorne Herefs 40 G5
Kingsthorpe Nhants 55 J8
Kingston Cambs 56 F9
Kingston Cnwll 7 L9
Kingston Devon 5 K7
Kingston Devon 9 K7
Kingston Dorset 11 J3
Kingston Dorset 11 M9
Kingston E Loth 116 D5
Kingston Hants 12 B4
Kingston IoW 12 H8
Kingston Kent 35 M12
Kingston W Susx 14 F10
Kingston Bagpuize Oxon 31 J3
Kingston Blount Oxon 31 Q2
Kingston Deverill Wilts 23 J6
Kingstone Herefs 40 F5
Kingstone Somset 21 N10
Kingstone Staffs 65 K6
Kingstone Winslow Oxon 30 F5
Kingston Lacy House & Gardens Dorset 11 N4
Kingston Lisle Oxon 30 G5
Kingston near Lewes E Susx 15 M9
Kingston on Soar Notts 66 E6
Kingston on Spey Moray 139 Q3
Kingston Russell Dorset 10 F6
Kingston St Mary Somset 21 K7
Kingston Seymour N Som 28 E9
Kingston Stert Oxon 31 Q2
Kingston upon Hull C KuH 87 K9
Kingston upon Thames Gt Lon 32 H8
Kingston upon Thames Crematorium Gt Lon 32 H8
Kingstown Cumb 98 E6
King's Walden Herts 44 H7
Kingswear Devon 5 Q6
Kingswells C Aber 133 L3
Kings Weston Bristl 28 H7
Kingswinford Dudley 52 G3
Kingswood Bucks 43 P8
Kingswood Gloucs 29 M4
Kingswood Kent 34 E12
Kingswood Powys 62 H11
Kingswood S Glos 29 K7
Kingswood Somset 20 H6
Kingswood Surrey 33 J11
Kingswood Warwks 53 M6
Kingswood Brook Warwks 53 M6
Kingswood Common Herefs 51 J10
Kingswood Common Staffs 64 F11
Kings Worthy Hants 24 H7
Kingthorpe Lincs 80 C8
Kington Herefs 51 J9
Kington S Glos 29 J4
Kington Worcs 53 J9
Kington Langley Wilts 29 Q7
Kington Magna Dorset 22 G9
Kington St Michael Wilts 29 P7
Kingussie Highld 130 D4
Kingweston Somset 22 C7
Kinharrachie Abers 141 M9
Kinharvie D & G 97 J5
Kinkell Bridge P & K 123 N9
Kinknockie Abers 141 N7
Kinleith C Edin 115 M8
Kinlet Shrops 52 D4
Kinloch Highld 126 G4
Kinloch Highld 148 H9
Kinloch Highld 149 M6
Kinloch P & K 124 C4
Kinlochard Stirlg 122 D12
Kinlochbervie Highld 148 F5
Kinlocheil Highld 128 D8
Kinlochewe Highld 136 E3
Kinloch Hourn Highld 128 C3
Kinlochlaggan Highld 129 Q7
Kinlochleven Highld 128 H12
Kinlochmoidart Highld 127 M9
Kinlochnanuagh Highld 127 N7
Kinloch Rannoch P & K 122 H1
Kinloss Moray 139 K3
Kinmel Bay Conwy 74 D7
Kinmuck Abers 141 K12
Kinmundy Abers 141 L12
Kinnabus Ag & B 102 B1
Kinnadie Abers 141 N7
Kinnaird P & K 123 N1
Kinneff Abers 133 K9
Kinnelhead D & G 106 D9
Kinnell Angus 125 M3
Kinnerley Shrops 63 K8
Kinnersley Herefs 51 K10
Kinnersley Worcs 41 P3
Kinnerton Powys 50 H8
Kinnerton Shrops 51 L1
Kinnerton Green Flints 75 K11
Kinnesswood P & K 124 D12
Kinninvie Dur 90 H2
Kinnordy Angus 124 G2
Kinoulton Notts 66 H6
Kinross P & K 124 C12
Kinrossie P & K 124 D6
Kinross Services P & K 124 C12
Kinsbourne Green Herts 44 G8
Kinsey Heath Ches E 64 C4
Kinsham Herefs 51 K7
Kinsham Worcs 41 Q4
Kinsley Wakefd 85 N12
Kinson Bmouth 11 P5
Kintail Highld 136 D12
Kintbury W Berk 30 H9
Kintessack Moray 139 J4
Kintillo P & K 124 C9
Kinton Herefs 51 L6
Kinton Shrops 63 L8
Kintore Abers 133 J1
Kintour Ag & B 111 K11
Kintra Ag & B 110 H11
Kintra Ag & B 119 K8
Kintraw Ag & B 120 F11
Kintyre Ag & B 103 K2
Kinveachy Highld 138 G12
Kinver Staffs 52 F4
Kiplin N York 91 M7
Kippax Leeds 85 N9
Kippen Stirlg 114 B2
Kippford D & G 96 G7
Kipping's Cross Kent 16 B3
Kirbister Ork 147 c5
Kirby Bedon Norfk 71 K11
Kirby Bellars Leics 67 J8
Kirby Cane Norfk 59 M2
Kirby Corner Covtry 53 P5
Kirby Cross Essex 47 M7
Kirby Fields Leics 66 E11
Kirby Grindalythe N York 86 G2
Kirby Hill N York 85 N2
Kirby Hill N York 91 J5
Kirby Knowle N York 91 Q9
Kirby-le-Soken Essex 47 M7
Kirby Misperton N York 92 F10
Kirby Muxloe Leics 66 E11
Kirby Sigston N York 91 P8
Kirby Underdale E R Yk 86 E3
Kirby Wiske N York 91 P9
Kirdford W Susx 14 E5
Kirk Highld 151 N5
Kirkabister Shet 147 i8
Kirkandrews D & G 96 C8
Kirkandrews upon Eden Cumb 98 D6
Kirkbampton Cumb 98 C7
Kirkbean D & G 97 K6
Kirk Bramwith Donc 78 G1
Kirkbride Cumb 97 P7
Kirkbridge N York 91 L8
Kirkbuddo Angus 125 K4
Kirkburn Border 107 J2
Kirkburn E R Yk 86 H4
Kirkburton Kirk 77 M1
Kirkby Knows 75 L4
Kirkby Lincs 79 Q5
Kirkby N York 92 B5
Kirkby Fleetham N York 91 M8
Kirkby Green Lincs 80 B12
Kirkby-in-Ashfield Notts 78 E12
Kirkby-in-Furness Cumb 88 H10
Kirkby la Thorpe Lincs 68 B3
Kirkby Lonsdale Cumb 89 P11
Kirkby Malham N York 84 D3
Kirkby Mallory Leics 66 D12
Kirkby Malzeard N York 91 L11
Kirkby Mills N York 92 E9
Kirkbymoorside N York 92 E9
Kirkby on Bain Lincs 80 E11
Kirkby Overblow N York 85 L5
Kirkby Stephen Cumb 90 C5
Kirkby Thore Cumb 89 Q2
Kirkby Underwood Lincs 67 Q7
Kirkby Wharf N York 85 Q7
Kirkby Woodhouse Notts 66 E1
Kirkcaldy Fife 115 P3
Kirkcaldy Crematorium Fife 115 N2
Kirkcambeck Cumb 98 G4
Kirkchrist D & G 96 D8
Kirkcolm D & G 94 E4
Kirkconnel D & G 105 N7
Kirkconnell D & G 97 K5
Kirkcowan D & G 95 L6
Kirkcudbright D & G 96 D8
Kirkdale Lpool 75 K5
Kirk Deighton N York 85 N5
Kirk Ella E R Yk 87 J9
Kirkfieldbank S Lans 105 R1
Kirkgunzeon D & G 96 H5
Kirk Hallam Derbys 66 D3
Kirkham Lancs 83 K9
Kirkham N York 86 D2
Kirkhamgate Wakefd 85 L10
Kirk Hammerton N York 85 P4
Kirkharle Nthumb 100 C2
Kirkhaugh Nthumb 99 K8
Kirkheaton Kirk 85 J11
Kirkheaton Nthumb 100 C3
Kirkhill Highld 137 P7
Kirkhope S Lans 106 C8
Kirkhouse Cumb 98 H6
Kirkhouse Green Donc 78 G1
Kirkibost Highld 135 K12
Kirkinch P & K 124 F4
Kirkinner D & G 95 M8
Kirkintilloch E Duns 114 B6
Kirk Ireton Derbys 65 P2
Kirkland Cumb 88 E3
Kirkland Cumb 99 J11
Kirkland D & G 105 N7
Kirkland D & G 105 Q11
Kirkland D & G 106 D11
Kirkland Guards Cumb 97 N10
Kirk Langley Derbys 65 P4
Kirkleatham R & Cl 92 C2
Kirkleatham Crematorium R & Cl 92 C2
Kirklevington S on T 91 Q5
Kirkley Suffk 59 Q2
Kirklington N York 91 N10
Kirklington Notts 78 H12
Kirklinton Cumb 98 E5
Kirkliston C Edin 115 L6
Kirkmabreck D & G 95 N7
Kirkmaiden D & G 94 G11
Kirk Merrington Dur 100 H12
Kirk Michael IoM 102 d4
Kirkmichael P & K 131 K12
Kirkmichael S Ayrs 104 F8
Kirkmuirhill S Lans 105 P1
Kirknewton Nthumb 108 E4
Kirknewton W Loth 115 L8
Kirkney Abers 140 D9
Kirk of Shotts N Lans 114 F8
Kirkoswald Cumb 98 H10
Kirkoswald S Ayrs 104 D8
Kirkpatrick D & G 106 B11
Kirkpatrick Durham D & G 96 F4
Kirkpatrick-Fleming D & G 98 C4
Kirk Sandall Donc 78 G2
Kirksanton Cumb 88 F10
Kirk Smeaton N York 85 Q12
Kirkstall Leeds 85 K8
Kirkstead Lincs 80 D11
Kirkstile Abers 140 E9
Kirkstile D & G 107 K11
Kirkstone Pass Inn Cumb 89 L5
Kirkstyle Highld 151 P2
Kirkthorpe Wakefd 85 M11
Kirkton Abers 140 G10
Kirkton D & G 97 K2
Kirkton Fife 124 G8
Kirkton Highld 135 Q10
Kirkton Highld 136 C7
Kirkton P & K 123 N9
Kirkton Manor Border 106 G2
Kirkton of Airlie Angus 124 F3
Kirkton of Auchterhouse Angus 124 G5
Kirkton of Barevan Highld 138 F6
Kirkton of Collace P & K 124 D6
Kirkton of Glenbuchat Abers 132 B1
Kirkton of Logie Buchan Abers 141 N10
Kirkton of Maryculter Abers 133 K4
Kirkton of Menmuir Angus 132 E11
Kirkton of Monikie Angus 125 K5
Kirkton of Rayne Abers 140 H10
Kirkton of Skene Abers 133 K3
Kirkton of Strathmartine Angus 124 H6
Kirkton of Tealing Angus 124 H5
Kirkton of Tough Abers 132 F2
Kirktown Abers 141 N3
Kirktown Abers 141 Q5
Kirktown of Alvah Abers 140 G4
Kirktown of Bourtie Abers 141 K10
Kirktown of Fetteresso Abers 133 K7
Kirktown of Mortlach Moray 139 P8
Kirktown of Slains Abers 141 P10
Kirkurd Border 106 F1
Kirkwall Ork 147 c4
Kirkwall Airport Ork 147 d5
Kirkwhelpington Nthumb 100 C1
Kirk Yetholm Border 108 D4
Kirmington N Linc 80 B1
Kirmond le Mire Lincs 80 D5
Kirn Ag & B 112 H6
Kirriemuir Angus 124 H2
Kirstead Green Norfk 59 L1
Kirtlebridge D & G 97 P4
Kirtling Cambs 57 N9
Kirtling Green Cambs 57 N9
Kirtlington Oxon 43 K8
Kirtomy Highld 150 D4
Kirton Lincs 68 F4
Kirton Notts 78 H10
Kirton Suffk 47 N4
Kirton End Lincs 68 F4
Kirtonhill W Duns 113 M6
Kirton Holme Lincs 68 E4
Kirton in Lindsey N Linc 79 M4
Kirwaugh D & G 95 M7
Kishorn Highld 135 Q8
Kislingbury Nhants 54 H9
Kitebrook Warwks 42 F5
Kite Green Warwks 53 M7
Kites Hardwick Warwks 54 D7
Kitleigh Cnwll 7 J5
Kitt Green Wigan 75 P3
Kittisford Somset 20 H9
Kittle Swans 26 E4
Kitt's Green Birm 53 M3
Kittybrewster C Aber 133 M3
Kitwood Hants 25 L7
Kivernoll Herefs 40 G5
Kiveton Park Rothm 78 E7
Knaith Lincs 79 L7
Knaith Park Lincs 79 L6
Knap Corner Dorset 22 H8
Knaphill Surrey 32 D10
Knapp Somset 21 M8
Knapp Hill Hants 24 G8
Knapthorpe Notts 79 J12
Knapton C York 85 R5
Knapton N York 92 H11
Knapton Norfk 71 L5
Knapton Green Herefs 51 M10
Knapwell Cambs 56 F8
Knaresborough N York 85 M4
Knarsdale Nthumb 99 K7
Knaven Abers 141 L7
Knayton N York 91 Q9
Knebworth Herts 45 J7
Knedlington E R Yk 86 D9
Kneesall Notts 78 H11
Kneeton Notts 66 H3
Knelston Swans 26 C5
Knenhall Staffs 64 G5
Knettishall Suffk 58 E4
Knightacott Devon 19 M5
Knightcote Warwks 54 C9
Knightley Staffs 64 E7
Knightley Dale Staffs 64 F7
Knighton C Leic 66 G12
Knighton Devon 4 H7
Knighton Dorset 10 F2
Knighton Poole 11 P5
Knighton Powys 51 J6
Knighton Somset 21 K4
Knighton Staffs 64 D4
Knighton Staffs 64 D7
Knighton Wilts 30 G8
Knighton on Teme Worcs 52 B6
Knightsbridge Gloucs 41 P6
Knightsmill Cnwll 6 F8
Knightwick Worcs 52 D9
Knill Herefs 51 J8
Knipton Leics 67 K6
Knitsley Dur 100 E8
Kniveton Derbys 65 N2
Knock Cumb 89 R1
Knock Highld 127 M2
Knock Moray 140 E5
Knock W Isls 152 g3
Knockally Highld 151 L10
Knockan Highld 144 F3
Knockando Moray 139 M7
Knockbain Highld 137 P7
Knockbain Highld 138 B5
Knock Castle N Ayrs 113 J8
Knockdee Highld 151 L4
Knockdow Ag & B 112 G7
Knockdown Wilts 29 N5
Knockeen S Ayrs 104 F10
Knockenkelly N Ayrs 103 Q4
Knockentiber E Ayrs 104 G2
Knockhall Kent 33 Q7
Knockholt Kent 33 N10
Knockholt Pound Kent 33 N10
Knockin Shrops 63 K7
Knockinlaw E Ayrs 104 H2
Knockmill Kent 33 Q10
Knocknain D & G 94 D5
Knockrome Ag & B 111 M7
Knocksharry IoM 102 c4
Knocksheen D & G 96 C2
Knockvennie Smithy D & G 96 F4
Knodishall Suffk 59 N8
Knodishall Common Suffk 59 N8
Knole Somset 22 B8
Knole Park S Glos 29 J6
Knolls Green Ches E 76 E8
Knolton Wrexhm 63 L4
Knook Wilts 23 L5
Knossington Leics 67 K10
Knott End-on-Sea Lancs 83 J5
Knotting Bed 55 P8
Knotting Green Bed 55 P8
Knottingley Wakefd 85 Q10
Knotty Ash Lpool 75 L5
Knotty Green Bucks 32 D4
Knowbury Shrops 51 P6
Knowe D & G 95 K4
Knowehead D & G 105 L11
Knoweside S Ayrs 104 E7
Knowle Bristl 29 J8
Knowle Devon 8 E4
Knowle Devon 9 J8
Knowle Devon 9 K8
Knowle Devon 19 J6
Knowle Shrops 51 Q6
Knowle Solhll 53 M5
Knowle Somset 20 E5
Knowle Cross Devon 9 K5
Knowlefield Cumb 98 E7
Knowle Green Lancs 83 P7
Knowle Hill Surrey 32 E9
Knowle St Giles Somset 9 Q2
Knowle Village Hants 13 J3
Knowle Wood Calder 84 D10
Knowl Green Essex 46 D3
Knowl Hill W & M 32 B6
Knowlton Dorset 11 N3
Knowlton Kent 35 N11
Knowsley Knows 75 M4
Knowsley Safari Park Knows 75 M5
Knowstone Devon 20 C8
Knox N York 85 L4
Knox Bridge Kent 16 D3
Knoydart Highld 127 P4
Knucklas Powys 51 J6
Knuston Nhants 55 M7
Knutsford Ches E 76 D8
Knutsford Services Ches E 76 D8
Knutton Staffs 64 F3
Krumlin Calder 84 G11
Kuggar Cnwll 2 H11
Kyleakin Highld 135 N10
Kyle of Lochalsh Highld 135 N10
Kylerhea Highld 135 P11
Kylesku Highld 148 F10
Kylesmorar Highld 127 P6
Kyles Scalpay W Isls 152 f6
Kylestrome Highld 148 F9
Kynaston Herefs 41 K4
Kynaston Shrops 63 K8
Kynnersley Wrekin 64 C9
Kyre Green Worcs 51 Q8
Kyre Park Worcs 52 B8
Kyrewood Worcs 51 Q7
Kyrle Somset 20 G9

L

La Bellieuse Guern 12 c3
Lacasaigh W Isls 152 f4
Lacasdal W Isls 152 g3
Laceby NE Lin 80 D2
Lacey Green Bucks 32 B2
Lach Dennis Ches W 76 D9
Lackenby R & Cl 92 B3
Lackford Suffk 57 Q6
Lackford Green Suffk 57 Q6
Lacock Wilts 29 Q8
Ladbroke Warwks 54 C9
Ladderedge Staffs 64 H1
Laddingford Kent 16 C1
Lade Bank Lincs 68 H1
Ladock Cnwll 3 L4
Lady Ork 147 e2
Ladybank Fife 124 F11
Ladycross Cnwll 7 L7
Ladygill S Lans 106 B4
Lady Hall Cumb 88 G9
Ladykirk Border 117 K11
Ladyridge Herefs 41 J5
Lady's Green Suffk 57 P9
Ladywood Birm 53 K3
Ladywood Worcs 52 F8
La Fontenelle Guern 12 d1
La Fosse Guern 12 c3
Lag D & G 96 H1
Laga Highld 127 L12
Lagavulin Ag & B 111 J12
Lagg N Ayrs 103 P5
Laggan Highld 129 K5
Laggan Highld 130 B5
Lagganlia Highld 130 F5
La Greve Guern 12 c1
La Grève de Lecq Jersey 13 a1
La Hougue Bie Jersey 13 d2
La Houguette Guern 12 b2
Laid Highld 149 J5
Laide Highld 143 N7
Laig Highld 126 H7
Laigh Clunch E Ayrs 113 N11
Laigh Fenwick E Ayrs 104 H1
Laigh Glenmuir E Ayrs 105 L6
Laighstonehall S Lans 114 C10
Laindon Essex 34 B4
Lairg Highld 145 N4
Laisterdyke C Brad 85 J8
Laithes Cumb 98 F11
Lake Devon 7 P7
Lake Devon 19 L7
Lake IoW 13 K8
Lake Wilts 23 P5
Lake District National Park Cumb 88 H5
Lakenheath Suffk 57 N4
Laker's Green Surrey 14 E4
Lakesend Norfk 57 K1
Lakeside Cumb 89 K9
Laleham Surrey 32 F8
Laleston Brdgnd 27 L6
Lamanva Cnwll 3 J8
Lamarsh Essex 46 F4
Lamas Norfk 71 K7
Lambden Border 108 B1
Lamberhurst Kent 16 B4
Lamberhurst Down Kent 16 B4
Lamberton Border 117 L9
Lambeth Gt Lon 33 K6
Lambeth Crematorium Gt Lon 33 K8
Lambfair Green Suffk 57 N10
Lambley Notts 66 G3
Lambley Nthumb 99 K6
Lambourn W Berk 30 G6
Lambourne End Essex 33 N3
Lambourn Woodlands W Berk 30 G7
Lamb Roe Lancs 83 Q7
Lambs Green W Susx 15 J3
Lambston Pembks 36 H7
Lamellion Cnwll 4 C4
Lamerton Devon 7 N9
Lamesley Gatesd 100 G7
Lamington S Lans 106 C4
Lamlash N Ayrs 103 Q4
Lamonby Cumb 98 E11
Lamorick Cnwll 3 P2
Lamorna Cnwll 2 C9
Lamorran Cnwll 3 L6
Lampen Cnwll 4 B3
Lampeter Cerdgn 49 K11
Lampeter Velfrey Pembks 37 M7
Lamphey Pembks 37 K10
Lamplugh Cumb 88 E3
Lamport Nhants 55 J6
Lamyatt Somset 22 F6
Lana Devon 7 K3
Lana Devon 7 L5
Lanark S Lans 106 A1
Lancaster Lancs 83 L3
Lancaster & Morecambe Crematorium Lancs 83 L2
Lancaster Services Lancs 83 L5
Lancaut Gloucs 28 H3
Lanchester Dur 100 F9
Lancing W Susx 14 H10
L'Ancresse Guern 12 c1
Landbeach Cambs 57 J7
Landcross Devon 19 J8
Landerberry Abers 133 J3
Landford Wilts 24 D9
Land-hallow Highld 151 M10
Landican Crematorium Wirral 75 J6
Landimore Swans 26 C4
Landkey Devon 19 L7
Landore Swans 26 G3
Landrake Cnwll 4 E4
Landscove Devon 5 N3
Land's End Cnwll 2 B9
Land's End Airport Cnwll 2 B8
Landshipping Pembks 37 K8
Landue Cnwll 7 L9
Landulph Cnwll 4 F4
Landwade Suffk 57 M7
Lane Cnwll 3 K2
Laneast Cnwll 7 J8
Lane Bottom Lancs 84 C8
Lane End Bucks 32 A4
Lane End Cnwll 6 F11
Lane End Hants 25 J8
Lane End Kent 33 Q8
Lane End Lancs 84 C6
Lane End Warrtn 76 C6
Lane End Wilts 22 H4
Lane Ends Derbys 65 N5
Lane Ends Lancs 84 B9
Lane Ends N York 84 E6
Lane Green Staffs 64 G11
Laneham Notts 79 K8
Lane Head Dur 91 J4
Lanehead Dur 99 N10
Lanehead Nthumb 99 M1
Lane Head Wigan 76 B4
Lane Head Wsall 64 H12
Lane Heads Lancs 83 K7
Laneshaw Bridge Lancs 84 D7
Lane Side Lancs 84 B10
Langaford Devon 7 M5
Langaller Somset 21 L8
Langar Notts 67 J5
Langbank Rens 113 M6
Langbar N York 84 G5
Langbaurgh N York 92 B4
Langcliffe N York 84 B2
Langdale End N York 93 J8
Langdon Cnwll 7 K7
Langdon Beck Dur 99 N12
Langdown Hants 12 G3
Langdyke Fife 124 G11
Langenhoe Essex 46 H8
Langford C Beds 44 H3
Langford Devon 9 J4
Langford Essex 46 E10
Langford N Som 28 F10
Langford Notts 79 K12
Langford Oxon 42 F11
Langford Budville Somset 20 H9
Langham Dorset 22 H8
Langham Essex 46 H5
Langham Norfk 70 E4
Langham Rutlnd 67 L10
Langham Suffk 58 E6
Langho Lancs 83 Q8
Langholm D & G 98 D1
Langland Swans 26 F5
Langlee Border 107 M3
Langley Ches E 76 H9
Langley Derbys 66 C2
Langley Gloucs 42 B6
Langley Hants 12 G4
Langley Herts 45 J7
Langley Kent 34 E12
Langley Nthumb 99 M6
Langley Oxon 42 G8
Langley Rochdl 76 F2
Langley Slough 32 E6
Langley Somset 20 H7
Langley W Susx 25 P7
Langley Warwks 53 M8
Langley Burrell Wilts 29 Q7
Langley Castle Nthumb 99 N6
Langley Common Derbys 65 P5
Langley Green Derbys 65 P4
Langley Green Essex 46 F7
Langley Green Warwks 53 M8
Langley Lower Green Essex 45 N5
Langley Marsh Somset 20 G7
Langley Mill Derbys 66 D3
Langley Moor Dur 100 G10
Langley Park Dur 100 G9
Langley Street Norfk 71 M11
Langley Upper Green Essex 45 N5
Langney E Susx 16 A10
Langold Notts 78 F6
Langore Cnwll 7 K7
Langport Somset 21 P8
Langrick Lincs 68 E2
Langridge BaNES 29 L8
Langridgeford Devon 19 L9
Langrigg Cumb 97 N9
Langrish Hants 25 M8
Langsett Barns 77 N4
Langside P & K 123 K10
Langstone Hants 13 M4
Langstone Newpt 28 E4
Langthorne N York 91 L8
Langthorpe N York 85 M2
Langthwaite N York 90 G6
Langtoft E R Yk 87 J2
Langtoft Lincs 68 C9
Langton Dur 91 K3
Langton Lincs 80 E10
Langton Lincs 80 G9
Langton N York 86 E2
Langton by Wragby Lincs 80 C8
Langton Green Kent 15 Q3
Langton Green Suffk 58 H6
Langton Herring Dorset 10 F8
Langton Long Blandford Dorset 11 L4
Langton Matravers Dorset 11 N9
Langtree Devon 19 J10
Langtree Week Devon 19 J10
Langwathby Cumb 98 H11
Langwell House Highld 151 K12
Langwith Derbys 78 E9
Langwith Junction Derbys 78 E10
Langworth Lincs 79 Q8
Lanhydrock House & Gardens Cnwll 3 Q2
Lanivet Cnwll 3 P2
Lanjeth Cnwll 3 N4
Lank Cnwll 6 F9
Lanlivery Cnwll 3 Q3
Lanner Cnwll 2 H6
Lanoy Cnwll 7 K9
Lanreath Cnwll 4 B5
Lansallos Cnwll 4 B6
Lanteglos Cnwll 6 F8
Lanteglos Highway Cnwll 4 A6
Lanton Border 107 P5
Lanton Nthumb 108 E3
La Passee Guern 12 c1
Lapford Devon 8 D3
Laphroaig Ag & B 111 J12
Lapley Staffs 64 G9
La Pulente Jersey 13 a2
Lapworth Warwks 53 M6
Larachbeg Highld 120 D3
Larbert Falk 114 F5
Larbreck Lancs 83 K7
Largie Abers 140 F9
Largiemore Ag & B 112 D4
Largoward Fife 125 J11
Largs N Ayrs 113 J9
Largybeg N Ayrs 103 Q5
Largymore N Ayrs 103 R5
Larkbeare Devon 9 K5
Larkfield Inver 113 K6
Larkfield Kent 34 C10
Larkhall S Lans 114 D11
Larkhill Wilts 23 P4
Larling Norfk 58 E3
La Rocque Jersey 13 d3
La Rousaillerie Guern 12 c2
Lartington Dur 90 G3
Lasborough Gloucs 29 N3
Lasham Hants 25 L5
Lashbrook Devon 7 M3
Lashbrook Devon 7 N4
Lashenden Kent 16 E3
Lask Edge Staffs 76 G12
Lasswade Mdloth 115 P8
Lastingham N York 92 E8
Latcham Somset 21 P4
Latchford Herts 45 M7
Latchford Oxon 31 N2
Latchford Warrtn 76 B6
Latchingdon Essex 34 F2
Latchley Cnwll 7 M10
Lately Common Warrtn 76 C4
Lathbury M Keyn 44 C3
Latheron Highld 151 M10
Latheronwheel Highld 151 M10
Lathones Fife 125 J11
Latimer Bucks 32 E3
Latteridge S Glos 29 K5
Lattiford Somset 22 F8
Latton Wilts 30 C3
Lauder Border 116 C11
Laugharne Carmth 37 Q8
Laughterton Lincs 79 L8
Laughton E Susx 15 P8
Laughton Leics 54 H3
Laughton Lincs 67 Q6
Laughton Lincs 79 L4
Laughton-en-le-Morthen Rothm 78 E6
Launcells Cnwll 7 J4
Launcells Cross Cnwll 7 K4
Launceston Cnwll 7 L8
Launton Oxon 43 M7
Laurencekirk Abers 132 H10
Laurieston D & G 96 D5
Laurieston Falk 114 G5
Lavendon M Keyn 55 M10
Lavenham Suffk 58 D10
Lavernock V Glam 28 A8
Laversdale Cumb 98 F6
Laverstock Wilts 23 P7
Laverstoke Hants 24 H4
Laverton Gloucs 42 C4
Laverton N York 91 L12
Laverton Somset 22 H3
La Villette Guern 12 c3
Lavister Wrexhm 75 L12
Law S Lans 114 E10
Lawers P & K 122 H5
Lawford Essex 47 K5
Lawford Somset 21 J6
Law Hill S Lans 114 E11
Lawhitton Cnwll 7 L8
Lawkland N York 84 A2
Lawkland Green N York 84 B2
Lawley Wrekin 64 C10
Lawnhead Staffs 64 F7
Lawns Wood Crematorium Leeds 85 K7
Lawrenny Pembks 37 K9
Lawshall Suffk 58 C10
Lawshall Green Suffk 58 C10
Lawton Herefs 51 M9
Laxay W Isls 152 f4
Laxdale W Isls 152 g3
Laxey IoM 102 f5
Laxfield Suffk 59 L6
Laxford Bridge Highld 148 F7
Laxo Shet 147 j5
Laxton E R Yk 86 E10
Laxton Nhants 55 N1
Laxton Notts 79 J10
Laycock C Brad 84 F7
Layer Breton Essex 46 G8
Layer-de-la-Haye Essex 46 G7
Layer Marney Essex 46 G8
Layham Suffk 47 J4
Layland's Green W Berk 30 H9
Laymore Dorset 10 B4
Layter's Green Bucks 32 E4
Laytham E R Yk 86 D7
Laythes Cumb 97 P7
Lazenby R & Cl 92 C3
Lazonby Cumb 98 G10
Lea Derbys 77 Q12
Lea Herefs 41 K7
Lea Lincs 79 L6
Lea Shrops 51 K3
Lea Shrops 63 L10
Lea Wilts 29 Q5
Leachkin Highld 138 B7
Leadburn Border 115 N10
Leadenham Lincs 67 N2
Leaden Roding Essex 45 Q9
Leadgate Dur 100 E8
Leadgate Nthumb 100 E6
Leadhills S Lans 106 A7
Leadingcross Green Kent 34 F12
Leadmill Derbys 77 N7
Leafield Oxon 42 G8
Leagrave Luton 44 F7
Leahead Ches W 76 C11
Lea Heath Staffs 65 J7
Leake N York 91 Q8
Leake Common Side Lincs 68 H2
Lealholm N York 92 F5
Lealholm Side N York 92 F5

180 Malden Rushett – Monk's Gate

Malden Rushett Gt Lon 32 H10
Maldon Essex 46 E10
Malham N York 84 D3
Maligar Highld 134 H3
Mallaig Highld 127 M5
Mallaigvaig Highld 127 M5
Malleny Mills C Edin 115 L8
Mallows Green Essex 45 N6
Malltraeth IoA 72 G10
Mallwyd Gwynd 61 Q9
Malmesbury Wilts 29 Q5
Malmsmead Devon 20 B4
Malpas Ches W 63 N3
Malpas Cnwll 3 K6
Malpas Newpt 28 D4
Malshanger Hants 25 J3
Malswick Gloucs 41 L7
Maltby Lincs 80 F7
Maltby Rothm 78 E5
Maltby S on T 91 Q4
Maltby le Marsh Lincs 81 J7
Malting Green Essex 46 H7
Maltman's Hill Kent 16 F2
Malton N York 92 F12
Malvern Worcs 41 M2
Malvern Hills 41 M3
Malvern Link Worcs 52 E11
Malvern Wells Worcs 41 M3
Mamble Worcs 52 C6
Mamhilad Mons 40 D11
Manaccan Cnwll 3 J9
Manafon Powys 62 F11
Manais W Isls 152 e6
Manaton Devon 8 E8
Manby Lincs 80 H6
Mancetter Warwks 53 Q1
Manchester Manch 76 F4
Manchester Airport Manch 76 F7
Manchester Crematorium Manch 76 F5
Mancot Flints 75 K10
Mandally Highld 129 K4
Manea Cambs 57 J3
Maney Birm 53 L2
Manfield N York 91 L4
Mangerton Dorset 10 D5
Mangotsfield S Glos 29 K7
Mangrove Green Herts 44 G7
Manhay Cnwll 2 H8
Manish W Isls 152 e6
Mankinholes Calder 84 E10
Manley Ches W 75 N9
Manmoel Caerph 40 A11
Mannel Ag & B 118 D5
Manningford Bohune Wilts 30 D10
Manningford Bruce Wilts 30 D10
Manningham C Brad 84 H8
Mannings Heath W Susx 14 H5
Mannington Dorset 11 P4
Manningtree Essex 47 K5
Mannofield C Aber 133 M3
Manorbier Pembks 37 L11
Manorbier Newton Pembks 37 K10
Manordeilo Carmth 38 G6
Manorhill Border 107 Q3
Manorowen Pembks 36 H3
Manor Park Gt Lon 33 M5
Manor Park Crematorium Gt Lon 33 M5
Mansell Gamage Herefs 40 E3
Mansell Lacy Herefs 40 F3
Mansergh Cumb 89 P10
Mansfield E Ayrs 105 L7
Mansfield Notts 78 E11
Mansfield & District Crematorium Notts 78 E12
Mansfield Woodhouse Notts 78 E11
Mansriggs Cumb 89 J10
Manston Dorset 22 H10
Manston Kent 35 P9
Manston Leeds 85 M8
Manswood Dorset 11 N3
Manthorpe Lincs 67 M5
Manthorpe Lincs 67 Q9
Manton N Linc 79 M3
Manton Notts 78 G8
Manton Rutlnd 67 L11
Manton Wilts 30 E8
Manuden Essex 45 P6
Manwood Green Essex 45 Q9
Maperton Somset 22 F8
Maplebeck Notts 78 H11
Maple Cross Herts 32 E4
Mapledurham Oxon 31 N7
Mapledurwell Hants 25 M3
Maplehurst W Susx 14 H6
Maplescombe Kent 33 Q9
Mapleton Derbys 65 M3
Mapleton Kent 15 N1
Mapperley Derbys 66 C4
Mapperley Park C Nott 66 F4
Mapperton Dorset 10 D5
Mappleborough Green Warwks 53 K7
Mappleton E R Yk 87 N6
Mapplewell Barns 77 Q2
Mappowder Dorset 10 H3
Marazanvose Cnwll 3 K4
Marazion Cnwll 2 E8
Marbury Ches E 63 P3
March Cambs 56 H1
March S Lans 106 C7
Marcham Oxon 31 K3
Marchamley Shrops 63 Q6
Marchamley Wood Shrops 63 Q6
Marchington Staffs 65 L6
Marchington Woodlands Staffs 65 L6
Marchros Gwynd 60 E7
Marchwiel Wrexhm 63 K3
Marchwood Hants 12 F3
Marcross V Glam 27 L8
Marden Herefs 40 H2
Marden Kent 16 D2
Marden Wilts 30 C10
Marden Ash Essex 45 Q11
Marden Beech Kent 16 C2
Mardens Hill E Susx 15 P4
Marden Thorn Kent 16 D2
Mardlebury Herts 45 K8
Mardy Mons 40 D8
Marefield Leics 67 J10
Mareham le Fen Lincs 80 E11
Mareham on the Hill Lincs 80 F10
Marehay Derbys 66 C3
Marehill W Susx 14 F7
Maresfield E Susx 15 N6
Marfleet C KuH 87 L9
Marford Wrexhm 75 K12
Margam Neath 27 J5
Margam Crematorium Neath 27 J5
Margaret Marsh Dorset 22 H9
Margaret Roding Essex 45 Q9
Margaretting Essex 34 B2
Margaretting Tye Essex 34 B2
Margate Kent 35 P8
Margnaheglish N Ayrs 103 Q3
Margrie D & G 96 C8
Margrove Park R & Cl 92 D4
Marham Norfk 69 N10
Marhamchurch Cnwll 7 J4
Marholm C Pete 68 C11
Marian-glas IoA 72 H7
Mariansleigh Devon 19 P9
Marine Town Kent 34 G7
Marionburgh Abers 132 H3
Marishader Highld 135 J3
Maristow Devon 4 G4
Marjoriebanks D & G 97 M2
Mark Somset 21 N4
Markbeech Kent 15 N2
Markby Lincs 81 J8
Mark Causeway Somset 21 N4
Mark Cross E Susx 15 Q4
Markeaton C Derb 65 Q5
Markeaton Crematorium C Derb 65 Q5
Market Bosworth Leics 66 C11
Market Deeping Lincs 68 C10
Market Drayton Shrops 64 C5
Market Harborough Leics 55 J3
Market Lavington Wilts 23 M3
Market Overton Rutlnd 67 M9
Market Rasen Lincs 80 B6
Market Stainton Lincs 80 E7
Market Warsop Notts 78 F10
Market Weighton E R Yk 86 G7
Market Weston Suffk 58 E5
Markfield Leics 66 D10
Markham Caerph 27 R2
Markham Moor Notts 79 J9
Markinch Fife 115 P1
Markington N York 85 L2
Markle E Loth 116 D6
Marksbury BaNES 29 K10
Mark's Corner IoW 12 H6
Marks Tey Essex 46 F7
Markwell Cnwll 4 E5
Markyate Herts 44 F8
Marlborough Wilts 30 E8
Marlbrook Herefs 51 N9
Marlbrook Worcs 52 H6
Marlcliff Warwks 53 L10
Marldon Devon 5 P4
Marle Green E Susx 15 Q7
Marlesford Suffk 59 L9
Marley Kent 35 L12
Marley Kent 35 P11
Marley Green Ches E 63 P3
Marley Hill Gatesd 100 G6
Marlingford Norfk 70 H10
Marloes Pembks 36 E9
Marlow Bucks 32 B5
Marlow Herefs 51 L5
Marlow Bottom Bucks 32 B5
Marlpit Hill Kent 15 N1
Marlpits E Susx 15 N5
Marlpits E Susx 16 C8
Marlpool Derbys 66 D3
Marnhull Dorset 22 H9
Marple Stockp 76 H6
Marple Bridge Stockp 76 H6
Marr Donc 78 E3
Marrick N York 90 H7
Marros Carmth 37 N9
Marsden Kirk 77 K1
Marsden S Tyne 101 K5
Marsden Height Lancs 84 C8
Marsett N York 90 E9
Marsh Bucks 44 A10
Marsh C Brad 84 F8
Marsh Devon 9 P3
Marshall's Heath Herts 44 H8
Marshalswick Herts 44 H10
Marsham Norfk 71 J7
Marsh Baldon Oxon 31 M3
Marsh Benham W Berk 31 J9
Marshborough Kent 35 P11
Marshbrook Shrops 51 M3
Marshchapel Lincs 80 G4
Marsh Farm Luton 44 F6
Marshfield Newpt 28 C6
Marshfield S Glos 29 M8
Marshgate Cnwll 6 H6
Marsh Gibbon Bucks 43 N7
Marsh Green Devon 9 P6
Marsh Green Kent 15 N2
Marsh Green Wrekin 63 Q9
Marshland St James Norfk 69 K10
Marsh Lane Derbys 78 C8
Marsh Lane Gloucs 41 J10
Marshside Sefton 83 J11
Marsh Street Somset 20 F4
Marshwood Dorset 10 B5
Marske N York 91 J6
Marske-by-the-Sea R & Cl 92 C3
Marsland Green Wigan 76 C4
Marston Ches W 76 C8
Marston Herefs 51 L9
Marston Lincs 67 M3
Marston Oxon 43 L10
Marston Staffs 64 F9
Marston Staffs 64 G7
Marston Warwks 53 N2
Marston Wilts 29 Q11
Marston Green Solhll 53 M4
Marston Jabbet Warwks 54 B3
Marston Magna Somset 22 D9
Marston Meysey Wilts 30 D3
Marston Montgomery Derbys 65 L5
Marston Moretaine C Beds 44 E3
Marston on Dove Derbys 65 N6
Marston St Lawrence Nhants 43 L3
Marston Stannett Herefs 51 P9
Marston Trussell Nhants 54 H3
Marstow Herefs 40 H8
Marsworth Bucks 44 C8
Marten Wilts 30 G10
Marthall Ches E 76 E8
Martham Norfk 71 N8
Martin Hants 23 N10
Martin Kent 17 P1
Martin Lincs 80 C11
Martin Lincs 80 E10
Martindale Cumb 89 L3
Martin Dales Lincs 80 D11
Martin Drove End Hants 23 N9
Martinhoe Devon 19 N4
Martin Hussingtree Worcs 52 G8
Martinscroft Warrtn 76 C6
Martinstown Dorset 10 G7
Martlesham Suffk 47 N2
Martlesham Heath Suffk 47 M3
Martletwy Pembks 37 K8
Martley Worcs 52 D8
Martock Somset 21 P9
Marton Ches E 76 F10
Marton Ches W 76 B10
Marton Cumb 88 H11
Marton E R Yk 87 M1
Marton E R Yk 87 M7
Marton Lincs 79 L7
Marton Middsb 92 B3
Marton N York 85 N3
Marton N York 92 E10
Marton Shrops 63 J11
Marton Warwks 54 C7
Marton-le-Moor N York 85 M1
Martyr's Green Surrey 32 F11
Martyr Worthy Hants 24 H7
Marwell Wildlife Hants 24 H9
Marwick Ork 147 b3
Marwood Devon 19 K6
Marybank Highld 137 N5
Maryburgh Highld 137 P4
Marygold Border 116 H9
Maryhill C Glas 113 Q7
Maryhill Crematorium C Glas 113 Q7
Marykirk Abers 132 G11
Maryland Mons 40 G10
Marylebone Gt Lon 33 K6
Marylebone Wigan 75 P2
Marypark Moray 139 M8
Maryport Cumb 97 L11
Maryport D & G 94 G11
Marystow Devon 7 N8
Mary Tavy Devon 7 P9
Maryton Angus 125 N2
Marywell Abers 132 F5
Marywell Abers 133 M4
Marywell Angus 125 M4
Masham N York 91 L10
Mashbury Essex 46 B9
Mason N u Ty 100 G3
Masongill N York 89 Q11
Masonhill Crematorium S Ayrs 104 G6
Mastin Moor Derbys 78 D8
Matching Essex 45 P9
Matching Green Essex 45 P9
Matching Tye Essex 45 P9
Matfen Nthumb 100 D4
Matfield Kent 16 B2
Mathern Mons 28 H4
Mathon Herefs 41 M2
Mathry Pembks 36 G4
Matlask Norfk 70 H5
Matlock Derbys 77 P11
Matlock Bank Derbys 77 P11
Matlock Bath Derbys 77 P12
Matlock Dale Derbys 77 P12
Matson Gloucs 41 N8
Matterdale End Cumb 89 L2
Mattersey Notts 78 H6
Mattersey Thorpe Notts 78 H6
Mattingley Hants 31 Q10
Mattishall Norfk 70 F10
Mattishall Burgh Norfk 70 F9
Mauchline E Ayrs 105 J4
Maud Abers 141 M6
Maufant Jersey 13 c2
Maugersbury Gloucs 42 E7
Maughold IoM 102 g4
Mauld Highld 137 L8
Maulden C Beds 44 F4
Maulds Meaburn Cumb 89 Q3
Maunby N York 91 N9
Maund Bryan Herefs 51 P10
Maundown Somset 20 G7
Mautby Norfk 71 P9
Mavesyn Ridware Staffs 65 K9
Mavis Enderby Lincs 80 G10
Mawbray Cumb 97 M9
Mawdesley Lancs 83 L12
Mawdlam Brdgnd 27 J6
Mawgan Cnwll 2 H9
Mawgan Porth Cnwll 6 B11
Maw Green Ches E 76 D12
Mawla Cnwll 3 J5
Mawnan Cnwll 3 K9
Mawnan Smith Cnwll 3 J9
Mawsley Nhants 55 K5
Mawthorpe Lincs 81 J9
Maxey C Pete 68 C10
Maxstoke Warwks 53 N3
Maxted Street Kent 17 K2
Maxton Border 107 P4
Maxton Kent 17 P2
Maxwell Town D & G 97 J3
Maxworthy Cnwll 7 J6
Mayals Swans 26 F4
May Bank Staffs 64 F3
Maybole S Ayrs 104 E8
Maybury Surrey 32 E10
Mayes Green Surrey 14 G3
Mayfield E Susx 15 Q5
Mayfield Mdloth 115 Q8
Mayfield Staffs 65 M3
Mayford Surrey 32 E11
May Hill Gloucs 41 L7
Mayland Essex 46 G11
Maylandsea Essex 46 F11
Maynard's Green E Susx 15 Q7
Maypole Birm 53 K5
Maypole Kent 35 M9
Maypole Mons 40 G8
Maypole Green Norfk 59 N2
Maypole Green Suffk 58 D9
Maypole Green Suffk 59 K7
May's Green Oxon 31 Q6
May's Green Surrey 32 F11
Mead Devon 18 E9
Meadgate BaNES 29 K10
Meadle Bucks 44 A10
Meadowfield Dur 100 G10
Meadowtown Shrops 63 K12
Meadwell Devon 7 M8
Meaford Staffs 64 G5
Meal Bank Cumb 89 N7
Mealrigg Cumb 97 N9
Mealsgate Cumb 97 P10
Meanwood Leeds 85 L8
Mearbeck N York 84 B3
Meare Somset 21 P5
Meare Green Somset 21 L9
Meare Green Somset 21 M8
Mearns E Rens 113 Q10
Mears Ashby Nhants 55 L7
Measham Leics 65 Q9
Meathop Cumb 89 L10
Meaux E R Yk 87 L7
Meavy Devon 4 H3
Medbourne Leics 55 K2
Meddon Devon 18 F10
Meden Vale Notts 78 F9
Medlam Lincs 68 F1
Medlar Lancs 83 K8
Medmenham Bucks 32 A5
Medomsley Dur 100 E7
Medstead Hants 25 L6
Medway Crematorium Kent 34 D10
Medway Services Medway 34 E9
Meerbrook Staffs 77 J11
Meer Common Herefs 51 K10
Meesden Herts 45 M5
Meeson Wrekin 64 C8
Meeth Devon 7 Q3
Meeting Green Suffk 57 P9
Meeting House Hill Norfk 71 L6
Meidrim Carmth 37 Q6
Meifod Powys 62 G9
Meigle P & K 124 F4
Meikle Carco D & G 105 P7
Meikle Earnock S Lans 114 C10
Meikle Kilmory Ag & B 112 F9
Meikle Obney P & K 123 Q5
Meikleour P & K 124 D5
Meikle Wartle Abers 140 H9
Meinciau Carmth 38 C9
Meir C Stke 64 H4
Meir Heath Staffs 64 H4
Melbourn Cambs 45 M3
Melbourne Derbys 66 C7
Melbourne E R Yk 86 D6
Melbur Cnwll 3 M3
Melbury Devon 18 H10
Melbury Abbas Dorset 23 K9
Melbury Bubb Dorset 10 F3
Melbury Osmond Dorset 10 E3
Melbury Sampford Dorset 10 E4
Melchbourne Bed 55 P7
Melcombe Bingham Dorset 11 J4
Meldon Devon 7 Q6
Meldon Nthumb 100 E1
Meldon Park Nthumb 100 E1
Meldreth Cambs 45 M2
Meldrum Stirlg 114 C1
Melfort Ag & B 120 F10
Meliden Denbgs 74 E7
Melinau Pembks 37 N8
Melin-byrhedyn Powys 61 P12
Melincourt Neath 39 K11
Melin-y-coed Conwy 73 P11
Melin-y-ddol Powys 62 F10
Melin-y-wig Denbgs 62 E2
Melkinthorpe Cumb 89 P2
Melkridge Nthumb 99 L5
Melksham Wilts 29 P9
Mellangoose Cnwll 2 H9
Mell Green W Berk 31 K7
Mellguards Cumb 98 F9
Melling Lancs 83 N1
Melling Sefton 75 L4
Melling Mount Sefton 75 L3
Mellis Suffk 58 G6
Mellon Charles Highld 143 M7
Mellon Udrigle Highld 143 N6
Mellor Lancs 83 P9
Mellor Stockp 77 J6
Mellor Brook Lancs 83 P9
Mells Somset 22 G4
Mells Suffk 59 N5
Melmerby Cumb 99 J10
Melmerby N York 90 H9
Melmerby N York 91 N11
Melness Highld 149 M4
Melon Green Suffk 58 C9
Melplash Dorset 10 D5
Melrose Border 107 N3
Melsetter Ork 147 b6
Melsonby N York 91 K5
Meltham Kirk 77 L2
Meltham Mills Kirk 77 L2
Melton E R Yk 86 H10
Melton Suffk 59 K10
Meltonby E R Yk 86 E5
Melton Constable Norfk 70 F5
Melton Mowbray Leics 67 J8
Melton Ross N Linc 79 Q2
Melvaig Highld 143 K8
Melverley Shrops 63 K9
Melverley Green Shrops 63 K8
Melvich Highld 150 F4
Membury Devon 9 P4
Membury Services W Berk 30 G7
Memsie Abers 141 N3
Memus Angus 124 H1
Menabilly Cnwll 3 Q4
Menagissey Cnwll 2 H5
Menai Bridge IoA 73 J9
Mendham Suffk 59 K4
Mendip Crematorium Somset 22 D5
Mendip Hills 22 C3
Mendlesham Suffk 58 G7
Mendlesham Green Suffk 58 G8
Menheniot Cnwll 4 D4
Menithwood Worcs 52 D7
Menna Cnwll 3 M4
Mennock D & G 105 Q8
Menston C Brad 85 J6
Menstrie Clacks 114 F2
Menthorpe N York 86 C8
Mentmore Bucks 44 C8
Meoble Highld 127 P7
Meole Brace Shrops 63 N10
Meonstoke Hants 25 K9
Meopham Kent 34 B9
Meopham Green Kent 34 B9
Meopham Station Kent 34 B8
Mepal Cambs 56 H4
Meppershall C Beds 44 G4
Merbach Herefs 40 D3
Mere Ches E 76 D7
Mere Wilts 22 H7
Mere Brow Lancs 83 K11
Mereclough Lancs 84 C9
Mere Green Birm 65 L12
Mere Green Worcs 52 H8
Mere Heath Ches W 76 C9
Meresborough Medway 34 E9
Mereworth Kent 34 B11
Meriden Solhll 53 N4
Merkadale Highld 134 G9
Merley Poole 11 N5
Merlin's Bridge Pembks 37 J7
Merrington Shrops 63 M8
Merrion Pembks 36 H11
Merriott Somset 21 P11
Merrivale Devon 7 Q9
Merrow Surrey 32 E12
Merry Field Hill Dorset 11 N4
Merry Hill Herts 32 G3
Merryhill Wolves 52 G1
Merry Lees Leics 66 D11
Merrymeet Cnwll 4 D3
Mersea Island Essex 47 J8
Mersey Crossing Halton 75 N7
Mersham Kent 17 J3
Merstham Surrey 33 K11
Merston W Susx 14 C10
Merstone IoW 13 J8
Merther Cnwll 3 L5
Merthyr Carmth 38 A7
Merthyr Cynog Powys 39 N4
Merthyr Dyfan V Glam 27 Q8
Merthyr Mawr Brdgnd 27 L7
Merthyr Tydfil Myr Td 39 P10
Merthyr Vale Myr Td 27 P2
Merton Devon 19 K11
Merton Gt Lon 33 J8
Merton Norfk 70 D12
Merton Oxon 43 M8
Meshaw Devon 19 P9
Messing Essex 46 F8
Messingham N Linc 79 M3
Metfield Suffk 59 L4
Metherell Cnwll 4 F3
Metheringham Lincs 79 Q11
Methil Fife 115 Q1
Methilhill Fife 115 Q1
Methley Leeds 85 N10
Methley Junction Leeds 85 N10
Methlick Abers 141 K8
Methven P & K 123 P7
Methwold Norfk 57 P2
Methwold Hythe Norfk 57 N2
Mettingham Suffk 59 M3
Metton Norfk 71 J5
Mevagissey Cnwll 3 P5
Mexborough Donc 78 D4
Mey Highld 151 N2
Meyllteyrn Gwynd 60 C6
Meysey Hampton Gloucs 30 D2
Miabhig W Isls 152 e3
Miavaig W Isls 152 e3
Michaelchurch Herefs 40 H6
Michaelchurch Escley Herefs 40 D5
Michaelchurch-on-Arrow Powys 50 H10
Michaelstone-y-Fedw Newpt 28 C5
Michaelston-le-Pit V Glam 27 Q8
Michaelstow Cnwll 6 F9
Michaelwood Services Gloucs 29 L3
Michelcombe Devon 5 L3
Micheldever Hants 24 H5
Micheldever Station Hants 24 H5
Michelmersh Hants 24 F8
Mickfield Suffk 58 H8
Micklebring Donc 78 E5
Mickleby N York 92 G4
Micklefield Leeds 85 N8
Micklefield Green Herts 32 F3
Mickleham Surrey 32 H11
Mickleover C Derb 65 P5
Micklethwaite C Brad 84 G7
Micklethwaite Cumb 98 C8
Mickleton Dur 90 F2
Mickleton Gloucs 42 D3
Mickletown Leeds 85 N9
Mickle Trafford Ches W 75 M9
Mickley Derbys 77 Q8
Mickley N York 91 L11
Mickley Green Suffk 58 B9
Mickley Square Nthumb 100 D6
Mid Ardlaw Abers 141 M3
Midbea Ork 147 c2
Mid Beltie Abers 132 F4
Mid Bockhampton Dorset 12 B5
Mid Calder W Loth 115 K8
Mid Clyth Highld 151 P9
Mid Culbeuchly Abers 140 G3
Middle Assendon Oxon 31 Q5
Middle Aston Oxon 43 K6
Middle Barton Oxon 43 J6
Middlebie D & G 97 P3
Middlebridge P & K 130 G11
Middle Chinnock Somset 21 Q10
Middle Claydon Bucks 43 P6
Middlecliffe Barns 78 C3
Middlecott Devon 8 D7
Middle Duntisbourne Gloucs 41 R10
Middleham N York 91 J9
Middle Handley Derbys 78 C8
Middle Harling Norfk 58 E3
Middlehill Cnwll 4 D3
Middlehill Wilts 29 N8
Middlehope Shrops 51 N3
Middle Kames Ag & B 112 D3
Middle Littleton Worcs 42 C2
Middle Madeley Staffs 64 E3
Middle Maes-coed Herefs 40 D5
Middlemarsh Dorset 10 G3
Middle Mayfield Staffs 65 L3
Middle Mill Pembks 36 F5
Middlemore Devon 7 P10
Middle Quarter Kent 16 F3
Middle Rasen Lincs 80 B6
Middle Rocombe Devon 5 Q3
Middle Salter Lancs 83 N3
Middlesbrough Middsb 92 A3
Middlesceugh Cumb 98 E10
Middleshaw Cumb 89 N9
Middlesmoor N York 91 J12
Middle Stoford Somset 21 J9
Middle Stoke Medway 34 E7
Middlestone Dur 100 H12
Middlestone Moor Dur 100 G11
Middle Stoughton Somset 21 P3
Middlestown Wakefd 85 K11
Middle Street Gloucs 41 M10
Middle Taphouse Cnwll 4 B4
Middlethird Border 107 R1
Middleton Ag & B 118 C4
Middleton Cumb 89 Q9
Middleton Derbys 65 P1
Middleton Derbys 77 M11
Middleton Essex 46 F4
Middleton Hants 24 G4
Middleton Herefs 51 P7
Middleton Lancs 83 K3
Middleton Leeds 85 L9
Middleton N York 84 H5
Middleton N York 92 F9
Middleton Nhants 55 L3
Middleton Norfk 69 M9
Middleton Nthumb 100 D1
Middleton Nthumb 108 H3
Middleton P & K 124 C11
Middleton Rochdl 76 F3
Middleton Shrops 51 P5
Middleton Shrops 63 K6
Middleton Suffk 59 N7
Middleton Swans 26 B5
Middleton Warwks 65 M12
Middleton Cheney Nhants 43 K3
Middleton Crematorium Rochdl 76 G2
Middleton Green Staffs 65 J5
Middleton Hall Nthumb 108 F5
Middleton-in-Teesdale Dur 90 F2
Middleton Moor Suffk 59 N7
Middleton One Row Darltn 91 N4
Middleton-on-Leven N York 91 Q5
Middleton-on-Sea W Susx 14 D10
Middleton on the Hill Herefs 51 P7
Middleton on the Wolds E R Yk 86 H5
Middleton Park C Aber 133 M2
Middleton Priors Shrops 52 B3
Middleton Quernhow N York 91 N11
Middleton St George Darltn 91 N4
Middleton Scriven Shrops 52 C3
Middleton Stoney Oxon 43 L7
Middleton Tyas N York 91 L5
Middletown Cumb 88 C5
Middle Town IoS 2 b3
Middletown N Som 28 F8
Middletown Powys 63 K9
Middle Tysoe Warwks 42 H3
Middle Wallop Hants 24 E6
Middlewich Ches E 76 C10
Middle Winterslow Wilts 24 D7
Middlewood Cnwll 7 K9
Middlewood Herefs 40 C3
Middle Woodford Wilts 23 P6
Middlewood Green Suffk 58 G8
Middleyard E Ayrs 105 J3
Middle Yard Gloucs 41 N11
Middlezoy Somset 21 N7
Middridge Dur 91 L2
Midford BaNES 29 M10
Midge Hall Lancs 83 L10
Midgeholme Cumb 99 J6
Midgham W Berk 31 L9
Midgley Calder 84 F10
Midgley Wakefd 85 K12
Mid Holmwood Surrey 14 H2
Midhopestones Sheff 77 N4
Midhurst W Susx 14 C6
Mid Lavant W Susx 13 Q3
Midlem Border 107 N4
Mid Mains Highld 137 M8
Midney Somset 22 C8
Midpark Ag & B 112 F9
Midsomer Norton BaNES 22 F3
Midtown Highld 149 M4
Midville Lincs 80 G12
Mid Warwickshire Crematorium Warwks 53 P8
Midway Ches E 76 G7
Mid Yell Shet 147 j3
Migvie Abers 132 C3
Milborne Port Somset 22 F9
Milborne St Andrew Dorset 11 K5
Milborne Wick Somset 22 F9
Milbourne Nthumb 100 E3
Milbourne Wilts 29 Q5
Milburn Cumb 99 J12
Milbury Heath S Glos 29 K4
Milby N York 85 N2
Milcombe Oxon 43 J5
Milden Suffk 46 G2
Mildenhall Suffk 57 N6
Mildenhall Wilts 30 E8
Milebrook Powys 51 K6
Milebush Kent 16 D2
Mile Elm Wilts 30 A8
Mile End Essex 46 H6
Mile End Gloucs 41 J9
Mile End Suffk 59 L3
Mileham Norfk 70 D8
Mile Oak Br & H 15 J9
Mile Oak Kent 16 B2
Mile Oak Staffs 65 M11
Miles Hope Herefs 51 P7
Milesmark Fife 115 K4
Miles Platting Manch 76 F4
Mile Town Kent 34 G7
Milfield Nthumb 108 E3
Milford Derbys 66 B3
Milford Devon 18 E9
Milford Powys 50 F2
Milford Staffs 64 H8
Milford Surrey 14 D2
Milford Haven Pembks 36 H9
Milford on Sea Hants 12 D6
Milkwall Gloucs 41 J10
Millais Jersey 13 a1
Milland W Susx 25 P8
Milland Marsh W Susx 25 P8
Mill Bank Calder 84 F11
Millbeck Cumb 88 H2
Millbreck Abers 141 N7
Millbridge Surrey 25 P5
Millbrook C Beds 44 E4
Millbrook C Sotn 24 F10
Millbrook Cnwll 4 F6
Millbrook Jersey 13 b2
Millbrook Tamesd 76 H4
Mill Brow Stockp 76 H6
Millbuie Abers 133 J2
Millbuie Highld 137 P5
Millcombe Devon 5 N7
Mill Common Norfk 71 L11
Mill Common Suffk 59 N4
Millcorner E Susx 16 E6
Millcraig Highld 145 P11
Mill Cross Devon 5 M4
Milldale Staffs 65 L1
Mill End Bucks 31 R5
Mill End Cambs 56 F4
Millend Gloucs 29 M3
Mill End Herts 45 L5
Millerhill Mdloth 115 P7
Miller's Dale Derbys 77 L9
Millers Green Derbys 65 P2
Miller's Green Essex 45 Q10
Millerston C Glas 114 B8
Millgate Lancs 84 D11
Mill Green Cambs 46 A3
Mill Green Essex 34 B2
Mill Green Herts 45 J9
Mill Green Lincs 68 E7
Mill Green Norfk 58 H4
Millgreen Shrops 64 C6
Mill Green Staffs 65 K12
Mill Green Staffs 65 K8
Mill Green Suffk 46 G3
Mill Green Suffk 58 E9
Mill Green Suffk 58 H8
Mill Green Suffk 59 L8
Millhalf Herefs 51 J11
Millhayes Devon 9 N4
Millhead Lancs 83 L1
Millheugh S Lans 114 D11
Mill Hill E Susx 16 A9
Mill Hill Gt Lon 33 J4
Millhouse Ag & B 112 D7
Millhouse Cumb 98 D10
Millhousebridge D & G 97 M1
Millhouse Green Barns 77 N3
Millhouses Barns 78 C3
Millhouses Sheff 77 Q7
Milliken Park Rens 113 N9
Millin Cross Pembks 37 J8
Millington E R Yk 86 F5
Millmeece Staffs 64 F5
Millness Cumb 89 N10
Mill of Drummond P & K 123 L9
Mill of Haldane W Duns 113 M5
Millom Cumb 88 G10
Millook Cnwll 6 H5
Millpool Cnwll 2 F8
Millpool Cnwll 6 G10
Millport N Ayrs 112 H10
Mill Side Cumb 89 M10
Mill Street Kent 34 C11
Mill Street Norfk 70 F8
Mill Street Suffk 58 F6
Millthorpe Derbys 77 P8
Millthrop Cumb 89 Q8
Milltimber C Aber 133 K4
Milltown Abers 131 N2
Milltown Abers 132 D1
Milltown Cnwll 3 Q3
Milltown D & G 98 D3
Milltown Derbys 78 B11
Milltown Devon 19 L5
Milltown of Auchindoun Moray 139 Q8
Milltown of Campfield Abers 132 G4
Milltown of Edinvillie Moray 139 N8
Milltown of Learney Abers 132 F4
Milnathort P & K 124 C11
Milngavie E Duns 113 Q6
Milnrow Rochdl 76 G1
Milnthorpe Cumb 89 M10
Milnthorpe Wakefd 85 M11
Milovaig Highld 134 C6
Milson Shrops 52 B6
Milstead Kent 34 F10
Milston Wilts 23 Q4
Milthorpe Lincs 68 C6
Milthorpe Nhants 43 M2
Milton C Stke 64 G2
Milton Cambs 57 J8
Milton Cumb 98 H6
Milton D & G 95 J8
Milton D & G 96 G4
Milton D & G 97 J2
Milton Derbys 65 P7
Milton Highld 135 N7
Milton Highld 137 N9
Milton Highld 137 Q6
Milton Highld 146 D10
Milton Highld 151 P6
Milton Inver 113 L7
Milton Kent 34 B7
Milton Moray 139 M12
Milton Moray 140 D3
Milton N Som 28 D10
Milton Newpt 28 E5
Milton Notts 78 H9
Milton Oxon 31 K4
Milton Oxon 43 K5
Milton P & K 131 K12
Milton Pembks 37 K10
Milton Somset 21 P9
Milton Stirlg 113 P1
Milton W Duns 113 N6
Milton Abbas Dorset 11 K4
Milton Abbot Devon 7 M9
Milton Bridge Mdloth 115 N8
Milton Bryan C Beds 44 D6
Milton Clevedon Somset 22 F6
Milton Combe Devon 4 G3
Milton Common Oxon 43 N11
Milton Damerel Devon 7 M3
Milton End Gloucs 30 D2
Milton End Gloucs 41 L9
Milton Ernest Bed 55 P9
Milton Green Ches W 75 M12
Milton Hill Oxon 31 K4
Milton Keynes M Keyn 44 B4
Milton Lilbourne Wilts 30 E10
Milton Malsor Nhants 55 J9
Milton Morenish P & K 122 G5
Milton of Auchinhove Abers 132 E4
Milton of Balgonie Fife 115 P1
Milton of Buchanan Stirlg 113 N3
Milton of Campsie E Duns 114 B6
Milton of Leys Highld 138 C7
Milton of Murtle C Aber 133 L4
Milton of Tullich Abers 132 B5
Milton on Stour Dorset 22 H7
Milton Regis Kent 34 F9
Milton Street E Susx 15 P10
Milton-under-Wychwood Oxon 42 F8
Milverton Somset 20 H8
Milverton Warwks 53 P7
Milwich Staffs 64 H6
Milwr Flints 74 G8
Minard Ag & B 112 E2
Minchington Dorset 23 L10
Minchinhampton Gloucs 29 P2
Mindrum Nthumb 108 D3
Minehead Somset 20 F4
Minera Wrexhm 63 J2
Minety Wilts 30 B4
Minffordd Gwynd 61 K4
Mingarrypark Highld 127 M10
Miningsby Lincs 80 F11
Minions Cnwll 7 K10
Minishant S Ayrs 104 F7
Minllyn Gwynd 61 Q9
Minnigaff D & G 95 M5
Minnonie Abers 141 J4
Minshull Vernon Ches E 76 C11
Minskip N York 85 M2
Minstead Hants 12 D3
Minsted W Susx 25 Q9
Minster Kent 34 G8
Minster Kent 35 P9
Minsterley Shrops 63 L11
Minster Lovell Oxon 42 G9
Minsterworth Gloucs 41 M8
Minterne Magna Dorset 10 G4
Minterne Parva Dorset 10 G4
Minting Lincs 80 D9
Mintlaw Abers 141 N6
Mintlyn Crematorium Norfk 69 M8
Minto Border 107 N6
Minton Shrops 51 M2
Minwear Pembks 37 K8
Minworth Birm 53 M2
Mirehouse Cumb 88 C4
Mireland Highld 151 P4
Mirfield Kirk 85 J11
Miserden Gloucs 41 Q10
Miskin Rhondd 27 P3
Miskin Rhondd 27 P6
Misson Notts 78 H5
Misterton Leics 54 F4
Misterton Notts 79 J5
Misterton Somset 10 C3
Mistley Essex 47 K5
Mistley Heath Essex 47 K5
Mitcham Gt Lon 33 K8
Mitcheldean Gloucs 41 K8
Mitchell Cnwll 3 L4
Mitchellslacks D & G 106 C10
Mitchel Troy Mons 40 G9
Mitford Nthumb 100 F1
Mithian Cnwll 3 J4
Mitton Staffs 64 G9
Mixbury Oxon 43 M5
Mixenden Calder 84 G9
Moats Tye Suffk 58 F9
Mobberley Ches E 76 E8
Mobberley Staffs 65 J4
Moccas Herefs 40 E3
Mochdre Conwy 73 P8
Mochdre Powys 50 E3
Mochrum D & G 95 K9
Mockbeggar Hants 12 B3
Mockbeggar Kent 16 C1
Mockerkin Cumb 88 E2
Modbury Devon 5 L6
Moddershall Staffs 64 G5
Moelfre IoA 72 H6
Moelfre Powys 62 G6
Moel Tryfan Gwynd 60 H1
Moffat D & G 106 E8
Mogador Surrey 33 J11
Moggerhanger C Beds 56 C10
Moira Leics 65 P9
Molash Kent 35 J12
Mol-chlach Highld 126 H2
Mold Flints 74 H11
Moldgreen Kirk 84 H12
Molehill Green Essex 45 Q7
Molehill Green Essex 46 C7
Molescroft E R Yk 87 J7
Molesden Nthumb 100 F1
Molesworth Cambs 55 Q5
Molland Devon 20 C7
Mollington Ches W 75 L9
Mollington Oxon 54 D11
Mollinsburn N Lans 114 C7
Monachty Cerdgn 48 H8
Mondynes Abers 133 J8
Monewden Suffk 59 K9
Moneydie P & K 123 Q7
Moneyrow Green W & M 32 C7
Moniaive D & G 105 P11
Monifieth Angus 125 K6
Monikie Angus 125 K5
Monimail Fife 124 F10
Monington Pembks 37 M2
Monk Bretton Barns 78 B2
Monken Hadley Gt Lon 33 J3
Monk Fryston N York 85 Q9
Monkhide Herefs 41 J3
Monkhill Cumb 98 D6
Monkhopton Shrops 52 B2
Monkland Herefs 51 M9
Monkleigh Devon 19 J9
Monknash V Glam 27 L8
Monkokehampton Devon 7 Q4
Monkseaton N Tyne 101 J4
Monks Eleigh Suffk 58 E11
Monk's Gate W Susx 14 H5

Over Norton – Pontfaen 183

Over Norton Oxon 42 G6
Over Peover Ches E 76 E9
Overpool Ches W 75 L8
Overscaig Hotel Highld 149 J12
Overseal Derbys 65 P9
Over Silton N York 91 Q8
Oversland Kent 35 J11
Oversley Green Warwks 53 L9
Overstone Nhants 55 K7
Over Stowey Somset 21 J6
Overstrand Norfk 71 K4
Over Stratton Somset 21 P10
Overstreet Wilts 23 N6
Over Tabley Ches E 76 D7
Overthorpe Nhants 43 K4
Overton C Aber 133 L2
Overton Ches W 75 N8
Overton Hants 24 H3
Overton Lancs 83 K4
Overton N York 85 Q4
Overton Shrops 51 N6
Overton Swans 26 C5
Overton Wakefd 85 K12
Overton Wrexhm 63 L4
Overton Bridge Wrexhm 63 K4
Overton Green Ches E 76 E11
Overtown Lancs 89 Q11
Overtown N Lans 114 E10
Overtown Swindn 30 D6
Overtown Wakefd 85 M12
Over Wallop Hants 24 D6
Over Whitacre Warwks 53 N2
Over Woodhouse Derbys 78 D9
Over Worton Oxon 43 J6
Overy Oxon 31 M3
Oving Bucks 43 Q7
Oving W Susx 14 C10
Ovingdean Br & H 15 L10
Ovingham Nthumb 100 E5
Ovington Dur 91 J4
Ovington Essex 46 D3
Ovington Hants 25 J7
Ovington Norfk 70 D11
Ovington Nthumb 100 D5
Ower Hants 12 H4
Ower Hants 24 E10
Owermoigne Dorset 11 J7
Owlbury Shrops 51 K2
Owlerton Sheff 77 Q6
Owlpen Gloucs 29 M3
Owl's Green Suffk 59 K7
Owlsmoor Br For 32 B10
Owlswick Bucks 43 R10
Owmby Lincs 79 P6
Owmby Lincs 79 Q3
Owslebury Hants 24 H8
Owston Donc 78 F1
Owston Leics 67 K10
Owston Ferry N Linc 79 K4
Owstwick E R Yk 87 P8
Owthorne E R Yk 87 Q9
Owthorpe Notts 66 H5
Owton Manor Hartpl 101 M12
Oxborough Norfk 69 P11
Oxbridge Dorset 10 D5
Oxcombe Lincs 80 F8
Oxcroft Derbys 78 D9
Oxen End Essex 46 B6
Oxenholme Cumb 89 N9
Oxenhope C Brad 84 F8
Oxen Park Cumb 89 J9
Oxenpill Somset 21 P5
Oxenton Gloucs 41 Q5
Oxenwood Wilts 30 G10
Oxford Oxon 43 L10
Oxford Airport Oxon 43 K8
Oxford Crematorium Oxon 43 L10
Oxford Services Oxon 43 N10
Oxhey Herts 32 G3
Oxhill Dur 100 F8
Oxhill Warwks 42 G2
Oxley Wolves 64 G11
Oxley Green Essex 46 F9
Oxley's Green E Susx 16 C6
Oxlode Cambs 57 J3
Oxnam Border 108 A6
Oxnead Norfk 71 J7
Oxshott Surrey 32 G10
Oxshott Heath Surrey 32 G10
Oxspring Barns 77 P3
Oxted Surrey 33 M11
Oxton Border 116 C10
Oxton N York 85 Q6
Oxton Notts 66 G2
Oxton Wirral 75 J6
Oxwich Swans 26 D5
Oxwich Green Swans 26 D5
Oxwick Norfk 70 D7
Oykel Bridge Hotel Highld 145 J5
Oyne Abers 140 G10
Oystermouth Swans 26 F5
Ozleworth Gloucs 29 M4

P

Pabail W Isls 152 h3
Packers Hill Dorset 10 H3
Packington Leics 66 B9
Packmoor C Stke 64 F1
Packmores Warwks 53 P7
Padanaram Angus 124 H2
Padbury Bucks 43 P5
Paddington Gt Lon 33 K6
Paddington Warrtn 76 B6
Paddlesworth Kent 17 M3
Paddlesworth Kent 34 B10
Paddock Wood Kent 16 B2
Paddolgreen Shrops 63 N6
Padfield Derbys 77 J4
Padgate Warrtn 76 B6
Padhams Green Essex 34 B3
Padiham Lancs 84 B8
Padside N York 84 H3
Padstow Cnwll 6 C9
Padworth W Berk 31 M9
Page Bank Dur 100 G11
Pagham W Susx 14 C11
Paglesham Essex 34 G4
Paignton Torbay 5 Q4
Pailton Warwks 54 D4
Paine's Cross E Susx 16 A6
Painleyhill Staffs 65 J5
Painscastle Powys 40 A2
Painshawfield Nthumb 100 D6
Painsthorpe E R Yk 86 F4
Painswick Gloucs 41 P9
Painter's Forstal Kent 34 H10
Paisley Rens 113 P8
Paisley Woodside Crematorium Rens 113 P8
Pakefield Suffk 59 Q3
Pakenham Suffk 58 D7
Pale Gwynd 62 D5
Pale Green Essex 46 B3
Palestine Hants 24 D5
Paley Street W & M 32 B7
Palfrey Wsall 53 J1
Palgrave Suffk 58 G5
Pallington Dorset 11 J6
Palmersbridge Cnwll 6 H9
Palmers Green Gt Lon 33 K4
Palmerston E Ayrs 105 J6
Palmerstown V Glam 27 Q8
Palnackie D & G 96 G7
Palnure D & G 95 N5
Palterton Derbys 78 D10
Pamber End Hants 31 M10
Pamber Green Hants 31 M10
Pamber Heath Hants 31 M10
Pamington Gloucs 41 Q5
Pamphill Dorset 11 N5
Pampisford Cambs 57 J11
Panborough Somset 21 Q4
Panbride Angus 125 L6
Pancrasweek Devon 7 K4
Pancross V Glam 27 P8
Pandy Caerph 27 Q5
Pandy Gwynd 61 K11
Pandy Gwynd 61 Q6
Pandy Mons 40 D7
Pandy Powys 62 B11
Pandy Wrexhm 62 H5
Pandy'r Capel Denbgs 62 F2
Pandy Tudur Conwy 73 Q11
Panfield Essex 46 C6
Pangbourne W Berk 31 N7
Pangdean W Susx 15 K8
Panks Bridge Herefs 52 B11
Pannal N York 85 L5
Pannal Ash N York 85 L4
Pannanich Wells Hotel Abers 132 B5
Pant Shrops 63 J8
Pantasaph Flints 74 G8
Panteg Pembks 36 H4
Pantersbridge Cnwll 4 B3
Pant-ffrwyth Brdgnd 27 M5
Pant Glas Gwynd 60 H3
Pantglas Powys 49 N1
Pant-Gwyn Carmth 38 E6
Pant-lasau Swans 26 G2
Pant Mawr Powys 49 P4
Panton Lincs 80 D8
Pant-pastynog Denbgs 74 E11
Pantperthog Gwynd 61 N11
Pant-y-dwr Powys 50 D6
Pant-y-ffridd Powys 62 G11
Pantyffynnon Carmth 38 F9
Pantygaseg Torfn 28 C2
Pant-y-gog Brdgnd 27 L4
Pantymenyn Carmth 37 M5
Pant-y-mwyn Flints 74 H10
Panxworth Norfk 71 M9
Papa Stour Airport Shet 147 g6
Papa Westray Airport Ork 147 d1
Papcastle Cumb 97 M12
Papigoe Highld 151 Q6
Papple E Loth 116 D7
Papplewick Notts 66 F2
Papworth Everard Cambs 56 F8
Papworth St Agnes Cambs 56 E8
Par Cnwll 3 Q4
Paramour Street Kent 35 N10
Parbold Lancs 75 N2
Parbrook Somset 22 D6
Parbrook W Susx 14 F6
Parc Gwynd 61 Q5
Parc Gwyn Crematorium Pembks 37 M7
Parcllyn Cerdgn 48 D10
Parc Seymour Newpt 28 F4
Pardshaw Cumb 88 E2
Parham Suffk 59 L8
Park D & G 106 B11
Park Nthumb 99 K6
Park Bottom Cnwll 2 G6
Park Bridge Tamesd 76 H3
Park Corner E Susx 15 P4
Park Corner Oxon 31 P5
Park Corner W & M 32 B6
Park Crematorium Hants 14 C1
Park Crematorium Lancs 83 J9
Park End Bed 55 N10
Parkend Gloucs 41 J10
Park End Nthumb 99 N3
Parkers Green Kent 15 R1
Parkeston Essex 47 M5
Parkeston Quay Essex 47 M5
Park Farm Kent 16 H3
Parkgate Ches W 75 J8
Parkgate Cumb 97 P9
Parkgate D & G 106 D12
Parkgate E Susx 16 C8
Parkgate Essex 46 B6
Park Gate Hants 13 J3
Parkgate Kent 16 F4
Parkgate Kent 33 P9
Park Gate Leeds 85 J7
Parkgate Surrey 14 H2
Park Gate Worcs 52 H6
Park Green Essex 45 N6
Park Green Suffk 58 H8
Parkgrove Crematorium Angus 125 M3
Parkhall W Duns 113 P7
Parkham Devon 18 H9
Parkham Ash Devon 18 G9
Park Head Derbys 66 B1
Park Hill Gloucs 28 H2
Parkhouse Mons 40 G11
Parkmill Swans 26 E4
Park Royal Gt Lon 32 H6
Parkside Dur 101 L8
Parkside N Lans 114 E9
Parkside Wrexhm 63 L1
Parkstone Poole 11 P6
Park Street Herts 44 G11
Park Street W Susx 14 G4
Parkway Herefs 41 L4
Park Wood Crematorium Calder 84 G10
Parley Green Dorset 11 Q5
Parmoor Bucks 31 R4
Parndon Wood Crematorium Essex 45 N10
Parracombe Devon 19 N4
Parrog Pembks 37 K3
Parsonby Cumb 97 N10
Parson Cross Sheff 77 Q5
Parson Drove Cambs 68 G10
Parson's Heath Essex 46 H6
Parson's Hill Derbys 65 P7
Partick C Glas 113 Q8
Partington Traffd 76 D5
Partney Lincs 80 H10
Parton Cumb 88 C3
Partridge Green W Susx 14 H7
Partrishow Powys 40 C7
Parwich Derbys 65 M1
Paslow Wood Common Essex 45 Q11
Passenham Nhants 43 Q4
Passfield Hants 25 P6
Passingford Bridge Essex 33 P3
Paston C Pete 68 D11
Paston Norfk 71 L5
Pasturefields Staffs 65 J7
Patchacott Devon 7 N5
Patcham Br & H 15 K9
Patchetts Green Herts 32 G3
Patching W Susx 14 F9
Patchole Devon 19 M5
Patchway S Glos 29 J6
Pateley Bridge N York 84 H2
Paternoster Heath Essex 46 G8
Pathe Somset 21 N7
Pathhead Fife 115 P3
Pathhead Mdloth 115 R8
Pathlow Warwks 53 M9
Path of Condie P & K 124 B10
Patmore Heath Herts 45 N6
Patna E Ayrs 104 H7
Patney Wilts 30 C10
Patrick IoM 102 c5
Patrick Brompton N York 91 L8
Patricroft Salfd 76 D4
Patrington E R Yk 87 P10
Patrington Haven E R Yk 87 P11
Patrixbourne Kent 35 L11
Patterdale Cumb 89 L4
Pattingham Staffs 64 F12
Pattishall Nhants 54 H10
Pattiswick Green Essex 46 E7
Patton Shrops 51 P2
Patton Bridge Cumb 89 P7
Paul Cnwll 2 D9
Paulerspury Nhants 43 P3
Paull E R Yk 87 M10
Paul's Dene Wilts 23 P7
Paulton BaNES 29 K11
Paunton Herefs 52 C10
Pauperhaugh Nthumb 108 H10
Pave Lane Wrekin 64 E9
Pavenham Bed 55 N9
Pawlett Somset 21 L5
Pawston Nthumb 108 D3
Paxford Gloucs 42 E4
Paxton Border 117 L10
Payden Street Kent 34 G11
Payhembury Devon 9 L4
Paynter's Lane End Cnwll 2 G6
Paythorne Lancs 84 B5
Paytoe Herefs 51 L6
Peacehaven E Susx 15 M10
Peak Dale Derbys 77 K8
Peak District National Park 77 M5
Peak Forest Derbys 77 L8
Peak Hill Lincs 68 E9
Peakirk C Pete 68 C11
Pearson's Green Kent 16 C2
Peartree Green Herefs 41 J5
Peasedown St John BaNES 29 L11
Peasehill Derbys 66 C2
Peaseland Green Norfk 70 F9
Peasemore W Berk 31 K7
Peasenhall Suffk 59 M7
Pease Pottage W Susx 15 J4
Pease Pottage Services W Susx 15 J4
Peaslake Surrey 14 F2
Peasley Cross St Hel 75 N5
Peasmarsh E Susx 16 F6
Peasmarsh Somset 21 M11
Peasmarsh Surrey 14 E2
Peathill Abers 141 M3
Peat Inn Fife 125 J11
Peatling Magna Leics 54 F2
Peatling Parva Leics 54 F3
Peaton Shrops 51 P4
Pebmarsh Essex 46 E5
Pebworth Worcs 42 D2
Pecket Well Calder 84 E9
Peckforton Ches E 75 P12
Peckham Gt Lon 33 L7
Peckleton Leics 66 D12
Pedairffordd Powys 62 F7
Pedlinge Kent 17 L4
Pedmore Dudley 52 G4
Pedwell Somset 21 P6
Peebles Border 106 H2
Peel IoM 102 c5
Peel Lancs 83 J9
Peel Common Hants 13 J4
Peel Green Crematorium Salfd 76 D4
Peene Kent 17 L3
Peening Quarter Kent 16 F5
Peggs Green Leics 66 C8
Pegsdon C Beds 44 G5
Pegswood Nthumb 109 L12
Pegwell Kent 35 Q9
Peinchorran Highld 135 J9
Peinlich Highld 134 G4
Pelcomb Pembks 36 H7
Pelcomb Bridge Pembks 36 H7
Pelcomb Cross Pembks 36 H7
Peldon Essex 46 H8
Pell Green E Susx 16 B4
Pelsall Wsall 65 J11
Pelsall Wood Wsall 65 J11
Pelton Dur 100 G7
Pelton Fell Dur 100 H8
Pelutho Cumb 97 M8
Pelynt Cnwll 4 B6
Pemberton Carmth 26 D2
Pemberton Wigan 75 P3
Pembles Cross Kent 16 F1
Pembrey Carmth 26 C2
Pembridge Herefs 51 L9
Pembroke Pembks 37 J10
Pembroke Dock Pembks 37 J10
Pembrokeshire Coast National Park Pembks 36 G6
Pembury Kent 16 A3
Pen-allt Herefs 40 H6
Penallt Mons 40 H9
Penally Pembks 37 M10
Penare Cnwll 3 N6
Penarth V Glam 28 B8
Penblewin Pembks 37 M7
Pen-bont Rhydybeddau Cerdgn 49 L4
Penbryn Cerdgn 48 E10
Pencader Carmth 38 C4
Pencaenewydd Gwynd 60 G4
Pencaitland E Loth 116 B7
Pencarnisiog IoA 72 F9
Pencarreg Carmth 38 E3
Pencarrow Cnwll 6 G8
Pencelli Powys 39 P7
Penclawdd Swans 26 E3
Pencoed Brdgnd 27 M6
Pencombe Herefs 51 Q10
Pencoyd Herefs 40 G6
Pencraig Herefs 40 H7
Pencraig Powys 62 E7
Pendeen Cnwll 2 B7
Penderyn Rhondd 39 M10
Pendine Carmth 37 P9
Pendlebury Salfd 76 E3
Pendleton Lancs 83 R7
Pendock Worcs 41 M5
Pendoggett Cnwll 6 E9
Pendomer Somset 10 E3
Pendoylan V Glam 27 P7
Pendre Brdgnd 27 L6
Penegoes Powys 61 N12
Penelewey Cnwll 3 K6
Pen-ffordd Pembks 37 L6
Pengam Caerph 27 R3
Pengam Cardif 28 B7
Penge Gt Lon 33 L8
Pengelly Cnwll 6 F8
Pengorffwysfa IoA 72 H5
Pengover Green Cnwll 4 D4
Pen-groes-oped Mons 40 D10
Pengwern Denbgs 74 D8
Penhale Cnwll 2 H10
Penhale Cnwll 3 M3
Penhale Cnwll 3 Q2
Penhale Cnwll 4 F6
Penhallow Cnwll 3 J4
Penhalurick Cnwll 2 H7
Penhalvean Cnwll 2 H7
Penhill Swindn 30 D5
Penhow Newpt 28 F4
Penhurst E Susx 16 C7
Peniarth Gwynd 61 K11
Penicuik Mdloth 115 N9
Peniel Carmth 38 C7
Peniel Denbgs 74 E11
Penifiler Highld 135 J7
Peninver Ag & B 103 K5
Penisarwaun Gwynd 73 J11
Penistone Barns 77 N3
Penjerrick Cnwll 3 J8
Penketh Warrtn 75 P6
Penkill S Ayrs 104 D10
Penkridge Staffs 64 H9
Penlean Cnwll 7 J5
Penleigh Wilts 23 J3
Penley Wrexhm 63 L4
Penllergaer Swans 26 F3
Pen-llyn IoA 72 F7
Penllyn V Glam 27 M7
Pen-lôn IoA 72 G10
Penmachno Conwy 61 N2
Penmaen Caerph 28 A3
Penmaen Swans 26 D5
Penmaenan Conwy 73 M8
Penmaenmawr Conwy 73 M8
Penmaenpool Gwynd 61 M8
Penmark V Glam 27 P8
Penmon IoA 73 K7
Penmorfa Gwynd 61 J4
Penmount Crematorium Cnwll 3 K5
Penmynydd IoA 72 H9
Penn Bucks 32 C4
Penn Wolves 52 G2
Pennal Gwynd 61 M12
Pennan Abers 141 K3
Pennant Cerdgn 48 H8
Pennant Denbgs 62 E5
Pennant Powys 49 Q1
Pennant-Melangell Powys 62 D7
Pennard Swans 26 E5
Pennerley Shrops 63 K12
Pennicott Devon 8 G4
Pennines 84 E8
Pennington Cumb 88 H11
Pennington Hants 12 E6
Pennington Green Wigan 76 B2
Pennorth Powys 39 Q6
Penn Street Bucks 32 C3
Pennsylvania S Glos 29 M7
Penny Bridge Cumb 89 J10
Pennycross Ag & B 119 N7
Pennygate Norfk 71 L7
Pennyghael Ag & B 119 N7
Pennyglen S Ayrs 104 E7
Penny Green Derbys 78 E8
Penny Hill Lincs 68 G7
Pennymoor Devon 8 G3
Pennywell Sundld 101 J7
Penparc Cerdgn 48 C11
Penparcau Cerdgn 49 K4
Penpedairheol Caerph 27 Q3
Penpedairheol Mons 40 D11
Penperlleni Mons 40 D10
Penpethy Cnwll 6 F7
Penpillick Cnwll 3 Q3
Penpol Cnwll 3 K7
Penpoll Cnwll 4 A6
Penponds Cnwll 2 G7
Penpont Cnwll 6 F10
Penpont D & G 105 Q11
Penpont Powys 39 M6
Penquit Devon 5 K6
Penrest Cnwll 7 L9
Penrherber Carmth 37 Q3
Pen-rhiw Pembks 37 P2
Penrhiwceiber Rhondd 27 P3
Pen Rhiwfawr Neath 38 H9
Penrhiwllan Cerdgn 38 B3
Penrhiw-pal Cerdgn 48 E11
Penrhos Gwynd 60 E5
Penrhos IoA 72 D7
Penrhos Mons 40 F9
Penrhos Powys 39 J9
Penrhos garnedd Gwynd 73 J9
Penrhyn Bay Conwy 73 P7
Penrhyncoch Cerdgn 49 L4
Penrhyn-coch Cerdgn 49 L4
Penrhyndeudraeth Gwynd 61 K4
Penrhyn-side Conwy 73 P7
Penrice Swans 26 D5
Penrioch N Ayrs 112 C12
Penrith Cumb 98 G12
Penrose Cnwll 6 C10
Penruddock Cumb 89 L1
Penryn Cnwll 3 J7
Pensarn Conwy 74 C8
Pensax Worcs 52 D7
Pensby Wirral 75 J7
Penselwood Somset 22 G7
Pensford BaNES 29 J9
Pensham Worcs 41 Q3
Penshaw Sundld 101 J7
Penshurst Kent 15 P2
Penshurst Station Kent 15 P2
Pensilva Cnwll 4 D3
Pensnett Dudley 52 G3
Penstone Devon 8 E5
Penstrowed Powys 50 E2
Pentewan Cnwll 3 P5
Pentir Gwynd 73 J10
Pentire Cnwll 3 K2
Pentlepoir Pembks 37 M9
Pentlow Essex 46 E2
Pentlow Street Essex 46 E3
Pentney Norfk 69 N9
Pentonbridge Cumb 98 F3
Penton Grafton Hants 24 E4
Penton Mewsey Hants 24 E4
Pentraeth IoA 73 J8
Pentre Denbgs 74 F11
Pentre Flints 75 K10
Pentre Mons 28 F2
Pentre Mons 40 D10
Pentre Powys 50 E3
Pentre Powys 50 G3
Pentre Powys 51 J2
Pentre Rhondd 27 M3
Pentre Shrops 63 L8
Pentre Wrexhm 63 J4
Pentre bâch Cerdgn 38 E2
Pentre Bach Flints 74 H8
Pentrebach Myr Td 39 P11
Pentre-bach Powys 39 L5
Pentrebeirdd Powys 62 G9
Pentre Berw IoA 72 H9
Pentre-bont Conwy 61 M2
Pentrebychan Crematorium Wrexhm 63 J3
Pentre-cagel Carmth 37 R2
Pentrecelyn Denbgs 62 G2
Pentre-celyn Powys 62 B11
Pentre-chwyth Swans 26 G3
Pentre-clawdd Shrops 63 J6
Pentre-cwrt Carmth 38 B4
Pentredwr Denbgs 62 H3
Pentrefelin Gwynd 61 J4
Pentrefelin IoA 72 G5
Pentre Ffwrndan Flints 75 J9
Pentrefoelas Conwy 61 Q2
Pentregalar Pembks 37 N4
Pentregat Cerdgn 48 F10
Pentre-Gwenlais Carmth 38 F8
Pentre Gwynfryn Gwynd 61 K7
Pentre Halkyn Flints 74 H9
Pentre Hodrey Shrops 51 K5
Pentre Isaf Conwy 74 D9
Pentre Llanrhaeadr Denbgs 74 E11
Pentre Llifior Powys 50 G1
Pentre-llwyn-llwyd Powys 50 C9
Pentre-llyn Cerdgn 49 K6
Pentre-llyn-cymmer Conwy 62 D2
Pentre-Maw Powys 62 B11
Pentre Meyrick V Glam 27 M7
Pentre-piod Torfn 40 C11
Pentre-poeth Newpt 28 C5
Pentre'rbryn Cerdgn 48 F9
Pentre'r-felin Cerdgn 49 K11
Pentre'r Felin Conwy 73 P10
Pentre'r-felin Powys 39 L5
Pentre Saron Denbgs 74 E11
Pentre-tafarn-y-fedw Conwy 73 P11
Pentre ty gwyn Carmth 39 K5
Pentrich Derbys 66 C2
Pentridge Dorset 23 M10
Pen-twyn Caerph 28 B2
Pen-twyn Mons 40 H10
Pen-twyn Torfn 40 C11
Pentwynmaur Caerph 28 B3
Pentyrch Cardif 27 Q6
Penwithick Cnwll 3 P3
Penwood Hants 31 J10
Penwyllt Powys 39 K8
Penybanc Carmth 38 F7
Penybont Powys 50 F8
Pen-y-bont Powys 62 H7
Pen-y-bont-fawr Powys 62 F7
Pen-y-bryn Pembks 37 N2
Pen-y-cae Powys 39 K9
Penycae Wrexhm 63 J3
Pen-y-cae-mawr Mons 28 F3
Penycaerau Gwynd 60 C6
Pen-y-cefn Flints 74 F8
Pen-y-clawdd Mons 40 F10
Pen-y-coedcae Rhondd 27 P5
Penycwn Pembks 36 G6
Pen-y-fai Brdgnd 27 L6
Pen-y-felin Flints 74 G9
Penyffordd Flints 75 J11
Penyffridd Gwynd 72 H12
Pen-y-garn Cerdgn 49 K3
Pen-y-Garnedd Powys 62 F7
Pen-y-genffordd Powys 40 A6
Pen-y-graig Gwynd 60 C5
Penygraig Rhondd 27 N4
Penygroes Carmth 38 E9
Penygroes Gwynd 60 H2
Pen-y-Gwryd Gwynd 61 L1
Pen-y-lan V Glam 27 N7
Pen-y-Mynydd Carmth 38 C11
Penymynydd Flints 75 J11
Pen-y-pass Gwynd 61 L1
Pen-yr-Heol Mons 40 F9
Pen-yr-Heolgerrig Myr Td 39 N10
Penysarn IoA 72 G5
Pen-y-stryt Denbgs 62 H2
Penywaun Rhondd 39 M10
Penzance Cnwll 2 D8
Peopleton Worcs 52 H10
Peover Heath Ches E 76 E9
Peper Harow Surrey 14 D2
Peplow Shrops 64 B7
Pepper's Green Essex 46 A9
Pepperstock C Beds 44 F8
Perceton N Ayrs 104 F2
Percyhorner Abers 141 M3
Perelle Guern 12 b2
Perham Down Wilts 24 D4
Periton Somset 20 E4
Perivale Gt Lon 32 H6
Perkins Village Devon 9 J6
Perkinsville Dur 100 H7
Perlethorpe Notts 78 G9
Perranarworthal Cnwll 3 J7
Perranporth Cnwll 3 J4
Perranuthnoe Cnwll 2 E8
Perranwell Cnwll 3 J4
Perranwell Cnwll 3 J6
Perran Wharf Cnwll 3 J7
Perranzabuloe Cnwll 3 J4
Perrott's Brook Gloucs 42 B10
Perry Birm 53 K2
Perry Barr Birm 53 K2
Perry Barr Crematorium Birm 53 K2
Perry Green Essex 46 E7
Perry Green Herts 45 N8
Perry Green Wilts 29 R4
Perrystone Hill Herefs 41 K6
Perry Street Somset 9 Q4
Pershall Staffs 64 E6
Pershore Worcs 41 Q2
Pertenhall Bed 56 B7
Perth P & K 124 C8
Perth Crematorium P & K 124 B8
Perthy Shrops 63 L5
Perton Herefs 41 J4
Perton Staffs 64 F12
Pertwood Wilts 23 K6
Peterborough C Pete 68 D12
Peterborough Crematorium C Pete 68 C11
Peterborough Services Cambs 56 C2
Peterchurch Herefs 40 D4
Peterculter C Aber 133 K4
Peterhead Abers 141 Q6
Peterlee Dur 101 L10
Petersfield Hants 25 N8
Peter's Green Herts 44 G8
Petersham Gt Lon 32 H7
Peters Marland Devon 19 J10
Peterstone Wentlooge Newpt 28 C6
Peterston-super-Ely V Glam 27 P7
Peterstow Herefs 40 H7
Peters Village Kent 34 C9
Peter Tavy Devon 7 P9
Petham Kent 35 K12
Petherwin Gate Cnwll 7 K7
Petrockstow Devon 7 P3
Petsoe End M Keyn 55 M10
Pet Street Kent 17 K1
Pett E Susx 16 F8
Pettaugh Suffk 58 H8
Pett Bottom Kent 35 L12
Petterden Angus 124 H5
Pettinain S Lans 106 C1
Pettistree Suffk 59 L9
Petton Devon 20 F8
Petton Shrops 63 M7
Petts Wood Gt Lon 33 N9
Pettycur Fife 115 N4
Petty France S Glos 29 M5
Pettymuk Abers 141 L11
Petworth W Susx 14 D6
Pevensey E Susx 16 B10
Pevensey Bay E Susx 16 B10
Pewsey Wilts 30 D10
Pheasant's Hill Bucks 31 R5
Phepson Worcs 52 H8
Philadelphia Sundld 101 J8
Philham Devon 18 E9
Philiphaugh Border 107 L4
Phillack Cnwll 2 F7
Philleigh Cnwll 3 L6
Philpot End Essex 45 R8
Philpstoun W Loth 115 K6
Phocle Green Herefs 41 J6
Phoenix Green Hants 25 N2
Phones Highld 130 C5
Pibsbury Somset 21 P8
Pica Cumb 88 D2
Piccadilly Warwks 53 N1
Piccotts End Herts 44 F9
Pickburn Donc 78 E2
Pickering N York 92 F10
Picket Piece Hants 24 F4
Picket Post Hants 12 C3
Picket Twenty Hants 24 F4
Pickford Covtry 53 P4
Pickford Green Covtry 53 P4
Pickhill N York 91 N10
Picklescott Shrops 63 M12
Pickmere Ches E 76 C8
Pickney Somset 21 K7
Pickstock Wrekin 64 D7
Pickup Bank Bl w D 83 Q10
Pickwell Devon 19 J5
Pickwell Leics 67 K10
Pickwick Wilts 29 P8
Pickworth Lincs 67 P5
Pickworth Rutlnd 67 N9
Picton Ches W 75 M9
Picton Flints 74 F7
Picton N York 91 P5
Piddinghoe E Susx 15 N10
Piddington Bucks 32 A3
Piddington Nhants 55 K9
Piddington Oxon 43 N8
Piddlehinton Dorset 10 H5
Piddletrenthide Dorset 10 H5
Pidley Cambs 56 F5
Piercebridge Darltn 91 L4
Pierowall Ork 147 c1
Piff's Elm Gloucs 41 P6
Pigdon Nthumb 109 J12
Pigeon Green Warwks 53 N8
Pig Oak Dorset 11 N4
Pig Street Herefs 51 L11
Pikehall Derbys 77 M12
Pilford Dorset 11 P4
Pilgrims Hatch Essex 33 Q3
Pilham Lincs 79 L5
Pill N Som 28 H7
Pillaton Cnwll 4 E4
Pillatonmill Cnwll 4 E4
Pillerton Hersey Warwks 53 P11
Pillerton Priors Warwks 53 P11
Pilleth Powys 51 J7
Pilley Barns 77 Q4
Pilley Hants 12 E5
Pilley Bailey Hants 12 E5
Pillgwenlly Newpt 28 D5
Pillhead Devon 19 J8
Pilling Lancs 83 J5
Pilling Lane Lancs 83 J5
Pilning S Glos 28 H5
Pilot Inn Kent 17 K7
Pilsbury Derbys 77 L11
Pilsdon Dorset 10 C5
Pilsgate C Pete 67 Q11
Pilsley Derbys 77 N9
Pilsley Derbys 78 C11
Pilson Green Norfk 71 M9
Piltdown E Susx 15 N6
Pilton Devon 19 L6
Pilton Nhants 55 P4
Pilton Rutlnd 67 M11
Pilton Somset 22 D5
Pilton Green Swans 26 C5
Pimbo Lancs 75 N3
Pimlico Herts 44 F10
Pimlico Lancs 83 R6
Pimlico Nhants 43 N3
Pimperne Dorset 11 L3
Pinchbeck Lincs 68 E7
Pinchbeck Bars Lincs 68 D7
Pincheon Green Donc 86 C11
Pinchinthorpe R & Cl 92 C4
Pincock Lancs 83 M11
Pinfold Lancs 75 L1
Pinford End Suffk 58 C8
Pinged Carmth 38 B11
Pingewood W Berk 31 P8
Pin Green Herts 45 J6
Pinhoe Devon 8 H6
Pinkett's Booth Covtry 53 P4
Pinkney Wilts 29 P5
Pinkneys Green W & M 32 B6
Pinley Covtry 54 B5
Pinley Green Warwks 53 N7
Pin Mill Suffk 47 M4
Pinminnoch S Ayrs 104 C11
Pinmore S Ayrs 104 D11
Pinn Devon 9 L7
Pinner Gt Lon 32 G4
Pinner Green Gt Lon 32 G4
Pinsley Green Ches E 63 P3
Pinvin Worcs 52 H11
Pinwherry S Ayrs 104 D12
Pinxton Derbys 66 D1
Pipe and Lyde Herefs 40 G3
Pipe Aston Herefs 51 M6
Pipe Gate Shrops 64 D4
Pipehill Staffs 65 K10
Piperhill Highld 138 F6
Pipers Pool Cnwll 7 J8
Pipewell Nhants 55 L3
Pippacott Devon 19 K6
Pippin Street Lancs 83 N10
Pipton Powys 39 R4
Pirbright Surrey 32 D11
Pirbright Camp Surrey 32 D11
Pirnie Border 107 Q4
Pirnmill N Ayrs 112 C12
Pirton Herts 44 G5
Pirton Worcs 52 G11
Pisgah Cerdgn 49 L5
Pishill Oxon 31 P4
Pistyll Gwynd 60 E4
Pitagowan P & K 130 E11
Pitblae Abers 141 N3
Pitcairngreen P & K 123 Q7
Pitcalnie Highld 146 E10
Pitcaple Abers 140 H10
Pitcarity Angus 131 Q11
Pitchcombe Gloucs 41 N10
Pitchcott Bucks 43 Q7
Pitcher Row Lincs 68 F5
Pitchford Shrops 63 P11
Pitch Green Bucks 43 Q11
Pitch Place Surrey 14 C3
Pitch Place Surrey 32 D11
Pitchroy Moray 139 M8
Pitcombe Somset 22 F7
Pitcot V Glam 27 L7
Pitcox E Loth 116 E6
Pitfichie Abers 132 G1
Pitglassie Abers 140 H7
Pitgrudy Highld 146 E7
Pitlessie Fife 124 G11
Pitlochry P & K 123 N1
Pitmachie Abers 140 G10
Pitmain Highld 130 D4
Pitmedden Abers 141 L10
Pitmedden Garden Abers 141 L10
Pitminster Somset 21 K9
Pitmuies Angus 125 L3
Pitmunie Abers 132 G1
Pitney Somset 21 P7
Pitroddie P & K 124 E8
Pitscottie Fife 124 H10
Pitsea Essex 34 C5
Pitses Oldham 76 H3
Pitsford Nhants 55 J7
Pitstone Bucks 44 D8
Pitt Devon 20 G10
Pitt Hants 24 G8
Pittarrow Abers 132 H9
Pitt Court Gloucs 29 M3
Pittenweem Fife 125 L12
Pitteuchar Fife 115 P1
Pittington Dur 101 J9
Pittodrie House Hotel Abers 140 H11
Pitton Wilts 24 C7
Pitt's Wood Kent 33 R12
Pittulie Abers 141 M2
Pityme Cnwll 6 D9
Pity Me Dur 100 H9
Pivington Kent 16 G2
Pixey Green Suffk 59 K5
Pixham Surrey 32 H12
Plains N Lans 114 E8
Plain Street Cnwll 6 E9
Plaish Shrops 51 N1
Plaistow Gt Lon 33 M6
Plaistow W Susx 14 E5
Plaitford Hants 24 D9
Plank Lane Wigan 76 B4
Plas Cymyran IoA 72 E8
Plastow Green Hants 31 L10
Platt Bridge Wigan 75 Q3
Platt Lane Shrops 63 N5
Platts Heath Kent 34 F12
Plawsworth Dur 100 H8
Plaxtol Kent 33 R11
Playden E Susx 16 G6
Playford Suffk 59 J11
Play Hatch Oxon 31 Q7
Playing Place Cnwll 3 K6
Playley Green Gloucs 41 M5
Plealey Shrops 63 M10
Plean Stirlg 114 F4
Pleasance Fife 124 E10
Pleasington Bl w D 83 P10
Pleasington Crematorium Bl w D 83 P10
Pleasley Derbys 78 E10
Pleasleyhill Notts 78 E11
Pleasurewood Hills Suffk 59 Q1
Pleck Dorset 10 H3
Pledgdon Green Essex 45 Q6
Pledwick Wakefd 85 M12
Pleinheaume Guern 12 c1
Plemont Jersey 13 a1
Plemstall Ches W 75 M9
Plenmeller Nthumb 99 K6
Pleshey Essex 46 B9
Plockton Highld 135 P9
Plowden Shrops 51 L3
Plox Green Shrops 63 L11
Pluckley Kent 16 G2
Pluckley Station Kent 16 G2
Pluckley Thorne Kent 16 G2
Plucks Gutter Kent 35 N9
Plumbland Cumb 97 N10
Plumgarths Cumb 89 M8
Plumley Ches E 76 D8
Plumpton Cumb 89 J11
Plumpton Cumb 98 G11
Plumpton E Susx 15 L8
Plumpton Nhants 54 F11
Plumpton End Nhants 43 P3
Plumpton Green E Susx 15 L7
Plumpton Head Cumb 98 G11
Plumstead Gt Lon 33 N6
Plumstead Norfk 70 H5
Plumstead Green Norfk 70 H5
Plumtree Notts 66 G5
Plumtree Green Kent 16 E2
Plungar Leics 67 J5
Plurenden Kent 16 G3
Plush Dorset 10 H4
Plusha Cnwll 7 J8
Plushabridge Cnwll 7 K10
Plwmp Cerdgn 48 F10
Plymouth C Plym 4 G6
Plymouth Airport C Plym 4 H5
Plympton C Plym 4 H5
Plymstock C Plym 4 H6
Plymtree Devon 9 K4
Pockley N York 92 D9
Pocklington E R Yk 86 E5
Pode Hole Lincs 68 D8
Podimore Somset 22 D8
Podington Bed 55 N8
Podmore Staffs 64 E5
Point Clear Essex 47 K8
Pointon Lincs 68 C6
Pokesdown Bmouth 11 Q6
Polbain Highld 144 C3
Polbathic Cnwll 4 E5
Polbeth W Loth 115 J8
Polbrock Cnwll 6 E11
Poldark Mine Cnwll 2 H8
Polebrook Nhants 55 Q3
Pole Elm Worcs 52 F10
Polegate E Susx 15 Q10
Pole Moor Kirk 84 G12
Polesden Lacey Surrey 32 G12
Polesworth Warwks 65 N11
Polgigga Cnwll 2 B9
Polglass Highld 144 C4
Polgooth Cnwll 3 N4
Polgown D & G 105 N9
Poling W Susx 14 F10
Poling Corner W Susx 14 F9
Polkerris Cnwll 3 Q4
Pollard Street Norfk 71 L5
Pollington E R Yk 86 B11
Polloch Highld 127 P10
Pollokshaws C Glas 113 Q9
Pollokshields C Glas 113 Q8
Polmassick Cnwll 3 N5
Polmear Cnwll 3 Q4
Polmont Falk 114 G6
Polnish Highld 127 N8
Polperro Cnwll 4 B6
Polruan Cnwll 3 R4
Polsham Somset 22 C5
Polstead Suffk 46 H4
Polstead Heath Suffk 46 H4
Poltalloch Ag & B 112 B2
Poltescoe Cnwll 2 H11
Poltimore Devon 8 H5
Polton Mdloth 115 P8
Polwarth Border 116 G11
Polyphant Cnwll 7 K8
Polzeath Cnwll 6 D9
Pomathorn Mdloth 115 N9
Pomeroy Derbys 77 L10
Ponde Powys 39 Q4
Pondersbridge Cambs 56 E2
Ponders End Gt Lon 33 L3
Ponsanooth Cnwll 3 J7
Ponsonby Cumb 88 E5
Ponsongath Cnwll 3 J11
Ponsworthy Devon 8 D10
Pont Abraham Services Carmth 38 E10
Pontac Jersey 13 d3
Pontamman Carmth 38 F9
Pontantwn Carmth 38 C9
Pontardawe Neath 38 H11
Pontarddulais Swans 38 E11
Pont-ar-gothi Carmth 38 D7
Pont-ar-Hydfer Powys 39 K6
Pont-ar-llechau Carmth 38 H7
Pontarsais Carmth 38 C6
Pontblyddyn Flints 75 J11
Pont Cyfyng Conwy 73 M12
Pontcysyllte Aqueduct Wrexhm 63 J4
Pont Dolgarrog Conwy 73 N10
Pontdolgoch Powys 50 D2
Pont-Ebbw Newpt 28 C5
Pontefract Wakefd 85 P11
Pontefract Crematorium Wakefd 85 N11
Ponteland Nthumb 100 F4
Ponterwyd Cerdgn 49 N4
Pontesbury Shrops 63 L11
Pontesbury Hill Shrops 63 L11
Pontesford Shrops 63 L11
Pontfadog Wrexhm 62 H4
Pontfaen Pembks 37 K4

Ringstead Nhants ... 55 N5
Ringstead Norfk ... 69 N4
Ringwood Hants ... 12 B4
Ringwould Kent ... 17 P1
Rinmore Abers ... 132 C1
Rinsey Cnwll ... 2 F9
Rinsey Croft Cnwll ... 2 F9
Ripe E Susx ... 15 P9
Ripley Derbys ... 66 C2
Ripley Hants ... 12 B5
Ripley N York ... 85 L3
Ripley Surrey ... 32 F11
Riplingham E R Yk ... 86 H9
Riplington Hants ... 25 L8
Ripon N York ... 85 L1
Rippingale Lincs ... 68 B6
Ripple Kent ... 35 P12
Ripple Worcs ... 41 P4
Ripponden Calder ... 84 F11
Risabus Ag & B ... 102 B1
Risbury Herefs ... 51 P9
Risby N Linc ... 86 G12
Risby Suffk ... 57 Q7
Risca Caerph ... 28 B4
Rise E R Yk ... 87 M7
Riseden E Susx ... 16 A5
Riseden Kent ... 16 C4
Risegate Lincs ... 68 D6
Riseholme Lincs ... 79 N8
Risehow Cumb ... 97 L11
Riseley Bed ... 55 P8
Riseley Wokham ... 31 P9
Rishangles Suffk ... 58 H7
Rishton Lancs ... 83 Q9
Rishworth Calder ... 84 F11
Rising Bridge Lancs ... 84 B10
Risley Derbys ... 66 D5
Risley Warrtn ... 76 C5
Risplith N York ... 85 K1
Rivar Wilts ... 30 G10
Rivenhall End Essex ... 46 E8
River Kent ... 17 N2
River W Susx ... 14 D6
River Bank Cambs ... 57 K7
Riverford Highld ... 137 P5
Riverhead Kent ... 33 P11
Rivers Corner Dorset ... 22 H10
Rivington Lancs ... 83 N12
Rivington Services
Lancs ... 76 B1
Roachill Devon ... 20 C9
Roade Nhants ... 55 J10
Road Green Norfk ... 59 K2
Roadhead Cumb ... 98 G3
Roadmeetings S Lans ... 114 F11
Roadside E Ayrs ... 105 K6
Roadside Highld ... 151 L4
Roadwater Somset ... 20 G6
Roag Highld ... 134 E7
Roa Island Cumb ... 82 F2
Roan of Craigoch
S Ayrs ... 104 E9
Roast Green Essex ... 45 N5
Roath Cardif ... 28 B7
Roberton Border ... 107 L7
Roberton S Lans ... 106 B4
Robertsbridge E Susx ... 16 C6
Robertown Kirk ... 85 J10
Roberton Wathen
Pembks ... 37 L7
Robgill Tower D & G ... 97 Q4
Robin Hill Staffs ... 76 G12
Robin Hood Lancs ... 75 N1
Robin Hood Leeds ... 85 L9
Robin Hood
Crematorium Solhll ... 53 L4
Robin Hood Doncaster
Sheffield Airport
Donc ... 78 G4
Robinhood End Essex ... 46 C4
Robin Hood's Bay
N York ... 93 J6
Roborough Devon ... 4 H4
Roborough Devon ... 19 L10
Roby Knows ... 75 M5
Roby Mill Lancs ... 75 N2
Rocester Staffs ... 65 L4
Roch Pembks ... 36 G6
Rochdale Rochdl ... 76 G1
Rochdale
Crematorium
Rochdl ... 76 G1
Roche Cnwll ... 3 N2
Rochester Medway ... 34 D8
Rochester Nthumb ... 108 D10
Rochford Essex ... 34 F4
Rochford Worcs ... 52 B7
Rock Cate Pembks ... 36 G6
Rock Cnwll ... 6 D9
Rock Neath ... 27 J4
Rock Nthumb ... 109 K6
Rock W Susx ... 14 G8
Rock Worcs ... 52 D6
Rockbeare Devon ... 9 J6
Rockbourne Hants ... 23 P9
Rockcliffe Cumb ... 98 D6
Rockcliffe D & G ... 96 C7
Rockcliffe Cross Cumb ... 98 D5
Rock End Staffs ... 76 G12
Rockend Torbay ... 5 Q4
Rock Ferry Wirral ... 75 K6
Rockfield Highld ... 146 G8
Rockfield Mons ... 31 P4
Rockford Devon ... 19 P4
Rockford Hants ... 12 B3
Rockgreen Shrops ... 51 N5
Rockhampton S Glos ... 29 J4
Rockhead Cnwll ... 6 F8
Rockhill Shrops ... 51 J5
Rock Hill Worcs ... 52 H7
Rockingham Nhants ... 55 L1
Rockland All Saints
Norfk ... 58 E1
Rockland St Mary
Norfk ... 71 L11
Rockland St Peter
Norfk ... 58 E1
Rockley Notts ... 78 H8
Rockley Wilts ... 30 D8
Rockliffe Lancs ... 84 C10
Rockwell End Bucks ... 31 N5
Rockwell Green
Somset ... 20 H9
Rodborough Gloucs ... 41 N10
Rodbourne Swindn ... 30 D5
Rodbourne Wilts ... 29 Q6
Rodd Herefs ... 51 K8
Roddam Nthumb ... 108 G6
Rodden Dorset ... 10 M8
Roddymoor Dur ... 100 F11
Rode Somset ... 22 H3
Rode Heath Ches E ... 76 E12
Rode Heath Ches E ... 76 F4
Rodel W Isls ... 152 d7
Roden Wrekin ... 63 P9
Rodhuish Somset ... 20 F5
Rodington Wrekin ... 63 P9
Rodington Heath
Wrekin ... 63 P9
Rodley Gloucs ... 41 M9
Rodley Leeds ... 85 K8
Rodmarton Gloucs ... 29 Q3
Rodmell E Susx ... 15 M9
Rodmersham Kent ... 34 F10
Rodmersham Green
Kent ... 34 G10
Rodney Stoke Somset ... 21 N3
Rodsley Derbys ... 65 M4
Rodway Somset ... 21 L6
Roecliffe N York ... 85 M2
Roe Cross Tamesd ... 77 J5
Roe Green Herts ... 45 J10
Roe Green Herts ... 45 K5
Roe Green Salfd ... 76 D3
Roehampton Gt Lon ... 33 J7

Roffey W Susx ... 14 H4
Rogart Highld ... 146 C5
Rogate W Susx ... 25 P8
Roger Ground Cumb ... 89 K7
Rogerstone Newpt ... 28 C5
Roghadal W Isls ... 152 d7
Rogiet Mons ... 28 F5
Roke Oxon ... 31 M4
Roker Sundld ... 101 K6
Rollesby Norfk ... 71 N9
Rolleston Leics ... 67 J12
Rolleston Notts ... 67 J2
Rolleston on Dove
Staffs ... 65 N10
Rolston E R Yk ... 87 N6
Rolstone N Som ... 28 E10
Rolvenden Kent ... 16 E4
Rolvenden Layne Kent ... 16 E5
Romaldkirk Dur ... 90 G2
Romanby N York ... 91 N8
Romano Bridge
Border ... 115 L11
Romansleigh Devon ... 19 P9
Romden Castle Kent ... 16 F2
Romesdal Highld ... 134 G5
Romford Dorset ... 11 P3
Romford Gt Lon ... 33 P4
Romiley Stockp ... 76 H5
Romney Street Kent ... 33 Q10
Romsey Cambs ... 57 J9
Romsey Hants ... 24 F9
Romsley Shrops ... 52 H5
Romsley Worcs ... 52 H6
Rona Highld ... 135 L4
Ronachan Ag & B ... 111 Q10
Rood Ashton Wilts ... 29 P11
Rookhope Dur ... 99 P9
Rookley IoW ... 12 H8
Rookley Green IoW ... 12 H8
Rooks Bridge Somset ... 21 N3
Rooks Nest Somset ... 20 H6
Rookwith N York ... 91 L9
Roos E R Yk ... 87 P9
Roose Cumb ... 82 F1
Roosebeck Cumb ... 82 G2
Roothams Green Bed ... 56 B9
Ropley Hants ... 25 L7
Ropley Dean Hants ... 25 L7
Ropley Soke Hants ... 25 L6
Ropsley Lincs ... 67 N5
Rora Abers ... 141 P6
Rorrington Shrops ... 63 J12
Rosarie Moray ... 140 B6
Rose Cnwll ... 3 J4
Roseacre Lancs ... 83 K8
Rose Ash Devon ... 20 B9
Rosebush Pembks ... 37 L5
Rosecare Cnwll ... 6 H5
Roseddiston Cnwll ... 3 L3
Rosedale Abbey N York ... 92 E7
Rose Green Essex ... 46 F6
Rose Green Suffk ... 46 G4
Rose Green Suffk ... 46 G4
Rose Green W Susx ... 14 C11
Rosehall Highld ... 145 L5
Rosehearty Abers ... 141 M2
Rose Hill E Susx ... 15 N7
Rose Hill Lancs ... 84 B9
Rosehill Shrops ... 63 M9
Rose Hill
Crematorium Donc ... 78 G3
Roseisle Moray ... 139 L2
Roselands E Susx ... 16 A10
Rosemarket Pembks ... 37 J9
Rosemarkie Highld ... 138 D4
Rosemary Lane Devon ... 21 J10
Rosemount P & K ... 124 D4
Rosenannon Cnwll ... 6 D11
Rosenithon Cnwll ... 3 K10
Roser's Cross E Susx ... 15 Q7
Rosevean Cnwll ... 3 P2
Rosevine Cnwll ... 3 L7
Rosewarne Cnwll ... 2 F7
Rosewell Mdloth ... 115 P9
Roseworth S on T ... 91 P2
Roseworthy Cnwll ... 2 F6
Rosgill Cumb ... 89 N3
Roskestal Cnwll ... 2 B10
Roskhill Highld ... 134 E7
Roskorwell Cnwll ... 3 K9
Rosley Cumb ... 98 C9
Roslin Mdloth ... 115 N8
Rosliston Derbys ... 65 N9
Rosneath Ag & B ... 113 K5
Ross D & G ... 96 D9
Ross Nthumb ... 109 J2
Rossett Wrexhm ... 75 L12
Rossett Green N York ... 85 L5
Rossington Donc ... 78 G4
Rossland Rens ... 113 N7
Ross-on-Wye Herefs ... 41 J7
Roster Highld ... 151 N8
Rostherne Ches E ... 76 D7
Rosthwaite Cumb ... 88 H4
Roston Derbys ... 65 L4
Rosudgeon Cnwll ... 2 E8
Rosyth Fife ... 115 L4
Rothbury Nthumb ... 108 H9
Rotherby Leics ... 66 H9
Rotherfield E Susx ... 15 Q5
Rotherfield Greys
Oxon ... 31 P6
Rotherfield Peppard
Oxon ... 31 P6
Rotherham Rothm ... 78 C5
Rotherham
Crematorium
Rothm ... 78 D5
Rothersthorpe Nhants ... 55 J9
Rotherwick Hants ... 31 P11
Rothes Moray ... 139 P6
Rothesay Ag & B ... 112 G8
Rothiebrisbane Abers ... 141 J8
Rothiemay Moray ... 140 E6
Rothiemurchus Lodge
Highld ... 130 H3
Rothienorman Abers ... 140 H8
Rothley Leics ... 66 F9
Rothley Nthumb ... 108 G12
Rothmaise Abers ... 140 G9
Rothwell Leeds ... 85 M9
Rothwell Lincs ... 80 C4
Rothwell Nhants ... 55 K4
Rotsea E R Yk ... 87 K5
Rottal Lodge Angus ... 132 B10
Rottingdean Br & H ... 15 L10
Rottington Cumb ... 88 C4
Roucan D & G ... 97 L3
Roucan Loch
Crematorium D & G ... 97 L3
Roud IoW ... 12 H8
Rougham Norfk ... 70 B8
Rougham Suffk ... 58 D8
Rough Close Staffs ... 64 G4
Rough Common Kent ... 35 K10
Roughley Lancs ... 84 C7
Roughpark Abers ... 131 Q2
Roughton Lincs ... 80 E10
Roughton Norfk ... 71 J5
Roughton Shrops ... 52 E2
Roughway Kent ... 34 A11
Roundbush Essex ... 34 F2
Round Bush Herts ... 32 G3
Roundbush Green
Essex ... 45 Q8
Round Green Luton ... 44 F7
Roundham Somset ... 10 C3
Roundhay Leeds ... 85 M8
Rounds Green Sandw ... 71 N9
Round Street Kent ... 34 B8
Roundstreet
Common W Susx ... 14 F5
Roundswell Devon ... 19 K7
Roundway Wilts ... 30 B9
Roundyhill Angus ... 124 H4

Rousay Ork ... 147 C3
Rousdon Devon ... 9 P6
Rousham Oxon ... 43 K7
Rous Lench Worcs ... 53 J10
Routenburn N Ayrs ... 113 J9
Routh E R Yk ... 87 K7
Rout's Green Bucks ... 31 R3
Row Cnwll ... 6 G9
Row Cumb ... 89 M9
Row Cumb ... 99 J11
Rowanburn D & G ... 98 E3
Rowardennan Stirlg ... 113 M2
Rowarth Derbys ... 77 J6
Row Ash Hants ... 25 J10
Rowberrow Somset ... 28 F10
Rowde Wilts ... 29 R10
Rowden Devon ... 8 C5
Rowen Conwy ... 73 N9
Rowfield Derbys ... 65 M2
Rowfoot Nthumb ... 99 K6
Rowford Somset ... 21 J8
Row Green Essex ... 46 D7
Rowhedge Essex ... 47 J7
Rowhook W Susx ... 14 G4
Rowington Warwks ... 53 M7
Rowland Derbys ... 77 N9
Rowland's Castle
Hants ... 13 M3
Rowlands Gill Gatesd ... 100 F6
Rowledge Surrey ... 25 P5
Rowley Dur ... 100 E8
Rowley E R Yk ... 86 H8
Rowley Shrops ... 63 J11
Rowley Hill Kirk ... 85 J12
Rowley Regis Sandw ... 52 H3
Rowley Regis
Crematorium
Sandw ... 52 H3
Rowlstone Herefs ... 40 E6
Rowly Surrey ... 14 F2
Rowner Hants ... 13 K4
Rowney Green Worcs ... 53 K6
Rownhams Hants ... 24 F10
Rownhams Services
Hants ... 24 F9
Rowrah Cumb ... 88 E3
Rowsham Bucks ... 44 B8
Rowsley Derbys ... 77 N10
Rows of Trees Ches E ... 76 F8
Rowstock Oxon ... 31 K4
Rowston Lincs ... 80 B12
Rowthorne Derbys ... 78 D10
Rowton Ches W ... 75 M11
Rowton Shrops ... 51 L4
Rowton Shrops ... 63 L9
Rowton Wrekin ... 63 P8
Row Town Surrey ... 32 E9
Roxburgh Border ... 108 A4
Roxby N Linc ... 86 G11
Roxby N York ... 92 H5
Roxton Bed ... 56 C9
Roxwell Essex ... 46 B10
Royal Leamington
Spa Warwks ... 53 Q7
Royal Oak Darltn ... 91 L2
Royal Oak Lancs ... 75 L3
Royal's Green Ches E ... 64 B4
Royal Sutton
Coldfield Birm ... 53 L1
Royal Tunbridge Wells
Kent ... 15 Q3
Royal Wootton
Bassett Wilts ... 30 C6
Royal Yacht Britannia
C Edin ... 115 N6
Roy Bridge Highld ... 129 J8
Roydhouse Kirk ... 77 L1
Roydon Essex ... 45 M9
Roydon Norfk ... 70 B7
Roydon Norfk ... 69 N7
Roydon Hamlet Essex ... 45 M10
Royston Barns ... 78 B1
Royston Herts ... 45 L4
Royton Oldham ... 76 G2
Rozel Jersey ... 13 c1
Ruabon Wrexhm ... 63 J3
Ruaig Ag & B ... 118 C3
Ruan High Lanes Cnwll ... 3 M6
Ruan Lanihorne Cnwll ... 3 L6
Ruan Major Cnwll ... 2 H11
Ruan Minor Cnwll ... 2 H11
Ruardean Gloucs ... 41 J9
Ruardean Hill Gloucs ... 41 K8
Ruardean Woodside
Gloucs ... 41 J9
Rubery Birm ... 53 J5
Rubha Ban W Isls ... 152 C12
Ruckcroft Cumb ... 98 G9
Ruckhall Herefs ... 40 F4
Ruckinge Kent ... 17 J4
Ruckland Lincs ... 80 F8
Ruckley Shrops ... 63 P12
Rudby N York ... 91 Q5
Rudchester Nthumb ... 100 E5
Ruddington Notts ... 66 F5
Ruddle Gloucs ... 41 K9
Ruddlemoor Cnwll ... 3 N3
Rudford Gloucs ... 41 M7
Rudge Somset ... 22 H3
Rudgeway S Glos ... 29 J5
Rudgwick W Susx ... 14 F4
Rudhall Herefs ... 41 J6
Rudheath Ches W ... 76 C9
Rudheath Woods
Ches E ... 76 D9
Rudley Green Essex ... 46 E11
Rudloe Wilts ... 29 N8
Rudry Caerph ... 28 B5
Rudston E R Yk ... 87 L2
Rudyard Staffs ... 76 H12
Ruecastle Border ... 107 P6
Rufford Lancs ... 83 K12
Rufford Abbey Notts ... 78 G10
Rufforth C York ... 85 Q5
Rug Denbgs ... 62 E3
Rugby Warwks ... 54 E5
Rugeley Staffs ... 65 K8
Ruishton Somset ... 21 L8
Ruislip Gt Lon ... 32 F4
Rum Highld ... 126 G5
Rumbach Moray ... 140 B5
Rumbling Bridge P & K ... 115 J1
Rumburgh Suffk ... 59 L4
Rumby Hill Dur ... 100 F11
Rumford Cnwll ... 6 C10
Rumford Falk ... 114 G6
Rumney Cardif ... 28 B6
Rumwell Somset ... 21 K8
Runcorn Halton ... 75 N7
Runcton W Susx ... 14 C10
Runcton Holme Norfk ... 69 M10
Runfold Surrey ... 14 B1
Runhall Norfk ... 70 F10
Runham Norfk ... 71 P10
Runham Norfk ... 71 Q10
Runnington Somset ... 20 H9
Runsell Green Essex ... 46 D10
Runshaw Moor Lancs ... 83 M11
Runswick N York ... 92 G3
Runtaleave Angus ... 131 P10
Runwell Essex ... 34 D3
Ruscombe Wokham ... 31 R7
Rushall Herefs ... 41 K5
Rushall Norfk ... 59 J4
Rushall Wilts ... 25 J2
Rushall Wsall ... 65 J12
Rushbrooke Suffk ... 58 C8
Rushbury Shrops ... 51 N2
Rushden Herts ... 45 K5
Rushden Nhants ... 55 M7
Rusher's Cross E Susx ... 15 R5
Rushford Devon ... 7 N9
Rushford Norfk ... 58 D4
Rush Green Essex ... 47 L8

Rush Green Gt Lon ... 33 P5
Rush Green Herts ... 45 J7
Rush Green Warrtn ... 76 C7
Rushlake Green E Susx ... 16 A7
Rushmere Suffk ... 59 N4
Rushmere St Andrew
Suffk ... 47 M2
Rushmoor Surrey ... 14 B3
Rushock Herefs ... 51 K9
Rushock Worcs ... 52 G6
Rushoime Manch ... 76 F5
Rushton Ches W ... 75 P11
Rushton Nhants ... 55 L4
Rushton Shrops ... 63 Q10
Rushton Spencer
Staffs ... 76 H11
Rushwick Worcs ... 52 F10
Rushyford Dur ... 91 M1
Ruskie Stirlg ... 114 B1
Ruskington Lincs ... 68 B2
Rusland Cross Cumb ... 89 K9
Rusper W Susx ... 14 H3
Ruspidge Gloucs ... 41 K9
Russell Green Essex ... 46 D9
Russell's Water Oxon ... 31 P4
Russel's Green Suffk ... 59 K6
Russ Hill Surrey ... 15 J3
Rusthall Kent ... 15 Q3
Rustington W Susx ... 14 F10
Ruston N York ... 93 J10
Ruston Parva E R Yk ... 87 K3
Ruswarp N York ... 92 H5
Ruthall Shrops ... 51 Q3
Rutherford Border ... 107 Q4
Rutherglen S Lans ... 114 B9
Ruthernbridge Cnwll ... 6 E11
Ruthin Denbgs ... 74 F12
Ruthrieston C Aber ... 133 M3
Ruthven Abers ... 140 D6
Ruthven Angus ... 124 F5
Ruthven Highld ... 130 D2
Ruthven Highld ... 138 G5
Ruthvoes Cnwll ... 3 M2
Ruthwaite Cumb ... 97 P11
Ruthwell D & G ... 97 M5
Ruxley Corner Gt Lon ... 33 N8
Ruxton Green Herefs ... 40 H8
Ruyton-XI-Towns
Shrops ... 63 L8
Ryal Nthumb ... 100 C3
Ryall Dorset ... 10 B6
Ryall Worcs ... 41 P3
Ryarsh Kent ... 34 B10
Rycote Oxon ... 43 P10
Rydal Cumb ... 89 K5
Ryde IoW ... 13 K6
Rye E Susx ... 16 G7
Ryebank Shrops ... 63 N6
Ryeford Herefs ... 41 K7
Rye Foreign E Susx ... 16 F6
Rye Harbour E Susx ... 16 G7
Ryehill E R Yk ... 87 N10
Ryeish Green Wokham ... 31 P9
Rye Street Worcs ... 41 M4
Ryhall Rutlnd ... 67 P10
Ryhill Wakefd ... 85 M12
Ryhope Sundld ... 101 K7
Rylah Derbys ... 78 D10
Ryland Lincs ... 79 P8
Rylands Notts ... 66 E5
Rylstone N York ... 84 E3
Ryme Intrinseca
Dorset ... 10 F3
Ryther N York ... 85 Q7
Ryton Gatesd ... 100 F5
Ryton N York ... 92 F11
Ryton Shrops ... 64 E11
Ryton Warwks ... 54 C3
Ryton-on-Dunsmore
Warwks ... 54 C2
Ryton Woodside
Gatesd ... 100 F6
RZSS Edinburgh Zoo
C Edin ... 115 M6

S

Sabden Lancs ... 84 B7
Sabine's Green Essex ... 33 Q3
Sacombe Herts ... 45 L8
Sacombe Green Herts ... 45 L8
Sacriston Dur ... 100 G9
Sadberge Darltn ... 91 N3
Saddell Ag & B ... 103 L3
Saddington Leics ... 54 H2
Saddlebow Norfk ... 69 M9
Saddlescombe W Susx ... 15 K8
Sadgill Cumb ... 89 M6
Saffron Walden Essex ... 45 Q5
Sageston Pembks ... 37 L10
Saham Hills Norfk ... 70 C11
Saham Toney Norfk ... 70 C11
Saighton Ches W ... 75 M11
St Abbs Border ... 117 K8
St Agnes Border ... 107 J4
St Agnes Cnwll ... 2 H4
St Agnes IoS ... 2 a3
St Agnes Mining
District Cnwll ... 2 H4
St Albans Herts ... 44 G10
St Allen Cnwll ... 3 K4
St Andrew Guern ... 12 c2
St Andrews Fife ... 125 K9
St Andrews Botanic
Garden Fife ... 125 K9
St Andrew's Major
V Glam ... 27 Q8
St Andrews Well
Dorset ... 10 D6
St Anne's Lancs ... 82 H9
St Ann's D & G ... 106 E11
St Ann's Chapel Cnwll ... 7 M10
St Ann's Chapel Devon ... 5 L7
St Anthony Cnwll ... 3 J9
St Anthony's Hill E Susx ... 16 A10
St Arvans Mons ... 28 H3
St Asaph Denbgs ... 74 E9
St Athan V Glam ... 27 P8
St Aubin Jersey ... 13 b2
St Austell Cnwll ... 3 N4
St Bees Cumb ... 88 C4
St Blazey Cnwll ... 3 P4
St Blazey Gate Cnwll ... 3 P4
St Boswells Border ... 107 P4
St Brelade Jersey ... 13 a2
St Brelade's Bay Jersey ... 13 a2
St Breock Cnwll ... 6 E10
St Breward Cnwll ... 6 G9
St Briavels Gloucs ... 40 H10
St Brides Pembks ... 36 F9
St Bride's Major V Glam ... 27 L7
St Brides Netherwent
Mons ... 28 F4
St Brides-super-Ely
V Glam ... 27 P7
St Brides Wentlooge
Newpt ... 28 C6
St Budeaux C Plym ... 4 G5
Saintbury Gloucs ... 42 D4
St Buryan Cnwll ... 2 C9
St Catherine BaNES ... 29 M8
St Catherines Ag & B ... 121 N11
St Chloe Gloucs ... 41 N11
St Clears Carmth ... 38 B8
St Cleer Cnwll ... 4 D5
St Clement Cnwll ... 3 L6
St Clement Jersey ... 13 c2
St Clether Cnwll ... 7 J8
St Colmac Ag & B ... 112 F8
St Columb Major Cnwll ... 3 M2
St Columb Minor Cnwll ... 3 N2
St Columb Road Cnwll ... 3 M3
St Combs Abers ... 141 P3

St Cross South
Elmham Suffk ... 59 L4
St Cyrus Abers ... 133 J11
St David's P & K ... 123 N9
St Davids Pembks ... 36 E5
St Davids Cathedral
Pembks ... 36 E5
St Day Cnwll ... 2 H6
St Decumans Somset ... 20 G5
St Dennis Cnwll ... 3 M3
St Devereux Herefs ... 40 F5
St Dogmaels Pembks ... 48 B11
St Dogwells Pembks ... 37 J5
St Dominick Cnwll ... 4 F3
St Donats V Glam ... 27 M8
St Edith's Marsh Wilts ... 29 R9
St Endellion Cnwll ... 6 E9
St Enoder Cnwll ... 3 L4
St Erme Cnwll ... 3 L5
St Erney Cnwll ... 4 E5
St Erth Cnwll ... 2 E7
St Erth Praze Cnwll ... 2 F7
St Ervan Cnwll ... 6 C10
St Eval Cnwll ... 6 C11
St Ewe Cnwll ... 3 N5
St Fagans Cardif ... 27 Q7
St Fagans: National
History Museum
Cardif ... 27 Q7
St Fergus Abers ... 141 Q5
St Fillans P & K ... 122 H8
St Florence Pembks ... 37 L10
St Gennys Cnwll ... 6 H5
St George Conwy ... 74 D8
St George's N Som ... 28 E10
St George's V Glam ... 27 Q7
St George's Hill Surrey ... 32 F10
St Germans Cnwll ... 4 E5
St Giles in the Wood
Devon ... 19 K9
St Giles-on-the-Heath
Devon ... 7 L7
St Gluvia's Cnwll ... 3 K7
St Harmon Powys ... 50 D6
St Helen Auckland Dur ... 91 K1
St Helens Cumb ... 97 L11
St Helen's E Susx ... 16 E8
St Helens IoW ... 13 K7
St Helens St Hel ... 75 N5
St Helens
Crematorium St Hel ... 75 N5
St Helier Gt Lon ... 33 J9
St Helier Jersey ... 13 c2
St Hilary Cnwll ... 2 E8
St Hilary V Glam ... 27 N8
St Illtyd Blae G ... 40 B11
St Ippollitts Herts ... 44 H6
St Ishmael's Pembks ... 36 G9
St Issey Cnwll ... 6 D10
St Ive Cnwll ... 4 D3
St Ive Cross Cnwll ... 4 D3
St Ives Cambs ... 56 F6
St Ives Cnwll ... 2 E6
St Ives Dorset ... 11 N8
St James's End Nhants ... 55 J8
St James South
Elmham Suffk ... 59 L4
St Jidgey Cnwll ... 6 D10
St John Cnwll ... 4 F6
St John Jersey ... 13 b1
St Johns Dur ... 100 D11
St John's IoM ... 102 C5
St John's Kent ... 33 P11
St Johns Surrey ... 32 D10
St Johns Worcs ... 52 F10
St John's Chapel
Devon ... 19 K7
St John's Chapel Dur ... 99 N10
St John's Fen End
Norfk ... 69 K9
St John's Highway
Norfk ... 69 K9
St John's Kirk S Lans ... 106 C3
St John's Town of
Dalry D & G ... 96 C2
St John's Wood Gt Lon ... 33 K6
St Jude's IoM ... 102 e3
St Just Cnwll ... 2 B8
St Just-in-Roseland
Cnwll ... 3 L7
St Just Mining District
Cnwll ... 2 B8
St Katherines Abers ... 141 J9
St Keverne Cnwll ... 3 K10
St Kew Cnwll ... 6 F9
St Kew Highway Cnwll ... 6 F9
St Keyne Cnwll ... 4 C4
St Lawrence Cnwll ... 6 E11
St Lawrence Essex ... 46 G11
St Lawrence IoW ... 13 J9
St Lawrence Jersey ... 13 b2
St Lawrence Kent ... 35 Q9
St Leonards Bucks ... 44 C10
St Leonards Dorset ... 11 Q4
St Leonards E Susx ... 16 E9
St Leonard's Street
Kent ... 34 B11
St Levan Cnwll ... 2 B10
St Lythans V Glam ... 27 Q8
St Mabyn Cnwll ... 6 F10
St Madoes P & K ... 124 D8
St Margarets Herefs ... 40 E5
St Margarets Herts ... 45 M9
St Margaret's at Cliffe
Kent ... 17 P2
St Margaret's Hope
Ork ... 147 c6
St Margaret South
Elmham Suffk ... 59 L4
St Marks IoM ... 102 d6
St Martin Cnwll ... 4 C6
St Martin Cnwll ... 3 K9
St Martin Guern ... 12 c3
St Martin Jersey ... 13 d2
St Martin's IoS ... 2 c1
St Martin's P & K ... 124 D7
St Martin's Shrops ... 63 K5
St Martin's Moor
Shrops ... 63 K5
St Mary Jersey ... 13 b1
St Mary Bourne Hants ... 24 G3
St Marychurch Torbay ... 5 Q3
St Mary Church V Glam ... 27 N8
St Mary Cray Gt Lon ... 33 N8
St Mary Hill V Glam ... 27 M7
St Mary in the Marsh
Kent ... 17 J5
St Marylebone
Crematorium
Gt Lon ... 33 J4
St Mary's IoS ... 2 b2
St Mary's Ork ... 147 c5
St Mary's Bay Kent ... 17 J5
St Mary's Grove N Som ... 28 G8
St Mary's Hoo Medway ... 34 E6
St Mary's Platt Kent ... 34 A11
St Maughans Mons ... 40 F8
St Maughans Green
Mons ... 40 G8
St Mawes Cnwll ... 3 L7
St Mawgan Cnwll ... 6 C11
St Mellion Cnwll ... 4 F4
St Mellons Cardif ... 28 B6
St Merryn Cnwll ... 6 C10
St Mewan Cnwll ... 3 M4
St Michael Caerhays
Cnwll ... 3 N6
St Michael Church
Somset ... 21 L8
St Michael Penkevil
Cnwll ... 3 L6
St Michaels Kent ... 16 F3
St Michaels Worcs ... 51 P8

St Michael's Mount
Cnwll ... 2 E8
St Michael's on Wyre
Lancs ... 83 K7
St Michael South
Elmham Suffk ... 59 L4
St Minver Cnwll ... 6 E9
St Monans Fife ... 116 C1
St Neot Cnwll ... 4 B3
St Neots Cambs ... 56 D8
St Newlyn East Cnwll ... 3 K3
St Nicholas Pembks ... 36 H3
St Nicholas V Glam ... 27 P7
St Nicholas-at-Wade
Kent ... 35 N9
St Ninians Stirlg ... 114 E3
St Olaves Norfk ... 71 N12
St Osyth Essex ... 47 K8
St Ouen Jersey ... 13 a1
St Owens Cross Herefs ... 40 H7
St Paul's Cray Gt Lon ... 33 N8
St Paul's Walden Herts ... 44 H7
St Peter Jersey ... 13 b1
St Peter Port Guern ... 12 c2
St Peter's Guern ... 12 b2
St Peter's Kent ... 35 Q8
St Peter's Hill Cambs ... 56 E6
St Petrox Pembks ... 37 J11
St Pinnock Cnwll ... 4 B4
St Quivox S Ayrs ... 104 H5
St Ruan Cnwll ... 2 H11
St Sampson Guern ... 12 c2
St Saviour Guern ... 12 b3
St Saviour Jersey ... 13 c2
St Stephen Cnwll ... 3 M4
St Stephens Cnwll ... 4 F5
St Stephens Cnwll ... 7 L7
St Teath Cnwll ... 6 F8
St Tudy Cnwll ... 6 F9
St Twynnells Pembks ... 37 J11
St Veep Cnwll ... 4 B6
St Vigeans Angus ... 125 M6
St Wenn Cnwll ... 6 D11
St Weonards Herefs ... 40 G7
St y-Nyll V Glam ... 27 P7
Salcombe Devon ... 5 M9
Salcombe Regis Devon ... 9 M7
Salcott-cum-Virley
Essex ... 46 G9
Sale Traffd ... 76 E5
Saleby Lincs ... 80 H8
Sale Green Worcs ... 52 H9
Salehurst E Susx ... 16 D6
Salem Carmth ... 38 B7
Salem Cerdgn ... 49 L4
Salen Ag & B ... 119 P4
Salen Highld ... 127 M11
Salesbury Lancs ... 83 P8
Salford C Beds ... 44 D4
Salford Oxon ... 42 G6
Salford Salfd ... 76 F4
Salford Priors Warwks ... 53 K10
Salfords Surrey ... 15 K2
Salhouse Norfk ... 71 L9
Saline Fife ... 115 J2
Salisbury Wilts ... 23 P7
Salisbury
Crematorium Wilts ... 23 P7
Salisbury Plain Wilts ... 23 N4
Salkeld Dykes Cumb ... 98 G10
Salle Norfk ... 70 G7
Salmonby Lincs ... 80 F9
Salperton Gloucs ... 42 C7
Salph End Beds ... 55 Q10
Salsburgh N Lans ... 114 F8
Salt Staffs ... 64 H6
Saltaire C Brad ... 84 H7
Saltash Cnwll ... 4 F5
Saltburn Highld ... 138 D2
Saltburn-by-the-Sea
R & Cl ... 92 D3
Saltby Leics ... 67 L7
Salt Coates Cumb ... 97 P7
Saltcoats Cumb ... 88 D6
Saltcoats N Ayrs ... 104 D2
Saltcotes Lancs ... 83 J9
Salterbeck Cumb ... 88 C1
Salterforth Lancs ... 84 C6
Salterswall Ches W ... 76 B10
Salterton Wilts ... 23 P6
Saltfleet Lincs ... 81 J5
Saltfleetby All Saints
Lincs ... 81 J5
Saltfleetby St
Clement Lincs ... 81 J5
Saltfleetby St Peter
Lincs ... 81 J6
Saltford BaNES ... 29 K9
Salthouse Norfk ... 70 G3
Saltley Birm ... 53 L3
Saltmarsh Newpt ... 28 D6
Saltmarshe E R Yk ... 86 E10
Saltney Flints ... 75 L10
Salton N York ... 92 E10
Saltrens Devon ... 19 J9
Saltwell Crematorium
Gatesd ... 100 G6
Saltwick Nthumb ... 100 F7
Saltwood Kent ... 17 L4
Salvington W Susx ... 14 G9
Salwarpe Worcs ... 52 G8
Salwayash Dorset ... 10 C5
Sambourne Warwks ... 53 K8
Sambrook Wrekin ... 64 D7
Samlesbury Lancs ... 83 N9
Samlesbury Bottoms
Lancs ... 83 N9
Sampford Arundel
Somset ... 20 H10
Sampford Brett
Somset ... 20 H5
Sampford Courtenay
Devon ... 8 B4
Sampford Moor
Somset ... 20 H9
Sampford Peverell
Devon ... 20 G10
Sampford Spiney
Devon ... 7 N11
Samsonlane Ork ... 147 e3
Samson's Corner
Essex ... 47 K8
Samuelston E Loth ... 115 B7
Sanaigmore Ag & B ... 110 F7
Sancreed Cnwll ... 2 C9
Sancton E R Yk ... 86 H8
Sand Somset ... 21 N4
Sandaig Highld ... 127 N5
Sandal Magna Wakefd ... 85 M11
Sandavore Highld ... 126 H7
Sanday Ork ... 147 e2
Sanday Airport Ork ... 147 e2
Sandbach Ches E ... 76 D10
Sandbach Services
Ches E ... 76 E11
Sandbank Ag & B ... 112 H5
Sandbanks Poole ... 11 P7
Sandend Abers ... 140 E3
Sanderstead Gt Lon ... 33 L10
Sandford Cumb ... 90 D4
Sandford Devon ... 8 H3
Sandford Dorset ... 11 M7
Sandford Hants ... 12 B4
Sandford IoW ... 13 J8
Sandford N Som ... 28 F10
Sandford S Lans ... 105 N1
Sandford Shrops ... 63 K6
Sandford Shrops ... 63 P6
Sandford-on-Thames
Oxon ... 43 L11
Sandford Orcas Dorset ... 22 E9

Sandford St Martin
Oxon ... 43 J6
Sandgate Kent ... 17 M4
Sandhaven Abers ... 141 M2
Sandhead D & G ... 94 G8
Sandhill Rothm ... 78 D4
Sandhills Dorset ... 10 F5
Sandhills Dorset ... 10 G3
Sand Hills Leeds ... 85 M7
Sandhills Oxon ... 43 L10
Sandhills Surrey ... 14 D3
Sandhoe Nthumb ... 100 B5
Sandholme E R Yk ... 86 F9
Sandholme Lincs ... 68 G5
Sandhurst Br For ... 32 B10
Sandhurst Gloucs ... 41 N7
Sandhurst Kent ... 16 D5
Sandhurst Cross Kent ... 16 D5
Sand Hutton N York ... 86 B4
Sandhutton N York ... 91 P10
Sandiacre Derbys ... 66 D5
Sandilands Lincs ... 81 K7
Sandiway Ches W ... 75 Q9
Sandleheath Hants ... 23 P10
Sandleigh Oxon ... 31 L2
Sandling Kent ... 34 D10
Sandlow Green Ches E ... 76 E10
Sandness Shet ... 147 h6
Sandon Essex ... 46 C10
Sandon Herts ... 45 L5
Sandon Staffs ... 64 H6
Sandon Bank Staffs ... 64 H6
Sandown IoW ... 13 K8
Sandplace Cnwll ... 4 C5
Sandridge Herts ... 44 H9
Sandringham Norfk ... 69 N6
Sands Bucks ... 32 B4
Sand Side Cumb ... 88 H10
Sandside Cumb ... 89 M10
Sandtoft N Linc ... 79 J2
Sandway Kent ... 34 F12
Sandwell Valley
Crematorium
Sandw ... 53 J2
Sandwich Kent ... 35 P10
Sandwick Cumb ... 89 L3
Sandwick Shet ... 147 i9
Sandwick W Isls ... 152 G3
Sandwith Cumb ... 88 C4
Sandwith Newtown
Cumb ... 88 C4
Sandy Beds ... 56 D10
Sandy Bank Lincs ... 68 E1
Sandycroft Flints ... 75 K10
Sandy Cross E Susx ... 15 Q7
Sandyford D & G ... 106 G11
Sandygate Devon ... 8 G9
Sandygate IoM ... 102 e3
Sandy Haven Pembks ... 36 G9
Sandyhills D & G ... 96 H7
Sandylands Lancs ... 83 K3
Sandy Lane C Brad ... 84 H8
Sandylane Staffs ... 64 D5
Sandylane Swans ... 26 E4
Sandy Lane Wilts ... 29 Q8
Sandy Lane Wrexhm ... 63 L4
Sandy Park Devon ... 8 E7
Sandysike Cumb ... 98 E5
Sandyway Herefs ... 40 G6
Sangobeg Highld ... 149 J3
Sangomore Highld ... 149 J3
Sankey Bridges
Warrtn ... 75 P6
Sankyn's Green Worcs ... 52 E7
Sanna Bay Highld ... 126 H10
Sannox N Ayrs ... 103 Q4
Sanquhar D & G ... 105 P8
Santon Cumb ... 88 E6
Santon IoM ... 102 d6
Santon Bridge Cumb ... 88 F6
Santon Downham
Suffk ... 58 B3
Sapcote Leics ... 54 D2
Sapey Common Herefs ... 52 D8
Sapiston Suffk ... 58 D6
Sapley Cambs ... 56 E6
Sapperton Derbys ... 65 M5
Sapperton Gloucs ... 41 Q11
Sapperton Lincs ... 67 P5
Saracen's Head Lincs ... 68 H5
Sarclet Highld ... 151 Q8
Sarisbury Hants ... 12 H3
Sarn Brdgnd ... 27 L6
Sarn Gwynd ... 60 D6
Sarn Powys ... 50 H2
Sarnau Carmth ... 37 Q8
Sarnau Cerdgn ... 48 E10
Sarnau Gwynd ... 61 P5
Sarnau Powys ... 39 N5
Sarnau Powys ... 62 G8
Sarn Bach Gwynd ... 60 D7
Sarnesfield Herefs ... 51 L10
Sarn Park Services
Brdgnd ... 27 L6
Saron Carmth ... 38 D8
Saron Carmth ... 38 F9
Saron Gwynd ... 72 H12
Saron Gwynd ... 73 J10
Sarratt Herts ... 32 F2
Sarre Kent ... 35 N9
Satley Dur ... 100 E9
Satmar Kent ... 17 N3
Satron N York ... 90 F7
Satterleigh Devon ... 19 N9
Satterthwaite Cumb ... 89 K8
Satwell Oxon ... 31 P6
Sauchen Abers ... 132 H2
Saucher P & K ... 124 D7
Sauchieburn Abers ... 132 G10
Saughall Ches W ... 75 K9
Saughtree Border ... 107 N8
Saundby Notts ... 79 J6
Saunderton Bucks ... 31 N3
Saunderton Bucks ... 44 A11
Saunderton Station
Bucks ... 32 A3
Saunton Devon ... 19 J5
Sausthorpe Lincs ... 80 G10
Saverley Green Staffs ... 64 H4
Savile Town Kirk ... 85 K11
Sawbridge Warwks ... 54 E7
Sawbridgeworth Herts ... 45 N8
Sawdon N York ... 93 J10
Sawley Derbys ... 66 D5
Sawley Lancs ... 84 B6
Sawley N York ... 85 K2
Sawston Cambs ... 57 J11
Sawtry Cambs ... 56 C4
Saxby Leics ... 67 K8
Saxby Lincs ... 79 P6
Saxby All Saints N Linc ... 87 J12
Saxelbye Leics ... 66 H8
Saxham Street Suffk ... 58 G8
Saxilby Lincs ... 79 M8
Saxlingham Norfk ... 70 F4
Saxlingham Green
Norfk ... 59 K1
Saxlingham
Nethergate Norfk ... 59 J1
Saxlingham Thorpe
Norfk ... 59 J1
Saxmundham Suffk ... 59 M7
Saxon Street Cambs ... 57 M9
Saxtead Suffk ... 59 K7
Saxtead Green Suffk ... 59 K8